# Remembering Elites

# A selection of previous *Sociological Review* Monographs

Actor Network Theory and After*
eds John Law and John Hassard
Whose Europe? The Turn Towards Democracy*
eds Dennis Smith and Sue Wright
Renewing Class Analysis*
eds Rosemary Cromptom, Fiona Devine, Mike Savage and John Scott
Reading Bourdieu on Society and Culture*
eds Bridget Fowler
The Consumption of Mass*
eds Nick Lee and Rolland Munro
The Age of Anxiety: Conspiracy Theory and the Human Sciences*
eds Jane Parish and Martin Parker
Utopia and Organization*
ed. Martin Parker
Emotions and Sociology*
ed. Jack Barbalet
Masculinity and Men's Lifestyle Magazines*
ed. Bethan Benwell
Nature Performed: Environment, Culture and Performance*
eds Bronislaw Szerszynski, Wallace Heim and Claire Waterton
After Habermas: New Perspectives on the Public Sphere*
eds Nick Crossley and John Michael Roberts
Feminism After Bourdieu*
eds Lisa Adkins and Beverley Skeggs
Contemporary Organization Theory*
eds Campbell Jones and Rolland Munro
A New Sociology of Work*
eds Lynne Pettinger, Jane Parry, Rebecca Taylor and Miriam Glucksmann
Against Automobility*
eds Steffen Böhm, Campbell Jones, Cris Land and Matthew Paterson
Sports Mega-Events: Social Scientific Analyses of a Global Phenomenon*
eds John Horne and Wolfram Manzenreiter
Embodying Sociology: Retrospect, Progress and Prospects*
ed. Chris Shilling
Market Devices*
eds Michel Callon, Yuval Millo and Fabian Muniesa

*Available from John Wiley & Sons, Distribution Centre, 1 Oldlands Way, Bognor Regis, West Sussex, PO22 9SA, UK

Most earlier monographs are still available from: Caroline Baggaley, The Sociological Review, Keele University, Keele, Staffs ST5 5BG, UK; e-mail srb01@keele.ac.uk

## *The Sociological Review* Monographs

Since 1958 The Sociological Review has established a tradition of publishing Monographs on issues of general sociological interest. The Monograph is an edited book length collection of research papers which is published and distributed in association with Blackwell Publishing. We are keen to receive innovative collections of work in sociology and related disciplines with a particular emphasis on exploring empirical materials and theoretical frameworks which are currently underdeveloped. If you wish to discuss ideas for a Monograph then please contact the Monographs Editor, Rolland Munro, at The Sociological Review, Keele University, Newcastle-under-Lyme, North Staffordshire, ST5 5BG, UK.

# Remembering Elites

Edited by Mike Savage and Karel Williams

Blackwell Publishing/The Sociological Review

BLACKWELL PUBLISHING
350 Main Street, Malden, MA 02148–5020, USA
9600 Garsington Road, Oxford OX4 2DQ, UK
550 Swanston Street, Carlton, Victoria 3053, Australia

First published 2008 by Blackwell Publishing Ltd

*Library of Congress Cataloging-in-Publication Data*

Remembering elites / edited by Mike Savage and Karel Williams.
    p. cm. – (The sociological review monographs)
    Includes bibliographical references and index.
    ISBN 978-1-4051-8546-2
    1. Elite (Social sciences)   2. Power (Social sciences)   3. Capitalism.
  I. Savage, Michael, 1959–   II. Williams, Karel.
    HM1263R46 2008
    305.5′201–dc22

                                                              2008009653

A catalogue record for this title is available from the British Library

Set in 10/12 Times NR MT

by SNP Best-set Typesetter Ltd., Hong Kong

Printed and bound in the United Kingdom by Page Brothers, Norwich

For further information on Blackwell Publishing, visit our website:
http://www.blackwellpublishing.com

# Contents

*Contents*

# Preface and acknowledgements

Both editors and more than half the contributors to this monograph are based in the Centre for Research in Socio Cultural Change (CRESC) whose activity spans the University of Manchester and The Open University. Our Centre's core funding from the UK Economic and Social Research Council made this book possible. The funding of our centre in 2004 created the space for an unusually broad interdisciplinary conversation about the remaking of present day capitalism around multiple logics yet predictable outcomes in terms of inequality. Out of this internal conversation came the strategic idea that different discourses and mixed methods could be used to revive elites studies and produce an understanding of elites that incorporated new ways of thinking in the social sciences and recognized a more financialized capitalism. The organization of an international workshop in 2005 at Manchester brought together CRESC researchers from anthropology, politics, sociology and business with distinguished international scholars including John Scott, Bill Carroll and Fredric Lebaron.

This volume of twelve essays grows out of that original workshop in Manchester, where half the contributions in this monograph were presented in draft form. The contributors themselves and The Sociological Review's Rolland Munro then made suggestions about further contributions. We are grateful to Rolland Munro for his intellectual encouragement of our project in this development phase when he insisted the issue was the quality and balance of the contributions not word limits and page length. We also owe a more practical debt to two other individuals. Caroline Baggaley of *The Sociological Review* was patient about various delays and firm about our final deadline; while Ebru Soytemel worked efficiently and quickly to put manuscripts from a dozen authors into the format required by our publisher Blackwells. As the project was finally coming together, the two editors turned to an introduction and they must take sole responsibility for the provocative argument about how social sciences forgot elites as they were being remembered in present day capitalism.

The monograph title 'remembering elites' may be misleading because this intellectual project is not about looking back. Readers will find the monograph does not encourage nostalgia for a golden age of social sciences or the glorious years of capitalism, even though we are respectful of, and inspired by, earlier giants like Wright Mills. The challenge for the contributors (and now for our readers) is to show how we can draw on diverse intellectual resources to reconceptualize the role of elites within a mobile and resourceful capitalism. This sets us against old established notions about the varieties of capitalism and about supposedly epochal change. But we are very definitely not trying to define a new elites orthodoxy around one discursive object or an approved set of methods and would insist that none of us have the answers without doing more empirical research. We will have succeeded if others are persuaded to join us in that research.

*Mike Savage and Karel Williams*, November 2007

# Elites: remembered in capitalism and forgotten by social sciences

## Mike Savage and Karel Williams

By any account, the last twenty years of the 20th century have seen the most rapid and dramatic shift of income, assets and resources in favour of the very rich that has ever taken place in human history. This 'raiding of the commons' has been most evident in the former communist nations, especially Russia after 1989, where an arriviste plutocracy emerged in little over a decade from the hasty, even squalid, privatization of state assets and public resources. We can see the rise of the 'super rich' in the 'old' capitalist nations, especially those such as the UK and USA, which have enthusiastically embraced neo-liberalism from the early 1980s. In both countries the top one or five percent of income earners have more or less doubled their share of total income since the early 1980s and we have now almost returned to pre-1914 levels of income inequality (Atkinson, 2003). There is no historical precedent for such regressive redistribution within one generation without either change in legal title or economic disaster such as hyper-inflation. For reasons which nobody yet understands, corporate chief executive officers have for two decades obtained real wage increases of 20 per cent each year and the much larger number of intermediaries earning multi-million $/£ incomes in and around finance has hugely increased.

Where, however, are the social theorists who focus on these processes as central to understanding the contemporary dynamics of social change? As the rich draw away and inhabit their ever more privileged worlds, one might expect a revival of elite studies from contemporary critical writers who are concerned about such developments. After all, earlier generations of theorists were in no doubt about the importance of elites and elite formations for understanding the social dynamics of their nations. Max Weber's first major sociological work was an account of the challenge to patriarchal relations on Prussian landed estates at the end of the 19th century (see Poggi, 2005, chapter 1). Karl Marx's focus on the ruling class needs no demonstration, and his famous chapter on 'Primitive Accumulation' in *Capital* (Marx, 1961), which focuses on how a new capitalist class enriched itself from the enclosure of land and thereby set in train the process of capital accumulation, certainly repays reading in light of current events. Other early 20th century sociologists, notably Pareto and Mosca, also saw the nature of elites as fundamental to understanding the characteristics of their societies (see the discussion in Scott, 1996: chapter 5). Yet, from the middle of the 20th century we can detect the erosion of this animating concern. Sociologists such as C Wright Mills (1956) who continued to focus on the 'power elite' were increasingly defined as 'leftists', whilst Pierre Bourdieu, one of the few leading sociologists to retain an interest in elites down to the end of the 20th century (notably Bourdieu, 1996) was more concerned in the cultural elites of academics and civil servants than in Chief Executive Officers (CEOs) or investment bankers. The leading British sociologist of elites, John Scott, has increasingly concentrated on general issues in sociological theory and analysis rather defining himself as an elite 'specialist' (though see his paper in this volume). In political science, critiques by Dahl (1961) and his colleagues (Polsby, 1963) of the methodology of Millsian elite theory led to a kind of *politikerstreit* in which over more than a decade the antagonists argued themselves to a position of mutual exhaustion. The cap on the whole thing was provided by Lukes (1975) who neatly placed the competing schools into a three-dimensional framework for the study of power and argued for the supremacy of a third, essentially structural, dimension, which did not require a developed theory of elites as such.

It is this glaring invisibility of elites that makes the chapters of this volume so important. Drawing on the interdisciplinary agenda of the ESRC Centre for Research on Socio-Cultural Change (CRESC), the chapters in this volume involve leading scholars from inside and outside the Centre who insist, in different ways, on the need to make elites visible again. Our contributors range across sociology, political economy, anthropology, political science, cultural studies and history, while the empirical focus ranges globally and includes British, English, French, Balkan, and Canadian case studies. Collectively, we seek to kick-start elite studies and engage with remembering elites in present day capitalism which have been forgotten by the social sciences.

Of course, we need to recognize at the outset that elites have not entirely escaped the attention of recent social writers, especially Sklair (2001) and Van Der Pijl (1998) with their emphasis on the rise of 'transnational classes'. We do not think, however, that the focus on globalization has proved helpful in unpacking the complexity and local specificities of contemporary elite formation. Revealingly, major social theorists of globalization struggle to find a conceptual vocabulary to understand elites. A good example is Manuel Castells' remarkable trilogy on 'The Rise of Network Society' which deploys sophisticated versions of globalization theory, as well as related conceptions of 'virtuality'. Castells recognizes the prominence of elites in this new global order.

> The fundamental form of domination in our society is based on the organizational capacity of the dominant elite that goes hand in hand with the capacity to disorganize those groups in society which, while constituting a numerical majority, see their interests partially (if ever) represented only within the framework of the fulfilment of dominant interests (Castells, 1996: 415).

Yet, despite the apparent importance of such a group, the other 1300 pages offer very little elaboration. We learn that elites live in global cities and help to define certain kinds of new urban space (Castells, 1996: 415–7), and they hang around with each other in exclusive resorts such as Davos (Castells, 1998:355–356) but we never learn who they are, what roles they have, how they gain access to elite positions, and so forth. A similar, rhetorical conjuring up of elites can be found in Bauman's work, which contrasts a global elite with a local 'mass' but never seriously investigates their actual characteristics.

This failure of social theory has taken place even though the idea of elite remains important in the popular, political imagination (see more generally Froud, Savage *et al.*, 2006). As Frank (2004) reminds us, the US Republicans prospered in the 1990s partly because they mobilized blue collar workers against what they saw as a liberal elite who were supposedly undermining American values; just as the British establishment had supposedly undermined economic performance 50 years previously (Sampson, 1962). But in this age of new business plutocracy and popular paranoia, the social theory of elites is moribund. Our introduction reflects on this peculiar situation, and lays out a controversial argument to remedy this problem. We do this not in the spirit of asserting old, dated, orthodoxies, but by building on important recent innovations and recognizing the distinctiveness of present day capitalism. The aim is to develop a new research agenda, not to uphold a fundamentalist view that 'nothing has changed', and that we simply need to reassert traditional conceptions of 'old boys' clubs' and bureaucratic power. We need to understand the dynamic and 'mobile' nature of present day elites which cannot be understood adequately using established empirical measures and arguments about, for example, interlocking directorates. Rather, as will become apparent in the chapters of this monograph, we need new theoretical tools and methodological innovations to understand the significance of elite formations in present day capitalism. In terms of intellectual strategy, our major concern is to connect elite theory with a social analysis of money, finance and power, which focuses attention on the rise of the new kinds of intermediaries who act as (often financial) brokers between diverse fields of action.

This introduction is therefore a ground clearing exercise which will lay the platform for the more substantive empirical contributions in this volume which cover both bases. We begin by explaining the demise of traditional elite studies, by unravelling the 'pincer movement' that dispelled traditional elite theory. One part of this pincer is the rise of orthodox, positivist or neo-positivist social science. Within the sociology of stratification and inequality, we can trace the eclipse of elite theory in favour of 'status attainment' and 'class structural' models of analysis. A central feature of this shift was the insistence by quantitative social scientists that the sample survey was the central research tool for analysing social inequality. Given their small size and invisibility within national sample surveys, elites thereby slipped from view. The other side of this pincer comes from structuralist and post-structuralist social theory. The anti-humanism which was central to the stucturalist movement of the 1960s led to a rejection of the focus on visible, human, elites, signalled most famously in Poulantzas's (1973) critique of Miliband's (1968) account of the capitalist state.[1] Foucault famously built on, and reworked, this reasoning through his critique of 'sovereign power' and his insistence that capillary power was central to contemporary liberal and neo-liberal governmentality. Actor network theory and currents within science and technology studies (STS) have further insisted on the distributed, local, and mobile character of socio-technical relations, thereby rejecting any obvious appeal to an 'elite' acting as a 'deus ex machina' which orchestrates society. Acting together, these two different arms of the pincer have theoretically and methodologically 'whipped the carpet' away from elite studies which became deeply unfashionable right across the social sciences from the mid 1970s onwards.

In the second part of our chapter, we explain how a more 'descriptive' account of elites can offer a valuable framework if it is set in the context of an account of the distinctiveness of present-day financialized capitalism. Here we deliberately sidestep epochalist readings of social change, associated with claims regarding Post-Fordism, disorganized capitalism, neoliberalism, and the like. The task of elite studies is not to choose the one correct concept of present day capitalism but to use the figure of elites to recognize, in the spirit of Walter Benjamin, how there are enduring continuities in the way that powerful groups organize society in their own interests. We argue that financialization provides a point of entrance for understanding changing elite fortunes in our time, because it revalues the power and rewards of the executive elites in giant firms who were supposedly crucial in the old power elite; just as financialization greatly expands the numbers of highly paid intermediaries in banking, corporate finance and coupon trading who are especially important in major global financial centres. This change of focus onto new groups fits with recent social theory which establishes the 'active' role of money as social agent. The third part of the chapter examines how we can further develop these interests by drawing on theoretical tools developed within Bourdieusian social theory to provide a new means of understanding elites, not as fixed, traditional pillars, but as a group of intermediaries whose power rests on being able to forge connections and bridge gaps.

## The pincer movement

*Surveys, stratification and networks*

Until the early 1970s, the study of social inequality placed great emphasis on the significance of elites. In the United States, the most eminent critical sociologist of his day, C Wright Mills, forged his reputation on his inspiring account of *The Power Elite* (1950), and these ideas were taken up by other leading scholars, notably Maurice Zeitlin (1989) and Richard Useem (1984). In the United Kingdom, the research programme on social mobility and stratification loosely associated with David Glass at the LSE placed great emphasis on understanding the role of elite professions, leading to studies of senior civil servants (Glass, 1954; Kelsall, 1955) and related groups. Studies of political elites were undertaken most notably by Guttsman (1963).

As CRESC researchers have argued, methods themselves are implicated in processes of social change (eg Savage and Burrows, 2007) and we need to understand how they are implicated in the identification of elites. The classic tradition of elite studies had a common methodological belief in the value of the focused case study, using a mixture of documentary sources, in-depth interviews, and ethnographic analysis. It was this pluralism which was to be dispelled by the rise of survey analysis in the 1960s, and which by the 1970s had become the hegemonic means of studying social inequality. In the United States, Blau and Duncan (1967) inaugurated the 'status attainment' approach. By giving all occupations a 'status score', it became possible to look at the determinants of people's scores, so refining inequality not as a set of social relations, but as a gradated hierarchy. This approach was bitterly contested by European sociologists (most famously John Goldthorpe, 1980; Erikson and Goldthorpe, 1992) who argued that occupations should be placed within a relatively small number of social classes. This then allowed researchers to treat classes as categorical variables and use methods such as log linear models to examine the relationship between origin and destination class (see generally, Savage, 1997; 2000).

There is no need for us to get involved in the dispute between these camps, which persists to this day. Actually, for all their differences, they shared a fundamental starting point: that the national sample survey offered the best means of exploring the nature and determinants of social inequality. The sample survey abstracts individuals from their context, and allows them to be arrayed through classification, none of which however, are amenable to researching 'small' groups – such as elites. Those within the class-structural tradition differentiated classes which had sufficient numbers in them to allow statistically significant findings to be drawn using methods such as log linear modelling. Goldthorpe's most 'elite' class, the 'higher service class' thus contains as many as 14.3 per cent of the male population in the UK, even in 1972[2]; anything smaller, as he readily acknowledges, is not amenable to survey analysis (see the debate between Penn 1981 and Goldthorpe, 1981).[3]

Within the status-attainment tradition, it was possible to give a high-status score to smaller occupational groups; but this had the effect of defining elites not as distinctive social entities but as the 'apex' of a status hierarchy. Interest in elites as specific social formations was subordinated to a concern with unravelling the determinants of 'who gets ahead'. Furthermore, this approach tended to define elite groups in terms of their social exclusiveness, rather than their wealth or political power. In the UK the closest appropriation to the 'status attainment' tradition, Blackburn and Prandy's (1997) 'Cambridge scale' involved giving a score to all occupations on the basis of the friendship patterns of their members. This has the effect of placing University academics, the group least likely to have 'ordinary' people as friends, as the 'highest' ranked occupational group. Although interesting in its own terms in demonstrating the sad lives of contemporary academics, this example makes it clear that this is a rather different conception of elites to that imagined by earlier generations of social theorists.

5

The issue here is that one of the unanticipated consequences of the rise of the sample survey, as the most powerful and legitimate social science research method of the late 20th century, is that elites become opaque from within its purview. It necessarily focuses on large social aggregates and/or decontextualized individuals. From within this perspective, the earlier prominence of elite studies depended on a certain pre- or non scientific framing which made a virtue of case study approaches. This point does not mean that quantitative analysis more generally is not essential to study elites. In those nations, such Scandinavia, where social scientists have access to individual tax return records, for instance, it is perfectly possible for quantitative analysis to unravel patterns of wealth-holding among small groups in the population. Similarly, quantitative analysis of corporate remuneration records, using documentary sources, is vital and informative (see Froud *et al.*, 2006). We should also note the welcome possibility, within the UK's National Statistics Socio-Economic Classification, of allowing the analysis of relatively small groupings. Thus, since 2001, it has been possible to differentiate 'class one' into 'Employers in large organizations', 'Higher managerial occupations', and 'higher professional occupations' (which can be further differentiated into 'traditional' employees; 'new' employees; 'traditional' self-employed and 'new' self-employed, see Rose and Pevalin 2003, and see also the ongoing work of CCSE researchers, eg LeRoux, Rouanet, Savage and Warde, 2007). In this vein, Majima and Warde in this volume show how survey sources can be used imaginatively to explore features of the top one per cent of households in Britain.

An important issue here is the marginal role of social network analysis within quantitative social sciences. Social network analysis, which explores the ties and connections between individuals, institutions, or groups, is a powerful tool for unravelling ties of influence and interlinkage. It developed from the 1950s (see Scott, 1990; Freeman, 2002; Knox *et al.*, 2006), yet because it ideally requires information on 'whole populations' rather than a sample, it has been marginalized, or at least strongly demarcated, from mainstream quantitative social sciences. Practically, data on whole populations can be collected using two approaches: detailed qualitative case studies of particular environments, for instance schools (Bearman *et al.*, 2004), or local neighbourhoods (Wellman, 1979), where all relevant members can be interviewed. Alternatively, publicly available documentary sources can be used. Data on the directors of leading corporations have been a mainstay of social network analysis since the work of Hobson in the early 20th century. The papers by Carroll, Froud *et al.*, and Griffiths *et al.*, in this volume all indicate how social network analysis can be used in the contemporary context, not just by exploring corporate linkages and networks articulated through 'interlocking directorships' but through broader lines of inquiry and more diverse data sources.

To be effective, network connections need to be linked to other lines of analysis. Important work on the social networks of interlocking directors by researchers like Windolf (2002) has not been able to keep the study of elites more generally centre stage within the social sciences. Within management studies, the observation that linkages between directors existed invited the 'so what' response from management researchers like Pettigrew (1992) who doubted whether such linkages made any difference to behaviour. Further, the familiar techniques for studying the position of directors are less valuable for addressing other kinds of elite connections, which may be more fluid and less formalized, but which may be increasingly significant in an era of neo-liberal, financialised capitalism where the giant firm is not the only – or even the main – locus of economic power. It is also clear that in an era of 'equal opportunities' and proceduralized governance, businesses of all kinds are increasingly keen not to be seen not to recruit 'old boys', if only because meritocratic recruitment at point of entrance and promotion is a way of justifying the privilege of those at the apex of the hierarchy. This kind of defence of the City is now commonplace in the UK, where there is a reflexive loop by which the criticisms about the existence of an 'inner circle' and an 'old boys' club' has informed the policies of key agents. It would be most unwise simply to rely on data of corporate directors alone (see Carroll, 2004 for a skilful examination of this point). We should not, therefore, assume that the choice for a quantitative researcher is simply between those who use sample surveys on national populations, and social network analysts who focus on directors and corporate interlocks alone. Our task, we argue, is to expand the repertoire of methods that can be used to address the issue of contemporary elite formation, and to use network methods in more fluid and dynamic ways than simply the study of company directors alone, and involving ethnographic as well as documentary sources (see generally Knox *et al.*, 2006, and the examples in this volume by Froud *et al.*, and Griffiths *et al.*).

We have argued that the invisibility of elites is dependent on the role of hegemonic social science methods, but we also detected some 'chinks in the armour'. Let us now consider the second part of the pincer movement, the various kinds of social theory which, by dispensing with notions of 'sovereign power' and the 'subject', have called into question the value of elite studies themselves.

*Cutting off the Sovereign's head: structuralist and post-structuralist critiques*

There seems little doubt that earlier interests in elites were related to humanistic models of social science that were concerned with attributing causal significance to motives and values. This is true in the early theorizing of both Weber and Marx, both of whom recognized in different ways the importance of the 'human' dimension of social relations. It is also clear that both these theorists also sought ways of developing a more structural sociology, in the case of Weber through his deployment of neo-Kantian distinctions between fact and value, and in the case of Marx through his much discussed, and still contested, 'epistemological break' which led to the downplaying of his earlier social theory that centred on alienation in favour of his later, more structural accounts of capitalism and modes of production.

The issue here is that classic theorizing allows (only) two different ways of recognizing the importance of elites, both of which have been subject to major criticism and seem unsustainable today. First, elites can be seen as important because they are active 'key agents', and hence shape social change. This of course, is the journalists' view. By virtue of being elite members, their actions have undue social significance, and can decide on courses of action that have fundamental significance in shaping the course of history. Secondly, and in tension with this first approach, elites can be seen in purely 'instrumental' ways, i.e. as passive supports of particular structural determinants, a framing which can be found in classical versions of Marxist theory. Versions of this position are most emphasized in the mainstream tradition of work on business elites, from Hilferding (1910) on 'finance capital' to Scott (1997) on the 'constellation of interests' where the individual director represents the interests of a fraction of capital. In the work of Giddens, the tension between these two different perspectives (Giddens, 1973) has itself been generalized into a concern with the relationships between 'agency' and 'structure' itself (Giddens, 1984).

This oscillation between 'humanism' and 'instrumentalism' runs through the history of social science's engagement with elites (and of course, more generally), and it is now widely recognized that this is a problematic framing. The most celebrated discussion of this issue is the 'Miliband-Poulantzas' debate of the early 1970s. Here, Ralph Miliband's (1969) careful dissection of the particular individuals involved in British elite circles, and the connections binding these different worlds together, was convincingly rebutted by Poulantzas (1973) who drew on Althusser's structuralism to insist that it was precisely the structural 'dis-connects' between different spheres of activity, what he termed their 'relative autonomy', that was essential for the reproduction of contemporary capitalism. This argument was further sustained by post-structuralist concerns with the 'distributed' nature of social relations, which deny that any particular groups themselves have any necessary efficacy or importance. It becomes more important to understand forms of neo-liberal 'governmentality', which define the possibilities for the production of contemporary social relations. A focus on the nature of 'capilliary power', organized through minute and localized interactions is evident both within Foucault's (1975) thinking, as well as within actor network theory (eg Latour, 1988; Law, 1986).

An important dimension of this current, visible in the work of both Foucault and Bourdieu, was increasing interest in the way that knowledge was not a neutral resource, which could be mobilized by different social groups, but was itself implicated in the production of society itself (see more generally, Mitchell, 2003). This focus had the indirect effect of encouraging research on the articulate and knowledge-saturated worlds of academia and professional expertise. Foucault's interests in criminalization and normalization led to burgeoning interests in the role of the police, social workers, teachers, and (notably in the work of Nikolas Rose, 1990) psychiatrists and 'psy-scientists' more generally. Bourdieu focused on academics, journalists, artists and other cultural producers. Insofar as a visible elite remains, it is now comprised of these professional and 'knowledge' groupings, recently and controversially trumpeted by Florida as the 'creative class'.

Although we have been influenced by this impressive body of work, to the extent that we include in this volume studies of cultural elites (Bennett and Warde, and Griffiths *et al.*) it is time to take stock of the absences it has promoted. There has been little attention paid to the new or expanded group of financial elites who, as Folkman *et al.* (2007) argue, are intermediaries, often operating without executive roles in giant corporations, and usually incentivized on the basis of sharing fees or profits. This descriptive concern with a new group connects to the disparate, more theorized arguments of Arrighi (1994), MacKenzie and his colleagues (2007), and Ingham (2004). All of these authors argue, in different ways, that money itself should not be seen as a 'neutral veil' but as a key social device and technology. The implication is that those who control money are establishing themselves as central social and political agents, who can also embed themselves in wider circuits of power. Our position can be read as an alternative to the standard sociological account, elegantly reformulated by Scott in this volume, which seeks to restrict the definition of elites to those who have a formal relationship to power in one of the established political or sociological usages of that term. We prefer to see power saturating the circuits of contemporary capitalism, and see the relationship between money and power as one under-investigated major driver of the remaking of present day capitalism.

Here, we are best off sidestepping the debate about precise definitions of elites, to pose the issue in a somewhat different way, where our attention is directed, in the first instance, towards how the wealthy have prospered and regrouped in contemporary financialized capitalism. Rather than seeking to impose *a priori* boundaries around putative elite groups, we might instead pose the descriptive question as to how the fortunes of particular individuals and groups have so signally prospered, and how they have managed to become economic, social, cultural and political agents in association with their enrichment? What is it about contemporary social life that sees such groups obtain such prominence, and what lessons does this have for social science research?

## Elites and financialization

We evoke financialization in this volume to emphasize the mobility and resourcefulness of present-day capitalism. This allows us to distance ourselves from epochal accounts of capitalism, couched in 'before and after' terms. Elites are both causes and products of an ongoing process of financialization which increases the number of elite financial intermediaries and which has effects that are conjunctural, contradictory and non-totalising.

Established accounts of the remaking of capitalism since the 1970s are typically associated with a master concept which crystallizes an epochal understanding of the difference of present day capitalism from what came before and which unjustifiably privilege one aspect or dimension of change. If the emphasis is placed on specific policies and institutions, Thatcherism and Reaganism denote the 1980s attack on the post-war settlement in the high-income countries just as 'Washington consensus' (Williamson 1989) epitomizes the policy fix for the rest of the world. If the period is foreshortened to consider the 15 'glorious years' of expansion and high employment since the early 1990s, then many would instead emphasize socio-technical innovation driven by digital technology and business re-organization. These processes are epitomized in the popular 1990s claims about a new economy which found a precursor in Drucker's (1969) concept of the knowledge economy and academic support in Castells (1996) concept of the 'network society'.

Financialization empirically focuses on the past thirty years of unprecedented innovation in the wholesale financial markets and in the mass consumption of retail financial services. These have both given capital markets new influence over firms and households and reworked previously established power relations. Even before the credit crunch of summer 2007, there had been a flurry of media and academic interest in financialization (eg Arrighi, 1994; Epstein, 2005; Harvey, 2005; Blackburn, 2002 and 2006; Financial Times, 19 June 2007, 27 June 2007). We do not have the scope here to review different conceptualizations (though see our discussion in Erturk *et al.*, 2008) and simply draw out its relevance for the remaking of elites and insist that it does not have to be developed as an epochal concept. The implication is that we can, when using the financialization concept in the early 2000s, learn from the earlier experience with the overselling of globalization in the mid 1990s as an epochal tendency bringing new and unprecedented changes which carry all before them. This offered an easy target for Hirst and Thompson's (1996) critique which emphasized the regional (not global) dimension of integration and the pre-1914 precdents; the medium term result was death by a thousand qualifications about the interpenetration of the global and the local.

Empirically, financialization is relevant to the good fortune of new intermediary financial elites since the 1980s in much the same way as European integration and globalization is relevant to the misfortunes of male manual workers in the UK since the 1970s. Financialization is associated with the remembering of elites because it manifestly expands the number of financial intermediary positions and apparently diminishes the role of previously dominant managerial elites.

One of the most striking developments in present-day capitalism is the increasing number of highly paid financial intermediaries whose role is not the executive management of 'men and things' within corporate hierarchies but the switching or servicing of the flows of money through market trading and corporate deals whose profits greatly increase the numbers of working rich. Certainly, as Folkman *et al.* (2007) demonstrate, high-income financial intermediaries now hugely outnumber high-income corporate executives. Newspaper stories about the chief executives (CEOs) of giant firms in the FTSE 100 earning £2 or £3 million per annum keep senior executives in the news but, even if we add chief financial officers (CFOs) and directors of major divisions, no more than some 600 senior managers/executive directors (including CEOs) in the FTSE earn more than £1 million per annum. By contrast, media reports in 2005 claimed that around 3,000 City bankers and traders then earned bonuses of £1 million or more. On our estimates (Folkman *et al.*, 2007), the total number of senior, highly paid intermediaries in the City of London adds up to some 15,000 if we include the total number of senior intermediaries employed at a principal or partner level in investment banking, hedge funds and other kinds of trading and private equity (as well as those providing support services in law and accounting). This new group of the 'working rich' in a financialized economy can be thought of as the present day analogues of Keynes 'hard faced men who had done well out of the war'. But the way to make money now is not defence contracting or arms manufacture but finance.

Analytically, the rise of the new intermediaries challenges the assumptions about managerial capitalism that underpinned the work of Wright Mills, the last great theorist of the interpenetration of business and political elites. The Millsian idea of a power elite is managerial because it assumes that strategic power is effectively held by a small number of actors at the apex of three bureaucracies (political, military and economic). Furthermore, as in other theories of managerial (or 'organized') capitalism, Mills credited the coordinating managers with the ability to impose their own discretionary priorities and indeed to formulate a specific project (in 1950s America, this was the prosecution of the cold war). Critical elite studies was then vested with the project of unmasking the unaccountability of the executive elite and explaining how social homogeneity (though common backgrounds and interchange of personnel) secured group solidarity and motivation. The pursuit of discretionary strategic objectives, however, by CEOs at the apex of the giant firms in the FTSE 100 or S and P 500 is now apparently qualified and constrained because CEO actions increasingly require the consent or endorsement of capital markets where articulate and active investors have strong views about the desirability of the next value-creating move and the consequences of the last.

Nevertheless, it would be wrong to suppose that such developments inaugurate a new 'epoch' of financialization or an era of intermediary capitalism with the old managerial bosses replaced by new 'non-executive masters of the universe'. As Erturk *et al.* (2008) argue, the process of financialization is about changing conjectural logics and multiple discrepancies (not about an entirely new financial logic of capitalism). Since the 1970s, mass savings now provide the feedstock for elite dealing. But the conjuncture changes every five to seven years, so that the 1996–2000 conjuncture of New Economy and Silicon Valley IPOs is different from the 2000–7 conjuncture of excess liquidity, hedge funds and private equity. While the conjuncture represents a temporarily organized space, it is marked by internal discrepancies, multiple contradictions and unintended consequences in terms of social inequality and economic instability which make financialization so much unfinished business. Consider, for example, the Froud *et al.* (2006) analysis of the response of UK and US giant firms to shareholder value in the 1990s and early 2000s. Here, capital market demands from institutional investors for increased profits stimulated narrative inventiveness and performative initiatives by giant firm managers who enriched themselves but did not raise profits (by Return on Capital Employed measures) which were limited by product market competition.

Thus, in one moment, a major intermediary group like US and UK fund managers in the 1990s cannot organize a conjuncture to produce intended consequences and prevent unintended free riding by CEOs. With conjunctural change, as Wall Street bond traders and LBO artists found out in the early 1990s, each new conjuncture diminishes or displaces the group of financiers previously hailed as 'masters of the universe' who typically retire on their banked bonuses. While we emphasize the importance of financialization in remembering elites, we would therefore expect the survival, regrouping and transformation of other elites (business, political, cultural or whatever) whose existence, organization and effects cannot be read off finance. All this raises theoretical and empirical questions about the power of finance which we consider in the next section.

## Finance and the power of temptation

This account relates to our earlier argument about how, after Polulantzas, new ideas of capillary and distributed power displaced older ideas of sovereign power. The power of finance is either overestimated or invisible because it does not fit with classical ideas about the organizing power of finance, nor with current ideas about power that works through sovereign disempowerment of subjects or capillary production of docile subjects. From our point of view, the challenge in present day capitalism is to understand the disorganizing power of finance materialized in a loose distributive coalition of intermediaries whose power works unpredictably through temptation. For this reason, LeBaron's analysis, in this volume, of the opposed and divergent policies and properties of central bankers is so timely.

In earlier accounts of capitalist business and elite formation, especially by Marxists from Hilferding (1910) onwards, the power of finance was an organizing power. Thus, in early 20th century Marxism, 'finance capital' was a stage in capitalism which (*inter alia*) involved monopolizing industrial corporations and cartels and the fusion of banking and industrial capital 'under the direction of high finance' (Hilferding, 1981, p. 30). This was practically represented in mainland Europe by the presence of outside directors from banks and insurance companies on the boards of industrial companies. Scott's later concept of 'control through a constellation of interests' (Scott, 1997: 51) represents a more nuanced, Weberian variant on Hilferding's original concept where the board of directors acts as a micro level executive committee of the bourgeoisie, representing and reconciling the sectional interests of different fractions of capital. In another variant of this approach to interlock in Europe, Windolf

(2002) emphasizes the 'big linkers' who bring broad perspectives to what would otherwise be narrowly sectional boardroom debates.

This all seems increasingly quaint and anachronistic when in present day corporate business 'everything is for sale' and the intermediary elite in finance is no more than a distributional coalition. Whereas giant firms were once long-lived survivors, they now typically have short lives, often involving changes of ownership. More than 70 of the FTSE 100 companies of the early 1980s no longer survive in the index and most of those giant companies have vanished to hostile takeover. Over the past twenty five years, giant companies in the UK and USA have spent as much or more on buying other companies as on fixed capital investment; and, if smaller, closely held companies have traditionally been much less saleable, private equity now aims to change all that by trading in mittelstand type operations. If the supposed task of Hilferding's business elite in the 1900s was keeping things going in a period of pressure on profits; the rather different effect of present day business elites in the 2000s is breaking things up and selling things on in a period of excess liquidity. The gains in this process are often windfall gains from rising markets or come from redistribution and 'breach of implicit social contract' with employees, suppliers or other stakeholders (Shliefer and Summers, 1988).

None of this requires a unitary elite, nor any kind of 'executive committee of the bourgeoisie', to reconcile sectionalism. The intermediaries are instead in Mancur Olson's (1982) sense a distributional coalition[4] which forms and reforms around the money-making deals and innovations in financial markets that change with each conjuncture. Meanwhile, the investment bankers who are on the same side in one takeover deal will be on opposite sides in the next deal; and, as Aeron Davis has emphasized (2002, 2006), the City consists of a multiplicity of little groups constructing their own small worlds. As we have argued elsewhere (Folkman *et al.*, 2007) the intermediaries are individually 'working for themselves', under arrangements of sharing revenue and profits, which operate within giant public company investment banks as much as in partnerships. These fee structures (like the 2 per cent management fee and 20 per cent of profits claimed by hedge fund managers and PE general partners) often operate in ways that create divisions within and between firms because only a few seniors in large-scale operations will get rich.

If we consider this process more abstractly and theoretically, financial power works through the interpellation of actors (whether as intermediaries, or senior corporate executives or ordinary retail investors and borrowers). All are individualized and tempted, in the sense of *Matthew 4.8,* by being offered whatever they want in the way of security, riches or freedom of action. Thus, in everyday life, the consumer's encounter with retail finance is prepared through the 'get a life' adverts which invariably show retired couples or happy families enjoying the security that comes from buying appropriate pension or life insurance products in a world where financial services companies have intuitively grasped Kahneman and Tversky's behavioural insight that subjects choose positive outcomes (Kahneman *et al.*, 1982). Financial power thus works through the social and cultural imaginary with unpredictable and variable effects which often include disappointment about the gap between promise and outcome. This then feeds secondary reactions with technical practices like corporate governance techniques or financial literacy campaigns mobilized ineffectually to produce companies and consumers worthy of financialized capitalism.

Some have presented the capital market as a disciplinary institution (Roberts *et al.*, 2006). This is only partly correct, since (divided) intermediaries sometimes encounter a motivated group with a different agenda and some basis for resistance. The different possibilities and outcomes here can be illustrated by contrasting the behaviour since the mid 1990s of British NEDs or Non Executive Directors and French PDGs or Chief Executive Officers. The British NEDs, who are now in a majority on FTSE 100 boards are the ciphers of the capital market as they enforce and operate the policy of 'everything for sale' in the UK; while French PDGs (or CEOs) have used the capital market to finance their discretionary policies of expansion which makes them eager purchasers in the UK and elsewhere. The cases are worth developing because they show so clearly how the effects of capital market pressures vary according to time and place so as to create willing sellers and buyers of British companies.

As Froud *et al.* explain in their contribution to this volume, the old British system of interlocking directors has been dramatically changed by the rise of proceduralized governance since the publication of the Cadbury Report in 1992. This brings in a new kind of outside, non-executive, director, who is typically not a banker but a serving or retired senior executive from another giant firm. From case study evidence, Froud *et al.* argue that the British NED director acts in a new way as a kind of enforcer of capital market priorities about auctioning the company off to any bidder who offers a suitable premium and thereby helping to ensure that 'everything is for sale'. Their arguments are complemented by Johal and Leaver's (2007) analysis of French CEO behaviour, where directors use the capital market in a traditional way to fund their discretionary policies of acquisition. Fund managers from the secondary market did attempt to discipline the relatively unprofitable French giant firm sector (Morin, 2000) but their efforts were negated by the way in which investment bankers from the primary market freely offered debt and equity issues to fund the overseas acquisitions which made French giant firms into global players. Since the early 1990s, French CEOs have got what they wanted by exploiting divisions within the intermediary elites while British NEDs have served their fund managers.

Some researchers from science and technology studies (STS) backgrounds have tried to short circuit these complications by invoking concepts of performativity which incidentally abolish the classic sociological questions about the motivation of British NEDs and French CEOs. But Mackenzie's (2004) empirical work on the adoption of the Black Scholes model and Aspers (2006) theoretical reflections on different kinds of markets, both show the limits of mechanical notions about financial markets performing economic theory. To understand more about the power of finance we need new analytic tools and a programme of empirical research.

## An empirical problem and some new tools

The power of the elite idea in the 1950s and 1960s in academic and popular usage stemmed partly from the way in which elites were credited with a unitary identity and a strategic role in promoting or frustrating any modernizing economic and social change. Thus, in academic discourse, Wright Mills power elite was a thoroughly 'modern' social entity whose mission was to manage the military-industrial complex so as to win the Cold War. In the same way, a historian like Edward Thompson saw the power of the British landed elite as central to the institution of the 'Black Acts' during the 18th century, whilst Barrington Moore (1967) saw the role of elites as fundamental to the different routes to modernity evident in capitalist, fascist and communist societies. But, during the 1950s, this interest in elites as modern phenomena was challenged by the lay and political view that elites were traditional, status groups who represented reactionary survivals and obstacles to modernization projected through concerns with meritocracy and 'efficiency'. Thus, in 1950s Britain the journalist Henry Fairlie and others (Thomas, 1959) popularized the idea of the 'Establishment' – a public-school educated officer class in business, the City and politics – and then attributed Britain's relative economic decline to the inaction and incompetence of this residual stratum. This then played an important role in the mobilization of the 1960s Labour Party under Harold Wilson as a movement for 'change' and 'modernization'.

In these academic and political usages, elites became unhelpfully identified as part of a conspiratorial throwback to some kind of 'ancient regime', rather than themselves as key agents of change. It has thus been possible for plutocrats to lead a populist politics which allows them to continue to prosper, all in the name of anti-elitism. Frank (2005) shows how in the USA Republicans invoke the idea of a liberal elite conspiracy to undermine American values (see also du Gay in this volume). Elites are set in opposition to the market, rather than identified as key market agents. In this respect the continued rhetorical identification of elites with 'old boy networks', the 'establishment', or 'inner circles' is deeply unhelpful – and is one more instance of how elites research has been stultified by those who know the answers to the questions before the empirical research has been done.

We need instead to ask for empirical investigation of the composition of elites, and explorations of the difference they make. Here, the papers of Griffiths *et al.* on the English cultural elite, Majima and Warde on the spending patterns of the very wealthy in Britain, and Harvey and MacLean on the French and British business elites, offer novel studies of elite composition, showing significant forms of change whilst also allowing us to see how old privileged groups are able to change their spots and adapt to contemporary conditions.

In pursuing this project, we need to deploy appropriate analytical tools. Here aspects of Pierre Bourdieu's influential thinking offer valuable guidance for the sociological analysis of elites, even though this analysis is also ultimately limited by its insistence on 'elite reproduction' and cannot be deployed uncritically (see also Savage *et al.*, 2005). Several of the chapters in this volume, notably LeBaron's study of central bankers, and Harvey and MacLean's study of business elites, are explicitly framed by Bourdieu's thinking. He sees elites as neither status residues nor modernizing agents, but as the dominant players within semi-autonomous 'fields' (see Bourdieu, 1993; 2005a, 2005b). This has the distinctive advantage of not (pre-) defining elites in terms of their putative roles or functions but, instead, in terms of their field specific dominance. Bourdieu differentiates between elite positions within any one field, and the formation of elites which span fields. Fields consist of a set of practices which are bound together by a set of common stakes and concerns, by an understanding of the 'rules of the game' which participants, reflexively and also in embodied and implicit ways, are aware of and abide by in their practices. They can thus encompass, at one extreme, the micro social world of enthusiasts – stamp collectors for instance. Within the field of philately, there is no doubt a distinct elite who have the best stamp collections, know who the best dealers are, get the best deals, and generally command respect and authority from other collectors. So it is that one can similarly talk about elite footballers, elite academics, elite television presenters and the like (Bourdieu, 2005b). In such situations, elites can command a certain cultural legitimacy. Some elites, however, are able to move between different fields, thereby connecting what are otherwise disconnected realms and, through this process, forging a more cohesive identity as a wide-ranging social elite (and here there is a link with the elite theory of Mosca and Pareto, see Scott in this volume).

This is extraordinarily suggestive if, as we have argued, financialization changes elite roles and tasks but does not establish a totalizing hegemony. The intermediaries of finance are important as the marine corps of an economy of permanent restructuring where everything is for sale; but this war of manoeuvre requires a supply corps to support each fresh assault and an occupying administration to co-opt other local elites. Hence, the new or renewed importance of individuals or groups who can move between the worlds of business, politics, media and so forth, and through this process act as a means of mediating connections between dispersed social circles. In Bourdieu's later work[5], he distinguishes between those elites who seek to maximise their position within a field – intellectuals for instance – from those who seek to import considerations from outside that field, notably industrialists. At certain times these groups can exist in a state of considerable tension, although in other contexts, and especially when threatened by interests from the 'dominated' positions within the field, they can more readily make common cause. In addition, in his later work as he seeks to resist 'neo-liberal' marketization, Bourdieu (2005a) is clear that it is money that facilitates movement between fields. Those who can mobilize economic capital are uniquely able to define themselves in elite terms.

Bourdieu's thinking has something in common here with developments within social network theory which has itself made a significant shift through switching attention away from the extent to which 'inner circles' interlock and towards the issue of how specific individuals can bridge 'structural holes'.[6]

Ronald Burt (1992, 2004) deploys a theory of social capital which shows that it is not those who necessarily have a large number of connections, so much as those whose connections bring together those who would otherwise not be in contact with each other, that enjoy social advantages. Contacts and networks are hence not to be seen simply as ascriptive 'hang-overs' from early life (eg going to the 'right school'), nor identified in purely quantitative terms, but are fundamentally to be identified in terms of their capacity to bridge diverse worlds or fields. We might also note that this idea is not entirely dissimilar from Bruno Latour's arguments about the role of 'immutable mobiles', objects that become 'obligatory points of passage' between diverse and heterogeneous actors. Godechot's chapter in this volume shows how aspects of Bourdieu's thinking can be incorporated with aspects of social network thinking to allow a 'performative' account of elite social capital.

We can see that Bourdieu's work allows us to see why elites should be increasingly significant insofar as financialization multiplies and differentiates fields, and may well produce new kinds of elites who span fields as well as those specific to particular fields. We need to differentiate this aspect of Bourdieu's thinking from his more familiar, and to some degree problematic, insistence on the power of class reproduction, the way that privileged groups are able to transmit their advantages to their children through inculcating an appropriate 'habitus'. This more reductive element (notable in Bourdieu and Passeron, 1990), has been widely appropriated within educational sociology. It is worth noting, however, that Bourdieu's actual focus here is not on elites so much as on the educated middle classes, the professional petit bourgeois, as it were, who seek to pass on their advantages through their educational, rather property, assets. By recognizing the multiplicity of fields, however, and the possible tensions between them, it is possible to develop a less reductive account.

A second limitation of Bourdieu's thinking, and one that he shares with many other sociologists (see the discussion in Ingham, 2004), is a reductive understanding of money. Bourdieu's substantial focus is the cultural field, which he portrays as a fluid and constructed one, where those who claim cultural superiority actively do so through promoting cultural forms which denigrate the cultural activity of the popular classes. By contrast, economic capital is not portrayed with such richness or vigour, and it is almost assumed that money exists as an 'obvious' object, not it itself subject to forms of production, mobilization, contestation, symbolization etc. In *The social structures of the economy* Bourdieu (2005a) does distinguish financial capital from commercial capital, and recognizes the significance of finance in opening up a new 'global field', yet these remarks are still under-developed. We need to see the processes of 'financialization' as themselves a complex field, requiring mobilizations, creativity, and innovation every bit as important as those that can be detected in the cultural domain. Capital does not accumulate automatically. If we recognize the creativity involved in these processes, we can develop a greater understanding of the role of various financial actors as players within a complex and differentiated economic field.[7]

## The chapters in this volume

The chapters in this monograph offer different kinds of resources for our project of rethinking, and restating, elites as a central site of analysis. They are organized into three sections under the headings of taking stock; money and finance; and cultural elites. The chapters in the first section all have an explicit 'then and now' theme and take up questions about how we recognize historical changes since the period when elite studies engaged with managerial capitalism and imagined an establishment. The second set of chapters examines new business elites, money and finance and takes up questions about dynamics and finance on the working assumption that finance is a major driver of the remembering of elites in present day capitalism. The third and final set of chapters provides the necessary counterweight and focuses on cultural elites and consumption of elites which drive home the argument that our object of study cannot be read off a general concept of financialization and the new positions that it allows in metropolitan capitalist countries.

The first set of chapters, which presents stock taking, is appropriately opened with an essay by John Scott who has for the last thirty years resisted the eclipse of elite studies and is established as one of the leading international sociologists of elites. His restatement of Weberian elite theory offers an essential reference point for other discussions in this book. He argues that elite studies were undermined from within by the 'indiscriminate' use of the term to denote many different kinds of group, including the high paid. From this point of view, it is important to limit the usage to groups who 'have a degree of power' and then to clarify the concept by distinguishing between different kinds of power. Readers will see that Scott's approach diverges from ours since we are especially concerned to elaborate a financialized and monetized conception of elites where, for example, the question of how small groups acquire high pay is a key issue in present day capitalism.

Canadian elite formation has been seriously and serially studied over the past forty years since the publication of John Porter's (1965) classic study. Bill Carroll is a leading Canadian sociologist of business elites who examines trends in the past forty years and reflects on how the social network approach to the study of elites has fared. Carroll notes the weakening and decentering of the Canadian business elite, which is no longer an ethnically homogeneous group of British ancestry, and also notes the new pressures from institutional shareholders for shareholder value. If these empirical observations are ambiguous, Carroll's analysis is notable because it restates the relevance of social network analysis for examining elites. An especially important feature of his account is his discussion of the different methods and data sources that can be used to study elites, and his chapter can hence be read as elaborating the emphasis we give in our chapter on the relevance of finding the right methods to recognize elites.

The distinguished political scientist Mick Moran represents all those in the social sciences over the past thirty years who have been perturbed by the decline of elite studies. Moran's analysis of the paradoxes of capitalist change starts from the very British paradox that if Thatcherism represented the victory of business over labour it also inaugurated the atrophy of organized business through various collective associations that represented business in the political realm. Moran sketches a new model for the containment of political opposition to big business as individual giant firms resort to 'do it yourself' representation while they try to neutralize and contain the opposition of groups who are hostile to business in a civil society where business is not popular. The implication is that this has given new power to a giant firm corporate elite, which Moran explicitly identifies as a plutocracy.

Paul Du Gay from Warwick Business School examines the rise of those like the political adviser to New Labour whose tactic is to criticize old elites and deny the existence of new elites and whose trick is to convince others that he does not exist. Du Gay's essay is important because he broadly agrees with Moran about the importance of bringing back elites so as to study new or remembered groups but focuses on a different group and arrives at his conclusion through forms of argument which are very different from those of Moran. Du Gay presents a cultural economy analysis which focuses on the discourses about elites. His arguments are most trenchant when he turns to the anti elite discourses of modernizing elites who justify themselves by disparaging opponents as part of an 'establishment' or historical residue which resists the economic and political needs of the present and the future.

The second set of essays on money, finance and business elites opens with a contribution from Harvey and Maclean which provides a bridge between the traditional analysis of business elites in terms of interlocking directorates and the radical novelties of conceptualization and method proposed by the other three essays on business elites. Harvey and Maclean define business elites in the orthodox managerial way as the directors of giant firms in France and the UK. They then reframe this traditional object, using a Bourdieusian theorization of the forms of capital with an associated interest in elite reproduction and how newcomers become accepted elite members. This highlights national differences, because in the absence of French style recruitment from '*grandes ecoles*' to elite career, the British rely much more heavily on networking via arts and sports institutions. If the Harvey and Maclean question is how far they can get by applying a Bordieuian theory of social dynamics to a traditional object, the other contributors want to look at different social groups and see Bourdieu more as source of imaginative methods and provocative metaphors.

This is certainly the position of Frederic Lebaron's study of central bankers. The traditional importance of this group has been greatly increased by the granting of political independence to central banks tasked with the pursuit of objectives like monetary stability in economies where governments have renounced other macro-economic instruments of policy. In Lebaron's analysis, Bourdieu figures not as the author of a typology about forms of capital but as the popularizer of the method of multiple correspondence analysis through which differences in the career trajectories of central bankers in Europe, the United States and Japan can be empirically tracked and visually represented in ways which allow us to distinguish Alan Greenspan from Jean Claude Trichet. In this context, Lebaron aims to understand policy differences in a social space as something other than the logic of economic necessity or the discretion of exceptional individuals.

The question of social motivation is taken up in Froud *et al.*'s study of non-executive directors, a new kind of outside director who, in the era of corporate governance, now accounts for a majority of directors on the boards of the giant British companies in the FTSE 100. Froud *et al.*'s question is whether and how NEDs make a difference to behaviour; and their starting point is that earlier studies have crucially failed to demonstrate this point in a way that convinces 'so what' sceptics. Their tactic is then to deploy mixed methods of research with new kinds of network analysis, to establish the point that corporate governance had set up a new kind of exchange of current and former giant firm executives in NED roles. The difference in outcomes is then tackled through a case study of Pilkington which shows how a NED dominated board in 2006 efficiently auctioned the company that had successfully resisted takeover 20 years previously.

The same kind of resourceful methodological radicalism informs Olivier Godechot's study of the heads of dealing rooms. This is the only chapter that engages specifically with one section in the new coalition of financial intermediaries, whose numbers and power have increased over the past 25 years in ways that, apparently, constrain the discretion of the top corporate managers whom Mills regarded as the industrial power elite. Godechot supplies an ethnography of heads of dealing rooms which is radically inflected by the way in which he focuses the issue of how heads of dealing rooms have captured increasing financial rewards partly at the expense of others in the dealing room. By way of explanation, Godechot invokes not the star system but 'the political division of labour'. The head of the dealing room, like the 'putter out' in the industrial revolution, divides and recombines tasks so as to ensure that he benefits and can threaten to transfer the whole team to another bank.

A third batch of chapters focuses specifically on the cultural aspects of elite formation. Picking up on Bourdieu's emphasis on the relationship between consumption, taste, and the accumulation of advantage, these chapters not only demonstrate how monetary and financialization processes are interrelated with wider aspects of elite formation, but also reinforce our point that elite formation cannot be read from financialization. Thus, Griffiths *et al.* examine the changing nature of the cultural elite in England. They engage with the familiar idea that the traditional Oxbridge intellectual class has lost its power in neo-liberal times. Although there is some evidence for this view, at the same time there is evidence of new kinds of 'brokers' within the cultural elite, who continue to have a traditional background. Through empirical study of the membership of quangos in the jurisdiction of the Department of Culture, Media and Sport, the authors show that those with old elite characteristics are over-represented but do not monopolize the quango boards. Their social network analysis then shows that those with traditional institutional affiliations are more important in mediating and spanning such quangos.

Consumption and taste figure as objects in their own right in the chapters by Majima and Warde and Bennett and Warde. Majima and Warde offer the fullest empirical account of changes in the spending patterns of the top one per cent in the UK ever to have been published. Their account is invaluable in demonstrating both continuities and change. They trace a process whereby from 1961 to 1981 there was a slight closing of economic inequalities but thereafter the top one per cent pulled away. Whereas in 1961, the very wealthy were concerned to accumulate durables, possessions and 'personal service', by 2004 they were more attuned to investment and ensuring the profitable deployment of resources. Bennett and Warde use eleven in-depth interviews with elite members to explore their contemporary cultural engagement. They portray a picture of significant involvement of elite members in the governance of culture and show how obligatory it is for such elites to be culturally well versed. At the same time, this research shows how this engagement rarely crosses over into enthusiasm, and mainly supports a conformist, conventional, 'middle of the road' orientation towards the cultural realm.

The final chapter, by Sarah Green, shows how anthropologists can contribute to the resumption of elite studies and provides a caution against the idea that the only elites that matter live in a few world cities at the leading edge of metropolitan capitalist development. Green draws on extensive ethnography of the Balkans and considers village presidents, lawyers and civil servants in a laggard Greek region. The ethnography shows show how popular conceptions of local elites draw on monetized notions, especially around the idea of elites 'eating money' in a regional economy where the input of EU regional funding does not produce the output of infrastructure and activity for sustainable development. If Green's object is highly specific, her analysis overlaps suggestively with that in other essays, particularly in its emphasis on elites as intermediaries and the circuits of finance and money through cultural tropes into waiting mouths or pockets.

## Notes

1 In a period when a leading businessman such as Silvio Berlusconi can become Prime Minister of Italy, when Rupert Murdoch is actively courted by politicians, and more generally when the interplay between business interests and political representatives seems more fluid than in the post war period, it might seem that Poulantzas's insistence on the 'relative autonomy' of the state seems overstated. But this is to jump ahead.

2 ONS figures for the UK in 2006, using the National Statistics Socio-Economic Classification (which in its new form has been strongly influenced by the Goldthorpe's Nuffield class schema), indicate that 15% of working-age men, and 7% of working-age women were in the highest class of 'higher managerial and professionals'.

3 Goldthorpe has always insisted that he is prepared to recognize that there is a small elite, which may be amenable to analysis using other methods (eg Goldthorpe, 1995: 314). However, since he

also argues that survey methods are the most powerful tools available to social scientists, and is generally critical of ethnographic and case study approaches, it is not clear that this admission amounts to very much.

4 While the inflection of the argument to cover intermediaries is our own, Edwards' (2007) historical study of the role of the City in British relative decline revisits Olson's work and develops the idea of a distributional coalition as a way of analysing a neglected, classic problem.

5 See especially Bourdieu 2005a where he also introduces a new concept of financial capital 'the direct or indirect mastery (through access to the banks) of financial resources, which are the main condition (together with time) of the accumulation and conservation of all other kinds of capital' (Bourdieu, 2005a: 194).

6 And see Bourdieu 2005a where he specifically engages with social network theorists Mark Granovetter and Harrison White.

7 As an aside which we cannot develop here, we see the potential of Deleuze's social theory. His insistence, borrowing from Spinoza, is on the world as in a state of 'becoming', premised on virtual flows of energy and matter,m which can become crystallized in more stable forms (Delanda, 2002). Much of Deleuze's interest focuses on processes of de- and re-territorialization that take place around these fluid processes of becoming (Deleuze and Guattari, 1987). Within this framing, we can see elites as mechanisms for stabilizing turbulence, acting as mediators and fixers.

# References

Arrighi, G., (1994), *The Long Twentieth Century: Money, Power and the Origins of Our Time,* London: Verso.

Aspers, P., (2006), 'Theory, reality and performativity in markets', *American Journal of Economics and Sociology,* **66**: 379–398.

Atkinson, A.B., (2003), 'Top income in the United Kingdom over the twentieth century', mimeo, Oxford: Nuffield College, available at: http://www.nuff.ox.ac.uk/users/atkinson/ TopIncomes2003.pdf

Bearman, P., (1995), *Relations into Rhetorics,* ASA Rose Monographs.

Bearman, P., Moody, J. and Stovel, K., (2004), 'Chains of affection: the structure of adolescent romantic and sexual networks', *American Journal of Sociology* **110**: 44–91.

Blau, P and Duncan, O.S., (1967), *The American Occupational Structure,* New York: Wiley.

Blackburn, R., (2002), *Banking on Death or Investing in Life,* London: Verso.

Blackburn, R., (2006), 'Finance and the fourth dimension', *New Left Review* **39**: 39–70.

Blackburn, B. and Prandy, K., (1997), 'The reproduction of social inequality', *Sociology,* **31**, 3: 491–505.

Bourdieu, P., (1993), 'Some properties of fields', in: *Sociology in Question,* London: Sage: 72–77.

Bourdieu, P., (1996), *The State Nobility,* Cambridge: Polity.

Bourdieu, P., (2005a), *The Social Structure of the Economy,* Cambridge: Polity.

Bourdieu, P., (2005b), 'The journalistic field, the social science field, and the journalistic field', in Benson, R., and Neveu, E., *Bourdieu and the Journalistic Field,* Cambridge: Polity.

Bourdieu, P. and Passeron, J-C., (1990), *Reproduction in Education, Society and Culture,* London: Sage.

Brenner, R., (2002), *The Boom and a Bubble: the US in the World Economy,* London: Verso Press.

Burt, R., (1992), *Structural Holes: A New Theory of Competition,* Harvard: Harvard University Press.

Burt, R., (2005), *Brokerage and Closure: An Introduction to Social Capital,* Oxford: Oxford University Press.

Carrol, W., (2004), *Corporate Power in A Globalizing World,* Toronto: Oxford University Press.

Castells, M., (1996), *The Rise of the Network Society,* Oxford: Blackwells.

Castells, M., (1998), *End of Millenium,* Oxford: Blackwells.

Dahl, R., (1961), *Who Governs? Democracy and Power in an American City,* New Haven: Yale University Press.

Davies, A., (2002), *Public Relations Democracy,* Manchester: Manchester University Press.

Davies, A., (2007), *The Mediation of Power,* London: Routledge.

Delanda, M., (2002), *Intensive Science and Virtual Philosophy,* London: Continuum.

Deleuze, G. and Guattari, F., (1987), *A Thousand Plateaus: Capitalism and Schizophrenia,* Minneapolis: University of Minnesota Press.

Drucker, P., (1969), *The Age of Discontinuity,* New York: Harper Row.

Epstein, G.A., (ed.), (2005), *Financialization and the World Economy,* Cheltenham: Edward Elgar.

Erikson, R. and Goldthorpe, J.H., (1992), *The Constant Flux,* Oxford: Clarendon.

Erturk, I., Froud, J., Johal, S., Leaver, A. and Williams, K., (2008), *Financialization at Work,* London: Routledge.

Folkman, P., Froud, J., Johal, S. and Williams, K., (2007), 'Working for themselves? Capital market intermediaries and present day capitalism', *Business History* **49** (4): 552–572.

Foucault, M., (1975), *Discipline and Punish,* London: Allen Lane.

Frank, T., (2004), *What's the Matter with Kansas?* New York: Henry Holt.

Froud, J., Johal, S., Leaver, A. and Williams, K., (2006), *Financialization and Strategy: Narrative and Numbers,* London: Routledge.

Froud, J., Savage, M., Tampubolon, G., Williams, K., (2006), 'Rethinking elite research', *CRESC Working Paper,* No 12.

Giddens, A., (1973), *The Class Structure of the Advanced Societies,* Hutchinson, London.

Giddens, A., (1984), *The Constitution of Society,* Cambridge: Polity.

Glass, D.V., (1954), *Social Mobility in Britain,* London: Routledge and Kegan Paul.

Goldthorpe, J.H., (1980), *Social Mobility and the Class Structure in Modern Britain,* Oxford: Clarendon.

Goldthorpe, J.H., (1981), 'The class schema of social mobility and class structure in modern Britain: a reply to Penn', *Sociology* **15**: 272–280.

Guttsman, W.L., (1963), *The British Political Elite,* London: MacGibbon and Kee.

Harvey, D., (2005), *A Brief History of Neoliberalism,* New York: Oxford University Press.

Hilferding, R, (1981), *Finance Capital,* London: Routledge, translation of 1910 original *Das Finanzkapital.*

Ingham, G., (2004). *The Nature of Money,* Cambridge: Polity.

Johal, S. and Leaver, A., (2007), 'Is the stockmarket a disciplinary institution? French giant firms and the regime of accumulation', *New Political Economy* **12**, 3: 349–368.

Kahneman, D., Slovic, P. and Tversky, A., (eds) (1982), *Judgement under Uncertainty: Heuristics and Biase,* New York: Cambridge University Press.

Kelsall, R.K., (1955), *Higher Civil Servants in Britain,* London: Routledge and Kegan Paul.

Knox, H., Savage, M. and Harvey, P., (2006), 'Social networks and the study of relations: networks as method, metaphor and form', *Economy and Society* **35** (1): 113–140.

Lash, S. and Urry, J., (1987), *The End of Organized Capitalism,* Cambridge: Polity.

Latour, Bruno, (1988), *The Pasteurization of France,* Cambridge, Mass.: Harvard University Press.

Law, John, (1986), 'On the methods of long distance control: vessels, navigation and the Portuguese route to India', in Law, J., (ed.) *Power, Action and Belief: A New Sociology of Knowledge? Sociological Review Monograph,* 32: 234–263, London: Routledge and Kegan Paul.

Lazonick, W. and O'Sullivan, M., (2000), 'Maximising shareholder value: a new ideology for corporate governance', *Economy and Society,* (29), 1: 13–35.

Leroux, B., Rouanet, H., Savage, M., Warde, A., (2007), 'Culture and class in Britain, 2003' *CRESC Working Paper forthcoming.*

Lukes, S., (1975), *Power: A Radical View,* Basingstoke: Palgrave.

MacKenzie, D., Fabian M. and Lucia Siu, (eds), (2007), *Do Economists Make Markets? On the Performativity of Economics,* Princeton: Princeton University Press.

Marx, K., (1961), *Capital* (Vol 1), London: Lawrence and Wishart.

Miliband, R., (1969), *The State in Capitalist Society,* New York: Basic.

Mills, C.W., (1956), *The Power Elite,* London: Oxford University Press.

Mitchell, T., (2003), *Rule of Experts,* Berkeley: University of California Press.

Moore, B., (1967), *The Social Origins of Dictatorship and Democracy*, Oxford: Oxford University Press.

Olson, M., (1982), *The Rise and Decline of Nations*, New Haven: Yale University Press.

Penn, R., (1981), 'The nuffield class categorization', *Sociology*, **15**: 265–271.

Pettigrew, A., (1992), 'On studying managerial elites'. *Strategic Management Journal*, **13**, 163–182.

Poggi, G., (2005), *Max Weber, A Short Introduction*, Oxford: Blackwells.

Polsby, N., (1963), *Community Power and Political Theory*, New Haven: Yale University Press.

Porter, J., (1965), *The Vertical Mosaic*, Toronto: University of Toronto Press.

Poulantzas, N., (1973), *Political Power and Social Classes*, London: Verso.

Roberts, J., Sanderson, P., Baker, R. and Hendry, J., (2006), 'In the mirror of the market: the disciplinary effects of company/fund manager meetings', *Accounting, Organizations and Society*, **31**, 3: 277–294.

Rose, D. and Pevalin, D., (eds), (2003), *A Researcher's Guide to the National Statistics Socio-Economic Classification,* London: Sage.

Rose, N., (1990), *Governing the Soul*, London: Routledge.

Sampson, A., (1962), *Anatomy of Britain*, London: Hodder and Stoughton.

Savage, M., (1997), 'Social mobility and the survey method: a critical analysis', in Bertaux, D. and P. Thompson (eds), *Pathways to Social Class: Qualitative Approaches to Social Mobility*, Oxford: Clarendon Press.

Savage, M., (2000), *Class Analysis and Social Transformation*, Milton Keynes: Open University Press.

Savage, M. and Burrows, R., (2007), 'The coming crisis of empirical sociology', *Sociology,* 41, 5: 885–889.

Savage, M., Warde, A. and Devine, F., (2005), 'Capitals, assets and resources: some critical issues', *British Journal of Sociology*, 56, 1: 31–48.

Scott, J., (1982), *The Upper Class,* Basingstoke: MacMillan.

Scott, J., (1992), *Social Network Analysis*, London: Sage.

Scott, J., (1996), *Stratification and Power*, Cambridge: Polity.

Scott, J., (1997), *Corporate Business and Capitalist Classes*, 1st Edition, Oxford: Oxford University Press.

Scott, J. and Griff, C., (1984), *Directors of Industry: the British Corporate Network 1900–1976*, Cambridge: Polity.

Shliefer, A. and Summers, L.H., (1988), 'Breach of trust in hostile takeovers', in Auerbach, A.J., (ed.) *Corporate Takeovers: Causes and Consequences*, Chicago: Chicago University Press/NBER: 33–56.

Sklair, L., (2001), *The Transnational Capitalist Class*, Oxford: Blackwells.

Soros, G., (1998), *The Crisis of Global Capitalism*, New York: Little, Brown and Company.

Thomas, H., (1959), *The Establishment*, London: Blond.

Useem, M., (1984), *The Inner Circle: Large Corporations and the Rise of Business Political Activity in the U.S. and U.K.*, New York: Oxford University Press.

Van Der Pijl, K., (1998), *Transnational Classes and International Relations*, London: Routledge.

Wellman, B., (1979), 'The community question: the intimate networks of East Yorkers', *American Journal of Sociology* **84**: 1201–1231.

Williamson, J., (ed.), (1989), *Latin American Readjustment: How Much has Happened*, Institute of International Studies, Washington.

Windolf, P., (2002), *Corporate Networks in Europe and the United States*, Oxford: Oxford University Press.

Zeitlin, J., (1989), *The Large Corporation and Contemporary Classes*, Oxford: Polity.

# Section 1
# Taking Stock of Elites: Recognizing Historical Changes

# Modes of power and the re-conceptualization of elites

## John Scott

The idea that societies can be seen in terms of dominant and competing elites was central to the research agendas of political and economic sociology through much of the twentieth century.[1] Investigations of economic and political power in the United States invariably involved an examination of the social background and connections of 'top decision-makers' (Hunter, 1953; Mills, 1956; Domhoff, 1967). By the early 1980s there was a substantial body of literature on this topic, especially concerning economic elites (see, for example, Dooley, 1969; Bunting and Barbour, 1971; Bearden and others, 1975; Mintz, 1975; Allen, 1978; Useem, 1984). Similar studies had been undertaken in Britain (Miliband, 1969; Giddens 1972; Urry and Wakeford, 1973; Stanworth and Giddens, 1974; Thomas, 1978), and comparative studies had been carried out (Stokman *et al.*, 1985). At the end of the decade, a compilation of classic studies (Scott, 1990) had aimed at consolidating these achievements. Through much of the 1980s and 1990s, however, this research paradigm had faltered. Investigations into substantive issues of economic and political power continued (Scott and Griff, 1984; Mintz and Schwartz, 1985; Carroll, 1986; Scott, 1991, 1997; Useem, 1993) but these studies sought to operate without the concept of an elite. Many works in political sociology concentrated, instead, on the development of structural theories of state power that minimized the part played by collective agency in the exercise of this power.

The weakness of elite research over the last three decades can, perhaps, be seen as a reaction to the overstated claims that had been made for the idea of the elite and as an implicit acceptance of the many critical attacks levelled at it. The claim that elite researchers tended to overstate the power and cohesion of elites was unintentionally reinforced by the tendency of sociologists to use the word indiscriminately. At the height of its popularity almost any powerful, advantaged, qualified, privileged, or superior group or category might be described as an elite. The term became one of the most general – and, therefore, one of the most meaningless – terms used in descriptive studies. It was applied to such diverse groups as politicians, bishops, intelligent people, aristocrats, lawyers, and successful criminals. Not surprisingly, elite research attracted sustained criticism. The most vociferous critics were those pluralists who challenged what they called 'positional' studies in the name of a more dynamic approach

© 2008 The Author. Editorial organisation © 2008 The Editorial Board of the Sociological Review. Published by Blackwell Publishing Ltd, 9600 Garsington Road, Oxford OX4 2DQ, UK and 350 Main Street, Malden, MA 02148, USA

to power and decision-making (Dahl, 1958, 1961, 1966; Polsby, 1962). It was such challenges that led many of those involved in power structure research to eschew the word 'elite' in their substantive studies. The idea simply seemed to carry too much unwanted intellectual baggage to warrant its continued use.

It is now time to reassess that conclusion. A number of powerful and sophisticated studies (Carroll, 2004; MacLean *et al.*, 2006) have once again made it central to their concerns. The term can play an important part in sociological research; and its meaning must be narrowed down and refined so that it can be retained as a powerful analytical concept and not inflated beyond its legitimate use. Elites must be distinguished from all those other social groups with which they are often confused; and their relations with other groups with which they may often be associated in real-world situations must be clarified.

The fundamental starting point must be that, at the very least, the word 'elite' should be used only in relation to those groups that have a degree of power.[2] Some but not all of the groups indiscriminately described as elites are holders of power; and my argument is that the concept should be limited to such groups. My concern will be to try to distinguish precisely what forms of power give rise to the formation of elites and, therefore, to set some limits on the ways in which the term should be used.

This emphasis on power means that people with high IQ, for example, do not constitute an elite in any sociologically meaningful sense. They may be very significant in many walks of life and it may be very important to study them, but they are not a category to which the word 'elite' should be applied. Similarly, highly-paid occupational groups should not be described as elites simply because of their high pay, however privileged or advantaged they may be. Such groups become elites only if their intelligence or high pay becomes a basis for significant power. To label superior or advantaged groups indiscriminately as 'elites' is to make it *more difficult* to study them, as it implies spurious similarities among them and with other groups. Such an approach masks their specific features and destroys all distinctiveness that the elite concept can have. Clarifying the concept of an elite, therefore, can help us to study both elites *and* those other groups with which they tend to be confused.

## Conceptualizing power and domination

Elites are most usefully seen, then, in relation to the holding and exercising of power. This implicitly raises a further problem, as power itself is a much-contested idea and has been defined in numerous different ways. It might seem at first glance, therefore, that a focus on power cannot really provide an answer to the problem of defining what is meant by an elite. Many recent arguments, especially those that draw on the work of Foucault (1975–6, 1982), have sought to reject all prior approaches and to argue that power, by its very nature, cannot be defined in a rigorous or systematic way. Such an argument is misleading. While it is important to recognize the contributions to the analysis of power that have been made by Foucault and his followers, there is far more consistency with earlier views than is often believed. Following Lukes (1974), I have argued elsewhere (Scott, 2001) that a viable concept of power underlies all the principal debates in the area. This view of power can be articulated into a conceptual framework that can help to make sense of the parallel debate over the concept of an elite.

Power, in its most general sense, can be seen as the production of causal effects, and social power is an agent's intentional use of causal powers to affect the conduct of other agents. At its simplest, then, social power is a bipartite relation between two agents, one of whom is the 'principal' or paramount agent, and the other the 'subaltern' or subordinate agent. The principal has or exercises power, while the subaltern is affected by the power of a principal. In the mainstream of power research, investigators have largely been concerned with the actual exercise of power by a principal over a subaltern: power consists in actually making someone do something. In a second stream of research, on the other hand, attention has been given to a principal's capacity or potential to do something. From this latter point of view, the central significance of power is to be found in the ability that certain actors have to facilitate things.

The paradigm for power relations in the mainstream view is the exercise of decision-making powers in a state through the use of electoral and administrative mechanisms. This view of power is extended to other kinds of sovereign organization, such as business enterprises, universities, and churches. According to this point of view, principals are those who make others do what they would not otherwise do. Conversely, agents may resist the attempts of others to place them in subaltern positions by making them act against their own wishes and preferences. In sovereign organizations, power relations are asymmetrical and are organized around the conflicting interests and goals of the participants. Power is fixed in quantity and, because some have more than others, one agent can gain only at the expense of another. Conflict over the distribution of power will always involve both winners and losers.

Lukes's (1974) critical commentary on power studies has concentrated, for the most part, on mainstream research. He followed Bachrach and Baratz (1962) in distinguishing between two faces of sovereign power – decision-making and nondecision-making – but he also went on to recognize a third facet. In discussing this third aspect of power, Lukes recognized the mobilization of bias within a social structure, but he also recognized the need to take social structure itself more seriously (see also Lukes, 1977). From this point of view, the analysis of power has to be extended from the 'discrete intervention by a social agent in the life of another social agent' (Wartenberg, 1990:72) to the enduring structural constraints that shape that exercise of power.

These issues were precisely those that have been central to the second stream of power research, though researchers have focussed on the cultural construction of institutional structures far more than they have on the relational structures emphasized by Lukes.[3] The second stream of research does not focus on specific organizations of power, but on the strategies and techniques of power.

Power is not concentrated in sovereign organizations but is diffused throughout a society, and so must be seen as a collective property of systems of co-operating actors. Instead of the repressive aspects of power, which tend to figure in the mainstream, the second stream stresses its facilitative or 'productive' aspects.

Developed in the work of Gramsci, Althusser, Arendt, and Parsons, the second stream view was most thoroughly elaborated by Foucault (1975, 1976). What Foucault has referred to as the 'discursive formation' of power operates through mechanisms of socialization and community building that constitute individuals as subjects with particular kinds of mental orientation and habitual routines of action. Discursively formed power can be a means of collective empowerment, as argued by Arendt (1969) and Parsons (1963), but Foucault stressed its negative aspects as a basis for 'discipline'. The principals in power relations are those formed as experts and who are 'authorized' to discipline others. Foucault makes the further point, however, that the most effective and pervasive forms of power occur where people have learned to exercise self-discipline over their own behaviour. They have been discursively formed into subalterns who conform without the need for any direct action on the part of a principal.

It is the combination of mainstream and second stream approaches to power that provides the basis for developing a nuanced understanding of the various forms that power can take. Each stream has highlighted different, but complementary, sets of mechanisms, and it is important to develop an understanding of these mechanisms, working from the elementary forms to the more complex patterns of domination that are found in states, economic structures, and associations.

There are two elementary forms of social power. *Corrective influence*, analysed principally within the mainstream, depends on the rational calculations made by agents and operates through punishments and rewards. *Persuasive influence*, a principal theme of the second stream, depends on the offering of arguments, appeals, and reasons that lead subalterns to believe that it is appropriate to act in one way rather than another. The two main forms of corrective influence are force and manipulation. Where force involves the use of negative physical sanctions to prevent the actions of subalterns, manipulation involves both positive and negative sanctions (eg, money, credit, and access to employment) as ways of influencing subaltern decisions. The two main forms of persuasive influence are signification and legitimation, operating respectively through shared cognitive meanings and shared value commitments. These discursive meanings make a particular course of action seem necessary or emotionally appropriate.

These elementary forms of power are the building blocks from which more fully developed power relations are built. These developed power relations occur in a number of modalities as structures of *domination*, forms of *counteraction* to domination, and the more amorphous patterns of *interpersonal power* that are rooted in face-to-face relations. These and related distinctions are shown in Figure 1.

| *Elementary forms of power* | Corrective influence | | Persuasive influence | |
|---|---|---|---|---|
| | Force | Manipulation | Signification | Legitimation |
| *Developed forms of power* | Domination | | | |
| | Through constraint | | Through authority | |
| | Coercion | Inducement | Expertise | Command |
| | Counteraction | | | |
| | Protest | | Pressure | |
| | Interpersonal power | | | |

**Figure 1:** *A Map of Power Relations.*
*Source*: Based on Scott (2002: Figure1.1)

Domination is power that is structured into stable and enduring relations of control, and Figure 1 identifies four forms of domination. *Coercion* and *inducement* are structures of constraint through corrective influence. *Expertise* and *command*, on the other hand, are discursively based structures of authority built through persuasive influence. Constraint is the form of domination that Weber (1914) referred to as 'domination by virtue of a constellation of interests' and that Giddens (1979:100–101) called 'allocative domination'. Constraint exists where principals are able to influence subalterns by determining the action alternatives open to them, either by direct force and repression or by offering inducements that influence a subaltern's calculations. Within the overall distribution of resources, the resources controlled by the principal determine the constellation of interests faced by principal and subaltern and within which both must act. Domination through discursive formation is what Giddens called 'authoritative domination'. Authority exists where principals influence subalterns through persuasion rooted in the institutionalized commitments, loyalties, and trust that organize command and expertise.

In relations of coercion, action alternatives are restricted through direct force or repression. Subalterns are coerced by power that exists independently of their preferences or wishes. They must take account of it in their subjective assessment of their situation, but it does not depend upon their giving it any discursive justification. Inducement, also, operates through the subjectivity of participants and without discursive justification. In this case, however, it relies on the preferences and desires of the subalterns by influencing the calculations that they make about how to act in particular situations. The leaders of an invading army of conquest, for example, may coerce a population into compliance through threatening or actually using violence against them. Bank managers, on the other hand, may induce clients to invest by altering rates of interest and other conditions attached to loans.

Agents who have internalized prevailing cultural values will tend to identify with those who occupy positions of domination defined in terms of these values.

31

This internalization and identification defines the powers of command and expertise available to principals in relation to subalterns. Relations of command are those where internalized values structure both the *rights* of principals to give orders and the corresponding *obligations* for subalterns to obey. Subalterns willingly comply because they are committed to a belief in the legitimacy of a specific command and of those who issue commands. Legitimacy exists when there is a belief that a pattern of domination is right, correct, justified, or valid (Held, 1989:102; Beetham, 1991:10–12). Relations of expertise are those where knowledge that is monopolized by one group is accepted by others as a legitimate basis on which they can offer authoritative expert advice. Subalterns are not obliged to treat this advice as an instruction, but there is a presumption that the experts can be trusted to offer valid and reliable guidance that ought to be followed. An executive manager in a bureaucratic hierarchy may hold a position of command over junior employees, while a lawyer or accountant may exercise expertise through the technical advice that he or she can offer to clients.[4]

## Reconceptualizing elites

This delineation and clarification of the forms of power and domination has had a purpose: to enable me to set out a defensible and useable concept of 'elite' as a specific kind of group involved in holding and exercising power. Specifically, elites are to be defined in relation to the structures of domination that constitute them. Elites are those groups that hold or exercise domination within a society or within a particular area of social life.

Corresponding to the four forms of domination are four types of elite (see Figure 2). Coercive elites and inducing elites are based in allocative control over resources. Coercers and inducers derive their power from the constraints that flow from the distribution of the resources involved in force and manipulation. They are the elites that Pareto (1916) referred to as the 'lions' and the 'foxes', using the language of fables. Expert and commanding elites are based in relations of authority. Experts and commanders derive their power from the discursive formation of signifying and legitimating principals and subalterns. Emulating Pareto's language, it can be suggested that the experts be referred to as 'owls' and the commanders as 'bears'.[5]

| Allocative domination | Coercive elite – lions (force) | Inducing elite – foxes (manipulation) |
|---|---|---|
| Authoritative domination | Commanding elite – bears (legitimacy) | Expert elite – owls (signification) |

**Figure 2:** *Types of Elite.*

Coercive and inducing elites can be identified in purely formal terms by the resources under their control. Those who control access to the use of the means of violence have the ability to coerce others into conformity and to act against their wishes, desires, and interests. Those with financial and industrial assets organized as economic capital are able to induce others to conform by influencing their rational, self-interested calculations of personal or group advantage.

Expert and commanding elites can be identified by the particular symbols and social meanings that they monopolize. Expert elites are those whose specialized bodies of technical knowledge are organized into 'professional' structures and practices. Lawyers, accountants, doctors, and investment advisers, for example, may all be involved in persuasive power on the basis of a claimed and accepted expertise. Commanding elites are those who legitimately occupy the top administrative positions in institutional hierarchies of management and control. In contemporary societies this characteristically takes the form of what Weber described as bureaucracy. Such 'top' bureaucratic positions are institutionally defined as those that carry strategic significance for a particular organization or form of association.

These four ideal types of elite overlap with each other in concrete situations and may only rarely be distinguishable in their particular forms. The analytical distinctions are, however, important to make as it is only through analysis that the complex interdependence of factors may be investigated. Thus, a commanding elite may also possess coercive powers that provide an ultimate, last-resort back-up for their authority. They may also be able to gain personal control over those resources that give them enhanced life chances and the ability to manipulate the behaviour of others. Holders of commanding positions in business enterprises – the executives and top managers – are especially likely to have further powers of financial inducement available to them. Under some conditions, however, it is possible for the mechanisms that structure the powers of particular elites to achieve a degree of differentiation from each other. In these circumstances, members of some or all of the types of elite may be able to act as autonomous and specialized agents. A commanding elite in the state, for example, may face a challenge from the coercive power held by the military forces of another state or from the financial inducements that can be offered by criminal syndicates. The concrete configuration of power in any particular situation is always a matter for empirical investigation; but such investigations must rest on a clear delineation of the various types of domination and their bases.

## Ruling elites and social classes

In its most general sense, then, the term 'elite' is most meaningfully and usefully applied to those who occupy the most powerful positions in structures of domination. Elites can be identified in any society by identifying these structural positions. As occupants of a purely formal category, the members of an elite need have few bonds of interaction or association and may not exist as a cohesive and solidaristic social group. Such solidarity occurs only if social mobility, leisure time socializing, education, intermarriage, and other social relations are such that the members of an elite are tied together in regular and recurrent patterns of association. Only then are they likely to show any unity or to develop common forms of outlook and social consciousness. A key area of elite research is to examine whether these links of background and recruitment exist and to chart their consequences for elite consciousness and commonality of action.

This elite structuring is especially likely to occur where recruitment to elite positions reflects larger processes of class and status formation. Elites are analytically distinguishable from social classes and status groups, no matter how entwined they may be in real situations. One of the recurrent problems in elite research, however, has been the tendency to confuse these concepts and to use them interchangeably. 'Economic elite' and 'capitalist class', for example, may be used interchangeably to describe various privileged, advantaged, or powerful economic groups. This tendency must be resisted if the analytical power of the elite concept is to be retained, as this is the only basis on which the dynamics of power can be clearly understood.

The resources involved in holding and exercising power are also relevant to the formation of class and status situations. It was for this reason that Weber held that class and status were to be seen as aspects of the distribution of power. When access to material resources is structured through property and market relations, the resource distribution forms the 'class situations' that determine the life chances of their occupants and become the bases of social class formation (Scott, 1996). Similarly, the symbolic resources of social prestige that comprise cultural capital may be formed into 'status situations' that determine styles of life and become the bases for the formation of social estates and status groups. Class structures are differentiated by divisions of property and employment that are the bases of the inequalities of wealth and life chances measured in class schema. Status situations are constituted by cultural definitions of factors such as gender, religion, and ethnicity that become the bases for judgements of social superiority and inferiority.

Studies of class and class situation have generally operated with occupational classification schemes, classifying occupations by their employment relations. They have generally failed to focus on the property relations that are also involved in class situations, and this has led to a confusion of class and elite ideas.[6] This is apparent in the work of Goldthorpe (1987), otherwise the most sophisticated and compelling writer on class. Goldthorpe has argued that the privileged section of property holders can be regarded as an 'elite' within the 'service class'. A service class, for Goldthorpe, is defined by the employment relations of its members, and its especially privileged members are, for Goldthorpe, those who additionally have propertied interests. However, those who are most advantaged by these employment relations or who have personal property holdings may not, thereby, have the ability to exercise authoritative or allocative domination over others. It is only where such domination exists that we are dealing with an elite. It is important to identify such a group, to theorize its property relations and its location within a class hierarchy, but it should not simply be regarded as an elite *per se*. Rather, we may be dealing with the occupants of a particular class situation, with a class or class fraction, or with those drawn from such a background.

Wealthy or propertied classes and honoured status groups are, in analytical terms, quite distinct from elites. The analysis of class and status as aspects of the distribution of power owes much to Weber, who was very clear about the need to distinguish these from, in particular, the powers of command that exist in structures of authority (see Scott, 1996). Elites are recruited from social classes and social estates – and they will, therefore, exhibit classed, gendered, racialized, and other characteristics. This means that in real situations it may be difficult to separate them. Nevertheless, the principles on which they operate and the mechanisms of power involved are quite distinct and a theoretically informed discussion of power must make the analytical distinction.

These arguments help us to understand the structuration of elite categories into substantive social groups. Weber did not use the term 'elite' in his work, but his pupil Roberto Michels (1927) drew out the implications of his work and linked these to parallel ideas in the work of Mosca (1896; 1923) and Pareto (1901; 1916). This work is central to any understanding of the structure and action of elites (see the readings in Scott, 1990; 1994). The work of these classical elite theorists shows, in particular, that the various elites of a society may overlap and combine to form a single, overarching elite. Those who occupy the leading positions of command and expertise within a state, an established church, and in capitalist enterprises, for example, may be forged into a single concrete elite, though it may still be fruitful to distinguish the varying mechanisms of domination in each of these areas.

Mosca introduced the term *classe dirigente* or 'ruling class' to describe this kind of ruling minority. In view of the confusions surrounding the language of 'class', however, it is preferable to follow Pareto's (1916) terminological innovation, and use the word 'elite'. *Classe dirigente*, then, can best be translated as 'ruling elite'. Mosca's aim in introducing this idea was to address such questions as whether a narrowly defined political elite forms part of a broader and more all-encompassing ruling elite. The argument of Mills (1956) that the American power structure involves a fusion of economic, political, and military dominants into a single 'power elite' follows this same approach.

Shared participation in the holding and exercising of power may forge a unity among the occupants of elite positions. It is, however, when the members of specialized or ruling elites are recruited from narrow and specific class and status backgrounds that they are most likely to develop a unity and cohesion of consciousness and action. Coming to the elite with a shared outlook and experiences, their unity as participants in power is reinforced by their wider commonality. As Alan Warde and Tony Bennett show in their chapter in this volume, elites may develop distinctive patterns of consumption. It must not be assumed, however, that elite unity is the norm. Even specialized political and economic elites may be internally divided along ideological, religious, ethnic, or other lines, and these divisions may preclude them from achieving any overall solidarity or from forming part of a larger ruling elite. Factions may divide a political elite to such an extent that it is better to consider it as comprising two or more rival sub-elites whose conflict and tension may be an important source of change. Michael Moran's chapter in this volume demonstrates the fragmentation within the business elite in Britain that developed during the 1980s and 1990s and some of the difficulties this poses for class-wide representation of business interests.

## Elite formation and dynamics

Elites can exist at various levels of a society and so are distinguishable by their degree of power. The commanding elite within a golf club, for example, may have autocratic control over club employees and other club members, but it will have little influence in the wider society unless its members individually have positions of power within other, more salient organizations and institutional hierarchies. Their power may also be enhanced if the golf club becomes a means of access to other channels of power: a venue for business meetings, for example. In most cases, however, the elites in particular organizations will have only locally specific power and will have little influence in the wider society. The main focus of elite studies has been on the central and most salient institutional hierarchies and systems of resources within a society.

I have concentrated so far on elites within specific formal organizations, whether these be states, business enterprises, churches, or other types of association that exhibit an institutionalized hierarchy of power. It is also important to recognize, however, that inter-organizational relations need to be taken into account in considering the formation of elites. In the case of a state, its various organizational units – the government, the judiciary, the military, the civil service, and so on – are generally unified through their inter-organizational links as branches of the higher-level organization of a state. This, however, is not so clearly the case for economic elites. It is relatively easy to identify an elite within a particular business enterprise, as the enterprise will have directors and top executives who hold its key positions of command. The same is true for such business associations as employers' federations and sales cartels, and it applies also to the top professionals in expert organizations relevant to business. These various economic elites, however, will often maintain inter-organizational links among themselves, and it is important to see how the overall power structure of business can be analysed. If an analysis remains at the level of the individual organization, then a false impression of a fragmented power structure may be obtained.

Structures of economic power are typically formed from intercorporate networks of personal, commercial, and capital relations within which the intraorganizational exercise of command and expertise is embedded (Scott and Griff, 1984:17). These are the bases on which interlocking directorships and other forms of intercorporate association are established as the bases through which individuals may be able to exercise power within two or more organizations. In these circumstances, the overlap of personnel is such that the overall economic or corporate elite is more than simply a collection of separate company-level elites. In addition to positions within particular organizations, its members have powers of command and/or expertise that result from the intercorporate connections among large numbers of enterprises and they may be able to bring about a degree of co-ordination among their activities across the economy as a whole. Froud and her colleagues, in their contribution to this volume, have shown how 'outsider' non-executive directors play an important part in intercorporate relations. Bankers and investment managers, for example, have powers of command within their own organizations and coercive or inducing power that derives from their ability to grant or withhold credit or venture capital for particular enterprises. Through, the interweaving of shareholdings, credit arrangements, and board positions, they may also occupy strategic positions in the overall flow of capital and so be able to exercise system-wide powers. Such intercorporate economic elites may be built from many diverse corporate elites with varying bases of power, and recent developments in the 'financialization' of capitalist economies, as shown by Michael Savage and Karel Williams in their introduction to this volume, have made this even more complex to explore. Hedge-fund managers, for example, combine numerous resources and bases of power that distinguish them from investment bankers, clearing bankers, stock-market equity traders, and pension fund managers (MacKenzie, 2003; Hardie and MacKenzie, 2007. And see the chapter by Oliver Godechot in this volume). Identification of an economic elite, therefore, rests upon a detailed and comprehensive mapping of intra- and inter-corporate relations.

The relevant inter-organizational relations should not be seen as confined to national societies and national economies, any less than nation states should be seen as isolated from transnational agencies and other nation states. The growing globalization of political economies and the extension of transnational networks of relations (Castells, 1996) has underlined the fact that 'societies' are not purely national (Urry, 2000). Neither specialized elites nor ruling elites and power elites need be understood as purely national phenomena, and it is important to locate elites within the relevant transnational flows (Fennema, 1982; Carroll and Fennema, 2002).

It is important, once again, to emphasize that an economic elite is not the same thing as a capitalist class. An economic elite is an inter-organizational group of people who hold positions of dominance in business organizations and who may, under certain circumstances, have certain additional powers available to them. A capitalist class, on the other hand, comprises the occupants of specific class situations, defined by the ownership of corporate property, who are generally able to secure their reproduction as a class through practices of inheritance and inter-marriage. To the extent that the members of such a class may secure a disproportionate representation within the economic elite, it may also consolidate and enhance its property and wealth. This, however, does not make the formal, analytical distinction between the class and the elite redundant. Indeed, one particularly important debate in this area has been that over the so-called 'managerial revolution' – the question of whether owning controllers have been replaced by propertyless managers (Scott, 1997) as the leading members of the corporate elite. Such questions simply cannot be asked, let alone answered, if the distinction between class and elite is not maintained. Similarly, Sklair's (2001) identification of global formations of economic, political, and cultural power should not be taken as evidence for the formation of a 'global capitalist class'. His analysis may have produced evidence for the formation of a global business elite (see Bauman, 1998) but not for a global capitalist class.

A further point about the dynamics of power must be underlined. I have shown that the two streams of power research have focused on both the *holding* and the actual *exercise* of power, and I have argued that both must be seen as integral elements of a viable research agenda. Important as it is, the identification of elites on the basis of positions within structures of domination is only one element in a comprehensive investigation. No conclusions about the power of an elite can be regarded as final until the actual exercise of their power potential and its effects on the behaviour of subalterns has been demonstrated. This argument was central to the pluralist critique of elite studies, and its importance must be recognized. Nevertheless, it is not necessary to accept the pluralist conclusion that elite research must be abandoned. Both facets of power have their part to play in the type of research agenda that is advocated here.

## Counteraction

I have emphasized that political and economic elites, organized around structures of domination, must not be seen in isolation from other forms of power. One of the errors made in much elite analysis, however, has been to assume, or at the very least to imply, that elites are all-powerful and that organizationally dominant groups will hold all the other power resources of a society. This implication has been reflected in many of the criticisms that have been levelled at forms of elite analysis: elite studies have been criticized for their naivety in assuming that even a ruling elite, as defined by Mosca, will face no effective challenge to its power.

Power is intrinsically tied to the possibility of resistance, and the power of any elite must be seen as open to challenge from the resisting counteraction of its subalterns. This may be manifest in inchoate resentment, hostility, or withdrawal, or in isolated acts of disruption or sabotage. The most important forms of counteraction, however, are those that involve co-ordinated or collective action against an elite: power from below rather than power from above. This counteraction derives its power from the number of subalterns that are able to unite together and the kind of solidarity that they are able to achieve as a collective.

Subaltern counteraction takes two principal forms. When oppositional action is institutionalized and counteracting groups are given a degree of recognition and legitimacy by the established elite, they can be said to exercise 'pressure' as members of the institutionalized structure of domination. Pressure groups, for example, have a legitimate role within the state and may exercise a countervailing power to that of a state elite. This interplay of state elites and pressure group leadership is central to pluralist models of politics (McLennan, 1995; Hirst, 1993, 1997).[7] 'Protest', on the other hand, is subaltern counteraction that occurs outside the formal institutions of power and that poses a challenge to those very structures. It is subaltern resistance exercised as a counter-mobilization to the existing structure of domination. Where protest movements are structured around formally organized groups, the leadership in these groups may properly be referred to as true 'counter-elites'. These are subalterns who hold dominant positions within oppositional movements. Thus, the trades union leadership within a labour movement may comprise a counteracting labour elite to the business elites that they encounter in the employment relations that bring them together. The chapter by Michael Moran in this volume has explored some of the conflict and contention that arises among the various business organizations operating within the corporate sphere.

These are, again, analytical distinctions that are often difficult to disentangle in concrete situations. Protest groups may achieve some of their goals and accommodate themselves to the established framework of power, transforming themselves into pressure groups; and pressure groups may be frustrated in their actions and mount progressively more confrontational protests. Pressure groups may be subverted from within, becoming progressively more challenging to the existing system; and protest groups may be subtly transformed into more quiescent resistance where their oppositional ideology obscures a *de facto* accommodation to the system.

While counter-elites, like the elites engaged in pressure politics, may be formally distinguished according to the forms of domination from which they are excluded and that they challenge – coercion, inducement, command, and expertise – they are also defined in terms of their organization around resistance *per se*. Their counteraction may be a far more important basis of their collective identity than the particular form of domination that they challenge. It is for this reason that alliances among counter-elites and their movements are a relatively common occurrence: it is the fact of exclusion and subordination that unites otherwise divergent protest movements around common patterns of resistance. It is, nevertheless, unusual to find distinct counter-elites fused into a single subaltern counter-elite of resistance, even where dominant groups are fused into a single ruling elite.

It was the confrontation between ruling elites and counter-elites that Pareto saw as central to the political process. He gave particular attention to the periodic replacement of ruling elites by counter-elites through revolutionary struggles. While Pareto's cyclical view of historical change may be questioned as a general framework of historical explanation, it is certainly important to explore the conflicts that are inherent in the challenges raised by the counter-action of subaltern organizations and social movements.

## Conclusion

I have tried to show that a clear and systematic delineation of the various forms of power produces a basis for building a viable usage for the word 'elite'. I have done this through exploring structures of domination and counteraction. Alongside these formal structures of power, and permeating them at every point, are relations of interpersonal power, which also need to figure in a full analysis. It is not possible fully to understand domination and counteraction without also recognizing the impact of interpersonal power. These relations are those of face-to-face encounters, where power depends on personal attributes and character-istics and is shaped by patriarchal and racialized attitudes. Unfortunately, there is no the space to explore this further here.

A research agenda for a renewed programme of elite studies must comprise four principal tasks, though these will rarely all figure in one project. There is, first, the identification and mapping of the various elites in the society, societies, or social sectors under investigation. Identification of the relevant dimensions of power involved in structures of domination and an investigation of the net-works of inter-organizational linkages through which they are connected allows the mapping of coercive, inducing, expert, and commanding elites and the boundaries that separate them from the other groups in their social world. Sec-ondly, it is important to examine the balances of power that exist among the various elites. This involves an investigation of the overlap and integration apparent in their composition and the relative salience of each elite *viz-à-viz* all others. Thirdly is the need to investigate the connections between the various elites and the class and status groups from which they may be recruited and whose interests they may – or may not – pursue. Such investigations are likely to form an integral part of any investigation into the institutional fusion of dis-tinct elites into a single 'ruling elite'. Finally, a comprehensive investigation must examine the relations of an elite to the counteracting pressure groups and protest movements that may challenge it. It must not be assumed that an elite – even a ruling elite – will be all-powerful and will always hold sway over the remainder of its society or social organization. Resistance is integral to power and must figure in any comprehensive research agenda.

I hope to have established not only that the idea of the elite has a legitimate usage in sociological research but also that this idea must be seen in narrower terms than has often been the case. Only if the concept is restricted to specific groupings arising in relation to structures of domination can it be of value to sociologists. Such a definition makes sense of the bulk of the research previ-ously undertaken, it implies a research programme that avoids the criticisms that have been levelled against it, and it points the way forward for a renewal of elite studies.

## Notes

1 The argument of this chapter has developed through earlier versions delivered at conferences on 'The Extremes of Social Space: Ways of Thinking About Changes at the Top and the Bottom of Advanced Transatlantic Societies' (Amsterdam School for Social Research, University of Amsterdam, June 11th, 2002), 'Occupations and Power' (University of Greenwich, November 22nd, 2002), and 'Reviving Elites Research' (CRESC, University of Manchester, March 8th, 2006). I am grateful to the participants in these conferences for their many useful comments on the chapter.
2 See the initial attempt to do this in Scott (1996). My argument in this paper modifies slightly some of those made in that book.
3 This distinction between institutional and relational structure is elaborated in López and Scott (2000).
4 Gouldner (1954) attempted to theorize the relations between these two processes in his distinction between 'punishment-centred' and 'representative' bureaucracy'.
5 In Scott (2001) I limited the term to commanding elites but it now seems more appropriate to recognize these four types of elite.
6 Nor have they rigorously analysed the differences of prestige that are associated with status situations. Where authority is considered in these classifications, this has been through the idea of the 'work situation', seen as a subsidiary and causally dependent aspect of the property and employment relations that constitute 'market situation'.
7 Pluralist theories have often been tied to the assumption of a relative equality of power among competing elites (for example, Dahl 1971), but this need not be the case. A recognition of the plurality of power can go hand-in-hand with a recognition of fundamental inequalities of power among contending groups.

## References

Allen, M. P., (1978), 'The structure of interorganizational elite cooptation', *American Sociological Review* 39: 393–406.
Arendt, H., (1969), *On Violence*, New York: Harcourt Brace and World.
Bachrach, P. and Baratz, M. S., (1962), 'The two faces of power' in Scott, John (ed.), *Power, Volume 2*, London: Routledge.
Bauman, Z., (1998), *Globalization*, Cambridge: Polity Press.
Bearden, J. et al., (1975), 'The nature and extent of bank centrality in corporate networks', in Scott, J. (ed.), (2002), *Social Networks, Volume 3*, London: Sage.
Beetham, D., (1991), *The Legitimation of Power*, Houndmills: Macmillan.
Bunting, D. and Barbour, J., (1971), 'Interlocking directorates in large american corporations, 1896–1964' in Scott, John (ed.), (2002), *Social Networks, Volume 3*, London: Sage.
Carroll, W. K., (1986), *Corporate Power and Canadian Capitalism*, Vancouver: University of British Columbia Press.
Carroll, W. K., (2004), *Corporate Power in a Globalizing World. A Study in Elite Social Organization*, Ontario: Oxford University Press.
Carroll, W. K. and Fennema, M., (2002), 'Is there a transnational business community?', *International Sociology* 17, 3: 393–419.
Castells, M., (1996), *The Rise of the Network Society, Volume 1 of the Information Age: Economy, Society and Culture*, Oxford: Blackwell Publishers.

Dahl, R. A., (1958), 'A critique of the ruling elite model' in Scott, John (ed.), (1990), *The Sociology of Elites, Volume 1*, Aldershot: Edward Elgar Publishing.

Dahl, R. A., (1961), *Who Governs?* New Haven: Yale University Press.

Dahl, R. A., (1966), 'Further reflections on "the elitist theory of democracy"', *American Political Science Review* 60: 296–305.

Dahl, R. A., (1971), *Polyarchy: Participation and Opposition*, New Haven: Yale University Press.

Domhoff, G. W., (1967), *Who Rules America?* Englewood Cliffs: Prentice Hall.

Dooley, P. C., (1969), 'The interlocking directorate' in Scott, John (ed.), (1990), *The Sociology of Elites, Volume 3*, Aldershot: Edward Elgar Publishing.

Fennema, M., (1982), *International Networks of Banks and Industry*, Hague: Martinus Nijhof.

Foucault, M., (1975), *Discipline and Punish*, (1977), London: Allen Lane.

Foucault, M., (1975–6), *Society Must Be Defended*, (2003), Harmondsworth: Penguin.

Foucault, M., (1976), *The History of Sexuality, Volume 1: An Introduction*, (1980), New York: Vintage Books.

Foucault, M., (1982), 'The subject and power' in Scott, John (ed.), (1994), *Power, Volume 1*, London: Routledge.

Giddens, A., (1972), 'Elites in the British class structure' in Scott, John (ed.), (1990), *The Sociology of Elites, Volume 1*, Aldershot: Edward Elgar Publishing.

Giddens, A., (1979), *Central Problems in Social Theory*, London: Macmillan.

Goldthorpe, J. H., (1987), *Social Mobility and Class Structure* (originally 1980), Oxford: Clarendon Press.

Gouldner, A. W., (1954), *Patterns of Industrial Bureaucracy*, New York: Free Press.

Hardie, I. and MacKenzie, D., (2007), 'Assembling an economic actor: the *agencement* of a Hedge Fund', *The Sociological Review* 55, 1: 57–80.

Held, D., (1989), *Political Theory and the Modern State*, Cambridge: Polity Press.

Hirst, P. Q., (1993), *Associative Democracy. New Forms of Economic and Social Governance*, Cambridge: Polity Press.

Hirst, P. Q., (1997), *From Statism to Pluralism*, London: Routledge.

Hunter, F., (1953), *Community Power Structure*, Chapel Hill: University of North Carolina Press.

López, J. and Scott, J., (2000), *Social Structure*, Buckingham: Open University Press.

Lukes, S., (1974), *Power: A Radical View*, 2nd Revised Edition 2004, London: Palgrave Macmillan.

Lukes, S., (1977), 'Power and Structure' in Lukes, Steven (ed.) *Essays in Social Theory*, London: Macmillan.

MacKenzie, D., (2003), 'Long-term capital management and the sociology of arbitrage', *Economy and Society* 32, 3: 349–80.

Maclean, M., Harvey, C. and Press, J., (2006), *Business Elites and Corporate Governance in France and the UK*, Basingstoke: Palgrave Macmillan.

McLennan, G., (1995), *Pluralism*, Cambridge: Buckingham.

Michels, R., (1927), *First Lectures in Political Sociology*, New York: Harper and Row.

Miliband, R., (1969), *The State in Capitalist Society*, London: Weidenfeld and Nicolson.

Mills, C. W., (1956), *The Power Elite*, New York: Oxford University Press.

Mintz, B., (1975), 'The President's cabinet, 1897–1972: A contribution to the power structure debate', in Scott, John (ed.), (1990), *The Sociology of Elites, Volume 2*, Aldershot: Edward Elgar Publishing.

Mintz, B. and Schwartz, M., (1985), *The Power Structure of American Business*, Chicago: Chicago University Press.

Mosca, G., (1896), 'Elementi di scienza politica, volume one' in Mosca, G. (ed.), (1939), *The Ruling Class, Chapters 1–11*, New York: McGraw Hill.

Mosca, G., (1923), 'Elementi di scienza politica, volume two' in Mosca, G. (ed.), (1939), *The Ruling Class, Chapters 12–17*, New York: McGraw Hill.

Pareto, V., (1901), *The Rise and Fall of Elites*, (1968), New York: Bedminster Press.

Pareto, V., (1916), *A Treatise on General Sociology*, (1963), New York: Dover.

Parsons, T., (1963), 'On the Concept of Political Power', *Proceedings of the American Philosophical Society* 107: 232–262.

Polsby, N. W., (1962), *Community Power and Political Theory*, second edition 1980, New Haven: Yale University Press.

Scott, J., (ed.), (1990), *The Sociology of Elites, Three Volumes*, Cheltenham: Edward Elgar Publishing.

Scott, J., (1991), *Who Rules Britain?* Cambridge: Polity Press.

Scott, J., (ed.), (1994) *Power*, Three volumes, London: Routledge.

Scott, J., (1996), *Stratification and Power: Structures of Class, Status and Command*, Cambridge: Polity Press.

Scott, J., (1997), *Corporate Business and Capitalist Classes*, Oxford: Oxford University Press.

Scott, J., (2001), *Power*, Cambridge: Polity Press.

Scott, J. and Griff, C., (1984), *Directors of Industry*, Cambridge: Polity Press.

Sklair, L., (2001), *The Transnational Capitalist Class*, Oxford: Blackwell Publishing.

Stanworth, P. and Giddens, A. (eds), (1974), *Elites and Power in British Society*, Cambridge: Cambridge University Press.

Stanworth, P. and Giddens, A., (1975), 'The modern corporate economy' in Scott, John (ed.), (1990), *The Sociology of Elites, Volume 1*, Aldershot: Edward Elgar Publishing.

Stokman, F., Ziegler, R. and Scott, J. (eds.), (1985), *Networks of Corporate Power*, Cambridge: Polity Press.

Thomas, A. B., (1978), 'The British business elite: the case of the retail sector' in Scott, John (ed.), (1990), *The Sociology of Elites, Volume 1*, Aldershot: Edward Elgar Publishing.

Urry, J., (2000), *Sociology Beyond Societies: Mobilities for the Twenty-First Century*, London: Routledge.

Urry, J. and Wakeford, J. (eds), (1973), *Power in Britain*, London: Heinemann,

Useem, M., (1984), *The Inner Circle*, New York: Oxford University Press.

Useem, M., (1993), *Executive Defence: Shareholder Power and Corporate Reorganization*, Cambridge, Mass.: Harvard University Press.

Wartenberg, T., (1990), *The Forms of Power: From Domination to Transformation*, Philadelphia: Temple University Press.

Weber, M., (1914), 'The economy and the arena of normative and de facto powers' in Roth, G. and Wittich, C., (eds), (1968), *Economy and Society*.

Whitley, Richard D., (1973), 'Commonalities and connections among directors of large financial institutions' in Scott, J. (ed.), (1990), *The Sociology of Elites, Volume 1*, Aldershot: Edward Elgar Publishing.

# The corporate elite and the transformation of finance capital: a view from Canada

*William K. Carroll*

Since 1905, when Otto Jeidels published the results of his research on the relationship of the big German banks to industry, the overlapping elite affiliations of corporate directors have been an issue of recognized importance for social scientists and political activists alike. In *Imperialism, the highest stage of capitalism* (1975 [1917]), one of the formative texts of the 20th-century revolutionary left, Lenin quoted Jeidels's study extensively, presenting the coalescence of different forms of capital under the control of the most powerful corporate directors as a criterial attribute of advanced capitalism:

> ... a personal link-up, so to speak, is established between the banks and the biggest industrial and commercial enterprises, the merging of one with another through the acquisition of shares, through the appointment of bank directors to the Supervisory Boards (or Boards of Directors) of industrial and commercial enterprises, and vice versa (Lenin, 1975:39).

According to Rudolf Hilferding (1981 [1910]), whose theorization of finance capital (also influenced by Jeidels's findings) provided part of the analytic basis for Lenin's pamphlet, the enormous concentrations of industrial and financial capital that issued from the merger movements at the turn of the century created a community of interests between directors of the largest banks (who controlled much of the available money-capital) and the directors of the largest corporations (who required great quantities of money-capital to finance the expansion of their industrial capital).[1]

What Hilferding saw, early on, was the tendency in advanced capitalism for the forms of capital to become functionally interwoven under the sway of a financial-industrial elite who derive unprecedented economic power from their ownership and/or control of key blocs and pools of financial capital (including, of course, corporate shares; Hussein, 1976:11). Arguably, this insight has been at the centre of critical sociological approaches to the analysis of economic elites ever since. Summarizing the sociological literature, Scott suggests that the interlocking directorships that weave the directorates of giant companies into a more or less cohesive network 'must be seen alongside the capital relations that undergird them' (Scott, 2003:159).[2] A corollary, of considerable interest in the current era of financialization, is that as the character of capital relations changes, so does the character of the corporate network. A key issue in contemporary analyses, considered below, is how changes in financial investment and ownership, the most recent of which fall under the rubric of *financialization*, introduce changes to the capital relations that undergird corporate-elite networks, modifying the form of finance capital.

In presenting a view from Canada, this chapter considers only a small piece of the puzzle. Nevertheless, Canada is an instructive case, in part because in Canada, even after sociology made its cultural turn in the 1980s, there has been a sustained interest in corporate-elite analysis, enabling us to chart changes in the organization of corporate power over the half century following World War Two. Below, I reflect on gains made in understanding Canada's corporate elite as a manifestation of business organization embedded in larger structures of capital and class.

## The *Vertical Mosaic* and its influence

A review of this kind must begin with the seminal text of Canadian sociology, John Porter's *Vertical Mosaic*. Published in 1965, when sociology in Canada was just coming of age, *The Vertical Mosaic* won the American Sociological Association's MacIver Award for the best sociology book (the only non-American book ever to do so), and established the credibility of macro-sociological analysis within the Canadian academy. Grounding his analysis in a Weberian framework that incorporated elements of functionalism, Porter described modern Canada as a configuration of several institutional subsystems and documented the organization and dynamics of each sub-system and their interrelations. Following methods similar to C. Wright Mills (1956), Porter showed that a small elite occupied the 'command posts' at the top of each societal sub-system, that the set of elites formed a 'confraternity of power' (Porter, 1965:541–2) reinforced by kinship and class, and that the 'preeminently powerful' group was the economic elite (Helmes-Hayes, 2002:88). Porter depicted the elite as an ethnically homogeneous group of British ancestry, whose members interacted not only in the boardrooms but in elite clubs reserved for those with the money and cultural credentials to gain admission.

Porter's student Wallace Clement published *The Canadian Corporate Elite* in 1975 and *Continental Corporate Power* two years later. By this time, the political economy tradition that had been formative to Canadian social science in the 1920s and 1930s, under the leadership of Harold Innis, had been revived with a distinctively left-nationalist bent. Marxist critiques of class inequality were combined with *dependentist* readings of Canada as the 'world's richest underdeveloped country' (Levitt, 1970). Clement did much more than replicate Porter's study with new data from the early 1970s; he resituated the entire project of corporate-elite analysis within the grand narrative of left-nationalist political economy. Clement viewed Canada's corporate elite as an assemblage of class fractions, drawing on R.T. Naylor's (1972) thesis that the Canadian bourgeoisie had followed an exceptional path that led not to autonomous national development but to the hegemony of a commercial-financial fraction, dependent on foreign-based industry. My own engagement with corporate-elite studies began with a Marxist critique of Clement's work and more broadly of the thesis of Canadian dependency in which it was ensconced (Carroll, 1981). Debates about the structure of the Canadian capitalist class raged throughout the 1980s, with much of the work informed by network-analytic approaches and Marxist class analysis (Brym, 1989; Carroll, Fox and Ornstein, 1982; Kellogg, 1989; Niosi, 1981; Richardson, 1982, 1988). And if, by the 1990s, the question of corporate power had been displaced from the top tier of the research agenda as sociology made its cultural turn (eg Valverde, 1991), that turn was far gentler in Canada than elsewhere. A critical political economy, reaching beyond the initial issues of class, state and nation had become paradigmatic within Canadian sociology (Clement and Vosko, 2003), affording space for continuing research on elites and class (Brownlee, 2005).

An accounting of lessons learned from the research programme that Porter inspired and that others enunciated within the language of political economy may thus be of value as scholars in Britain and elsewhere revive the tradition of elites research 'in the context of post 1979 economic reform and permanent restructuring of the public and private sector' (Froud, Savage, Tampubolon and Williams, 2006:16). To be sure, the advent of neoliberal capitalism has transformed corporate power, but the issue of how elites are articulated to and implicated in practices of capital accumulation and cultural hegemony remains an important one for sociology. Analyses of Canada provide both methodological and substantive insights on these relationships.

## Methodological advances 1: conceptual refinements

Although Clement (1975) introduced a class-analytic dimension to corporate-elite analysis in Canada, he continued to depict the elite as a more or less unified entity, consistent with Bottomore's claim that 'top managers and the owners of property are so intimately connected as to form, in the main, a single social group' (Bottomore, 1964:81). In a critique that spanned two books, Jorge Niosi (1978, 1981) contested the assumption of elite homogeneity – the notion that in occupying an elite position, each corporate director has more or less the same power as other directors – and clarified the class character of corporate directorates. Through biographical analysis of corporate directors, Niosi initially disaggregated the elite into large stockholders (the owners of control blocs) and their 'advisors'. The latter, conceptualized as organic intellectuals in the Gramscian sense, included corporate lawyers, financial advisors (including investment dealers), career managers and the owners or managers of other companies (Niosi, 1978:134). Niosi was able to show that most of Canada's largest firms were controlled by clearly identifiable families, individuals and groups (sometimes through intercorporate pyramiding of ownership). Yet restriction of capitalist class membership to major shareholders introduced problems of its own. Although ownership of corporate Canada never became as dispersed as in the US (a finding Porter noted in an appendix to *The Vertical Mosaic*), the classification of CEOs as mere advisors ignored the obvious extent to which in advanced capitalism the function of capital is exercised by a set of interdependent strata that includes top managers (Carchedi, 1977:84). Ultimately, Niosi rightly concluded that top executive officers serve not simply as advisors but as 'dependent and subordinate' members of the capitalist class (1981:16). The upshot was a view of the corporate elite as the capitalist class's dominant and most organized stratum – *a configuration of capitalists* (major shareholders and top executives) *and organic intellectuals* occupying positions of ultimate authority within leading corporations.

An issue related to the class positioning of the corporate elite was that of its boundaries. Mills, Porter, Clement and others included within the elite all directors of the largest corporations. Yet Ashley (1957), in an early review of Porter's work, and McKie (1976) two decades later suggested that this was an over-inclusive definition. Most corporate directors hold only a single directorship. They belong to the organizational elites at the top of each corporation, but do not participate in the *inter*-organizational elite (Scott, 2003:158) that actually constitutes the corporate elite as a dominant stratum of the capitalist class – an 'inner group' of corporate interlockers whose multiple directorships foster class-wide rationality in mobilizing economic, political and cultural resources (Useem, 1979, 1981). Of course, as Useem (1979) went on to note, members of the dominant stratum can themselves be arrayed along an axis of centrality, with the highly-connected 'big linkers' positioned at the core, an issue that highlights the need for analytic methods to map the social organization of the corporate elite's dominant segment.

## Methodological advances 2: network analysis

Mills, Porter, and other researchers of the 1950s and 1960s made minimal use of network analysis, which at the time was centred in the specialized field of sociometry (Gronlund, 1959). By the late 1970s, sociologists were applying these techniques in studies of the Canadian corporate elite, mindful of the substantive issues at the intersection of elite analysis and political economy. These issues included the question of alignments and cleavages within the Canadian corporate elite, the articulation of the elite to the structure and dynamics of capital accumulation, the relation between individual corporate directors as members of a class and corporations as units of capital accumulation, and the reach of the corporate elite into civil society and the state.

Canadian research initially probed these issues by mapping the entire national network and assessing its integration and differentiation. Network *integration* refers to the density of social relations, the connectedness of the network and the relative integration of firms vis-à-vis the network's core – that is, relative centrality. Network *differentiation* refers to both intersectoral relations within the network (eg, between finance and industry) and to the possible existence of subgroups and cliques (Carroll *et al.*, 1976). An initial investigation, based on data for 1972, found that the 100 largest Canadian firms made up a single connected network, with most pairs of firms mutually reachable through one intermediary. Canadian controlled companies, firms with large assets and financial institutions were positioned relatively close to the network's centre (Carroll *et al.*, 1976, 1982). This study also made use of nonmetric multidimensional scaling – a precursor to spring-embedded algorithms – as a visualization technique for mapping the whole network into a two-dimensional space in which distances between points are monotonically related to distances between nodes in the network. Finally, we explored the integrating effect of Canada's five big banks, whose profligate boards contained directors from many of the leading corporations. Prohibited by law from sharing directors, the big banks were found to share directors with common firms, creating a dense web of *overlapping social circles* and mitigating any tendency toward differentiation into subgroups.

If these findings cast the Naylor-Clement thesis into doubt, a more extensive investigation gave definitive reasons for rejecting the exceptionalist notion of 'merchants against industry' (MacDonald, 1976). Focusing on multiple-director interlocks, which Sonquist and Koenig (1975) had identified as a good indicator of institutionalized relations between firms, in my doctoral dissertation I examined successive 'Top 100' Canadian corporates, at five-year intervals over a thirty-year period beginning in 1946 (Carroll, 1981). This study explored elite differentiation by cross-tabulating companies according to (a) the country in which controlling interest was held and (b) the broad economic sector. This enabled an analytic carving of the network to test for possible elite fractions (eg 'indigenous' vs. 'comprador', 'industrial' vs. 'financial'). The distribution of companies and their assets revealed that the indigenous fraction controlled virtually all large-scale financial capital and a substantial proportion of big industrial capital throughout the postwar era; and that its control of industry, though challenged by the massive influx of American-based capital in the first post-war decade, had recovered to 1946 levels by 1976. The distribution of interlocks showed that a preponderance of multiple-director interlocks linked Canadian controlled companies, both financial and industrial, with the strongest intersectoral densities occurring between the Canadian controlled financial institutions and Canadian controlled industrial corporations. By contrast, the density of interlocking between Canadian financials and American-controlled industrials was no higher than the overall network density in each year. I concluded that the dominant fraction of the Canadian capitalist class comprises financial-industrial elite, controlling an integrated bloc of finance capital. In concert with a *densification* of interlocking, this elite's accumulation base was in the process of being further consolidated through the formation of investment companies that exerted control over large industrial corporations, as well as through the proliferation of Canadian foreign investments, whose growth in the 1970s began to overtake that of foreign direct investment in Canada (Carroll, 1982).

A more qualitative analysis of cliques and subgroups in the network of multiple interlocks added nuance to the account of structural differentiation. Adopting Alba's (1973) graph-theoretic definition of a clique (namely, a connected subnetwork of high internal density and few external ties), I compared the 1946 corporate elite with its 1976 counterpart. The data showed a shift from a network dominated by one large Montreal-based grouping of 20 industrial corporations and financial institutions to a structure organized around six cliques, five of which interpenetrated to some extent and four of which were predominantly centred in Toronto. In both years, cliques had extensive peripheries, composed of companies interlocked with clique members but not sufficiently integrated into any one clique to qualify as a member, and the trend over time was for the network's clique structure to include a greater swathe of the Top 100, indicating a more extensive national network. A parallel analysis of overlapping social circles between the major centres of financial capital – the big banks and the key investment companies – revealed that by 1976 several investment companies were at the centre of compact cliques organized around intercorporate share ownership, as 'enterprise groups' (Berkowitz *et al.*, 1995). In this 'increasingly integrated yet differentiated structure' (Carroll, 1986:156), big banks served as articulation points, linking intercorporate groupings at one remove and drawing into the inner circle company boards that otherwise would have been quite peripheral.

My collaborators and I took advantage of our data's three-decade timespan to conduct several kinds of longitudinal analysis, which shed light on the reproduction and transformation of the elite network in the post-war era. My own work combined the rudimentary analysis of successive temporal cross-sections (as above) with an analysis of *turnover* in both the corporate constituents of the network and the links between them. The *stable* part of the network was defined as the set of multiple-director interlocks that were maintained throughout 1946–76 among firms that consistently ranked in the Top 100. Of the 21 companies that met these criteria, twelve formed a connected component whose members heavily overlapped with the main Montreal-based clique in both 1946 and 1976. These firms – the bedrock of Canadian finance capital in the 20th century, included several of the largest industrial corporations and financial institutions, and in several cases, the mean yearly number of directors shared by their boards reach remarkable levels, indicating a highly institutionalized coalescence of industrial and financial capital, sustained across successive cohorts of interlocking directors.[3] It was around this stable core that the major structural transformations occurred, as differential rates of accumulation as well as major corporate reorganizations led companies to enter or exit from the Top 100, and as board interlocks emerged or disappeared with corporate realignments.

John Fox and Michael Ornstein's (1988) longitudinal study of linkages across the Canadian state and corporate elites explored not only concurrent relations (interlocks) but the *flow* of people from elite positions in the economic sphere into elite positions in the political sphere, and *vice versa*. Covering the same three decades, the study included the major federal and provincial state organizations as well as a number of sectors ancillary to state (eg, university and hospital boards of governors) and capital (eg, major law firms and business-dominated policy groups). Fox and Ornstein found an increase in the density of elite ties between private and public sectors, from 3.2 per cent in the first post-war decade to 6.0 per cent in the third (1986:493), with concurrent relations making up 68 percent of all ties, state-to-capital flows making up 21 per cent of flows, and capital-to-state flows accounting for 10 per cent. There were wide sectoral variations, however, in these kinds of relations. Ties connecting the federal and provincial cabinets (as well as civil service elites) to the corporate sector typically took the form of flows from state to capital, presumably as retiring politicians and senior bureaucrats were recruited onto corporate boards as well-connected advisors. In contrast, ties linking the Senate of Canada as well as the boards of crown corporations to the corporate sector tended to be concurrent. The empirical findings led Fox and Ornstein to endorse Miliband's (1983:65) formulation that the relationship between the state and the dominant class in advanced capitalism is 'one of *partnership between two different, separate forces*, linked to each other by many threads, yet each having its own separate sphere of concerns'.

Beyond the macrosociological mapping of the national network, Michael Ornstein's (1984) work on *broken ties* shifted the focus to a micro-analytic level: that of the interlocks themselves, viewed as relations in time that may disappear when an incumbent director retires, or may be reconstituted via the appointment of another interlocking director. The latter, clearly, are the stronger, purposive, more institutional relations; indeed, interlocks that disappear when an incumbent retires may simply be secondary by-products of stronger ties. Of the 5354 interlocks among large corporations in Canada that were broken at some point during the first three post-war decades, 29.5 per cent were reconstituted. Through a quantitative analysis, Ornstein established that interlocks carried by executives in one of the interlocked firms, and interlocks that were part of a multiple-interlock relation or a relation of intercorporate ownership between firms, were substantially more likely to be reconstituted. Moreover, interlocks among companies controlled domestically were far more likely to be reconstituted than were interlocks between Canadian- and American-controlled firms. A multiple regression analysis showed that, after controlling for a battery of predictors such as country of control, industry and location of head office, financial-industrial interlocks were more likely to be reconstituted than other interlocks.

Ornstein's analysis demonstrated that the basic architecture of the Canadian corporate elite – the coalescence of domestically controlled finance and industry – shapes not only the network of existing interlocks but also the network's *reproduction* when ties are broken. It also showed that not all interlocks are created equally: interlocks carried by executives, for instance, are more likely to be reconstituted. At issue here is the *duality* of corporate-elite networks – their character as interpersonal networks of directors and interorganizational networks of corporations, with the implication that that the positions of individuals and corporations are interdependent.[4] I explored this interdependence in a study of the Canadian inner group of interlocked directors in 1976 (Carroll, 1984; cf. Bearden and Mintz, 1987)). Remarkably, only 14 per cent of the 288 inner group members were organic intellectuals, although another 28 per cent were owners or executives in companies not large enough to qualify for the Top 100. The 58 per cent of inner group members who were principal shareholders or executives in one of the Top 100 firms (ie, 'insiders') were assigned the corporate-level attributes of those companies, enabling an analysis conducted at the level of individual directors, but including contextual information on the firms with which they were principally affiliated. Fully 79 per cent of these insiders were executives or owners of Canadian-controlled corporations. The interpersonal network of directors was decomposable into densely connected cliques, whose corporate affiliations followed intercorporate ownership relations closely and whose peripheries overlapped substantially, supporting a highly centralized interpersonal network. The corporations whose insiders belonged to cliques or were positioned on their peripheries were overwhelmingly controlled in Canada and ensconced in the industrial or financial sectors. These results led me to conclude that 'at the centre of Canadian corporate power – and at the apex of the Canadian bourgeoisie – we find groups of interlocked capitalists who own or manage supra-corporate blocs of indigenous finance capital' (Carroll, 1984:265).

The final significant contribution from the first wave of corporate network analysis served to place the Canadian corporate elite in comparative perspective. In the late 1970s the so-called Ten Nations study (Stokman *et al.*, 1985) gathered a massive amount of data on national corporate networks in nine European countries and the United States, circa 1976. Ornstein's (1989) comparative analysis of Canada (circa 1980) with these ten established that the Canadian network was at the time one of the most integrated of the advanced capitalist formations – a claim whose credibility was enhanced, a decade later, in the comparison of Canadian and Australian networks (circa 1992) that Malcolm Alexander and I undertook (Carroll and Alexander, 1999).

The 1980s, in short, was when the methodology of social network analysis was applied extensively to the study of corporate power in Canada, with interesting results. In contrast to the exceptionalist theses that dominated Canadian studies in the 1970s (eg, notions of a dependent bourgeoisie, of 'merchants against industry') research revealed a form of corporate organization consistent with the periodization of the post-war era as one of consolidating *nationally-focused organized capitalism*, even as transnational investments proliferated. The Canadian corporate elite appeared as the leading edge of a well-integrated, domestically based capitalist class, organized through an extensive network of interlocks that brought together the leading lights of big industry and high finance. It was only toward the end of the 1980s, as Lash and Urry (1987) proclaimed *The End of Organized Capitalism*, that issues such as the precise character and trajectory of organized capitalism in Canada and the incipient impact of emergent forces such as neoliberalism, globalization and financial-ization of investment, would begin to be broached.

## The turn to British and continental perspectives

In the transition to a more nuanced treatment of financial-industrial coales-cence, John Scott's (1987, 1997) comparative-historical framework of national business systems was helpful. Scott distinguished between two forms of power that accrue to controllers of financial capital: *allocative* power over capital flows (exercised mainly by financial institutions) and *strategic control* over corpor-ate management (achieved through ownership of large blocs of shares). If Germany's system of 'oligarchic bank hegemony' centralized both allocative and strategic power in a few big banks,[5] in France and Belgium the separation of investment banking and commercial banking and the rapid centralization of share capital within investment companies, created a 'holding system' wherein rival investment companies took up controlling interests in a range of operat-ing companies. The Anglo-American system of 'polyarchic financial hegemony', for which the United States is the best example, involved both a separation of investment and commercial banking and a transition to the impersonal form of 'control through a constellation of interests', as institutional investors built up shareholdings that gave them influence (but not control) over various firms.

These different systems of finance capital were evident in the post-war struc-tures of national corporate networks. As epicenters of allocative power, big banks tended to be centrally positioned in each network (Fennema and Schijft, 1979), but in the German network banks were extraordinarily prominent and interlocks with their industrial affiliates were very strong, while in Belgium and France the network tended to clump around the corporate webs of the major holding companies (Stokman *et al.*, 1985). American and British networks were looser, even if bank-centred (Mintz and Schwartz, 1985), and did not easily divide into corporate groups, except on a regional basis (Sonquist and Koenig, 1975).

Scott held that behind all the diversity was 'a common move towards bank hegemony of a loosely structured kind' (Scott, 1987:227). However, as Scott Lewis and I found in our longitudinal analysis of the 1970s and 1980s (Carroll and Lewis, 1991), Canada's resemblance to the Anglo-American system was complicated by the consolidation of several corporate groups centred around investment companies. Moreover, the big chartered banks' financial hegemony was eroded in the 1960s as new centres of allocative power, some of them aligned with the corporate groups, gained sway. In the 1980s, deregulation of the financial sector enabled the big banks to buy up the major investment dealers, ending the traditional separation of commercial and investment banking and opening the prospect for German-style universal banking. By the late 1980s, Canada's system of finance capital appeared to be hybridizing, with elements of all three patterns combining to structure the corporate network (Carroll and Lewis, 1991). The situation was further complicated by a massive upswing in the internationalization of investment in which Canadian banks, corporate groups and individual firms were all active participants – raising the prospect of a system of 'transnational finance capital' (Andreff, 1984) coexisting with and perhaps attenuating nationally organized finance capital.

These trends underlined the importance of not only placing the corporate elite in comparative perspective but exploring the elite's relationship to the changing political-economic order, both nationally and globally. On this matter I found the neo-Gramscian perspective of the 'Amsterdam Project' in international political economy (Overbeek, 2004) of great value. Gaining initial prominence with Kees van der Pijl's *The Making of an Atlantic Ruling Class* (1984), researchers at the University of Amsterdam theorized the historical relation between capital structure and political strategy as a succession of comprehensive 'concepts of control', each of which offers a paradigm for managing capitalism from a specific fractional standpoint. The functional division of capital into industrial and financial forms gives rise respectively to the 'productive capital concept' and the 'money capital concept' (Van der Pijl, 1984:33–4).

> The former reflects the particularities of the productive process and its social context, in which the real subsumption of labour to capital takes shape, while the peculiar nature of money capital as capital-in-general and its indirect relation with labour taint the latter. These comprehensive concepts function as rallying points for those (coalitions of) bourgeois groups and their allies which contest political leadership (Overbeek, 2004:119).

Explicit in this formulation is a recognition of the inherent tension that haunts the coalescence of industrial and financial capital: the contradiction between capital as abstract labour (epitomized by mobile money capital) and capital as surplus-value production (epitomized by the management of industry). The era of post-war Fordism and corporate liberalism saw the ascendancy of a productive-capital concept of control rooted in the exigencies of managing mass production for mass consumption and providing ancillary state programs and regulations to buoy effective demand. Although this regime 'implied a subordination of independent bank capital and the rentier element in the bourgeoisie to an integrated, state-supported finance capital' (Van der Pijl, 1986:26), the rentier class fraction was never euthanized. If banking and rentier interests were subordinated to productive capital, via financial regulations, capital controls and the like, the crisis of Fordism that became evident in the early 1970s, and the associated rise of neoliberal policies, set in motion a restructuring that would recompose the bourgeoisie's dominant stratum (Carroll, 1989:86).

Scott's thesis of a common move in national corporate networks toward bank hegemony of a loosely structured sort captures the predominant organizational form that finance capital took during the fordist/Keynesian era. Although banks were central hubs in the network, their activities were strictly regulated and their allocative power was predominantly exercised in such a way as to promote industrial capital formation by maintaining long-term relations with corporate debtors. For their part, industrial corporations were able to self-finance to a considerable extent from (substantial) retained earnings, and the long-term tendency toward share dispersal strengthened the position of industrial managers.

But in the 1970s, American abrogation of Bretton Woods and the rise of the Eurodollar freed money capital from national regulation by central banks (Edwards, 1985:181), and a generalized international recession forced banks further into the international arena (MacEwan, 1986:194). In the process,

> The existing relation between money capital and productive capital broke down and was replaced by a hypertrophy of the international circuit of money capital managed by the international banking system [as] . . . monetary authorities were unable to maintain the Keynesian nexus between money capital and productive capital at the international level (Fennema and Van der Pijl, 1987:305).

The upshot was twofold: 1) the emergence of transnational finance capital, as internationalizing banks established closer relations with transnational corporations (Andreff, 1984) and 2) the resurgence of money capital – and of the money capital concept of control – in the major capitalist economies. The strategically dominant position that money capital came to re-occupy in the circuits of finance capital was evident in several trends that subsequently were conceptualized under the rubric of *financialization*: 1) the abolition of New Deal financial regulations and the rapid internationalization of bank capital; 2) a general shift in the distribution of profits from productive to money capital and an associated increase in external financing of industry; and 3) a reorientation, even among 'industrial' corporations, towards the financial sphere, with increased holdings of liquid assets (including corporate shares, Fennema and Van der Pijl, 1987:307–10).

Comparison of the 1976 and 1986 Canadian corporate networks documented some of these tendencies, including the proliferation of investment companies as vehicles of strategic control (which partly displaced the big banks from their strategic locations) and the weakening of relations between banks and industrials as the former came to hold vast foreign currency holdings. The imminent deregulation of the financial sector (Canada's 'little bang' of 1987) portended a recomposition of finance capital, 'from a system of loosely-structured financial hegemony to a system within which power is wielded in deregulated and increasingly international circuits by means of strategic concentrations of money capital' (Carroll, 1993:227). But the fuller implications of these developments for the Canadian corporate elite would await further exploration.


## A corporate elite in transition

In *Corporate Power in a Globalizing World*, I extended the longitudinal network analysis of Canada's corporate elite into the last two decades of the twentieth century, and took up the issues of structural and cultural transitions associated with liberalization, financialization and globalization.

The diffusion of a discourse of improved 'corporate governance' in the 1990s, through stock-exchange task forces and think-tank initiatives, marked a key cultural transition. Analysis of the Canadian business press in the late 1990s (Carroll, 2004:33–8) revealed a value framework centred around (1) a meritocratic professionalism and cosmopolitanism, incorporating concerns for representation of women and ethnic minorities; (2) effective board decision-making; and especially (3) the priority of *shareholder value* – of ever-rising share prices for stockholders. Beyond embodying a transition in corporate elite *culture*, the new norms carried implications for the *structural* organization of corporate power.

In 1995 the Toronto Stock Exchange placed non-binding regulations on corporate boards, mandating that they become more active stewards, more independent of management and other non-shareholding interests, and small enough to facilitate effective decision-making (Carroll, 2004:34). The structural impact was immediate. By 1996, interlocks involving non-CEO corporate officers had greatly diminished, bankers had left the boards of industrials, and banks had slimmed their elephantine directorates. This left a looser elite structure in which the banks continued to participate alongside transnational corporations, at the centre of a network of information flows across outside directorships.[6]

The corporate governance reforms of the 1990s hastened a shift underway since the 1980s, from leisure to activism as a leitmotif for corporate-elite culture. As the old boys' network thinned and the ranks of women and non-British ethnicities grew, the corporate elite became less mono-cultural, less petrified, less a fixture of exclusionary corporate boards and private clubs, and more diverse. Along with the elaboration of a network of neoliberal policy boards heavily interlocked with leading corporate directorates, these developments modernized the face of Canadian corporate capital. Transitions from oligarchy to meritocracy and from leisure to activism seem integral to a new form of hegemony – a more porous elite social organization offering greater possibilities for the ruling class's reach into civil society, for civil society's reach into the ruling class, and thus for more effective business leadership (Carroll, 2004:210–215).

If the catalyst for corporate governance reform was financial scandal (in particular, the collapse in 1994 of Confederation Life), its most immediate causal agent was the rise of active institutional shareholders interested in corporate strategy. As major institutional investors come to claim the lion's share of corporate securities and become locked in to their equity stakes, they turn to the exercise of voice as a profit-maximization strategy, exerting 'steadily increasing pressure' on corporate managers to improve performance and 'working to improve the governance of firms in which they invest' (Morck and Nakamura, 1995:497).[7]

This enhanced strategic power comprises another aspect of the transition to *a new form of finance capital.* In the process, *the constellations of interests atop major firms have shifted from salaried managers and bankers, toward institutional shareholders and, at certain junctures of corporate restructuring, private equity outfits.* But even as the elite network thins, the coalescence of financial and industrial capital remains discernable. As of 1996, the last year for which complete Canadian data are currently available, 79 per cent of all interlocks among Canada's Top 250 corporations were created by the multiple affiliations of finance capitalists (Carroll, 2004:102).[8] Indeed, as mentioned earlier, the takeover (after deregulation) of all major Canadian investment dealers by the big banks gave the latter enhanced roles in corporate finance, even if the form of finance shifted from long-term loans to securitized transactions. In a functional sense, increasingly 'universal' banks, may be *more* important to the circuitry of finance capital now than before financial deregulation – even if they command less central positions in the elite network.

One way of interpreting these shifts – the weakening of 'patient money' relations between commercial banks and corporations, the ascendance of shareholder value and institutional investors – is to speak of financialization. In a financialized economy the dynamics of accumulation shift toward the dominance of financial circuits. 'New forms of financial competition reflect the requirement to meet the expectations of the capital market as much or more than those of consumers in the product market' (Thompson, 2003:366). The enhanced salience of money capital is evident on both sides of the industrial/financial divide. Industrial capital comes to resemble financial capital, as stock options align corporate management with a money-capital standpoint and as firms issue their own commercial paper and come to depend less on productive activities and more on income from financial sources, the case of Enron being the most notorious (Krippner, 2005). Financial institutions come to prefer liquidity over long-term loans;[9] deregulation spurs capital centralization into universal banks whose activities range from financing production to speculation in derivatives, and institutional investors controlling capitalized deferred wages become important centers of allocative as well as strategic power.

The clamour by institutional investors for shareholder value is part of these trends, as are the looser and more episodic relations between commercial banks and corporations. In the case of Canada, however, it would be wrong to infer that institutional investors relate to corporations in their portfolios purely as bundles financial assets. The example of the Ontario Teachers Pension Plan, one of the largest and most influential funds and a major Canadian player in private equity, is instructive. Inspection of Teacher's 24-member board, as of summer 2006, reveals interlocks with several of its affiliates, which number among the largest corporations in Canada.[10] These relations are relatively stable but not immune to fundamental change as profit opportunities present themselves. In July 2007, when BCE, Canada's largest telecommunications utility, was put on the auction block, Teachers, already BCE's largest shareholder, allied itself with two US-based private equity firms and won majority control in a highly leveraged buyout that took BCE private. Developments of this sort indicate both continuity and change in the coalescence of financial and industrial capital. To some extent, private equity players like Teachers and Onex Corp act as investment companies (in the classic manner of the Belgian holding system), establishing board interlocks with the firms in which they place major stakes, and thereby effecting a close integration of financial and industrial capital. But they are ever willing to cash out those stakes if immediate profit prospects favour such a move. The dust has yet to settle on the BCE acquisition, but it is likely that BCE, one of Canada's most venerable corporations, will be broken up and sold off in pieces.

What we can conclude from these examples is that the extent to which financialization disembeds institutional investors from productive capital and weakens the financial-industrial nexus should not be overestimated. True, the old nationally organized axis of finance capital, whose backbone was long-term bank loans to corporations, weakens as bankers decline corporate directorships in the new governance framework. But it also transmutes into a more flexible coalescence of capital in which institutional investors have enhanced roles. Finance capital becomes more loosely organized and more transnational in its circuitry. Yet national business communities such as Canada's persist, held together by a range of factors, including the need to exercise hegemony locally and to access the business scan that interlocking directorates enable.

The implications of transnationalization of investment for national corporate elites are particularly complex. Scott (1997) has suggested that capitalist globalization leads to a disarticulation of national elite networks, as TNCs become disembedded. In the last two decades of the 20th century, however, no such disarticulation of the Canadian network was evident. Overall, foreign control of large firms actually fell, and although among the largest Canadian companies there was a dramatic shift to greater transnational investment, the growing transnational segment of Canadian-based corporate capital remained densely interlocked at the board level, and extensively linked to the sub-transnational segment of Canadian firms relatively uninvolved in foreign direct investment. Transnational finance capital radiated from Canada in a way that did *not* disorganize the national network but *embedded* it more extensively in a circuitry of global accumulation. In the process, the Canadian corporate elite became re-centred around an expanding sector of Canadian-based TNCs, both industrial and financial (Carroll, 2004:85).

In the years since 2003, however, rising commodity prices along with the logic of North American economic integration have driven a series of spectacular foreign takeovers, as 10 of the Toronto Stock Exchange's TSX 60 disappeared from the corporate landscape. Canadian institutional investors, typically the major shareholders in the firms that have been acquired, have been criticized for their willingness simply to 'jump at any buyer offering a higher price than current market values' (Crane, 2007). This willingness was heightened by the abolition in 2005 of the longstanding restriction on public pension funds' foreign investments. Deregulation enabled funds to redeploy investments from Canadian equities to foreign assets (Cakebread, 2006), weakening their capacity to form consortia capable of making counterbids against foreign takeovers

(Olive, 2007). The spate of such takeovers shows another side of the transnationalization of finance capital, as the industrial capital controlled by Canadian-based institutional investors becomes fully consolidated into larger transnational enterprises based in Europe, the US, and even Brazil.[11] The long-term implication of such capital centralization may well be a disarticulation of the national corporate elite. Montreal billionaire and shareholder activist Stephen Jarislowsky's remark that by allowing a hollowing-out of corporate Canada, the country was committing 'economic suicide' (Moore, 2007), seconded by numerous other business leaders, including the CEO of the Royal Bank of Canada, captured a wider public concern about declining economic 'sovereignty'.[12]

The transnational mergers that are now reshaping Canada's corporate elite signal not the end of finance capital but its further globalization. As Aglietta (1979) noted in the work that launched regulation theory, waves of massive corporate reorganization were always integral to finance capital; indeed, finance capital arose precisely through such capital centralization.[13] The same applies to the more flexible form that finance capital has assumed in recent years, with the rise of financial engineering and what Blackburn calls 'grey capitalism': 'the financial elite and the corporate elite need one another and financialized techniques have helped to cement the pact between them' (Blackburn, 2006:40). Moreover, the sub-prime mortgage crisis, whose full ramifications have yet to play out as I write this, cautions us not to extrapolate the dynamic of financialization too far. The bubble economy that has driven much of the speculative churning so important to private equity is collapsing. In the current transition, the allocative power of the world's major financial institutions reasserts itself, denying the funding that has heretofore enabled the likes of KKR, Blackstone and Carlyle to spearhead massively leveraged buyouts.[14]

## Conclusion

A century after Jeidels, we can reflect on an enormous accumulation of knowledge about the social organization of corporate power, which, however, has struggled to keep pace with a frenetic accumulation of corporate capital into larger units and new forms. Canada offers a helpful comparison with Britain, where the corporate network has always been rather sparse and only weakly organized around large financial institutions that developed an exceptionally international orientation early on (Scott, 1997).

In Canada, over the past half century we can discern two eras in corporate-elite formation. In the 1940s-1970s, Canada followed the 'common move' towards loosely structured bank hegemony. The national network was extended, densified and consolidated following the principles of organized capitalism, along a Montreal-Toronto axis. Since the 1970s – with financial deregulation in the 1980s, corporate governance reform in the 1990s, and an ongoing process of globalization and financialization – we find an erosion of those organizational principles. This has meant a weakening of bank hegemony and of stable, financial-industrial interlocking within the corporate elite, the emergence of new and often more ephemeral forms of financial-industrial integration, and a further transnationalization of finance capital from within and without.

The research has documented both cultural and structural transitions in the elite, culturally, from old-boys oligarchy to multicultural meritocracy, from leisure to activism, from a productive-capital to a money-capital concept of control. Structurally, the key transition has seen a highly organized national network in which constellations exerting strategic and allocative power were directly represented on (interlocked) directorates give way to a loosely organized, more transnationalized formation. What has changed is the institutional structuring of allocative and strategic power; this is why it is appropriate to speak of a *new form of finance capital*, rather than 'the end' of finance capital. In the emergent configuration, constellations of interest are recomposed and even repositioned. Banks have lost hegemony yet they remain strategically important sites in finance capital's circuitry. Institutional investors have gained prominence within the constellations, and their influence may be exerted without recourse to representation on corporate boards. Most recently, massive foreign takeovers have wrested major industrial corporations from longstanding control by Canadian-based capitalist interests.

Within the broader context of financialization and globalization, these developments point to a far more complicated pattern of financial-industrial coalescence than Hilferding knew. In the new regime of finance capital, *the symbiosis of financial and industrial capital is partially displaced from the network of interlocking directorates*, into less formalized and durable venues such as one-on-one meetings between CEOs and institutional investors (Beckmann, 2006:6), and the interlock network itself becomes structured less around bank hegemony and more around the often transnational deal-making that has driven 'permanent restructuring' (Froud *et al.*, this volume). Yet the corporate topography continues to be organized around the dominance of finance capitalists – of 'those who by controlling large concentrations of financial capital wield power within integrated capital circuits' (Carroll, 1989:82), even if the means through which strategic control and allocative power are expressed have been partially transformed. In the circumstances, researchers need to consider how longstanding and emergent forms of elite social relations, along with the capital relations that undergird them, are being rearticulated into new configurations.

# Notes

1 Although Hilferding is often misinterpreted as having proposed a theory of bank control, John Scott has noted that the operative metaphor in Hilferding's finance capital is that of *fusion*: 'Large enterprises, whatever their primary area of economic activity, are increasingly likely to be involved in both "financial" and "non-financial" activities, and they are likely to enter into various forms of organizational alignment and co-operation. It is this fusion of the financial and the industrial that Hilferding described as the system of "finance capital" (1997:104).

2 Scott continues: 'These relations arise where families invest in a number of different companies, where banks, insurance companies, and other institutions invest in a number of companies, and where bank lending creates links between institutions and those who borrow from them' (2003:159).

3 For instance, Canada's largest industrial corporation, the Canadian Pacific Railway, shared an average of *seven* directors per year with the country's largest bank, the Bank of Montreal.

4 The centrality of a corporation, for instance, depends on how well connected the individuals are who sit on its board; yet the centrality of an individual director depends on how well connected the boards are on which (s)he sits (Everett and Borgatti, 2005).

5 A combination of strategic and allocative power has also characterized the *kigoyoshudan* that dominate the Japanese economy (Scott, 1997:191–5).

6 Subsequently, the TSX relinquished responsibility for setting corporate governance standards to provincial securities regulators – chiefly the Ontario Securities Commission (Howlett, 2003).

7 The increasingly directive role of institutional investors in corporate-governance reform was underlined with the founding in 2003 of the Canadian Coalition for Good Governance, a group composed of 19 institutional investors, which lobbies individual companies to implement governance norms (McFarland, 2003).

8 Based on Soref and Zeitlin's (1987:62) operationalization of finance capitalists as 'directors who sit simultaneously on the boards of top industrial corporations and major banks or other financial institutions.'

9 Including currency speculation and syndicated bought deals. The latter, pioneered in the 1980s, involve purchase of an entire issue of securities by a group of financial institutions. The relationship between 'creditor' and 'debtor' lasts only as long as it takes to complete the transaction. Between 1990 and 1998 the proportion of assets held by Canada's five biggest banks as traditional loans fell from nearly three-quarters to barely one-half. In 1998, their non-lending business activities exceeded their net interest income for the first time (Stanford. 1999:58).

10 In 2006, two executive Teachers directors sat on the board of Cadillac Fairview, a major property developer that Teachers owned. Nonexecutive Teachers directors also sat on the boards of such major corporations as Nenex Inc (of which Teachers owned 11.5%), Manulife Financial (of which Teachers owned 7.8%) and BCE Inc (of which Teachers owned 4.8%).

11 Among the recent foreign acquisitions, mining giants Inco and Falcolnbridge were acquired in 2006 by Brazil-based CVRD and Swiss-based Xstrata respectively; steel producer Dofasco was acquired by French-based Arcelor in the same year; aluminum giant Alcan was taken over by London/Melbourne-based Rio Tinto in July 2007. At the time of writing, Canada's largest steel company, Stelco, was being acquired by Pittsburg-based US Steel.

12 Polls in the spring of 2007 showed a strong majority of Canadians concerned about foreign takeovers, with only 16% expressing a lack of concern (Aubry, 2007).

13 As Aglietta put it, in the era of finance capital, 'the question of capitalist power over production takes the form of the control over property exercised in the enterprise by coalitions of capitalists who wield the weapon of financial centralization to their own advantage. The name *finance capital* is properly given to the mediation by which coalitions of capitalists exercise proprietary control over the structural forms necessary for the continuing cycles of valorization of productive capital, thanks to the centralized money capital at their disposal' (1979:253).

14 Global private equity deals hit a peak of $US150 billion in May 2007 but by August 2007 had crashed to $US17.8 (Berman, 2007).

# References

Aglietta, M., (1979), *A Theory of Capitalist Regulation*, London: NLB.
Alba, R.D., (1973), 'A graph-theoretic definition of a sociometric clique,' *Journal of Mathematical Sociology* 3: 113–26.

Andreff, W., (1984), 'The internationalization of capital and the reordering of world capitalism', *Capital & Class* 25: 58–80.

Ashley, C.A., (1957), 'Concentration of economic power,' *Canadian Journal of Economics and Political Science* 23: 105–8.

Aubrey, J., (2007), 'Most Canadians believe foreign takeovers a major concern', *Vancouver Sun*, 28 May: E2.

Bearden, J. and Mintz, B., (1987), 'The structure of class cohesion: the corporate network and its dual,' in Mizruchi, M.S. and Schwartz, M., (eds), *Intercorporate Relations*, Cambridge: Cambridge University Press: 187–207.

Beckmann, M., (2006), 'Institutional investors and the transformation of the European economy', presented at *Finance, Industry and Power: The Capitalist Corporation in the 21st Century*, Toronto: Department of Political Science, York University, April.

Berkowitz, S.D. and Fitzgerald, W., (1995), 'Corporate control and enterprise structure in the Canadian economy: 1972–1987,' *Social Networks* 17: 111–27.

Berman, D., (2007), 'Mergers can survive without private equity', *National Post*, 7 September: FP7.

Blackburn, R., (2006), 'Finance and the fourth dimension', *New Left Review* 39: 39–70.

Bottomore, T.B., (1964), *Elites and Society*, Harmondsworth, UK: Penguin.

Brownlee, J., (2005), *Ruling Canada: Corporate Cohesion and Democracy*, Halifax, Nova Scotia: Fernwood Publishing.

Brym, R.J., (1989), 'Canada', in Bottomore, T. and Brym, R.J., (eds), *The Capitalist Class*, Toronto: Harvester Wheatsheaf: 177–206.

Cakebread, C., (2006), 'Global Warming', *Benefits Canada* 30 (4): 61–3.

Carchedi, G., (1977), *On the Economic Identification of Social Classes*, London: Routledge.

Carroll, W.K., (1981), *Capital Accumulation and Corporate Interlocking in Post-War Canada*, Doctoral Dissertation, Toronto: York University.

Carroll, W.K., (1982), 'The Canadian corporate elite: financiers or finance capitalists?', *Studies in Political Economy* 8: 89–114.

Carroll, W.K., (1984), 'The individual, class, and corporate power in Canada', *Canadian Journal of Sociology* 9: 245–68.

Carroll, W.K., (1986), *Corporate Power and Canadian Capitalism*, Vancouver: University of British Columbia Press.

Carroll, W.K., (1989), 'Neoliberalism and the recomposition of finance capital in Canada', in *Capital and Class* 38: 81–112.

Carroll, W.K., (1993), 'Canada in the crisis: transformations in capital structure and political strategy', in: H. Overbeek (ed.), *Restructuring Hegemony in the Global Political Economy*, London: Routledge: 216–45.

Carroll, W.K., (2004), *Corporate Power in a Globalizing World*, Toronto: Oxford University Press.

Carroll, W.K. and Alexander, M., (1999), 'Finance capital and capitalist class integration in the 1990s: networks of interlocking directorships in Canada and Australia', *Canadian Review of Sociology and Anthropology* 36: 331–54.

Carroll, W.K. and Lewis, S., (1991), 'Restructuring finance capital: changes in the Canadian corporate network 1976–1986', *Sociology* 25: 491–510.

Carroll, W.K., Fox, J. and Ornstein, M.D., (1976), 'A network analysis of interlocking directorates among the one hundred largest Canadian corporations', Annual Meetings of the Western Anthropological and Sociological Association: Calgary.

Carroll, W.K., Fox, J. and Ornstein, M.D., (1982), 'The network of directorate interlocks among the largest Canadian firms', *Canadian Review of Sociology and Anthropology*: 245–68.

Clement, W., (1975), *The Canadian Corporate Elite*, Toronto: McClelland and Stewart.

Clement, W., (1977), *Continental Corporate Power*, Toronto: McClelland and Stewart.

Clement, W. and Vosko, L., (eds), (2003), *Changing Canada: Political Economy as Transformation*, Montreal: McGill-Queen's University Press.

Crane, D., (2007), 'Striking a balance on foreign ownership', *Toronto Star*, 23 July: B5.

Edwards, C., (1985), *The Fragmented World*, New York: Methuen.

*William K. Carroll*


Everett, M. and Borgatti, S.P., (2005), 'Extending centrality.' in Carrington, P.J., Scott, J. and Wasserman, S., (eds), *Models and Methods in Social Network Analysis*, Cambridge: Cambridge University Press: 57–76.

Fennema, M. and Van der Pijl, K., (1987), 'International bank capital and the new liberalism', in Mizruchi, M.S. and Schwartz, M., (eds), *Intercorporate Relations*, Cambridge: Cambridge University Press: 298–319.

Fennema, M. and Schijf, H., (1979), 'Analysing interlocking directorates: theory and methods', *Social Networks* 1: 297–332.

Fox, J. and Ornstein, M.D., (1986), 'The Canadian state and corporate elites in the post-war period', *Canadian Review of Sociology and Anthropology* 23: 481–506.

Froud, J., Savage, M., Tampubolon, G. and Williams, K., (2006), 'Rethinking elite research', CRESC Working Paper No. 12, University of Manchester, available at www.cresc.ac.uk, accessed 6 November, 2007.

Froud, J., Tampubolon, G. and Williams, K., (2008), 'Everything for sale: an alternative view of corporate governance and the role of NEDs within and beyond the FTSE 100', this volume.

Gronlund, N.E., (1959), *Sociometry in the Classroom*, New York: Harper.

Helmes-Hayes, R., (2002), 'John Porter: Canada's most famous sociologist (and his links to American sociology)', *The American Sociologist* 33 (1): 79–104.

Hilferding, R., (1981 [1910]), *Finance Capital*, London: Routledge.

Howlett, K., (2003), 'TSX no longer governance cop', *Toronto Globe and Mail*, 20 September: B1.

Hussein, A., (1976), 'Hilferding's finance capital', *Bulletin of the Conference of Socialist Economists* 5 (1): 1–18.

Kellogg, P., (1989), 'State, capital and world economy: Bukharin's Marxism and the 'dependency/class' controversy in Canadian political economy', *Canadian Journal of Political Science* 22: 337–362.

Krippner, G.R., (2005), 'The financialization of the American economy', *Socio-Economic Review* 3: 173–208.

Lash, S. and Urry, J., (1987), *The End of Organized Capitalism*, Cambridge: Polity Press.

Lenin, N., (1975 [1917]), *Imperialism, the Highest Stage of Capitalism*, Moscow: Progress Publishers.

Levitt, K., (1970), *Silent Surrender*, Toronto: Macmillan of Canada.

MacDonald, L.R., (1975), 'Merchants against industry: an idea and its origins', *Canadian Historical Review* 56: 263–81.

MacEwan, A., (1986), 'International debt and banking: rising instability within the general crisis', *Science and Society* 50: 177–209.

McFarland, J., (2003), 'Good governance group set', *Toronto Globe and Mail*, 12 April: B3.

McKie, C., (1976), 'Review of Wallace Clement's *The Canadian Corporate Elite*', *Canadian Journal of Sociology* 1 (4): 547–9.

Miliband, R., (1983), *Class Power and State Power*, London: Verso.

Mills, C. W., (1956), *The Power Elite*, New York: Oxford University Press.

Mintz, B. and Schwartz, M., (1985), *The Power Structure of American Business*, Chicago: University of Chicago Press.

Moore, L., (2007), 'Alcan deal called economic suicide', *Vancouver Sun*, 14 July: D4.

Morck, R., and Nakamura, M., (1995), 'Banks and corporate governance in Canada', in Daniels, R.J. and Morck, R., (eds), *Corporate Decision-Making in Canada*, Calgary: University of Calgary Press: 481–502.

Naylor, R.T., (1972), 'The rise and fall of the third commercial empire of the St Lawrence', in Teeple, G., (ed.), *Capitalism and the National Question in Canada*, Toronto: University of Toronto Press: 1–41.

Niosi, J., (1978), *The Economy of Canada: Who Controls It?* Montreal: Black Rose Books.

Niosi, J., (1981), *Canadian Capitalism*, Toronto: Lorimer.

Olive, D., (2007), 'Canada beating industrial retreat', *Toronto Star*, 13 May: A1.

Ornstein, M.D., (1984), 'Interlocking directorates in Canada: intercorporate or class alliance?' *Administrative Science Quarterly* 29: 210–31.

Ornstein, M.D., (1989), 'The social organization of the Canadian capitalist class in comparative perspective', *Canadian Review of Sociology and Anthropology* 26: 151–77.

Overbeek, H., (2004), 'Transnational class formation and concepts of control: towards a genealogy of the Amsterdam Project in international political economy', *Journal of International Relations and Development* 7: 113–41.

van der Pijl, K., (1984), *The Making of an Atlantic Ruling Class*, London: Verso.

van der Pijl, K., (1986), 'Neoliberalism vs. planned interdependence: concepts of control in the struggle for hegemony', paper presented at *The Conference on Interdependence and Conflict in the International System*, Groningen: Polemologisch Instituut.

Porter, J., (1965), *The Vertical Mosaic*, Toronto: University of Toronto Press.

Richardson, R.J., (1982), 'Merchants against industry: an empirical study', *Canadian Journal of Sociology* 7: 279–96.

Richardson, R.J., (1988), 'A 'Sacred Trust?' The trust industry and Canadian economic structure', *Canadian Review of Sociology and Anthropology* 25 (1): 1–22.

Scott, J., (1987), 'Intercorporate structures in western Europe: a comparative historical analysis', in Mizruchi, M.S. and Schwartz, M., (eds), *Intercorporate Relations*, Cambridge: Cambridge University Press: 208–32.

Scott, J., (1997), *Corporate Business and Capitalist Classes*, New York: Oxford University Press.

Scott, J., (2003), 'Transformations in the British economic elite', *Comparative Sociology* 2 (1): 155–73.

Sonquist, J.A. and Koenig, T., (1975), 'Interlocking directorates in the top U.S. corporations: a graph theory approach', *Insurgent Sociologist* 5 (3): 196–229.

Soref, M. and Zeitlin, M., (1987), 'Finance capital and the internal structure of the capitalist class in the United States', in Mizruchi, M.S. and Schwartz, M., (eds), *Intercorporate Relations*, Cambridge: Cambridge University Press: 56–84.

Stanford, J., (1999), *Paper Boom*, Toronto: Lorimer.

Stokman, F.N., Ziegler, R. and Scott, J., (1985), *Networks of Corporate Power: A Comparative Analysis of Ten Countries*, Cambridge: Polity Press.

Thompson, P., (2003), 'Disconnected capitalism: or why employers can't keep their side of the bargain', *Work, Employment and Society* 17: 359–78.

Useem, M., (1979), 'The social organization of the American capitalist class', *American Sociological Review* 44: 553–71.

Useem, M., (1981), 'Business segments and corporate relations with U.S. universities', *Social Problems* 29: 129–41.

Valverde, M., (1991), 'As if subjects existed: analysing social discourses', *Canadian Review of Sociology and Anthropology* 28: 173–87.

# Representing the corporate elite in Britain: capitalist solidarity and capitalist legitimacy

*Michael Moran*

## Strangers and brothers

The study of elites lies at the meeting points of sociology, history and political science. This chapter is about the third partner in the meeting. Understanding what has happened to business elites certainly demands a sense of their history and social structure; but it also demands a sense of how they are organized politically, and how that organization in turn is shaped by the wider political environment of business.

These points have particular force in the study of business representation in Britain. The United Kingdom occupies an especially important place in debates about the political power of business, notably debates conducted over the last generation. Part of that importance is substantive: the UK economy is the fourth largest in the world, so it is an outstandingly important case in the population of capitalist democracies. But this substantive significance is only part of the story. Among the leading capitalist nations, the UK saw perhaps the most profound changes in policy during the turmoil following the end of the capitalist 'long boom' in the mid 1970s. The reforms associated with Thatcherism produced radical change in the political economy of Britain, notably in labour relations, corporate ownership and competitive practices. Moreover, many of these changes, most obviously in privatization, made the UK an international pioneer among capitalist democracies. These policy innovations were designed to shift power in the economy, to the benefit of business. They did indeed achieve this result. But I shall argue that the consequences – massive enrichment of parts of the corporate elite and huge increases in inequality – have exacerbated legitimacy problems for the corporate order. Thus the UK is not only an important case in the general debate about the power of business under democratic capitalism; it is a critical case in estimating what the great changes in the political economy of capitalism since the end of the 'long boom' have done to that power.

Understanding the political power of business elites depends on understanding how they are represented in the political system, for the following reason. Virtually all observers of business power recognize that a key issue for business is its capacity, or otherwise, to mobilize collectively. The problem of group solidarity is, naturally, crucial to all interest mobilizations, but there are good reasons why it is especially problematic for business interests in a market economy. The problem is encapsulated in Marx's often quoted observation that capitalists are 'hostile brothers' (Marx, 1894/1959:253) and in Vogel's modern summary of business interests as 'kindred strangers' (Vogel, 1996). Business interests, as these phrases attest, are simultaneously united by common interests and divided by competitive struggles. Collective action has proved especially difficult for British business; and this difficulty has deep structural and cultural roots. In the last thirty years, structural change, institutional evolution, and changes in the cultural environment of business have intensified the problem of collective action, even while they have empowered individual businesses and enriched parts of the corporate elite. This helps explain the oddity that in an age when political elites have competed to seem 'business-friendly', the legitimacy of business as a system of power in Britain has proved fragile; and it helps explain why the corporate elite in Britain has become at once fabulously wealthy and deeply despised.

## Structural power and capitalist solidarity

Viewed historically and comparatively, business power in Britain has three striking features: 1) a long established symbiosis between a particular economic sector and the state; 2) the relative political subordination of key interests created by the industrial revolution; and 3) a business culture which put a premium on the autonomy of the individual enterprise. This last feature in turn helps explain the late and partial development of 'class-wide' systems of representation – in other words, of institutions claiming credibly to speak for the collective interests of business (Useem, 1984:16–18).

The first of these features originates in the rise of a key state formation at the end of the 17th century: the development in the City of London of a system of 'service sector' capitalism organically connected to the ruling elite (Cain and Hopkins, 1993 and 1993a). This gave a particular cast to the practice of business representation, laying the foundations for a distinctive kind of social world: a tightly integrated social and cultural community, concentrated in a small space in London (Lisle-Williams, 1984; Kynaston, 1995, 1996 and 1999). It also gave a particular cosmopolitan cast to the business elite, for this City prospered on the back of global enterprises associated with imperialism.

The second characteristic – the relatively subordinate place of industrial interests – grew out of the best known feature of British economic development: its pioneering role in creating the first industrial society. The new elite born in the Industrial Revolution was local in scope, parochial in outlook, and often hegemonic in its little local world. A predominant theme of industrial representation for the first two thirds of the 20th century was the unsuccessful struggle to organize manufacturing interests in a stable nationwide institution capable of pursuing collective interests (Blank, 1973:13–20). Industry lacked the solidarity of commercial capital.

One reason why it proved difficult to organize manufacturing was connected to the third feature identified above: a belief in the autonomy of the individual firm. That belief was historically embedded in the very foundations of company law. The firm was pictured as a 'private association, which should have the minimum of government regulation and interference' (Gamble and Kelly, 2001:111). A wide range of sectoral studies show that, in its dealings with firms, the state stressed the autonomy of the enterprise: that meant self-regulation – where public institutions stood in the background – or co-operative and consensual regulation when there already existed public regulatory bodies (Carson, 1970, 1970a, 1974, 1979, 1980, 1982).

All this immensely empowered individual firms but greatly complicated the task of organizing business representation. It left trade associations weak in the face of firms, with few resources and little authority over members. Thus originated a feature, which was to characterize business organization throughout the 20th century: a stress on voluntarism which greatly limited the ability of associations to 'deliver' on behalf of their members.

In these circumstances of informality, fragmentation and firm autonomy, how could the class interests of business be identified and promoted? In a nutshell: in three ways.

First, after World War One the historically dominant part of business – the commercial-financial sector rooted in the City of London – developed powerful institutional and social mechanisms of cohesion. The most important organizing institution was the Bank of England which, under the long tenure of its first permanent Governor (Montagu Norman, 1920–44), commanded a key role both in the regulation of City markets and in managing the relations between the markets and the central state (Clay, 1957:272–317; Kynaston, 1999:42–4).

Second, as a by-product of the First World War the partisan cohesion of business in the new formal democracy was greatly strengthened. The destruction of the Liberal Party left the Conservatives as the unchallenged voice of business interests in the partisan arena.

Third, again under the immediate pressure of war, manufacturing for the first time created a putative single national voice, in the form of the Federation of British Industries (1916). But while the Federation's founding figure, Dudley Docker, had envisioned it as the collective voice of business, that vision came to nothing: separate employers' associations jealously guarded their 'turf' in negotiations over pay and conditions, and supported a rival peak association, the British Employers' Confederation (Davenport-Hines, 1984:84–7; Wigham, 1973:103–4; Middlemas, 1979:116–8; Grieves, 1989:169). The FBI also had a tense relationship with the National Union of Manufacturers, which was dominated by small manufacturing firms, while commercial and financial interests worked through the City networks described above (Blank, 1973:20).

These divisions persisted for nearly fifty years, but the decade after 1965 was a critical period in efforts to mend institutional fragmentation. That year saw the foundation of the Confederation of British Industry. This attempt to end half a century of institutional rivalry in business representation was encouraged by the central state, which from the early 1960s actively looked for a single business 'partner' in its new ventures into economic planning. But even the CBI had from the beginning a restricted view of its role as the collective voice of business, a view that betrayed the extent to which it was the child of the FBI (Federation of British Industries). The old tensions with employers' associations resurfaced (Grant and Marsh, 1977:59–60; Wigham, 1973:216). The Confederation accepted the special separate role of City representation by relegating banks and other parts of the commercial sector like finance houses to the status of associate membership; and it did the same with what in the next thirty years turned out to be one of the most dynamic parts of the economy, retail distribution and marketing (Grant and Marsh, 1977:31–2, 61).

The three main instruments for the collective representation of business interests described so far all had strengths, but all patently had weaknesses: the City was immensely effective but only within its restricted domain; the Conservative Party was very successful in managing the new democracy but to do so had to be something more than the instrument of business; while the representation of manufacturing was fragmented.

The reader might at this point wonder whether there were any mechanisms by which something as general as a class interest could have been identified and promoted. In a nutshell, again, there were two: structural and ideological.

The institutional divisions in business interest representation were partly transcended, after the First World War, by a reorganization of corporate control. This created a dense system of interlocked ownership and cross directorships, which bound together the largest corporations and straddled the conventional finance/industry divide. The work of Scott and others shows that this network became even more dense and encompassing in the years after the Second World War, up to the 1970s (Fidler, 1981, esp: 89–90 summarily tabulates the studies to that point; Scott and Griff, 1984 and Scott, 1991, 1997 and 2003).

A standard difficulty in interpreting this kind of 'interlock' data has been that of demonstrating how the simple fact of interlock could convert into class consciousness and action. But Useem's comparative study of 'class wide' business perspectives and actions in the US and the UK, based on analysis of interlock data, interviews with corporate elites conducted in 1979 and 1980, and close analysis of business engagement with the policy process, showed precisely how the sociological fact of interlock converted into a capacity for class mobilization (Useem, 1984:42–57).

This capacity for mobilization through informally created networks was greatly reinforced by the prior existence of a hegemonic ideology that legitimized business control of its own affairs. In the financial markets it was expressed in the language of 'self-regulation': the assertion that markets were the best regulators of their own affairs. In areas where the state had a historically established regulatory presence – in health and safety, in environmental regulation, in the regulation of competition – it was expressed in philosophies of 'co-operative regulation': the view that any legally based regulatory order could only be carried on with the cooperation of the regulated business interests – and was therefore constrained by what those interests found tolerable. In fundamental areas of corporate governance, the ideology silently 'organized out' of politics key issues to do with the internal government of the firm – who should do the governing, what standards of behaviour should apply, how corporate reward should be decided (Clift *et al.*, 2000; Bowden, 2000).

By the middle of the 1970s, the fact that business in Britain was a fragmented, often incompetent, political actor and had an unreliable partisan ally in the Conservative Party, did not matter greatly for the representation of class interests. The organized capitalism incarnated in densely interlocked networks, and the hegemonic regulatory ideology, proved highly effective. The most important clue to what happened to business politically over the next thirty years was that these conditions changed. Institutionally, business became more fragmented and even less able to organize collectively for lobbying purposes, while the structural foundations and ideologically created silences that compensated for everyday political incompetence were transformed.

## The decay of class wide representation

The direction of institutional change over the last three decades can be summed up in contradictory developments. There has been a sharp decline in the institutional solidarity of business as an organized interest but a sharp increase in the extent to which firms, especially big firms, have mobilized to voice their own narrow interests. Representing the class interests of business has become increasingly problematic; representing individual big businesses has become increasingly effective. This also provides a clue to another apparent contradiction, one to which I return in the conclusion: the business elite has become more embattled and more unpopular; but sections of that elite have been able to exercise power and privilege on a historically unprecedented scale.

A key underlying change bears on the original structural conditions for class solidarity: the dense system of interlocks that created organized capitalism over the first two thirds of the 20th century has partly dissolved. The 'headline' signs of structural change are well known. From the early 1970s there were momentous developments in the advanced capitalist economies: the collapse of the Bretton Woods system; the end of the long boom, ushering in a period of difficult structural change in the leading industrial economies; a new burst of globalization; and the onset of an era of financial deregulation. The UK was, as we noted at the start of this chapter, in the vanguard of structural change during the 1980s. One development, not restricted to Britain, we may note in passing as a symptom of the larger global structural upheavals: from the mid 1980s there was a sharp acceleration in Europeanization following the revitalization of the project to create a single market in the (then) European Economic Community, signalled by the passage of the Single European Act of 1986.

It was the twin mechanisms of financial deregulation and globalization which produced the most profound changes in the historic cohesion of the corporate elite. Two landmark events were the abolition of exchange controls in 1979 and the 'big bang' of 1986 in the City. The latter transformed ownership structures that had been central to the old system of corporate interlocks. Family firms that had dominated City markets were displaced by financial conglomerates, typically foreign controlled and globally organized. The changes in economic structures as a result of the competitive revolution also produced wider structural change, notably the contraction (or even disappearance) of much domestically owned manufacturing capacity. A boom in foreign direct investment, which still continues, saw the displacement of domestically owned enterprises in key sectors by branches of foreign owned multinationals.

Scott's preliminary data for the late 1980s and early 1990s showed the beginning of the twin impact of financial deregulation and globalization on the cohesion of the old system. The century-long trend that had consolidated the corporate elite into a single nationally-embedded network was reversed. The density of interlock declined, as a direct result of the fact that much business ownership in Britain was now part of a wider internationalized system. One immediate sign of this was a transformation in corporate ownership. Over the last thirty years individuals became less important as holders of equities. A long term securitization of assets has led to the utter dominance of financial institutions in equity markets. There has occurred a substantial internationalization of share ownership, and a consequential weakening of the density of the nationally embedded system of interlocks. Scott first spotted this disruption when reporting his preliminary findings for the early 1990s (Scott, 2003:170). More recent figures bear out his preliminary suppositions. In the decade after 1994 there was a sharp internationalization of ownership in the UK equity market: in 1994 foreign investors owned just over 16 per cent of stock; ten years later the figure was 32.6 per cent. The fragmenting impact on corporate management is neatly caught by a remark of the MD of Goldman Sachs: 'The relationships you need to have now are very different to 15 years ago when you only needed to know the top 10 funds and their top managers.' (Tassell and Saigol, 2005).

We can now turn to trace the impact of these great structural changes on the way business was organized for representation. One landmark development concerns the organization of business as an employer. As we saw earlier, the prior existence of employers' associations, and their determination to defend their institutional 'turf', was an important historic obstacle to the creation of a unified system of business organization. A seismic shift in economic power took place during the 1980s in the balance between organized labour and the corporation. But the very forces that dismantled trade union power also led to the decline of industry-wide or sector-wide collective bargaining in the private sector. The resulting decline of unions has been well documented; less well recognized is the decay of collective employer organization, as bargaining shifted away from the industry and sector level. This decay is strikingly recorded in the aggregate data: Milward and his colleagues report that over the decade of the 1980s the 'density' (coverage) of sectoral employers' associations fell by nearly a half (Milward *et al.*, 1992:45–6). Perhaps partly as a result, in the decade after 1994 Greenwood reports that a large number of associations simply went out of existence, either through amalgamation or simple cessation (Greenwood, 2004:8).

Estimating what has happened to trade associations, the meso level 'twin' of employers' associations, is harder because they form a large, institutionally diverse population subject to no systematic central 'mapping': May and his colleagues estimated numbers in the early 1990s at around 1300 (May *et al.*, 1998:263). The Devlin Report had painted an unflattering picture of the inefficiency and incompetence of trade associations in the early 1970s (Devlin, 1972). The 1990s saw a conscious effort by parts of the governing and business elites to improve their working. That is exactly the response – formally to organize more effectively – that we would expect, given the way ideological and structural change had eroded the 'natural' solidarity of business. In 1993 Michael Heseltine, then President of the Board of Trade, proposed that the DTI sponsor the emergence of a small number of 'lead' associations that would be closely integrated into policy making. He also urged enterprises to press for more efficiency and effectiveness in their own associations (May *et al.*, 1998:261–2). In 1997 the DTI and the CBI jointly sponsored the creation of the Trade Association Forum, designed to disseminate best practice. But May and his colleagues, reviewing experience after 1979, could find little evidence of a 'Heseltine' effect. Their work stressed the continuity of experience during the years from the late 1970s. They did find that a higher proportion of associations passed the financial test for minimum effectiveness than had been revealed by Devlin in 1972; but even more than two decades after Devlin they still found that over two-thirds of associations failed this bare test of likely operational effectiveness (May *et al.*, 1998:265).

The impression that, beyond a few well funded and effective instances, most trade associations are poorly funded and politically useless is strengthened by MacDonald's (2001) survey. He identified an elite of about 20 effective associations. The existence of that elite is important. It shows that not all collective action by business was weakened. Where firms could effectively pursue collective goods by common action, and only effectively do so in that manner, the associations prospered: that seems to explain the vigour of associational life in an industry like pharmaceuticals (Froud *et al.*, 2006:149ff). The point is particularly important because of an argument to which I return at the close: that the most striking feature of the political power of business in recent decades is not so much a story of growth or decline but one of divergence: different parts of the business elite have enjoyed rather different fortunes. The fate of trade associations is emblematic of that point. Beyond MacDonald's elite, associational performance was laughable: incompetence in presenting a case to government; lack of elementary knowledge about how government works; primitive technologies for communicating with members. As a sign of the impact of the structural change discussed in the previous section, he reports 'disconcerting examples' of a new trend: country managers of foreign multinationals who play the minimum possible role in associational life (Macdonald, 2001:24).

Of course collective organization at the meso level is not the most important means of class mobilization, indeed, only involves its partial realization. As the structural conditions for the kind of class-wide coordination documented by Scott and Useem disappeared, and as the hegemonic ideology of business regulation became more fragile, formal class wide organization became more imperative. But the obvious institution to organize this, the CBI, also weakened during this period. Even at the height of its prestige in the 1970s, the Confederation was, we have seen, a highly imperfect vehicle of class mobilization: it had only very partial coverage; it was pressured by the employers' associations to keep off their 'turf'; and it was continually subject to the stress of reconciling the interests of the very different interests of its diverse membership. It had also inherited from the FBI an 'insider' style that locked it, often profitably, into the world of the Whitehall elite. But that world was seriously disrupted by the new policies and styles of the Thatcher Governments after 1979. The resulting tactical difficulties are illuminated by a famous episode: the promise of the Director General in 1980 to have a 'bare knuckle fight' with a government that was at that very moment presiding over a recession highly destructive of traditional manufacturing – the very foundations of the Confederation. The threat produced serious dissent inside the Confederation, and some very public resignations (Grant and Sargent, 1993:124 on this episode). Although the CBI has now abandoned the restrictive membership policies of the 1970s and actively recruits across the whole of business, it is still dominated by the old industrial economy and, measured by staff size, was in the new millennium actually a smaller organization than in the 1970s (Grant, 2000:12).

The relative decline of the CBI reflected the fact that in the 1980s and 1990s it became increasingly difficult to organize business into a single cohesive class force, for a mix of ideological, institutional and structural reasons. In the Thatcher years the Institute of Directors was revitalized and became a rival national voice to the CBI. Its emergence – and pursuit of a line which was more consistently sympathetic to the Thatcher revolution – reflected ideological divisions in the corporate elite about how to react to a world after the great Thatcherite reforms.

A second kind of fragmentation involved a sector that the CBI had always found hard to represent, small business. In part the problem lay, paradoxically, in the revitalization of rival representative institutions. These included the Chamber of Commerce movement, which was incorporated into a variety of public roles in local economies and in the workforce-training regime from the mid 1980s; and the rise in membership and resources of the Federation of Small Businesses (Fallon and Brown, 2000; Jordan and Halpin, 2003 and 2004). But the rise of these institutions at the local level still leaves a highly fragmented system where most small businesses have no connection with representative organizations (see Curran *et al.*, 2000).

Some of these developments reflected tactical contingencies: the political entrepreneurship that created the Federation of Small Businesses, for example, was able to exploit the CBI's difficulties in accommodating this diverse sector into its already heterogeneous membership. But fragmentation also reflected ideological and structural shifts. In the 1980s and 1990s, after a generation of neglect, policy makers in the core executive arrived at a new consensus – that in the small business sector lay the key to economic dynamism (May and McHugh, 2002).

Just how far the economic structure had indeed shifted to one where small business was the driver of jobs and competitiveness is hard to estimate. But what is demonstrable is that the most innovative and dynamic part of the small business sector was, by the 1990s, disconnected from the established institutions of business representation, especially nationally organized business institutions. The most dynamic element in small business growth in the 1980s and 1990s was composed of small business service firms – knowledge-based enterprises like design and IT consultancies. Survey data assembled by Bryson *et al.* show that these firms were highly unlikely to have connections with nationally organized peak business institutions. They operated, if at all, through local Chambers of Commerce and a diffuse network of professional associations (Bryson *et al.*, 1997:356).

This disconnection from class, or even sector, wide business representation reflects a wider change in the business representation system which Grant first noticed in the 1980s (Grant, 1984). He then identified the development of the government relations function within big firms – an institutionalized alternative to collective representation. In the intervening years this individualization of representation has become much more extensive, spreading beyond the giant firm. We noted earlier that 'business service' firms were among the fastest growing parts of the economy in the 1980s and 1990s, and within this category particularly rapid growth has been seen in a series of linked categories: those offering professional business lobbying, corporate public relations, brand image management, and management of investor relations (Davis, 2000; Miller and Dinan, 2000). These firms offer services that allow enterprises to manage their own representation.

This growing individualization of representation can be traced to four influences.

First, the shift is exactly what we might expect in an age when the old nationally embedded, structurally cohesive system has become 'disembedded'. The new age of disembedded capitalism in Britain is also an age of deregulated capitalism marked by fierce competitive struggle. The process is strikingly illustrated by securities markets, where executives have to manage large institutional investors who make buy/sell decisions under short-term profit horizons; as Savage and Williams graphically put it in the introduction to this volume, in present day corporate business everything is for sale. In this world, professional investor relations firms, and corporate PR firms, fulfil defensive and offensive functions. Defensively, they manage volatile investors, at the extreme in circumstances where the enterprise is threatened by a hostile take-over. Offensively, they have become vital when the enterprise is itself mounting a hostile take-over. Some of the systemic consequences are explored in Davis's case study of the Granada/Forte take-over struggle in 1995–6: competitors swap knocking copy about each other, in the process contributing to the low general public esteem in which big business is held (Davis, 2000:286–93).

Second, Europeanization has spurred this process of individualization. In part this is a matter of 'demand': successive Commissions have shown themselves highly receptive to direct dealings with (big) individual enterprises (Coen, 1998:75–9). But it is also a matter of supply: commercial consultancies, professional lobbying firms, and multinational law firms combining legal services and specialized lobbying have all established a prominent presence in Brussels, notably since the inauguration of the Single Market project. (Lahusen, 2002). Nor is this surprising: European Union wide sectoral associations replicate all the problems of cohesion in national trade union associations, but of course now magnified to a multinational level. The professionalization of the lobbying function offers firms a much more direct way to fix their problems.

Third, investments in corporate PR and brand management have allowed individual firms to buck a damaging trend: disenchantment with, and distrust of, big business as a social institution. The survey data show that, while big business as a whole is disliked and distrusted, this does not necessarily extend to *individual* businesses (Lewis, 2003; Davis, 2000; and Miller and Dinan, 2000). Assiduous image cultivation and brand management, including assiduous cultivation of media business reporting, can do wonders for public perceptions of individual firms, at least in the short term. The data even show that where firms have been involved in PR fiascos – like the oil giant Shell over Brent Spar and cooperation with tyrannical regimes in Nigeria – heavy investment in good public relations can substantially change public perceptions for the better. (Whether it can create a stable reputation is a matter to which I return in the conclusion). These developments also explain why firms have now gone well beyond reliance on the specialized government relations departments originally identified by Grant; they recognize that specialized lobbying has to be integrated into a more comprehensive strategy to manage public perceptions of enterprises and their brands. Public opinion is highly sensitive to quite nuanced changes and this can be exploited by enterprises and individuals. For instance, when members of the public are asked their views, not of big business, but of some individual enterprises, they often respond highly positively (Audit Commission/MORI, 2005:30).

A fourth and final influence prompting 'individualization' of representation also springs from greater competition, but not of an economic kind. Business now inhabits a much more turbulently competitive lobbying environment than was the case in the past. This arises from changes in civil society that I discuss in more detail in the next section, but is strikingly illustrated by some of the most ambitious (and successful) instances of individual enterprise management.

Multinational oil firms like Shell and BP, faced with vocal and well organized environmental movements, have been obliged to respond with highly innovative programmes of corporate PR. Likewise, firms in mass retail markets have been forced, by movements lobbying for ethical employment and sourcing practices, to invest heavily in defensive brand management.

I now examine the wider challenge from civil society to the capacity of business to realize its individual and collective interests.

## Business solidarity and the challenge from civil society

Examining the cultural climate of business activity forces us to confront one of the puzzles which lie at the heart of this chapter: why, in an era of business-friendly government, does business find itself so unpopular? One obvious explanation – that greed and arrogance bred this hostility – is not fully convincing. Business has often behaved outrageously and scandalously; but this kind of behaviour now seems much more capable of arousing disapproval than do scandalous revelations about other powerful groups. For instance, the survey evidence indicates that confidence and trust in big business was damaged by scandals like Enron and Worldcom – hardly a surprising outcome (MORI, 2003). But contrast the experience of another group faced with an even more outrageous scandal, the murderous spree of the doctor Harold Shipman, a spree which reflected serious defects in the medical regulatory system: in the wake of the Shipman revelations public confidence in doctors actually rose (MORI, 2002). There is plainly something in the cultural climate which is working against business, especially big business. To borrow the language of Habermas, business authority now lives in an atmosphere that contains the seeds of legitimation crisis – it no longer seems quite part of the natural order of things (Habermas, 1976:37, 68–75, 96).

There are two main reasons why legitimacy has been damaged in this way, and since the first of these has cropped up earlier we can deal with it summarily. As we saw in the preceding section, while *individual* firms greatly strengthened their lobbying and image management capacities, the *collective* voice of business was actually weakened over the decades. In some instances the rise of individual lobbying was collectively damaging. For instance in hostile takeovers, the PR and lobbying activities of the battling parties were often dedicated to damaging the reputation of opponents – and by extension of business more generally.

This turn to investment in representation and image management for the individual firm was, however, itself a response to the second great source of damage to business legitimacy: the growth in civil society of networks of organizations that challenged both the legitimacy of the primacy of the pursuit of profits, and the authority of enterprise executives, especially executives in the largest firms. Despite the fact that governing elites have competed to seem ever more business-friendly, in the wider civil society business, especially big business, has had to operate in increasingly contentious conditions. A number of overlapping changes can be identified. They include the rise of the Corporate Social Responsibility movement; the rise of challenges from coalitions of active institutional shareholders; and the rise of challenging coalitions uniting NGOs and pressure groups, both domestically and globally.

It is often hard to disentangle these changes, because the networks that are producing them overlap. To economize on space, I concentrate for a moment on one set of cases here: the rise of church-led movements critical of business. Take first the special case of the Catholic Church. Globally, especially during the pontificate of John Paul II, the Church's ideology shifted: from a mildly conservative critique of capitalism, coupled with alliances in many parts of the globe with reactionary business elites, to a much more comprehensive critique of the most advanced practices of global business. This global shift was reflected within the UK, as the instance of the Church's most important NGO in the area, the Catholic Fund for Overseas Development (CAFOD), shows. CAFOD originated in a single act of charity entirely consistent with the Church's traditional social ideology: the organization of a national Family Fast Day in 1961 by the National Board of Catholic Women, in response to a request from the Caribbean island of Dominica for help with a mother-and-baby health-care programme. CAFOD itself was established by the Catholic Bishops of England and Wales in 1962 to provide a focus for these kinds of charitable initiatives. In the intervening generation its resources have grown greatly – from an income of £25,000 in its first year, to £47 million in 2004–5. But more important, CAFOD has also been transformed into a highly radical voice in debates, notably about trade and the individual practices of globally organized businesses. By 2007 this radicalism had begun to invade individual parishes, especially in inner cities. Globalization of labour markets was dramatically changing the composition of congregations as new migrants to Britain, many of them illegal, turned up at church services and, in some cases, involved parishes in bruising struggles with immigration authorities. In other words the radicalization of CAFOD was succeeded by a wider radicalization of the institutional church as it encountered the sharp edge of globalization in its pastoral ministry.

The importance of an institution like CAFOD lies partly in its position in a wider global network of over 160 like-minded Catholic NGOs coordinated in Caritas Internationalis. It lies partly in the way CAFOD, like similar NGOS, now intervenes in what were once only esoteric processes of corporate regulation, such as the DTI Company Law Reform Review (see CAFOD 1999 for this). But it lies above all in the fact that CAFOD here is only one part of a dense network of groups challenging numerous business practices. The character of the network is well illustrated by the example of the Ecumenical Council for Corporate Responsibility, founded in 1995 to focus, in particular, on the activities of British based multinationals. The Council unites numerous religious groups with many different roles: it stretches from religious orders with substantial corporate investments of their own, to the high profile Christian aid organizations. It has developed benchmarks for corporate responsibility, and has applied these benchmarks to a wide range of individual enterprises, forcing the enterprises in turn to respond to critical, damaging reports.

The significance of this attempt by ecumenical activists to exert pressure on enterprises is reinforced by the fact that these groups are in turn integrated into wider networks in civil society. The rapid growth of the NGO sector, both domestically in Britain and globally, is now well documented, and this growth is largely a phenomenon of the last two decades (Freehauf, 2003:5, for the UK; for global data, Glasius *et al.*, 2002:3). The result has been an extraordinary alphabet soup of groups, and coalitions of groups, spanning religious and secular NGOs, specialized ethical investment service organizations, and even more specialized shareholder activism groups – a whole new organizational population challenging managerial authority, one that simply did not exist a couple of decades ago. Of course as a challenge to business this organizational population operates under very serious limits, partly due to the lack of any single ideological agenda or common institutional cohesion: the wider so-called 'anti-globalization movement' is, in the words of Green and Griffith, 'neither solidly anti-globalization, nor a movement'(Green and Griffith, 2002:50). But it nevertheless represents a tumultuous wave of dissent from neo-liberal hegemony after the end of the long boom.

### 'Do it yourself' representation and capitalist solidarity

Many contradictions surround the political position of business in contemporary Britain. Political elites compete to seem business-friendly; but people at large dislike and distrust the corporate elite. There is contempt for big business as a system of power; but respect, and even affection, for individual big business figures and particular brands. Many powerful traditional opponents, like trade unions, have seen their influence greatly reduced; but new critics have appeared, often born in institutions, like churches, that historically were friendly to business privilege. And the greatest contradiction of all is that in an era when political leaders jostle to pay respect to the business system, it has become ever more difficult to supply leadership for that system – to voice its *common* interests and to represent those interests.

One important effect of this weakness in voicing common interests has been, paradoxically, to unleash the most rapacious parts of the corporate elite. As class discipline has weakened individual greed has grown. For instance, the data on trends on top executive pay assembled by Erturk (Erturk *et al.*, 2005; and see Savage and Williams, this volume) systematizes what is widely known anecdotally: that sections of this elite have appropriated a historically unprecedented share of corporate wealth. They have done this by using their insider status in the corporation and manipulating the tax system; and have produced staggering increases in inequality as a result. It has never been a better time to be a greedy chief executive and rarely been a more difficult one to be either a defender of the corporate order or the organizer of business into some solidaristic block.

Sectional interests within business are more powerfully defended than ever. The corporate elite has at its disposal, in the form of the new apparatus of image and brand management, tools of propaganda and public opinion manipulation that were beyond the ken of business leaders a generation ago. 'Do it yourself' representation works wonders in the short-term but only at the most narrowly sectional level. The new corporate plutocracy has appropriated wealth but has no moral foundations to justify that wealth; hence the general contempt in which big business is held, and the fragility of all corporate reputations, even those constantly burnished by the most sophisticated system of public relations. In this anomic environment reputation, in Power's words, 'is infused with both fear and opportunity' (Power, 2007:129). One might add: and with danger and opportunity. In this dangerous, fearful world some parts of the corporate elite prosper by a mixture of luck and the ruthless exploitation of the instruments of reputation management. Others, like Arthur Andersen in the wake of the Enron crisis, see both their reputation and organization vanish in a puff of smoke.

# Note

I am grateful to the editors, and to two anonymous referees, for valuable comments on an earlier version.

# References

Ashby, E. and Anderson, M., (1981), *The Politics of Clean Air*, Oxford: Clarendon Press.
Audit Commission/Mori, (2005), Trust in Public Institutions, London: Audit Commission, accessed at www.mori.com/sri, 28/1/05.
Blank, S., (1973), *Government and Industry in Britain*, Farnborough: Saxon House.
Bowden, S., (2000), 'Corporate governance in a political climate: the impact of public policy regimes on corporate governance in the United Kingdom' in Parkinson, *et al.*, (eds), 175–94.
Bryson, J., Keeble, D. and Wood, P., (1997), 'The creation and growth of small business service firms in post-industrial Britain', *Small Business Economics* 9: 345–60.
CAFOD (Catholic Fund for Overseas Development). *Cafod Submission on the Company Law Review.* (1999) www.cafod.org.uk/archive/policy/policylawreview 28.1.05.
Cain, P.G. and Hopkins, A.G., (1993), *British Imperialism: Innovation and Expansion, 1688–1914*, London: Pearson Longman.
Cain, P.G. and Hopkins, A.G., (1993a), *British Imperialism: Crisis and Deconstruction, 1914–1990*, London: Pearson Longman.
Carson, W.G., (1970), 'Some sociological aspects of strict liability and the enforcement of factory legislation', *Modern Law Review*, 33/4: 396–412.
Carson, W.G., (1970a), 'White-Collar crime and the enforcement of factory legislation', *British Journal of Criminology*, 10/4: 383–98.
Carson, W.G., (1974), 'Symbolic and instrumental dimensions of early factory legislation: a case study in the social origins of criminal law' in R. Hood, (ed.), *Crime, Criminology and Public Policy: Essays in Honour of Sir Leon Radzinowicz*, London: Heinemann: 107–38.
Carson, W.G., (1979), 'The conventionalization of early factory crime', *International Journal for the Sociology of Law*, 7/1: 37–60.

Carson, W.G., (1980), 'The institutionalization of ambiguity: early British factory acts' in G. Geis and E. Stotland (eds), *White-Collar Crime: Theory and Research*, London: Sage: 142–73.

Carson, W.G., (1982), *The Other Price of Britain's Oil: Safety and Control in the North Sea*, Oxford: Martin Robertson.

Cheffins, B., (1997), *Company Law: Theory, Structure and Operation*, Oxford: Clarendon Press.

Clay, H., (1957), *Lord Norman*, London: Macmillan.

Clift, B., Gamble, A. and Harris, M., (2000), 'The Labour Party and the Company' in Parkinson, J., Gamble, A. and Kelly, G., (eds), (2000) *The Political Economy of the Company*, Oxford: Hart: 51–81.

Coen, D., (1998), 'The European business interest and the nation state: large-firm lobbying in the European Union and the member states', *Journal of Public Policy*, 18:1: 75–100.

Curran, J., Rutherford, R. and Lloyd Smith, S., (2000), 'Is there a local business community? Explaining the non-participation of small business in local economic development', *Local Economy*, 15:2: 128–43.

Davenport-Hines, R.T.P., (1984), *Dudley Docker: The Life and Times of a Trade Warrior*, Cambridge: Cambridge University Press.

Davis, A., (2000), 'Public relations, business news and the reproduction of corporate elite power', *Journalism*, 1, 3: 282–304.

Devlin, Lord, Chairman, (1972), *Report* of the Commission of Inquiry into Industrial and Commercial Representation. London: Association of British Chambers of Commerce and Confederation of British Industry.

Erturk, I., Froud, J., Johal, S. and Williams, K., (2005), 'Pay for corporate performance or pay as social division? Rethinking the problem of top management pay in giant corporations', *Competition and Change* 9:1: 49–74.

Fallon, G. and Brown, R., (2000), 'Does Britain need public law status Chambers of Commerce?', *European Business Review*, 12:1: 19–27.

Fidler, J., (1981), *The British Business Elite: Its Attitude to Class, Structure and Power*, London: Routledge.

Froud, J., Sohal, S., Leaver, A., and Williams, K., (2006), *Financialization and Strategy: Narrative and Numbers*, London: Routledge.

Fruehauf, A., (2003) *The British Council and UK NGOs: A Report Commissioned by the British Council*, Institute for Public Policy Research, London.

Gamble, A. and Kelly, G., 'Shareholder value and the stakeholder debate in the UK', *Corporate Governance*, 9:2: 110–17

Glasius, H., Kaldor, M. and Anheier, H., (2002), *Global Civil Society Yearbook*, Oxford: Oxford University Press.

Grant, W., (1984), 'Large firms and public policy in Britain', *Journal of Public Policy*, 4: 1–17.

Grant, W., (2000), *Globalization, Big Business and the Blair Government*, Coventry: Centre for the Study of Globalization and Regionalization, working paper 58/00.

Grant, W. and Marsh, D., (1977), *The Confederation of British Industry*, London: Hodder and Stoughton.

Grant, W. and Sargent, J., (1993), *Business and Politics in Britain*, Basingstoke: Macmillan.

Green, D. and Griffith, M., (2002), 'Globalization and its discontents', *International Affairs*, 78:1: 49–68.

Greenwood, J., (2004), 'The association of small and medium-sized enterprises in the United Kingdom hhttp://www.rgu.ac.uk 15.2.05.

Grieves, Keith, (1989), *Sir Eric Geddes: Business and Government in War and Peace*, Manchester: Manchester University Press.

Habermas, J., (1976), *Legitimation Crisis*, translated by T. McCarthy, Cambridge: Polity Press.

Jordan, G. and Halpin, D., (2003), 'Cultivating small business influence in the UK: the Federation of Small Businesses' journey from outsider to insider', *Journal of Public Affairs*, 3:4: 313–25.

Jordan, G. and Halpin, D., (2004), 'Olson triumphant? Recruitment strategies and the growth of a small business organization', *Political Studies*, 52:3: 431–49.

Kynaston, D., (1995), *The City of London, Volume I, A World of its Own 1815–90*, London: Pimlico.
Kynaston, D., (1996), *The City of London, Volume II, Golden Years 1890–1914*, London: Pimlico.
Kynaston, D., (1999), *The City of London, Volume III, Illusions of Gold 1914–45*, London: Pimlico.
Lahusen, C., (2002), 'Commercial consultancies in the European Union: the shape and structure of professional interest intermediation', *Journal of European Public Policy*, 9:5: 695–714.
Lewis, S., (2003), *Reputation and Corporate Responsibility*, London: MORI.
Lisle-Williams, M., (1984), 'Merchant banking dynasties in the English class structure: ownership, solidarity and kinship in the City of London, 1850–90', *British Journal of Sociology*, XXXV/3: 333–62.
MacDonald, A., (2001), *The Business of Representation: The Modern Trade Association*, London: Trade Association Forum.
Marx, K., (1894/1959), *Capital: A Critique of Political Economy*, Volume III London: Lawrence and Wishart.
May, T., McHugh, J. and Taylor, T., (1998), 'Business representation in the UK since 1979: the case of Trade Associations', *Political Studies*, XLVI:2: 260–75.
May, T. and McHugh, J., (2002,) 'Small business policy: a political consensus?', *The Political Quarterly*, 73:1: 76–85.
Middlemas, Keith, (1979), *Politics in Industrial Society: The Experience of the British System since 1911*, London: Deutsch.
Miller, D. and Dinan, W., (2000), 'The rise of the PR industry in Britain, 1979–98', *European Journal of Communication*, 15:1: 5–35.
Milward, N., Stevens, M., Smart, D. and Hawes, W.R., (1992), *Workplace Industrial Relations in Transition*, Dartmouth: Aldershot.
MORI, (2002), *The Public's Trust in Doctors Rises*, www.mori/polls/2002/bma-topline – accessed, 18 August 2005.
MORI, (2003), *The Business World Will Never Be The Same: The Contribution Of Research To Corporate Governance Post-Enron*, www.mori.com/publicinfo/bg/esomar2003 – accessed, 27 January 2005.
MORI, (2003a), *The Public's View of Corporate Responsibility*, London: MORI.
Parkinson, J., Gamble, A. and Kelly, G., (eds), (2000), *The Political Economy of the Company*, Oxford: Hart.
Power, M., (2007), *Organized Uncertainty: Designing a World of Risk Management*, Oxford: Oxford University Press.
Scott, J., (1991), *Who Rules Britain?* Cambridge: Polity Press.
Scott, J., (1997), *Corporate Business and Capitalist Classes*, Oxford: Oxford University Press.
Scott, J., (2003), 'Transformations in the British economic elite,' *Comparative Sociology*, 2:1: 155–73.
Scott, J. and Griff, C., (1984), *Directors of Industry*, Cambridge: Polity Press.
Tassell, T. and Saigol L., (2005), 'International investors in the UK are buying up the keys to the kingdom', *Financial Times*, 22 June: 21.
Useem, M., (1984), *The Inner Circle: Large Corporations and the Rise of Business Political Activity in the U.S. and the U.K.* Oxford: Oxford University Press.
Vogel, D., (1996), *Kindred Strangers: The Uneasy Relationship Between Politics and Business in America*, Princeton, NJ: Princeton University Press.
Wigham, Ec., (1973), *The Power to Manage: A History of the Engineering Employers' Federation*, London: Macmillan.

# Keyser Süze elites: market populism and the politics of institutional change

*Paul du Gay*

Like 'authority' and 'hierarchy', to which they are unfailingly attached, elite and elitism are negatively coded terms in contemporary political discourse. The current British New Labour Government is absolutely opposed to them, the BBC derides them, as do almost all other organs of the media; and many public organizations, from schools to universities, line up to assure us that they won't stand for them. To talk positively of the idea of elites – to defend elitism, in no matter how nuanced a manner – seems unacceptable in polite company.

If the terminology of elites and elitism has become a potent, if entirely negative, component of contemporary political discourse, it might be expected that sociologists who, like many other social scientists, have been busy taking a cultural or 'discursive' turn in recent years, would have focused attention upon this phenomenon. But, while the turn to discourse within the social sciences has resulted in a proliferation of studies of almost anything one might care to imagine, from end stage renal failure to car mechanics, little attention has so far been paid to anti-elite discourse. This seems all the more surprising given that social constructionist work in the social sciences often regards itself as self-evidently political, and that discourses of anti-elitism have played such a crucial role in the rhetoric of political modernization and the restructuring of governmental institutions over the last three decades. Could it be that anti-elitism is such a powerful discourse that it even affects elite research? Or is it simply the case with elite research, as Alan Dawe (1970), noted many years ago, that sociologists rarely solve problems because they tend to get bored with them relatively easily? One thing seems certain, as the editors of this collection note: the study of elites and elite discourse is no longer a central topic of sociological analysis; and this is a remarkable anomaly given the importance of (anti)elite discourse in the restructuring of institutional life in a range of settings, from government to big business and from public broadcasting to higher education.

In this chapter, I seek to show how certain anti-establishment and anti-elite discourses have played a critical role in establishing an environment in which a range of public institutions could be represented as in need of radical reform. My main focus will be upon the ways in which a particular anti-elite discourse, one that Thomas Franks (2002) calls 'market populist' in tone and substance, helped reframe the purposes and norms of conduct of the senior civil service in Britain – the Mandarinate – thus severely curtailing and, indeed, fundamentally compromising its traditionally proclaimed office as independent, institutionalized counsel of government. In this way, I hope to show that anti-elite discourse has material effects upon, among other things, elite membership, character and style. In so doing, I will also have cause to consider some of the broader implications of the eclipse of a class of public service elites who ran this and other public institutions. The irony or paradox is that there is now a new breed of public sector elites, which, in keeping with equivalent elites in business and politics, denies its own elite status. I argue that the rise of this new elite of anti-elitists has some potentially serious consequences for traditional expectations of political accountability and the tenets of responsible government. If the members of an elite do not believe that they are in any sense part of an elite (and if the public at large appears to agree), then it is to be expected that they will not adjust to their status or to the responsibilities that inevitably come with it (Zakaria, 2003). Clearly, these elites will not lack power simply because they refuse to see themselves, and are not seen by others, as elites. Quite the opposite. Like Keyser Süze in the film *The Usual Suspects*, it is possible, I want to suggest, to get away with an awful lot if you can convince people that you don't actually exist.

### Filling the gap: market populism and the elite of anti-elitists

If by the beginning of the new millennium elite research had become something of a backwater in contemporary sociology, this did not signify a complete absence of sociological talk about elites. Sociological, or more correctly, perhaps, social theoretical texts have been liberally scattered with references to elites in an abstract sense. Theorists such as Bauman (1998), Castells (2000) and Lash and Urry (1994), for instance, frequently draw distinctions between mobile, cosmopolitan elites and a more static general populus in their accounts of globalization, network society and economies of signs, for instance. Yet the status of elites in such epochally framed work is often predominantly metaphorical and remarkably under-described. It has therefore been left to others to fill the gap and in recent years there has been a veritable explosion of texts, predominantly journalistic or popular academic in tone, on the changing character or constitution of elites. Coming at a time of dramatic, and by now well catalogued, increases in social polarization in the wealthiest nations on earth, it is perhaps not that surprising that elites and elite formation are regarded as matters of topical concern. Books such as *The New Elites* (2001), by the former Conservative MP George Walden, *One Market Under God* (2002), by the American commentator Thomas Franks, Christopher Lasch's *The Revolt of the Elites* (1995), and Anthony Sampson's *Who Runs this Place?* (2004), to name but a few of the best known examples, are united by a concern with the character of emerging new elites in business and government – even if this interest is, again, often empirically under-developed – and, in particular, with what they consider to be the market populist stripe of the new elites' rhetoric and governing style. Even if the empirics can on occasion leave much to be desired, however, the questions posed and the claims made in these and related texts are of considerable sociological interest.

As I indicated above, it was Franks (2002) who coined the term 'market populism', by which he referred to a 'powerful new political mythology' in which:

> The market and the people – both of them understood as grand principles of social life . . . were essentially one and the same. By its very nature the market was democratic, perfectly expressing the popular will through the machinery of supply and demand, poll and focus group, superstore and Internet. In fact, the market was more democratic than any of the formal institutions of democracy – elections, legislatures, government . . . The market was infinitely diverse, permitting without prejudice the articulation of any and all tastes and preferences. Most importantly of all, the market was militant about its democracy. It had no place for snobs, for hierarchies, for elitism . . . and it would fight these things by its very nature (2002:29).

As Franks argues, this form of market populism went hand-in-hand with a virulent anti-elitism, to the extent that democratic governance was explicitly equated with acts of buying and selling in a market, and that those who tried to interfere with the workings of the market were represented as both anti-democratic and setting themselves ultimately 'against nothing less than the almighty will of the people' (Franks, 2002:47). This symbiosis of market and people, Franks (2002:47) argued, effectively made any mechanism of government that sought to regulate or control the workings of the market suspect. Almost inevitably, the agents of 'Big' government were represented as part of a nefarious elite operating in a 'political' and therefore fundamentally corrupt and hopeless realm, as far removed from the world where the people's will was done – the corporate world – as was possible to imagine.

If 'The Market' in market populist discourse functions as something akin to a 'rigid designator',[1] in Bourdieu's (2000) terms (borrowed from Kripke), that which seeks to 'designate the same object in every possible world, that is concretely in different states of the same field, or in different fields at the same time', requiring the same basic solutions to any conceivable number of problems, then part of what this rigid designator demanded was a thorough-going exorcism of elites, because for market populists the market is the natural enemy of privilege, the great social equalizer.

It was, of course, public institutions that were most clearly subject to this virulent anti-elitism. For marketizers, public service professionals, or bureaucratic 'experts', were basically rent-seekers, trying to force the price of their labour above what the market would bear. Their self-proclaimed 'public service ethic', likewise, was nothing but a puff to legitimize a web of monopolistic cartels whose effects were to rip off consumers by denying them access to that which would really serve their best interests: the market (Marquand, 2004).

But while public institutions might have born the brunt of the market populist onslaught, they were not alone. Any hierarchical organization, any organization not considered the product of pure market forces, was likely to find itself similarly maligned. Thus, it was that large corporations found themselves under attack too, represented in market populist discourse as authoritarian hierarchies, seemingly dedicated to stifling initiative and enterprise. The particular quality that distinguished the management of large corporations from resolutely enterprising – ie, thoroughly marketized – firms was '*elitism*, that combination of class snobbery, intellectual certainty, defiance of nature, of the People, and of the market that so imbued each of the demon figures of market populism' (Franks, 2002:194).

For market populists, the senior management of public and private institutions are evidently un-enterprising precisely because they are elitist, and clearly elitist because they are in some way or another averse to subjecting themselves to the rigours of full scale marketization, or what Tom Peters (1992), a key figure in market-populist management literature, termed 'total businessing'. By failing to allow the market to flourish fully in their own organizations and, indeed, within themselves, they can only preserve their own power, privileges and standing at the expense of their own organization's future success and, of course, the liberation of their employees and of their most beloved rhetorical figure, 'the consumer', that very embodiment of 'the people'.

This imbrication of The Market and The People in market populist discourse, finds its expression in a range of contexts, from the endless efforts of media magnates such as Rupert Murdoch, entrepreneurs such as Richard Branson, or management gurus such as Tom Peters to cast themselves as outsiders, friends of the ordinary, of the people, continually battling away against the 'vested interests', to Tony Blair's insistence that he bore scars on his back from his attempts to modernize British politics and society in the face of hostility and truculence from 'the forces of conservatism . . . the elites, the Establishment'.

At one level, such rhetorical posturing is unremarkable, being a recurrent refrain in the rough and tumble of mobilizing friend enemy distinctions – the very stuff of politics – in any number of fields: journalism, business, and party politics, most obviously. At another level, though, it is of course very important. While there may be a sense in which, as Nietzsche had it, there is no action without illusion, the nature of the illusion motivating the action is not a marginal concern. Market populism is, as Franks (2002:29) argues, a very distinctive 'political mythology' and one which, when acted upon or operationalized, has describable material effects, including the wholesale reframing of the purposes of particular public institutions and the ethical reformatting of the persons deemed best to lead and manage them. It is to the relationship between market populist discourse and the politics of institutional modernization in the public sector that I now wish to turn.

## The strange after-life of 'The Establishment'

The idea of 'The Establishment' which caused such excitement in British political debate in the late 1950s and early 1960s, was always a rather vague concept. Indeed, in much popular and party political usage, it often functioned as little more than a pejorative term, depicting the centres of power in Britain, including notably, the Senior Civil Service, as composed of an exclusive, unrepresentative and small-knit group, bound together by the same schools, universities and family connections. In many ways, the idea of 'The Establishment' provided a much-needed domestic scapegoat for perceptions of national decline which had developed from the 1950s and which had an impact across the political spectrum in the late 1950s and 1960s. From the late 1950s, members of the intelligentsia began to declare a nationwide state of crisis. A series of events and apparent trends contributed to this sense of unease, including the Suez Crisis, declining rates of economic growth, and neglect of and then rejection by the European Economic Community (Blick, 2006:350).

The 1959 collection *The Establishment*, edited by Hugh Thomas provided a classic delineation of the presumed problems facing Britain and some clear indications of the solutions necessary for 'those who desire to see the resources and talents of Britain fully developed and extended', first and foremost of which was the destruction of the 'the fusty Establishment' (Thomas, 1959:20).

This collection contained an essay on the Senior Civil Service by Thomas Balogh, an economic adviser to Harold Wilson, entitled 'The Apotheosis of the Dilettante'. Balogh's critique of the Senior Civil Service as elitist, amateurish and complacent, echoed, in rather more dramatic and unqualified terms, some of the conclusions reached by R.K. Kellsall (1955) in his groundbreaking work *Higher Civil Servants in Britain*. As the first major academic study to be published on part of the 20th century civil service, Kellsall's book had a considerable impact, most notably in drawing attention to the advantages enjoyed by those candidates for the senior civil service who had been to public schools and Oxbridge, and suggesting that previous reforms designed to redress this social imbalance or unrepresentativeness in selection had signally failed to achieve their aims. If anything, Balogh's less qualified and more inflammatory essay had even greater impact, feeding into, as it did, the fashionable, if frequently superficial, criticisms of public institutions then in vogue (Chapman, 1988:35–36). Balogh's solution to the problem of the Establishment in the governmental domain was to replace it with a new Socialist one, since in his view 'So long as Labour hankers after being accepted by the old "Establishment", instead of creating its own, so long will it be in an awkward position, forced mainly on the defensive; so long, moreover, will the country remain uneasily poised on the brink of crisis, sinking behind its more dynamic competitors' (Balogh, 1959:126). For Balogh, one of the foremost barriers to a successful Socialist government was the 'ignorantly dilettante bureaucracy'. For him, only a wholesale purge of existing senior civil service 'amateurs' and their replacement by technically competent, expert, socialist bureaucracy, could guarantee Britain's survival and future prosperity.

Balogh's blistering attacks on the (Administrative Class) were followed by similarly provocative critiques by Brian Chapman (1963) in his British *Government Observed* and by a more nuanced but still highly critical Fabian Society tract entitled *The Administrators* (1964) which proved particularly influential in helping to formulate many of the ideas that came to the fore in the Fulton Committee Report on the Civil Service (1968). In essence, these highly critical texts highlighted the perceived elitism of the civil service at its highest levels, and the role its 'amateur generalists' had played and were continuing to play in Britain's relative post-war economic decline (O'Toole, 2006:105). In this sense the 'Establishment', while difficult to pin down empirically, provided a rhetorical godsend, enabling the mobilization of political support behind the banner of modernization: in this particular instance, the Wilson government's 'white heat' phase of technological modernization and economic and political reform ('New Britain' as the cover of the 1964 Labour Party manifesto had it).

As Froud *et al.* (2006:5) have argued, the important intellectual and political legacy of this idea of 'the Establishment' is its representation of a set of public institutions as some kind of 'historical residue', undemocratic, performing badly and therefore ripe for reform. For Balogh, and for other academic commentators of the time, the economic, political and social deficits associated with the dominance of the Establishment could only be overcome by a vociferous policy of evicting the 'old officer class and acquiring more appropriate and technically competent leadership in . . . the civil service' (Froud *et al.*, 2006:5).

Thus the Establishment form of anti-elite discourse always represents particular elites as obstacles to reform. Labour politicians of the 1960s, like 1980s Tories, and the New Labourites of recent vintage, have all been able to present their projects as the replacement of outmoded elite structures with efficient managerialism, technocratic capitalism or market structures which operated on different lines (Froud *et al.*, 2006:5). Elites are here framed as 'an establishment', a historical residue, out of temporal alignment with the economic and political needs of the present and future.

Interestingly, even some of those who did most to popularize this notion of the establishment, in the 1960s and since, have begun to see the limits of this form of anti-elite discourse. Anthony Sampson, for instance, whose various texts on the changing nature of British institutions have made much of the idea of an establishment, often precisely in the critical mode outlined above, has in recent years begun to change his tune. Many of the earlier volumes in his *Anatomy of Britain* series (1962; 1965) are quite scathing about civil service amateurism and echo the critical comments of Balogh, Chapman and the Fabians, in asking, for instance whether the 'monastic order' of Whitehall (quite the metaphor of historical residue) can be broken into by modernizing forces (notably in the very earliest volumes, the Wilson Labour government). Similarly, as a new Tory government under Margaret Thatcher is demanding revolution in the Civil service and deriding it as an 'establishment' antiquity, Sampson's (1982:420–421) dominant representations of the Civil Service are those of an immobile, increasingly irrelevant historic residue unable or unwilling to embrace modernization.

> Of all the legacies of empire the most dangerous is surely an immobile bureaucracy which can perpetuate its own interests and values, like those ancient hierarchies which presided over declining civilisations: the Pharaonic bureaucracy which still casts its spell over the chaos of contemporary Egypt; or the Byzantine bureaucracy which grew up in the Ottoman Empire; or the court of Imperial Spain which could not face the new challenges of the sixteenth century . . . As the British Mandarins reinforce their defences, awarding each other old imperial honours, do they hear any echoes from Castile or Byzantium?'

It is only recently, in what was to be his last Anatomy, *Who Runs This Place?* (2004) that Sampson begins to question the explanatory usefulness and reach of this notion of the establishment as 'historical residue'. For the later Sampson (2004:354–5), that particular conception of 'the Establishment', undoubtedly the most pervasive, effectively marginalized other, more interesting, and more benign, conceptions. He points, in particular, to the use of the term to refer to 'a network of liberal-minded people who could counteract the excesses of auto-cratic and short-sighted governments' (Sampson, 2004:354).[2] Sampson indicates that the man generally credited with coining the term 'the Establishment' in the pejorative sense, the journalist Henry Fairlie, also deployed the term in this more benign manner, as when he wrote that 'Men of power need to be checked by a collective opinion which is stable and which they cannot override: public opinion needs its counter; new opinion must be tested. These the Establishment provides: the check, the counter and the test' (Fairlie, 1956, quoted in Sampson, 2004:355).

Sampson goes on to argue that the popular representation of the Establish-ment as a nepotistic club was at actually odds with the picture he was trying to paint in the first edition of his *Anatomy of Britain* of a set of intersecting but relatively autonomous institutions: the law courts, the universities, the commons, and the church, for instance. 'This image seemed to convey the pattern of pluralistic power and influence. Each . . . had its own autonomy, which impinged on the others but maintained its own loyalties and social atmos-phere' (2004:355). According to Sampson, the popular image of 'the Establish-ment' as an all-powerful, undemocratic and unaccountable network has certainly proved a useful rhetorical device for those, such as Margaret Thatcher or Tony Blair, who have sought to change the terms of political debate and to do so through depicting those opposed to their policies as part of an outmoded and exclusionary elite. The downside of the predominance of such an image, though, was and is the way in which it served to evacuate these various, non-reducible institutions of the other 'establishment' – the universities, the law courts and so forth – of their determinate purposes, content and modus operandi. Each became a simple mirror image of the other when all that was allowed to matter about them was their 'elitism'.

It seems churlish to point out that Sampson himself could be said to be guilty of precisely such an approach to the extent that his various *Anatomies of Britain* have deployed this notion of the Establishment as a vehicle for criticizing public institutions, whilst simultaneously under-describing them empirically. It seems slightly odd that Sampson only begins to seek to pluralize 'the establishment' when he sees his own cherished beliefs under attack from 'new elites' who have no truck with, or simply oppose, political and institutional arrangements and ethics that Sampson holds dear.

In an often quite savage review of Sampson's *Who Runs This Place*, Marquand's *Decline of the Public* and le Carré's novel *Absolute Friends*, the New Labourite commentator John Lloyd (2004:25–27) castigates these 'old men' for their nostalgia, and suggests they are angry with and alienated from Blair's Britain precisely because they now represent a historical residue that New Labour is in the process of transcending. Lloyd suggests that given their own previous 'anti-establishment' pedigrees, they do not really have a political or moral leg to stand on. Their nostalgia blinds them to the need to carry on the anti-establishment revolution rather than becoming complicit with the 'forces of conservatism'. The fact that Sampson, Marquand and Le Carré had rather a different understanding of 'the establishment' only serves to draw attention to the dangers of deploying the term without adequate specificity or description. The idea of the 'establishment' as historic residue is a blunt conceptual instrument, its deployment more often a rhetorical move in a political polemic rather than a precision tool in an empirical analysis.

As Sampson continues his tirade against the monochrome image of the establishment that he sees contemporary politicians and mediasts deploying to achieve ends the very opposite of those he himself champions, his argument begins to exhibit two distinctive traits. First, he begins to be increasingly distrustful of the idea of the establishment as a historic residue. For Sampson (2004:357), as for Thomas Franks, the continued political potency of this popular image of the establishment, at a point when it has absolutely no empirical explanatory reach, is related to the dominance of market populism on both the Right and Left of the political spectrum. For both the latter, it was only by answering to the market that an institution could avoid elitism, and thus answer to the 'people', in this way becoming a legitimate as opposed to a fundamentally illegitimate actor in the democratic life of the nation. As Sampson (2004:357) goes on to argue, the market populist pair of spectacles through which both Left and Right now view the world has played a crucial role in framing their preferred reforms of that intersecting set of intermediate institutions of the public domain, which Sampson regards as the more realistic (and interesting) meaning of the establishment – the check, the counter, and the test. The reforms undermined the established purposes of these institutions and in effect turned them 'all of one colour . . . the colour of money'.[3] Secondly, Sampson becomes more specific about what it is that contemporary political discourse of 'the establishment' is intent on undermining and why it might need protecting (hence his use of Fairlie's more positive alternative definition of the Establishment). At certain key points, the level of generality at which his argument is pitched declines and an appreciation of particular institutional arrangements and specific mechanisms and techniques of governance begins to take fuller shape (as for instance in his discussion of the governmental role of the Joint Intelligence Committee (JIC) and the problems posed by the Blair government's desire to have the Iraq WMD (Weapons of Mass Destruction) Dossier published in the JIC's name (Sampson, 2004:153–160).

Sampson's references to the 'the establishment' in his final *Anatomy* seem less an expression of what Lloyd (2004:27) calls a 'nostalgia for the past' than an acceptance on Sampson's part both of the explanatory (and political) problems of deploying the term simply to define a 'historic residue' and of the costs associated with the related, political and academic, practice of moralizing *before* describing. The more judicious and contextually nuanced approach to the use of the term 'establishment' in the later Sampson, compared with that deployed in earlier *Anatomies*, finds a mirror in the differences framing the respective analyses of Kelsall and Balogh at the high-point of political and public controversy about 'the establishment' in general, and the 'establishment of Mandarins' (Balogh, 1959), in particular.[4]

## The 'establishment of Mandarins' revisited

As I indicated earlier, Kelsall's book, published in 1955, provided an important, perhaps the first really significant, social scientific study of the social background of administrative class civil servants. Its impact was great, extending beyond the boundaries of academe to stimulate and influence public debate about the educational and class backgrounds of the 'other governing profession', the senior civil service. As Kelsall explained in his preface, the book formed part of a wider research programme at the London School of Economics, the first main results from which were published in 1954 as *Social Mobility in Britain*, edited by D.V. Glass. As the title of the latter text suggests, the programme was primarily concerned with exploring the relationship between educational opportunity and social mobility in Britain. Kelsall's study drew particular attention to the advantages enjoyed, in the recruitment process to the senior echelons of the Civil Service, by those candidates who had been to public school and, in particular, to the universities of Oxford and Cambridge.

While conducting his research, Kelsall was given unusually generous assistance by officials in the Treasury and the Civil Service Commission (assistance they came to regret once the book was published) and a considerable amount of official information was made available for use in the study. In the book, Kelsall referred to evidence given to royal commissions on the civil service and made an analysis of published and unpublished recruitment statistics. In particular, he examined evidence given to the MacDonnell Royal Commission on the Civil Service, which reported in 1914 and focused on the cost to the candidate of competing for a place in the administrative class. He indicated, for example, that candidates would have to pay for a week's residence in London, to attend the examination, and that cramming was more a necessity than a luxury to ensure exam success; in 1910, of the 33 successful Cambridge candidates, 21 received tuition at a private college for six months. What Kelsall pointed out was that, while political patronage may have been removed by the introduction of open competition, openness and fairness did not of themselves ensure representativeness. The educational and social class backgrounds of candidates were by no means irrelevant to their success or failure in obtaining a position in the administrative class.

Kelsall's detailed and carefully argued study was accompanied by certain recommendations for reform, such as increased promotion to the Administrative Class from within the lower ranks of the Civil Service in order 'to ensure that those whose failure to go to a university was due to factors other than inability to reach the required standard should be given an opportunity to use and develop their talents to the greater benefit of the Service' (1955:193). He was careful to point out though, that such a policy needed to be accompanied by wider social changes which were not within the power of the Civil Service to effect by itself, namely 'the improvement of the educational ladder outside the service' (1955:193). A more socially representative Administrative class therefore depended in large part upon the development of a more egalitarian society.

Similarly, Kelsall recommended that more specialists, such as scientists, engineers and even social scientists, should be encouraged and able to join the highest ranks of the Service and that, as a consequence, the grip of the ethos of the so-called generalist administrator on the senior echelons of the Service might have to be weakened. Once again, though, Kelsall's recommendations were nuanced. He acknowledged that the generalist administrator had considerable virtues in relation to the fulfilment of the political duties associated with work at the senior levels of a constitutional bureaucracy, and that, as a result, those without the breadth of vision and judgment that such generalists exhibited 'may well err in the direction of narrowness, dogmatism, and unwillingness to admit the validity of any point of view but their own. The specialist-turned-administrator does not always prove a success; and in those countries where this is the normal route of entry to the highest appointments in the Civil Service, the need for senior officials with a general rather than a specialist training and approach is keenly felt' (Kelsall, 1955:194). Overall, on almost every occasion, Kelsall eschews making broad brush-stroke statements about the 'nature' of the senior civil service that are not backed up by his data or which do not refer specifically to the limited aims of his study. He concludes with a call to the Civil Service for more factual information concerning 'the ranks and routes of entry of members of the Administrative Class; their distribution according to type of school and university might even be given . . . In these and many other ways the provision of more adequate statistical information could increase our understanding of, and our justifiable pride in, the British Civil Service' (1955:203).

As Chapman (2004:225–226) has indicated, Kelsall's book had an effect 'not known outside the Civil Service Commission at that time'. In particular, it drew attention to facets of the education system and civil service selection procedures that had not previously received sustained attention. As Chapman indicates, this is illustrated by a memorandum to the First Commissioner and others, dated 18 October, 1955, which said that

> I have had a list made of the more regular members of CSSB (Civil Service Selection Board) Directing Staff since the Open Competitions began to see how representative the list looks . . . On the psychological side we are beyond reproach but otherwise, except for John Swindale, we are all public school boys . . . Do you think we ought to consider this angle in future? (Quoted in Chapman, 2004:225).

The list showed that eight of the nine Group Chairmen had been educated at Oxford or Cambridge Universities and one at the London School of Economics; of the twelve Observers, eleven had been educated at Oxford or Cambridge and one at Aberdeen; but the five psychologists had all attended universities other than Oxford or Cambridge.

In these and other ways, Kelsall's keen but nuanced criticisms had considerable effect, and helped to shift expectations of recruitment practice, and indeed practice itself (Chapman & Greenaway, 1980:169–170) in a more egalitarian direction. They were not, however, aimed at a wholesale critique of the Senior Civil Service as an institution of government, and Kelsall never felt the need to deploy a rhetorical designation such as 'the Establishment' in order to get his point across. He clearly wanted to see a more representative senior civil service, but that did not mean he was an anti-elitist in any populist or knee-jerk sense of the term. The senior civil service he envisaged might become more representative but would still be to all intents and purposes 'the elite of the elite'. Indeed, as Chapman and Greenaway (1980:170) suggest, Kelsall was aware that his was only a partial study, concerned exclusively with the social background of the administrative class and with looking at problems related to the wider research programme – social mobility in Britain – of which it was a part. As commentators have indicated, Kelsall had limited knowledge, for instance, about the specific nature of the work that senior civil servants actually did on a day-to-day basis. As a result, he had very little to say about their constitutional and political roles and how the latter formed their institutional persona in as direct (if not more direct) a fashion, than did their class background alone (Chapman, 1970:86).

Nonetheless, Kellsall's analysis of the social background of the senior civil service stimulated further debate in academic and political circles, as well as the civil service itself, and, at first sight, appears to share certain family resemblances with the arguments put forward by Balogh in his provocative attack on the 'Establishment of Mandarins' (though Balogh does not refer to Kelsall's work directly at any point in the essay).

While Balogh's arguments may have been influenced at some level by Kelsall's findings, Balogh's form of critique was a world apart from that informing Kelsall's analysis and recommendations. In many ways, Balogh's generalized, epochal, flamboyant and dramatic critique (epitomized by his reduction of the entire Senior Civil Service, its purposes and modus operandi, to the negative designation of 'the establishment of Mandarins') mirrors the style and strategy of contemporary market populist anti-elitism.

As Theakston (2004:5) has indicated, 'Balogh loathed and was loathed by the civil service'. Certainly, Balogh's assessment of the civil Service contained none of the subtlety or nuanced critique of Kelsall's analysis but instead sought, as I suggested earlier, a wholesale purge of the Senior Civil Service and its replacement (a recurring theme in socialist narratives of governance) by a cadre of expert mangers and technical specialists, able to implement the will of the government in an efficient and effective manner and supervised, in part, by new classes of adviser including personal aides, selected in accordance with the personal preference of ministers, who would provide the latter with general assistance and help promote their policies. In this way, a radical socialist government would gradually replace the hopelessly dilettante 'Establishment of Mandarins' with a new Establishment formed in its own image (Balogh, 1959; Bevir and Rhodes, 2003).

Balogh reserved his strongest condemnation of the 'ignorantly dilettante bureaucracy' for its Oxbridge bias and organizational amateurism, embodied in the so-called cult of the generalist. In this respect he referred to 'that special mysterious art, Administrative Capacity', which was said to depend on 'an attitude of effortless superiority, combined with cultured scepticism'. He added: 'Positive knowledge and imagination, assertion of the social against the private interest, were obviously not looked for. The negative qualities were thought to be best attained by a judicious mixture of breeding, "character building" and a purposefully useless, somewhat dilettante, erudition which would keep "dangerous thoughts" well away . . . Anything smacking of vocational training and technical knowledge was severely discountenanced' (Balogh, 1959:86–87).

Unlike Kelsall, who could see obvious political and organizational benefits in such generalism even if he felt these could be over-egged, Balogh was so caught up in the idea of the mandarinate as class conspirators who did not, indeed could not, tolerate anything smacking of socialism; and as managerial dilettantes, amateur administrators with no specialist knowledge and thus lacking in the ability to 'deliver' socialist programmes, that for him only a wholesale purge of the senior echelons would do.

As Harold Wilson's Economic Adviser in the 1964–1970 Labour Government, Balogh is frequently to be found railing against his civil servants at every turn. As Theakston (2004:5) indicates, Balogh bombarded the Prime Minister with complaints that he was being stymied by officials who were denying him access to crucial documents (we find David Blunkett saying something not dissimilar in the 1997 Labour government). 'A large part of the bureaucracy does not share our views', Balogh told Wilson. For him, ministerial responsibility must be seen as a fiction precisely because it was really the officials, not the governing politicians, who controlled information and hammered out their own inter-departmental agreements outside of political control. Wilson publicly scorned such views, and generally speaking, the suspicions found in some sections of the Labour Party, of the civil service as a politicized class-based organization, were proved to be unfounded, at least by most of those not on the left of the party. There was in fact considerable good will on the part of the Civil Service towards the incoming Labour government in 1964 (as there was to the incoming New Labour government in 1997), after thirteen years of Conservative rule. Initially suspicious on class and ideological grounds, James Callaghan, for instance, soon developed a good working relationship with his Treasury civil servants. Notions of a 'continuous battle' and 'real resistance or obstruction' were rejected by Anthony Crosland, who insisted that the key issue was successfully to harness the bureaucracy's 'large fund of knowledge and expertise'. Comments by other incoming Labour ministers such as Barbara Castle, Denis Healey and Roy Jenkins echo these sentiments. Theakston (2004:6–21) concludes that:

> As with their counterparts in the 1945–51 Labour government, most Labour ministers in the 1964–1970 administration came to rely upon and admire their officials for their bureaucratic professionalism, policy advice, and neutral competence. However, on the left of the party the experience of office rekindled the traditional suspicions of the civil service . . . as obstructing or sabotaging radical reform, fuelling calls after 1970 (and still more during and after the 1974–1979 Labour term of office) for major reform of Whitehall . . .

Despite the experience of most of those in office, the discourse of the 'establishment of Mandarins' as a historic residue, set upon undermining radical programmes of government both on class ideological grounds and by sheer lack of competence, continued. Familiar sounding reforms to check bureaucratic and strengthen political power – such as the use of more specialists, the deployment of politically-committed advisers and the development of techniques designed to increase individual official accountability for securing 'results' – were rekindled; but it was not to be a 'truly' socialist Labour administration (whatever that might be) that would do for the Mandarinate but, rather, first a radical right wing Conservative government and then an equally radical right wing Labour one. For the discourse of the 'establishment' was to be given a different inflection, one we have already outlined as 'market populist' in style.

It is possible to see this market populist animus in action if attention is focused upon recent and ongoing reforms of the British Civil Service, reforms that seek fundamentally to reconstruct this institution, changing it from a political-administrative institution of government, a constitutional bureaucracy, into a market-mimicking delivery mechanism.

## The civil service; from constitutional bureaucracy to delivery mechanism

It is not too difficult to see why the Senior Civil Service should be viewed with hostility by those wedded to market populism, as much as for those encumbered by visions of class conspiracy and ideological obstruction. For over a century, the British state has been directed by a governing mandarinate, the most important legacy of the 19th century battle against 'Old corruption'. These professional, non-partisan, career civil servants have lived their institutional lives according to values that, while in no sense explicitly antithetical to capitalistic behaviour, for instance, have nonetheless been informed by recognition of the appropriate limits of such conduct, and by the need for an ethic appropriate to serving the state, as opposed to the business world. For instance, professional career civil servants have been expected to be very careful in their dealings with people who represented concentrations of business power and to maintain, in this regard, some sense of the public interest that is 'both different from and superior to the sum of individual business ambitions, or of what could be induced from such ambitions' (Crouch, 2004:97).

To begin to look at the Mandarinate in this way, as a permanent and politically impartial elite bound together by a particular regime of norms and techniques of conduct rather than simply as a self-selecting and perpetuating upper class cabal intent on preserving its own power, enables us to transcend the terms of debate established in both older and more recent versions of 'establishment' discourse. A focus on the purposes of the job the Mandarins perform and the environment in which they operate provides a context for thinking about some of their attributes, caution and disinterestedness for instance, in a rather more positive way than is generally to be found in market populist or older 'establishment' representations of this elite.

The norms regulating the conduct of these high ranking, professional career civil servants have traditionally included, *inter alia*, party political neutrality or professional bi-partisan loyalty, permitting an official to serve any government without a crisis of conscience; willingness to offer frank and fearless advice without considering personal consequences; the obligation to set aside 'private' interests and commitments in the performance of public duties and to abstain from the use of official position or information for private gain; rigorous and demonstrable dispassionateness, integrity and propriety, including appropriate attention to criteria of efficiency, economy and effectiveness (understood in their statist or governmental context and not simply or primarily in commercial terms) in the conduct of official business; resistance to the temptation to cut corners, make generous gestures, relax discipline, take risks or 'innovate' unless clearly and unambiguously ordered or authorised by government policy and authority so to do; acceptance of the obligations of confidentiality, security and anonymity; expectation that decisions which could affect the public will be guided by a fair and full consideration of the likely effects of those decisions and not just by enthusiasm or hunch; an appropriate sense of pride in serving the state, constitution, and the public interest, and of preserving and enhancing the reputation and integrity of the civil service as a institution of government (the 'constitutional bureaucracy'). Through adherence to these and other elements of its 'ethos of office' (du Gay, 2002:466), the senior civil service was widely thought to fulfil its constitutional role as a sort of 'gyroscope of state', helping to provide, for example, the stability, continuity and institutional memory deemed necessary to the realization of responsible government. Its presence at the heart of the state was thus deemed a crucial safeguard, 'both against a lurch back into the favouritism and nepotism of the eighteenth and early nineteenth centuries and against infiltration by the "universal pandar" of market power' (Marquand, 2004:108).

This was the ideal. It may not have always been fully practised, as Kelsall pointed out in relationship to recruitment to the Administrative Class, but it is clear that it did play an important part in framing and regulating the conduct of the senior civil service (Bogdanor, 2001; Chapman, 2004). To market populists, as we saw earlier, it was and is anathema. On their assumptions such an ideal is doubly suspect. First, it is elitist, and this makes it an object of profound suspicion, if not hatred. For market populists, the ideal of public service is a con, perpetrated by an unelected elite who have the arrogance to think that their official role and ethos furnishes them with privileged relationship to some chimera called 'the public interest'. Secondly, this elite, with its lack of exposure to the chill winds of the market, was closeted from the real world of the 'people'. The senior civil service was a refuge for snobbish wimps who wouldn't know a real person if they saw one, and who couldn't hack it in the rough and tumble world of wealth creation and enterprise. Detachment, disinterest, 'without affection of enthusiasm' (Weber, 1994) – the ethos of public service was simply a fantasy, cloaking obstructionism, defeatism and failure.

Thus, what has in effect been an unbroken series of 'market populist'governments, stretching from the 1980s to the present, have all sought to change 'the culture' of the Senior Civil Service to accord with their own priorities.[5] Thus, market populist 'conviction' politicians have wanted to be surrounded by people who would work within and conform to the political convictions which they themselves held, and not challenge those convictions, or question if they had identified the issues correctly, or ask whether what they were trying to achieve was practically realisable. Ministers made it clear to Senior Civil Servants that dispassionate advice and careful consensus building arguments were out. The ideal of the professional civil servant was instead re-imagined as a 'can do' type, who would deliver on the market populist agenda by 'adding value, and not asking clever questions' (Grade 2 Civil Servant quoted in du Gay, 2000:114).

The long-standing Mandarin focus on deliberation and procedure, in protecting legality, consistency, fairness and other values, was not given a high priority by Ministers in successive Conservative administrations of then 1980s and 1990s. Rather, this ethos was contrasted negatively with the decisiveness and rapidity of action that was presumed to be the norm in the commercial world. The programme of creating 'arms-length' executive agencies began the process of bringing a greater number of outsiders, predominantly from the commercial world, into the civil service to run what was described as the 'operational' side of government. This pluralization of the civil service, in which government policies and programmes were to be delivered through diverse agencies or by the private sector under contract, was given an extra spin by idea that private sector pay and conditions should be made to apply to senior civil servants, reconceived as 'manager-leaders'. New recommendations were made by the Conservative Major administration to the effect that there should be much greater open competition, to allow the best outside people to compete for the most senior civil service positions, as well as the introduction of more flexible, and performance related, pay and conditions of employment. This was given further impetus by the related recommendation that 'market rates' of pay should be offered in order to encourage applications from those in the private sector.

Like their Conservative predecessors, the market populism of Britain's current Labour government has bred a pervasive suspicion of the civil service as an anachronistic 'establishment' institution, run by a privileged and out of touch elite, desperately in need of 'modernization'. Given the radical reforms of the civil service undertaken by successive Conservative regimes over the preceding eighteen years, such an image of the service seems remarkably naïve or deliberately provocative. That the latter was nearer the truth was quickly established when the government's plans for Civil Service modernization were published (Cabinet Office, 1999). For all the praises they lavished on an abstraction called 'public service', the organization and purpose of the senior civil service was once again negatively contrasted with the virtues of private entrepreneurial conduct.

The practicalities of 'modernization' under new Labour have involved a thorough going deinstitutionalization of the senior civil service, to the point where it no longer appears to be possess any distinctive purpose or constitutional significance. As Christopher Foster (a former Wilson government 'irregular', ie, special adviser) (2005:218–219) has argued, senior civil servants under New Labour were:

> treated as simple subordinates with little or no recognition they had a constitutional function of institutional scepticism, of speaking truth to power; of helping ministers to ensure fairness in their decision-making; of helping them achieve objectivity and accuracy in their public statements and documents. They were no longer allowed to make 'full submissions' challenging and appraising ministers' policy ideas or suggesting alternatives that might be more practical. However absurd, redundant or administratively flawed, whatever was in the election manifesto, or later emanated from No. 10 or No. 11, was beyond criticism, as never before.

Indeed, the established doctrine that public administration should be conducted by a disinterested, non-partisan, permanent and unified civil service, embodying a professional ethic of office, and with a career path protected from overt political interference has been systematically undermined by the New Labour administration in ways that make earlier Conservative market populists look positively restrained by comparison. Most obviously, and troublingly, policy-making has increasingly become the preserve of politically appointed special advisers, working in close political partnership with their political sponsors and exercising, in some departments of state, as much influence on political and governmental decisions as junior ministers (Daintith, 2002; Jones, 2002; O'Toole, 2006).[6] On some issues, the proliferating policy units housed in No. 10

Downing Street, again staffed by party political enthusiasts and can-do civil servants (frequently external appointments), find themselves with as much governmental decision-making power as some Cabinet Ministers, and, perhaps in some cases even more.[7]

If successive Conservative administrations broke the back of the 'ethos of office' of the senior civil service, then New Labour's attempts to turn it into a delivery mechanism, whose only purposes was to do whatever ministers insisted it should do, has helped to undermine the last vestiges of its role as a crucial guardian of the public domain – the check, counter and test, in Fairlie's terms. In particular, New Labour's policy of intensifying the number of outsiders recruited into the senior echelons of the Civil Service in order to ensure that the right sort of management skills and passionate commitment is available to make the 'delivery mechanism' work as the government requires, is now close to destroying the political impartiality of the Civil Service. Recent reports suggest that in only a matter of four or five years time, most senior positions in the service will be occupied by people recruited from outside the Civil Service (Levitt and Solebury, 2005). This matters precisely because the political neutrality of the service and its 'institutional memory' is a product of its career basis. If one joins the service for life, one will inevitably serve administrations of differing political hues. One is not likely to succeed in this unless one can successfully display political impartiality. As Bogdanor (2001:296) put it

> New recruits coming in from outside will generally lack the traditional patterns of experience, such as those gained by being private secretary to a minister, which help to socialise civil servants as neutral advisers. Moreover, someone recruited from outside by virtue of relevant knowledge is very likely to arrive with political baggage, policy commitments derived from previous experience. That is in a sense inevitable if civil servants are required to be 'creative', and to display 'leadership'. It will not be easy, however, to recruit civil servants who possess those qualities and yet are at the same time willing to conform to the principle that they possess no constitutional personality, their views being those of their minister. It is not clears, therefore, how far outside recruitment to senior policy positions in the service can avoid the dangers of politicisation, or at least a degree of prior policy commitment, incompatible with traditional notions of political neutrality.[8]

Sometime soon, as indicated above, the number of outsiders in the senior civil service will outweigh those career civil servants who have traditionally dominated the mandarinate. This is likely to have a number of effects. For one thing, it will signal that the senior civil service has been fundamentally altered, probably irreversibly, since the policy commitments of its senior echelons are unlikely to be acceptable to the main alternative government of the day. Because the senior civil service belongs to the state, and not to any one government, the introduction of too many people with prior policy commitments, sympathetic only to the government in power, will transform the senior civil service by effectively politicizing it. The governmental and administrative virtues associated with the Civil Service's role as 'institutional memory', 'gyroscope of state' and 'test, counter and check' will have been squandered.

As Michael Lind (2005) has recently argued, the bureaucratic 'mandarinate' – that other governing profession – having helped to deliver the state from the dangers of 'mobocracy' in the early 20th century now finds itself scapegoated by a range of powerful forces: managerialist, populist, libertarian and religious. To the managerialist, the bureaucrat is an amateur; to the libertarian, a statist; to the populist, an elitist; and to the religious fundamentalist, a heathen. Lind (2005:37) asks the rhetorical question: 'What could be worse than a society run by such people?' His answer is simple: 'a society without them'. The contemporary US, he argues, shows the consequences of turning a modern democracy into a 'mandarin free zone'. Britain be warned, he continues, for you are heading down the same path. Lind refers, in particular, to the vast social experiment with market populism that has taken place in these and other representative democracies, an experiment 'as audacious, in its own way, as that of Soviet collectivism' (2005:37).

Referring explicitly to developments in America Lind (2005:37) writes:

> The US ship of state veers now in one direction, now the other. From a distance, one might conclude that the captain is a maniac. But a spyglass reveals that there is no captain or crew at all, only rival gangs of technocrats, ideologues, populists and zealots devoted to Jesus Christ or Adam Smith, each boarding the derelict vessel and capturing the wheel briefly before being tossed overboard.

For Lind something important is being registered: the crucial role of the Mandarinate as a 'gyroscope of state', helping to provide, for example, the stability, continuity and institutional memory that were once deemed crucial to the realization of responsible and effective governance. It is precisely this *etatiste* role and status-conduct that constitutes the distinctiveness and virtue of the civil servant's ethos of bureaucratic office, and yet is also exactly this, as we have seen, which cannot be registered in the pervasive language of market populism, as it could not in the earlier criticisms of the 'Establishment of Mandarins' proffered by Balogh *et al.*, either.

## Concluding comments: the eternal return of 'The Establishment' and the politics of institutional modernization

Pity the poor mandarinate in a modern western democracy. These days, as Lind (2005:34) has argued, the mandarinate, in government but out of it, is rarely respected, let alone loved. It has a sort of aristocratic role, checking, testing, and sometimes countering the elective 'monarchy' of democratic executives and the majority 'tyranny' of elective democratic legislatures. This governmental role is a crucial one but it is not destined to make the mandarinate many friends amongst political enthusiasts of either left or right, who rail against the constraints that the mandarinate 'ethic of office' imposes upon the instant translation of their political desires into practical action, often in the name of the 'public interest'. Because the ethic of office regulating the conduct of the mandarinate makes them likely to greet the panaceas of all political parties with a degree of caution, inevitably this leads them to embrace party political programmes with less fervour than party enthusiasts would wish. But this is part of their job. And in fulfilling it they can be seen as servants of the state. This statist role, though, makes them ideal targets in the eyes of party political enthusiasts, who have found it easy to represent them precisely as a historic residue (their aristocratic role), with no democratic mandate, and therefore as an illegitimate governmental actor. Perhaps this is why denigration of this elite, 'the establishment of mandarins', has found such favour historically on both left and right (Greenaway, 1992). A Balogh and a Thatcher, for instance, found common cause in their distaste for the Mandarinate, a mutual language to describe this antipathy, 'the Establishment', and some not entirely dissimilar suggestions for a reduction in their authority and influence. What Balogh's socialist critique of the 'dilettante' administrator helped to begin, it took the market populist critique of Thatcher and Blair to deliver: the end of the Mandarinate.

As Franks (2002:189) has made clear, for both Left and Right of the political spectrum, Market Populism has proven a powerful weapon in the politics of institutional modernization. For market populists, any institution that does not ultimately answer to the market, in no matter how imagined or virtual a manner, and thus in so doing answer to the 'people', is effectively 'elitist' and therefore a fundamentally illegitimate actor in the political life of a state.

Market populist discourse has been a powerful mobilizing force in contemporary politics, fuelling a number of important institutional changes. In the name of taking on a chimera called 'the establishment', for example (represented as an historical residue, an old closed order, enjoying immense privilege at the expense of ordinary folk), market populist governments in the UK have sought to effect a remarkable transformation in the purposes and modus operandi of a range of public institutions, in the process eclipsing the class of elites who ran these institutions. More broadly, market populism has waged war on the very idea, though not the reality, of elites, making it difficult for authority to be claimed unless articulated in terms of market based criteria and popular support. Indeed, market populism so denigrates the idea of elites, routinely represented as closed and exclusive groups, united by status and undemocratic ties, that its advocates, whether Rupert Murdoch fighting the cartoon British Aristocracy or Tony Blair battling the phantom forces of conservatism dominating the public services, cannot but deny their own elite status, presenting themselves instead as simply champions of the people and 'pretty straight guys'. It is the dominance of this elite of market populists that led George Walden (2001:43) to write, somewhat tongue in cheek, that in Britain for the first time in its democratic history, politics 'is dominated by an elite of anti-elitists'.

This elite of anti-elitists can represent itself as 'ordinary' precisely because it refuses to acknowledge its own elite status. Because they see elites in market populist terms, as referring exclusively to a clan of people united by outmoded and undemocratic ties and links, the powerful and the wealthy can deny being part of an 'elite'. In the discourse of market populism, they are just like the rest of us, regular folk. But this claim is false and damaging. These people wield enormous power and influence. Denying that they are part of elite doesn't change this. But what it does do is help them to avoid the responsibilities that come with their status. As Zakaria (2003:235) has argued, 'if neither they nor the country believes that they are in any sense an elite, then neither will adjust to their status. Elites will not lack power because they go unnoticed – far from it'. Rather, as I suggested ealier these Keyser Süze elites can get away with an awful lot if they can pull off the trick of making people believe they do not actually exist.

As I indicated in relationship to reform of the Senior Civil Service, by representing that institution as elitist, dominated by an exclusive and socially closed group, united by undemocratic ties, and through linking its democratization to the dynamism of the market (or imagined market), market populists have ended up not only destroying the mandarinate but also undermining the very purposes for which it was instituted and the values it embodied. Among the latter was the belief in a distinction between the ethics appropriate to the conduct of public service and those appropriate to the conduct of private business. People in public service were expected to be fastidious in their dealings with persons who represented concentrations of business power for example, and to ensure that the idea of a public interest was not allowed to equate to the sum of individual business ambitions. Such values have been cast aside by the new elite of anti-elitists precisely because they are represented as part of an 'establishment' way of thinking unsuited to the dynamics of a populist market democracy. Because markets and marketization are seen as the source of legitimacy as well as efficiency, it appears obvious now that what Sampson (2004:357) calls 'the masters of the marketplace' should have a special place in reforming institutions like the Civil Service, and running them in their own image. The presumed competitiveness, energy and dynamism of the new hyper-mobility between boardroom and cabinet office, City and Whitehall, nonetheless erodes guides to action, barriers, checks and balances (the counter, the check, the test) that have historically been crucial to the practical realisation of responsible, stable and equitable government (Craig, 2006; Marquand, 2004). The result – increased politicization and opportunities for personal enrichment, combined with reduced political accountability – seems too high a price to pay. One can imagine a democratic polis that still contained within it some important formal and informal constraints, sacrificing some of its energy and dynamism for other values, such as equity, reliability, integrity and stability. But to do so, it would be necessary to resurrect, in some form, the institutions and elites that market populists have spent the last three decades tearing down.

*Paul du Gay*

# Notes

1 So what exactly is the relationship between 'The Market' as rigid designator and the idea of markets in the plural, with their distinctive non-reducible arrangements undergoing relatively constant transmutation but nonetheless, as Callon (2005) puts it in his critique of Danny Miller 'equipped to act on the basis of accumulation and maximisation'? It seems to me that the idea of 'the market' as rigid designator – the 'imagined' or 'virtual' market in the singular – has been a remarkably powerful rhetorical/ideological device, and much has been achieved in its name, not least the reconception and reformation of a number of public institutions along new lines, with often unfortunate consequences for the ability of those institutions to live up to the obligations and the purposes they embodied. In this guise of ideological rigid designator, 'the market' really does seem to be exactly what Callon (1998) suggests it can't be, 'cold, implacable and monstrous, imposing its laws while extending them ever further'.

2 In this liberal-pluralist definition, Sampson's 'establishment' comes close to resembling Marquand's (2004) intermediate institutions of the 'public domain'.

3 As Marquand (2004:193), has argued, '[I]t hardly needs saying that this approach struck hard at the foundations of the public domain. Populism is monist. The populist seeks to concentrate the popular will so that it flows into a single channel. The logic of the public domain is quintessentially pluralist . . . Variety is of its essence. Though Britain has never had a fundamental law entrenching the checks and balances on which pluralist politics depend, informal codes, inherited usages and unwritten rules nurtured a vast range of more or less autonomous intermediate institutions . . . [T]hese codes, usages and rules were the perimeter walls of the public domain . . .'

4 Thomas Balogh's (1959) essay 'The Apotheosis of the Dilettante, the Establishment of Mandarins' was one of the most widely cited and influential contributions to Hugh Thomas's (1959) classic collection *The Establishment*, the book that really helped to popularize the latter term. In his contribution, Balogh criticized the elitism and hidebound traditionalism of the senior civil service, and the negative role he felt it had played in the relative economic decline Britain had undergone in the post Second-World War period. The criticisms voiced in Balogh's essay formed part of the backcloth both to the setting up of the Fulton Committee and indeed, to its eventual findings.

5 There are, of course explanatory dangers in reducing the multiple logics informing the institutional reform of the Civil Service over the last three decades to a simple narrative of 'market populism'. However, for the purposes of this chapter, what matters is the broad thrust – the *leitmotif* – not the details. And the thrust is quite clear: as Tom Peters would have it: 'blasting the chill winds of the marketplace', real or virtual, into as many nooks and crannies of the Civil Service as was practically possible, all other things being equal.

6 For example, part of the reason for the resignation of Estelle Morris as Education Secretary was apparently related to the influence of Andrew (now Lord) Adonis, then one of the Prime Minister's senior special advisers, now a minister of the Crown. Morris is reported to have been very unhappy with the policies developed by Adonis and other special advisers at No.10, but because they had the support of the Prime Minister, she felt her position increasingly untenable.

7 Enthusiasts such as Michael Barber, Louise Casey and Geoff Mulgan, who have held or still do hold, senior policy advising positions – often as outside appointments to the Civil Service – within the New Labour administration would be good examples.

8 That the elitism of the Civil Service can be overcome and its efficiency and effectiveness increased via a dose of openness is a standard trope in the market populist lexicon. By opening up the Civil Service to the 'full range of talents', as New Labour has it, the Civil Service can become more like a proper business. As Bogdanor (2001: 295) argues, though, '[T]he main argument for this change is that an 'open' Civil Service is preferable to a 'closed' one. This argument would seem at first sight to be unanswerable. Yet, if the Civil Service is . . . a genuine profession, ought it not in fact to be closed? It would not, after all, be very sensible to suggest to someone who objected to unqualified doctors or lawyers that he or she favoured 'closed' medical or legal professions.

For professions are, almost by definition, closed. The question, then, is whether the Civil Service is to remain a profession, based on its own particular expertise of public administration, or whether civil servants are to become a somewhat undifferentiated and undefined species of 'manager'.

# References

Balogh, T., (1959), 'The Apotheosis of the dilettante: the establishment of Mandarins', in H. Thomas (ed.), *The Establishment,* London: Anthony Blond.
Bauman, Z., (1998), *Globalization: The Human Consequences,* Cambridge: Polity Press.
Bevir, M. and Rhodes, R.A.W., 'Searching for civil society: changing patterns of Governance in Britain', *Public Administration* 81: 41–62.
Blick, A., (2006), 'Harold Wilson, labour and the machinery of government', *Contemporary British History*, 20 (3): 343–362.
Bogdanor, V., (2001), 'Civil service reform: a critique', *The Political Quarterly*: 291–9.
Bourdieu, P., (2000), 'The biographical illusion', in P. du Gay, J. Evans & P. Redman (eds), *Identity: A Reader,* London: Sage.
Cabinet Office, (1999), *Modernizing Government,* London: HMSO.
Callon, M., (1998), 'Introduction', in M. Callon (ed.) *The Laws of the Markets,* Oxford: Blackwell: 1–57.
Callon, M., (2005), 'Why Virtualism paves the way to political impotence: Callon replies to Miller', *Economic Sociology European Electronic Newsletter*, 6 (2): 3–19.
Castells, M., (2000), *The Rise of the Network Society,* Oxford: Oxford University Press.
Chapman, B., (1963), *British Government Observed,* London: Allen & Unwin.
Chapman, R., (1970), *The Higher Civil Service in Britain,* London: Constable.
Chapman, R., (1996), 'The end of the civil Service' in P. Barberis (ed.), *The Whitehall Reader,* Buckingham: Open University Press.
Chapman, R., (2004), The *Civil Service Commission 1855–1991: A Bureau Biography*, London: Routledge.
Chapman, R. and Greenaway, J., (1980), *The Dynamics of Administrative Reform,* London: Croom Helm.
Craig, D. with Brooks, R., (2006), *Plundering the Public Sector,* London: Constable.
Crouch, C., (2004), *Post-Democracy,* Cambridge: Polity Press.
Daintith, T., (2002), 'A very good day to get out anything we want to bury', *Public Law*, Spring: 13–21.
Dawe, A., (1970), 'The two sociologies', *British Journal of Sociology*, 21 (2): 207–218.
Du Gay, P., (2000), *In Praise of Bureaucracy,* London: Sage.
Du Gay, P., (2002),'How responsible is 'responsive' Government?', *Economy & Society* 13 (3): 461–482.
Fabian Society, (1964), *The Administrators: The Reform of the Civil Service* (Fabian Tract 355), London: Fabian Society.
Foster, C., (2005), *British Government in Crisis,* Oxford: Hart Publishing.
Franks, T., (2002), *One Market under God,* London: Vintage.
Froud, J., Savage, M., Tampubolon, G. and Williams, K., (2006), 'Rethinking elite research, CRESC working paper No. 12, CRESC, Manchester: University of Manchester.
Fry, G., (1995), *Policy and Management in the British Civil Service,* London: Prentice-Hall.
Greenaway, J., (1992), 'British conservatism and bureaucracy', *History of Political Thought*, XIII(1).
Hennessy, P., (1995), *The Hidden Wiring,* London: Weidenfield & Nicolson.
Jones, N., (2002), *The Control Freaks,* London: Politicos.
Kelsall, R. K., (1955), *Higher Civil Servants in Britain,* London: Routledge and Kegan Paul.
Lash, C., (1995), *The Revolt of the Elites and the Betrayal of Democracy,* New York: W.W. Norton.

Lash, S. and Urry, J., (1994), *Economies of Signs and Space,* London: Sage.

Levitt, R. and Solesbury, W., (2005), *'Evidence-informed policy: what differences do outsiders make in Whitehall',* working paper 23, ESRC UK, London: Centre for Evidence Based Policy and Practice.

Lind, M., (2005), 'In defence of Mandarins', *Prospect,* 115 October: 34–37

Marquand, D., (2004), *The Decline of the Public,* Cambridge: Polity.

O'Toole, B., (2006), *The Ideal of Public Service,* London: Routledge.

Peters, T., (1992), *Liberation Management,* Basingstoke: Macmillan.

Sampson, A., (1962), *Anatomy of Britain,* London: Hodder & Stoughton.

Sampson, A., (1965), *Anatomy of Britain Today,* London: Hodder & Stoughton.

Sampson, A., (1982), *The Changing Anatomy of Britain,* London: Hodder & Stoughton.

Sampson, A., (1993), *The Essential Anatomy of Britain,* London: Coronet.

Sampson, A., (2004), *Who Runs This Place?* London: John Murray.

Scott, A., (1996), 'Bureaucratic revolutions and free market utopias', *Economy & Society* 25 (1): 89–110.

Theakston, K., (2004), 'The 1964–1970 Labour Governments and Whitehall Reform', POLIS working paper No.2, Leeds: University of Leeds.

Walden, G., (2001), *The New Elites,* Harmondsworth: Penguin.

Weber, M., (1994), 'The profession and vocation of politics', in P. Lassman and R. Speirs (eds) *Weber: Political Writings,* Cambridge: CUP.

Zakaria, F., (2003), *The Future of Freedom: Illiberal Democracy at Home and Abroad,* New York: W.W. Norton.

# Section 2
## Money, Finance and Business Elites: Dynamics and Outcomes

# Capital theory and the dynamics of elite business networks in Britain and France

## Charles Harvey and Mairi Maclean

'Capital', wrote Pierre Bourdieu, 'represents a power over the field . . . The kinds of capital, like aces in a game of cards, are powers that define the chances of profit in a particular field . . .' (1985: 724). For Bourdieu (1986b), capital is a generalized resource, which may be monetary or non-monetary in form, tangible or intangible. The four aces in the pack of cards to which Bourdieu refers are economic, cultural, social and symbolic capital (1986b). The power that these afford, however, is not stable and static; capital formation is an on-going, dynamic process, subject to accumulation or attrition. Like a game of cards, the hand which players are dealt must still be played – with greater or lesser skill, and to greater or lesser effect. Some individuals are endowed with significantly better life chances than others; although the patterns of social class formation are looser in present times than in the past, economic class divisions continue to exercise a considerable impact on life chances (Scott, 2002). That said, none of this is entirely deterministic. Human agency and responsibility continue to matter – career success is not preordained, although successful people still use their allotted capital to best effect, as Laird (2006) amply demonstrates. One condition of success, however, according to Bourdieu (1991), for all those who are privileged to play, is investment in the game itself, a recognition that the game, a priori, is worth playing. This unspoken contract unites all participants, fundamentally committed to and respectful of the game and its stakes.

The purpose of this article is twofold. On the one hand, it explores capital theory, studying the typology of forms of capital possessed by elite directors, drawing in particular on the work of Pierre Bourdieu. On the other, it examines the dynamics of elite business networking by directors in Britain and France. Bourdieu's ideas on capital theory are brought to life by empirical data from a comparative study on business elites in both countries. We are particularly interested in questions related to the reproduction and regeneration of business elites. How do business elites reproduce and regenerate themselves, in spite of the fact that their membership is constantly changing? What qualifies someone for membership of an elite business group, and how do newcomers gain acceptance? How does an ambitious individual acquire and display the capabilities and behavioural characteristics that mark him or her out as suitable material for recruitment? We focus here on some of the newcomers who were part of our study of French and British business elites (1998–2003), interviews with whom shed light on the experience of those who have gained admission to elite business groups. Elite organization and networking remain very different in the two countries. Our research points overwhelmingly to the strength of cultural reproduction among business elites, including at board level, despite the regular admission of newcomers to the boards of the leading companies of Britain and France, or of *nouveaux riches* into the 'old guard' business elite communities.

## The research

The research on which this article is based stems from a longitudinal, cross-nationally comparative study on business elites and corporate governance in Britain and France (Maclean *et al.*, 2006; 2007). The project has been conducted by the authors since 1999, and consists of four related sub-projects: first, a study of the institutional histories of the top 100 companies in 1998 in France and the UK respectively; second, a prosopographical study or 'collective biography' of 2,291 directors of the top 100 French and UK companies, examining their education, qualifications, careers, networks, roles and responsibilities; third, an in-depth study of the social backgrounds and accomplishments of the top 100 most powerful directors in France and the UK respectively, the 'super elite', analysing their social origins and career trajectories; and fourth, a study of the social reality of business elites based upon a set of semi-structured interviews with past and present business leaders in France and the UK. A 'census date' of 1 January 1998 was selected to ascertain organizational and individual membership of the corporate elites of France and the UK. The study period covers the years 1998 to 2003 inclusive: a length of time considered sufficiently long to reveal patterns and trends but sufficiently short to constitute a distinct historical period. Data were gathered from a wide range of publicly available sources on each of the directors identified as belonging to the business elites of France and the UK in 1998, including annual reports and accounts of French and UK companies for the years 1997 to 2004 inclusive, Datamonitor company reports, *Le Guide des Etats Majors des Grandes Entreprises* for 1998–2004 inclusive, *Who's Who* in France and the UK, and Hemscott Company Guru Academic director profiles.

## Bourdieu's concept of capital

Bourdieu's concept of capital is intimately related to his concept of field (*champ*), defined by DiMaggio and Powell as a 'totality of relevant actors' (1991:65), which together comprise 'a recognized area of institutional life' (1991:64). Bourdieu depicts modern society as highly differentiated and stratified, marked by specialization and the progressive splitting of fields into sub-fields, resulting in an order distinguished by a complex configuration of interweaving fields, 'differentiated social microcosms operating as spaces of objective forces and arenas of struggle . . . which refract and transmute external determinations and interests' (Calhoun and Wacquant, 2002:6). Fields are characterized by an on-going struggle for capital, as struggles over access or stakes ensue within structured systems of social relations (Oakes *et al.*, 1998; Wacquant, 1989). Stratification arises in fields because actors possess different amounts of capital. In the UK, for example, general practitioners have arguably enjoyed greater success in their struggle for resources than schoolteachers, faced with recent government reform agendas, for reasons which have to do with their respective locations in the field of professions (Laughlin and Broadbent, 1998).

Domination within any field or sub-field is contingent on possessing the right quantities and combinations of economic, cultural, social and symbolic capital. At the same time, homologies exist between fields that lead dominant actors to share similar dispositions across domains, so that structurally equivalent actors may be substitutable to a degree (Anheier *et al.*, 1995; Bourdieu, 1986a). Members of the elite within any field are capital rich, and can apply this in a variety of ways to maintain their dominant position. In this way, they reap the rewards of capital accumulation, control, legitimacy and distinction.

To some extent, the various types of capital – economic, cultural, social and symbolic (see Figure 1) – are transmutable, although they differ in their liquidity, i.e., the extent to which they may be converted into other types of capital, as well as the extent to which they are prone to erosion or inflation. Economic capital, for example, may be used to purchase cultural capital, in the form of an education at a prestigious establishment, while educational credentials in the form of qualifications may be converted in turn into a lucrative appointment. As Bourdieu explains, 'the volume of cultural capital . . . determines the aggregate chances of profit in all games in which cultural capital is effective, thereby helping to determine positions in the social space' (1985:724). The conversion of economic to cultural capital, however, cannot be taken for granted. The *nouveaux riches* are often rich in economic capital, but lacking in cultural capital (Anheier *et al.*, 1995; Crook, 1999). As one interviewee, who came from a

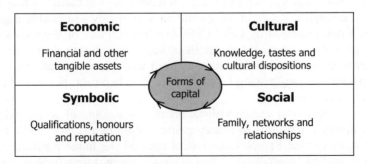

**Figure 1:** *Bourdieu's Concept of Capital.*
Source: Adapted from Maclean *et al.*, 2006: 29.

'very poor' background, lamented, this deficit is not necessarily something which can be made up retrospectively:

> I think I was better prepared as a 17-year-old coming from that background than any public school kid, who doesn't figure it out until he's 25. What you don't have is the education. The thing I most regret is that I was never given a French lesson. If I could speak four or five languages . . . the opportunities are so great. I'm lucky that I'm in the television business, which is predominantly English, but I have friends who can speak four or five languages in any accent, and it is a huge advantage.[1]

The elite member concerned pulled himself up by the bootstraps to become the founder of a leading international entertainment company, accumulating in the process considerable wealth and the trappings of wealth (the interview was held at a gentleman's club). He makes an important point when he highlights the importance of language: power and domination are linked to language (Oakes *et al.*, 1998). That linguistic capital, the way one speaks, is inseparably bound up with economic capital is something of which Bourdieu, hailing from southwestern France with its pronounced, provincial accent, was fully aware (1977b). Bourdieu (1991) warns us to be wary of language and the power of words, recognizing that whilst words may be ostensibly neutral in themselves, they are nevertheless used for symbolic profit. Words, however, do not reflect reality; rather, they are bound up with ritual, culture, convention, and hence class, and are instead 'an agreed way of speaking and carrying out activities' (Oakes *et al.*, 1998:257).

Cultural capital, in the form, say, of attendance at a good school, converts relatively easily into social capital, as scholarship children attending elite British public schools might appreciate – including one interviewee, who at age ten won a scholarship to Bromsgrove School, and later a Royal Navy scholarship to University College London. This interviewee went on to enjoy an illustrious career in law and business, heading a national business association, and subsequently attracting multiple, lucrative directorships. He believes Britain has become more of a meritocracy than previously, claiming: 'I am very proud of Britain in rising to the top. It has become less of a "who you know" and more of a meritocracy. It matters not where you went to school, it really does not matter as long as you are good enough.'[2] Belief in the meritocracy confirms and credits individual success, a point stressed by Laird (2006:11): 'Biographies of the successful . . . follow this pattern, replete with details of social factors, but crediting individual factors nonetheless'. This strikes a chord with France, a nation ostensibly built on a meritocracy, having rid itself more than two centuries ago of a hated monarchy and aristocracy.

To credit individual agency without taking full account of social and family factors, however, amounts to misrecognition (Bourdieu, 1986a; 1996; Bubolz, 2001). Many of our French interviewees stressed the humble nature of their origins, described on occasion as 'très modeste'; on enquiring further, these regularly emerged as less lowly. In one interview, a 'very modest' background turned out to imply a father who headed a company and a mother who owned a vineyard and ran an agricultural business.[3] In fact, our study of the social back-grounds of French directors found these to be drawn proportionately more from the upper and upper-middle classes than the British cohort, with 76.59 per cent of French directors belonging to these categories, as against 63.74 of British directors. Just over 4 per cent of French directors came from the lower classes, compared to almost 11 per cent of British directors (Maclean *et al.*, 2006). It is extremely rare to find, in the pages of *Who's Who in France*, a company direc-tor whose father is described as working class (*ouvrier*).

At interview, however, some French business leaders struck an overt populist tone, one director of a leading cosmetics company explaining that his passion was football, though he also played polo: 'I play football, which is the most popular sport. And I play polo, which is the most elitist'.[4] While social class pat-terns are more indeterminate than in the past, as noted, Bourdieu nevertheless describes this type of dichotomy as a 'condescension strategy', occurring when 'the person "naturally" associated with a Rolls Royce, a top hat or golf . . . takes the metro, sports a flat cap . . . or plays football' (1986a:472), thereby focusing attention on the gap between the two activities.

Symbolic capital, in the form of titles and reputation, is arguably less liquid and harder to acquire than cultural capital. This point was highlighted in the UK by the 'cash for honours' scandal, which blighted Tony Blair's final year as premier, allegedly proposing an exchange of economic for symbolic capital, cir-cumventing in the process the conventional channels of capital accumulation and conversion. Distinction, however, requires legitimacy in order to have power (Bourdieu, 1986a; 1994). The affair emphasizes the importance of the appear-ance of disinterestedness. Symbolic capital demands subtlety as part of the *modus operandi* of capital conversion: the link between alleged loans to politi-cal parties and proposed peerages was arguably too evident. A strategy, to be effective, should appear to be 'on the hither side of all calculation' (Bourdieu, 1977a:214; Swartz, 1997:70). The affair also sheds light on one of the key dif-ferences between senior elite members and newcomers or challengers. In Britain and also, to a lesser extent, in France, the honours system has the special func-tion of legitimizing the right of the elite to rule.[5] Symbolic power works pri-marily through a mechanism of naming and categorization (Oakes *et al.*, 1998). Challengers to the 'old guard', like the *nouveaux riches* of the Victorian and Edwardian eras (Crook, 1999), may lack (and therefore crave) the symbolic capital, in the form of titles and honours, which would cement, confirm and authenticate their arrival among the 'true' elite.

One feature which may distinguish the 'new elite' from the 'old guard' is the potential capacity for the former to exercise greater reflexivity. Lacking the 'unselfconscious belonging of those born to wealth, cultural pedigree and elite accents' (Calhoun and Wacquant, 2002:2), they have greater opportunity for, and arguably need of, more self-conscious reflection on the practices of busi-ness elites (Bourdieu, 1977a; 1990a; 1990b; Bourdieu and Wacquant, 1992). This is important in acquiring and demonstrating the personal dispositions and behaviours needed to function effectively alongside others in a strategic leadership role. Cultural practices are essentially reflective of deep-rooted class distinctions, while lifestyles give practical expression to the symbolic dimension of class identity. A practice approach therefore suggests paying close attention to accents, gestures, expressions and habits normally acquired unconsciously through being immersed in a community or environment (Chia and MacKay, 2007). Such self-awareness is exhibited by one French CEO, who speaks poignantly of how the military uniform worn at the elite *grande école* where he studied, Ecole Polytechnique, helped to iron out the sense of difference he felt as a southerner:

> I remember that in my younger days, wearing the school's uniform meant a lot to me. For the young man coming from Nice (in the South of France) that I was, it was a way to erase all the differences that existed between students coming up from the provinces and those brought up in the prestigious Parisian preparatory courses, such as the Lycée Louis-le-Grand.[6]

Of course, much of human behaviour is the product not of conscious decisions, but of 'habitus', the ingrained and socially constituted dispositions of social classes that lead actors to make choices and decisions that reproduce existing social structures and status distinctions. 'Habitus' is defined by Bourdieu as 'structured structures predisposed to function as structuring structures, that is, as principles which generate and organize practices and representations' (1990a:53). It is the means by which life chances are 'internalized and converted into a disposition' (Bourdieu, 1986a:170), and is thus primarily a mechanism for social reproduction. Habitus serves as a binding force between various fractions within a class, leading to common though not orchestrated action on the basis of categories of 'perception and appreciation' (Bourdieu, 1986a:170). In this way, it reconciles the co-existence of subjective and objective conditions within society.

The objective conditions of existence include the consumption of goods, which may be valued more for their social meaning than for their functional use (Solomon, 1983). A reflexive practice, therefore, is not just a mode of being-in-the-world but includes a relationship with products and things – emblems, and lesser emblems, of distinction – indicative of choices and preferences. Le Wita (1994:141) argues that 'trivia . . . have a particular function, namely to create distinction', a view shared by Bourdieu: 'Taste', he points out, 'classifies, and it classifies the classifier' (1986a:6). Tastes originate not from internally generated artistic preferences but from the socially conditioning effect of habitus and the availability of economic and cultural capital. Ultimately, in Bourdieu's view, the exercise of taste confirms the right to rule. The practical value of Bourdieu's thinking thus stems from the insight that those who advance in society into elite positions do so both by consciously acquiring personal capital (qualifications, experience, connections and goods) and by unconsciously assimilating knowledge and dispositions through habitus.

Ambitious newcomers arguably require, therefore, as suggested, greater self-consciousness in their efforts to acquire a 'feel for the game' in their new environment. One elite member, who claimed to come from humble origins, explained at interview, in minute detail, how he painstakingly acquired the dispositions necessary for membership of an elite business group. He did so by closely observing his father-in-law, a member of minor Scottish aristocracy, copying his habits and practices, paying acute attention to details, from the cutlery he used to the wine he ordered, to the pursuits of shooting and golf in which he engaged. He recognized the importance of speech – as he put it, 'the Scots are "pigeon-hole people": because I didn't have a Scottish accent they didn't know that I was not well born' – and strove to emulate the accent of the class into which he was marrying.[7]

Reflexive practice arguably includes marriage, viewed by Bourdieu (1972) as a strategy, fundamental to the perpetuation (or in the above case acquisition) of economic power on the part of business elites, though at times functioning more subconsciously than consciously. Hall and de Bettignies (1968), who established the occupations of fathers-in-law of their sample of French business leaders, found that marriage in the 1960s was very much an 'intra-class affair', with 75 per cent of their sample having wives belonging to the same social class. Our own research confirms the popularity of marriage amongst contemporary business elites, with almost all of the top 100 super elite in both countries having married, and just two elite directors from each cohort remaining single. The mean number of children of top 100 French and British directors was 2.9 and 2.4 respectively, above the national average in both cases. The impression of conventionality and family stability is reinforced by a lower than average divorce rate of just seven per cent among top French directors and 11 per cent among the British. In both countrieś nearly all the divorcees married again. The implication is that the symbols and rituals of married life – emphasizing constancy, reliability and a belief in family values – are seen in themselves to bear witness to the fitness of a person to hold high office in business; as one leading British CEO expressed it: 'I'm married with three children and am dog-thoroughly boring'.[8]

## The power of social capital

One of the most important 'aces' in the game is social capital, defined as the resources that inhere in the structure of relationships between actors (Bourdieu, 1986b; Coleman, 1988; Burt, 1992; 1997; Burt *et al.*, 2000; Oh *et al.*, 2004), or the 'sum of the actual and potential resources that can be mobilized through membership in social networks of actors and organizations' (Anheier *et al.*, 1995:862).

It is social capital that determines who advances in business and who does not (Finkelstein *et al.*, 2007:112–120). The distinction between membership and non-membership, inclusion and exclusion, is critical (Bourdieu 1986a:476). Discrimination, Laird insists, is two-way, pulling in and pushing out, such that no one makes it entirely on his or her own: 'what the rare rags-to-riches story and *all* success stories prove is another rule, one to which there is no exception: that of the necessity for connections and connectability – the rule of social capital' (2006:1–2). Even Andrew Carnegie, perhaps the most celebrated American rags-to-riches story, would not have enjoyed such prodigious success, she argues, without the invaluable assistance provided at the start of his career first by his uncle and then by his mentor, Tom Scott. Laird shows how this applies equally to the other ostensibly 'self-made' men included in her investigation, such as Benjamin Franklin, Bill Gates, J.P. Morgan and Thomas Mellon, pinpointing the social connections – the networks, mentors, role models and gatekeepers – that helped them to climb the ladder.

Many elite members who participated in this study illustrated the potency of social capital from their own, individual perspectives. One interviewee, a Chairman and non-executive director of several public limited companies, including a major international bank, spoke candidly at interview of the individuals who had facilitated his success, acting as beacons of his career. These included Sir William Hayter, Warden of New College, Oxford, who urged him not to go into the Foreign Office, and later Jimmy Goldsmith, described as an 'unconventional thinker' and a 'brilliant gambler', who taught him 'to think outside the box'.[9] Another interviewee, who rose to head the European operation of a global IT company, attributed his success, first, to the foresight of his working-class parents in sending him to university: 'My father was a porter and my mother was a waitress. To the great credit of my parents, they believed their children should go to university . . . and their attitude was very much that you could achieve what you wanted to'; and second, to his closest friend at university, with whom he formed a company, selling up in the early 1990s for a sum that meant neither of them would ever need to work again.[10] Another, unable, as he put it, 'with my sort of background to get in the front door to the BBC', or any of the major studios, required the connections of his father-in-law to find a way into television.[11] Yet another, who won a scholarship to independent school, spoke warmly of the help given him by his primary school headmaster:

> A headmaster at my state primary school, who clearly thought his job was to equip you for life, not just for exams, started me on this road of enormous love for history and our role in the world. He used to say to me, at age seven or eight, never be frightened of asking why, and never pretend that you know when you don't. I can remember him standing there and saying so. I have never forgotten him. He put me through three exams for a scholarship when I was ten-and-a-half, one was for the local grammar school, the second one was for King Edward School, and the third one was for Bromsgrove School. I got them all.[12]

## The dynamics of elite business networking in Britain and France

Few studies of the ties that bind elite business members (Palmer *et al.*, 1986) are cross-national and comparative (Hughes *et al.*, 1977; Useem, 1982; Scott, 1991;

Burt *et al.*, 2000; Maclean *et al.*, 2006). One key insight gleaned from the present study is the finding that elite networking by directors is achieved very differently in France and the UK. While the ties that bind the French business elite tend to be institutional and strong, sustained and supported by the state, those that unite the business elite in Britain are in part social in nature and tend to be relatively weak. In this they conform more closely to Granovetter's notion of weak ties (1973) than the tightly networked French business system. The French cohort displays a propensity towards more endogenous ties, while their British counterparts appear more willing to engage in more diverse, heterogeneous relationships. In France, networking is found to be an institutional feature, systemically embedded, whereas in the UK the onus is not on institutions but on individuals. The latter is more haphazard, relying largely on the social ambition and networking skills of aspiring individuals, often through sport or arts charities.

In fact, our research found that British directors were almost twice as likely to be involved with sports or arts institutions, displaying a participation rate of 28 per cent as against 15 per cent for the French group. Elite British directors are also more than four times as likely to engage in charitable work as French directors (Maclean *et al.*, 2006). One interviewee, indeed, who grew up on a tough housing estate in West Yorkshire, and was given his first pair of shoes by a charity, points to the importance of knowing what it feels like to be the beneficiary of charity, a rarity among elite directors: 'I'd rather take a child and teach them something; don't give the third world money, give them help'.[13] By contrast, French directors were more likely to serve on the boards of business associations, which tend to attract similar types of individual. One interviewee, the Human Resource Director for Europe of a world leader in industrial gases, explained how he had developed together with four colleagues a network of 15–20 international human resource directors across Paris, called the HR Exchange.[14]

Strong ties, as Granovetter (1973) observed, are more likely to induce conformity, exposing participants to richer but less diverse information. The French cohort exhibits a tendency towards more endogenous ties, corresponding in this way to a 'bonding' social capital perspective. French business, political and administrative elites share a common education, fostering local cohesion (Kadushin, 1995; Maclean, 2002; Maclean *et al.*, 2006). They are helped in this by the compact size of the French business elite, facilitating relationships amongst them. The numbers graduating each year from an elite *grande école* such as Polytechnique, for example, are far smaller than those that graduate each year from Oxford or Cambridge. British directors, on the other hand, appear more willing to engage in more diverse relationships with a variety of external constituencies, more typical of 'bridging' social capital (Adler and Kwon, 2002; Burt, 1992, 1997; Geletkanycz and Hambrick, 1997). Such relationships are more likely to bridge 'structural holes', defined by Burt as the 'disconnections between nonredundant contacts in a network' (1997:339). One French CEO of a leading international financial company, who lives and works in both Paris and London, stressed the importance to British business elites of a social life, in contrast to which French elites value their privacy:

> People in the UK find a social life is very important to them. In France people feel that private life is private life. Of course, there are those who break the rule, but even the CEOs of big companies like to have a private life. When you're not working you go to the movies or a restaurant and don't have your weekend interrupted by a business relationship.[15]

The state-sponsored nature of networking among the French business elite was amply illustrated by the same CEO, who spoke openly at interview of useful relationships gleaned from his days at the Ecole Nationale d'Administration (ENA), a leading *grande école*, which later revolved around the Ministry of Finance and the Treasury, forming a cohesive subgroup of relations:

> To be frank, it is more a subset, because the classes at ENA consisted of around 140 people. Some people go to the Foreign Office and some to the Health Ministry. You may know them personally, but you don't have business directly with them. So the subset was more being able to go to the Minister of Finance at the Treasury and meet people there, and the Treasury is traditionally (as I believe in the UK) a very active part of the Finance Ministry. At that time, people didn't stay in the Treasury for life. After civil service school you would stay in the Ministry of Finance for six or seven years, so repaying your debt for studies to the French State. Then people would stay in the Treasury for 10 to 15 years. . . . The CEO of Suez was in the Treasury. The CEO of Renault was in the Budget and Ministry of Finance at the time. The Head of the French Banking Federation was at the French Treasury at the same time as me. This must have been around 1974 . . . I suppose I have a kind of network in the world. Knowing people makes it easier to deal with people, because knowing them personally means I can call them.[16]

Our research found that 49 per cent of elite French directors in 1998 had moved from the public to the private sector, beginning their career, as this CEO did, working for the state. Indeed, the *grandes écoles* in France have a state-serving ethos, several of them having been established in revolutionary times, or later under Napoleon, specifically to provide the trained elite administrators and teachers needed to serve the state. This notion of the state as a sponsor and facilitator of elite ties is not encountered in the UK (Bauer and Bertin-Mourot, 1996). Just 3 per cent of top British directors began their careers in the public sector (Maclean *et al.*, 2006). Like the prestigious *grandes écoles*, the *grands corps*, the pinnacle of France's civil service elite, foster an *esprit de caste*, resembling forms of extended family, freemasonry or 'placement bureaux' (Barsoux and Lawrence, 1990; Marceau, 1989; Suleiman, 1978:197). The *grands corps* consecrate social identities that are both in competition and complementary, such that, despite the rivalry that exists between individual *corps*, all *corpsards* are 'united by a genuine organic solidarity' (Bourdieu, 1994:142).

In his study of the French financial elite in the early 1990s, Kadushin (1995) found that elite members serving as directors on multiple boards were more likely to have attended the 'right' schools, and to be members of the 'right' clubs.

Such schools and clubs, often endowed with a political dimension, function as policy circles, and come to serve as 'proxies' for membership of the upper social classes. Elite clubs frequented by leading French directors in our study include the Association du Siècle, Maxim's Business Club, the Racing Club of Paris, Polo de Paris, the Cercle du Bois de Boulogne, Entreprise et Cité and the Club des 100. What this commonality of membership gives elite French directors above all is a high degree of 'enforceable trust' (Kadushin, 1995:219). As Portes and Sensenbrenner explain, this is the means by which 'social capital is generated by individual members' disciplined compliance with group expectations'. In this it resembles reciprocity exchanges, except that 'the actor's behaviour is not oriented to a particular other but to the web of social networks of the entire community' (1993:1325). Trust therefore serves as an 'expectational asset' (Knez and Camerer, 1994), cementing relationships and building confident expectations regarding the future, inducing optimism among the business elite (De Carolis and Saparito, 2006).

Meanwhile, more that half of Britain's top 100 directors in 1998, 54 in all, belonged to a London club, many located in and around Pall Mall, including the Athenaeum, Brooks's and the RAC. Many more were members of elite sport clubs, with golf the most popular sporting club to join, one fifth of the British super elite being members of a golf club. This is in stark contrast to French directors. As one French CEO put it: 'The only thing you might get in France is tennis'. In declining invitations from British elites to go hunting or fishing, this particular CEO felt quite clearly that he had missed a connection: 'I've been invited to go shooting, but I say, "No, I don't know how to shoot", and you see very clearly that you've missed some connection. It's the same with fishing'.[17] From the personal accounts of top executives interviewed as part of our study, it is difficult to overestimate the importance of sport in the British context. One British CEO (whose father worked as a school janitor) cited sport as one of the main reasons why he had risen so swiftly up the corporate ladder, telling of a cricket match he had played in at the start of his career, when his company's cricket team had thrashed that of a leading high street bank:

> We sat down in the changing room afterwards and we suddenly realised that we had 10 internationals, nine full county players, and six blues. I'd only been in the company six months and saw what a company I'd joined. Ever since that day I've always known that it wouldn't matter what challenge was set. I could turn out an orchestra tomorrow, a football team, a rugby team, a cricket team, and we'd take anybody on.[18]

For ambitious British executives, sport serves as a proving ground, a means of building personal confidence. It provides a mechanism for social bonding and the development of solidarity between individuals. And, perhaps most tellingly of all, it is an enduring source of personal distinction. The popularity of exclusive clubs, sporting and social, among the British super elite underlines the social nature of many of the ties that enable individuals to connect. Major sporting events such as tennis at Wimbledon, racing at Ascot, the Henley regatta and sailing at Cowes provide similar symbolically loaded opportunities for elite networking.

## Discussion and conclusions

The notion that membership of a social institution or institutions can serve unconsciously to form the potentialities of an individual actor is an important one, implying that the life chances of individuals are forged uniquely, and in no small way, through their membership of a series of institutions, of which family, educational institutions, and corporate and professional organizations and associations are among the most fundamental. Boards also serve as structuring structures for the power elite of corporate capitalism, being essentially small, elite communities which function in accordance with established norms and cultural practices, requiring conformity of behaviour from the individuals who serve on them. In France, the state arguably serves as a further structuring structure, though this does not apply to anywhere near the same degree in the UK (Bauer and Bertin-Mourot, 1996). It is by getting the most out of membership of families, educational institutions and corporate and professional organizations that individuals add to their stock of capital, and position themselves for recruitment into the corporate elite (Bubolz, 2001).

It is also clear from our research that in both Britain and France there is a strong tendency towards cultural reproduction, inducing continuity without preventing change. We have been struck continually by the power of cultural reproduction in organizations, the reassertion of social and cultural patterns, often in the face of apparent change. Culture is the product and assimilation of lived experience, imposing discipline and compliance to the rules of the organizational game. It is manifest in, and generated by, practice. Change, on the other hand, may be misrecognized and exaggerated, partly because it is typically superficial, not structural. This chimes with the explanation offered by Bourdieu (1986a), who argues that the deep-rooted and socially constructed dispositions of classes induce actors to make choices and decisions which reinforce in turn pre-existing social structures and status distinctions. A board is also a culture in its own right, whose practices are internalized by board members, created by habitus and manifest of it. Through the recognition of signs and symbols, visual and verbal clues, individuals tend to act along pre-ordained lines laid down by habitus, which serve as an economizing device or 'shorthand'.

Habitus is assumed most wholly when one is born to a particular environment: 'to know is to be born with' (*'connaître, c'est naître avec'*). It follows that to be accepted by the elite as one of its own can only happen 'by birth or by a slow process of co-option and initiation which is equivalent to a second birth' (Bourdieu, 1990a:67–68). Newcomers who succeed in advancing their fortunes and legitimacy, of whom we have highlighted several examples in this article, typically seek to embrace – at times painstakingly, at others unawares – the social and cultural practices of the established elite into which they desire to become integrated. To gain acceptance requires that they display internalized behaviours that define them as boardroom material. This goes beyond a 'state of mind' to embrace a 'state of the body', to a greater or lesser degree of 'unawareness', since, as Bourdieu puts it: 'It is because agents never know completely what they are doing that what they do has more sense than they know' (1990a:67–69). For such newcomers, acceptance as authentic members of the business elite constitutes the ultimate prize.

The dominant culture of the US, according to Laird (2006), has sought to render class less visible, its principal manifestations attributed to individual achievement alone. The US prefers to see itself as a meritocracy, thereby overlooking the powerful part played by social capital, of which class is a key determinant. The former British Prime Minister, Margaret Thatcher, once famously said that there was 'no such thing as society, only individuals'; and individual agency and responsibility undeniably play a critical role. Yet to credit individual agency without fully acknowledging social and family factors is tantamount to misrecognition (Bourdieu, 1986a, 1996; Bubolz, 2001). As Laird points out (2006), there is a sense in which self-made business success, *stricto sensu*, is ultimately impossible. The point to emphasize here is that, as our interview data suggests, actors are positioned in a 'topography' of social relations, occupying 'positions of possibility' which are not permanent, but which are instead reflective of underlying power relations determined by their particular allocation or acquisition of economic, social, cultural and symbolic capital (Anheier *et al.*, 1995:859; Bourdieu, 1990a; Oakes *et al.*, 1998:260). Amongst these capital assets, connections and connectability, mentoring and networking, arguably provide a *sine qua non* for individual advancement and admission into elite business groups.

This is not to imply, however, that we are headed for international convergence. As we have demonstrated, elite organization and networking are still very different in both countries. Our research points overwhelmingly not to convergence, but rather to continuing diversity among national business systems, to the persistence of national distinctiveness and the strength of cultural reproduction. National business systems are, to a significant degree, self referring, supported and informed by pre-existing social structures, and possessing a coherence or cognitive similarity of organizing principles which restricts their capacity to adapt to new influences whilst not precluding change (Crouch, 2005; Hall and Soskice, 2001; Maclean and Harvey, 2008; Schmidt, 2003; Whitley, 1999). In the context of the present article, our research has pointed, albeit tentatively, to British society being rather more open than French society. Opportunities for upward social mobility appear somewhat more in evidence in Britain than in France. While Britain is well known for extolling 'blue blood', and while France projects itself as a meritocracy, our research suggests that an individual's chances of ascending the social ladder through a career in business may be higher in the former.

## Acknowledgement

The authors wish to thank the Leverhulme Trust and Reed Charity for funding the research which has informed the present article, the French and British business leaders concerned for kindly agreeing to be interviewed, and the reviewers for their helpful comments.

## Notes

1 Interview with Chairman of international entertainment company, 5 September, 2003, London.
2 Interview with business leader, 4 March, 2004, Bristol.
3 Interview with former Chairman and CEO, 3 January, 2003, Paris.
4 Interview with director of leading cosmetic company, 10 March, 2003, Paris.
5 While the French do not possess name-changing honours like the British, they do award various categories of the *Légion d'honneur*, introduced by Napoleon, and the *Ordre national du Mérite*, introduced by de Gaulle.
6 *McKinsey Quarterly* (1989) 3: 6.
7 Interview with Chairman of international entertainment company, 5 September, 2003, London.
8 *Maclean's* (2003), 116, 9: 32.
9 Interview with non-executive director of major international bank, 5 November, 2003, Bristol.
10 Interview with business leader, 24 April, 2003, London.
11 Interview with Chairman of international entertainment company, 5 September, 2003, London.
12 Interview with business leader, 4 March, 2004, Bristol.
13 Interview with UK managing director of global IT company, 23 April, 2004.
14 Interview with director of leading industrial gases company, Paris, 26 May, 2003.
15 Interview with French CEO, 7 November, 2003, London.
16 Interview with French CEO, 7 November, 2003, London.
17 Interview with French CEO, 7 November, 2003, London.
18 Interview with UK managing director of global IT company, 23 April, 2004.

## References

Adler, P. and Kwon, S., (2002), 'Social capital: the good, the bad and the ugly', in Lesser, E., (ed.), Knowledge and Social Capital: Foundations and Applications, Boston: Butterworth-Heineman: 80–115.
Anheier, H.K. *et al.*, (1995), 'Forms of capital and social structure in cultural fields: examining Bourdieu's topography', American Journal of Sociology, **100**, 4, January: 859–903.
Barsoux, J.-L. and P. Lawrence, (1990), *Management in France*, London: Cassell.
Bauer, M. and Bertin-Mourot, B., (1996), *Vers un modèle européen des dirigeants? Comparaison Allemagne/France/Grande-Bretagne*, Paris: CNRS/Boyden.
Bourdieu, P., (1972), 'Les stratégies matrimoniales dans le système de reproduction', *Annales Econ. Soc. Civil*, **4–5**: 1105–1127.
Bourdieu, P., (1977a), *Outline of a Theory of Practice*, translated by R. Nice, Cambridge: CUP.
Bourdieu, P., (1977b), 'The Economics of Linguistic Exchanges', *Social Science Information*, **16**, 6: 645–668.
Bourdieu, P., (1985,) 'The social space and the genesis of groups', *Theory and Society*, **14**: 723–744.
Bourdieu, P., (1986a), *Distinction: a Social Critique of the Judgement of Taste*, translated by R. Nice. London: Routledge and Kegan Paul.
Bourdieu, P., (1986b,) 'The Forms of Capital', in Richardson, J.G. (ed.), *Handbook of Theory and Research for the Sociology of Education*, New York: Greenwood: 241–258.

Bourdieu, P., (1990a), *The Logic of Practice*, translated by R. Nice, Stanford: Stanford University Press.

Bourdieu, P., (1990b), *In Other Words: Essay Toward a Reflexive Sociology*, Stanford: Stanford University Press.

Bourdieu, P., (1991), *Language and Symbolic Power*, translated by G. Raymond and M. Adamson, edited and introduced by J.B. Thomson, Cambridge: Polity Press.

Bourdieu, P., (1993), *The Field of Cultural Production*. edited and introduced by R. Johnson, Cambridge: Polity Press.

Bourdieu, P., (1994), *The State Nobility: Elite Schools in the Field of Power*, translated by L.C. Clough, Cambridge: Polity Press.

Bourdieu, P., (1996), 'On the family as a realized category', *Theory, Culture and Society*, **13**, 3: 19–26.

Bourdieu, P. and L. Wacquant, (1992), *An Invitation to Reflexive Sociology*, Cambridge: Polity Press.

Bubolz, M.M., (2001), 'Family as source, user and builder of social capital', *Journal of Socio-Economics*, **30**: 129–131.

Burt, R.S., (1992), *Structural Holes: the Social Structure of Competition*, Cambridge MA: Harvard University Press.

Burt, R.S., (1997), 'The contingent value of social capital', *Administrative Science Quarterly*, **42**: 339–365.

Burt, R.S., (2000), 'The Network structure of social capital', in Staw, B.M. and Sutton, R.I. (eds), *Research in Organizational Behavior*, New York: Elsevier: 345–423.

Burt, R.S., Hogarth, R.M. and Michaud, C., (2000), 'The social capital of French and American managers', *Organization Science*, **11**, 2, March-April: 123–147.

Calhoun, C. and Wacquant, L., (2002), 'Social science with a conscience: remembering Pierre Bourdieu (1930–2002)', *Thesis Eleven*, **70**: 1–14.

Chia, R. and MacKay, B., (2007), 'Post-processual challenges for the emerging strategy-as-practice perspective: discovering strategy in the logic of practice', *Human Relations*, **60**, 1: 217–241.

Coleman, J.S., (1988), 'Social capital in the creation of human capital', *American Journal of Sociology*, **78**: S95-S120.

Crook, J.M., (1999), *The Rise of the Nouveaux Riches*, London: John Murray.

Cross, R., Parker, A. and Sasson, L., (eds), (2003), *Networks in the Knowledge Economy*, New York: Oxford University Press.

Crouch, C., (2005), *Capitalist Diversity and Change: Recombinant Governance and Institutional Entrepreneurs*, Oxford: OUP.

De Carolis, D.M. and Saparito, P., (2006), 'Social capital, cognition, and entrepreneurial opportunities: a theoretical framework', *Entrepreneurship, Theory and Practice*, January: 41–56.

DiMaggio, P.J. and Powell, W.W., (1991), 'The iron cage revisited: institutional isomorphism and collective rationality in organizational fields', in Powell, W.W. and DiMaggio, P.J., (eds), *The New Institutionalism in Organizational Analysis*, Chicago: University of Chicago Press: 63–82.

Finkelstein, S., Harvey, C. and Lawton, T., (2007), *Breakout Strategy: Meeting the Challenge of Double Digit Growth*, New York: McGraw-Hill.

Frank, K.A. and Yasumoto, J.Y., (1998), 'Linking action to social structure within a system: social capital within and between subgroups', *American Journal of Sociology*, **104**, 3: 642–686.

Geletkanycz, M., and Hambrick, D.C., (1997), 'The external ties of top executives: implications for strategic choice and performance', *Administrative Science Quarterly*, **42**: 654–681.

Granovetter, M.S., (1973), 'The strength of weak ties', *American Journal of Sociology*, **78**: 1360–1380.

Hall, D. and de Bettignies, H-C., (1968), 'The French business elite', *European Business*, **19**, October: 52–61.

Hall, P.A. and Soskice, D., (2001), 'An introduction to varieties of capitalism', in Soskice, D. and Hall, P.A., (eds), *Varieties of Capitalism: the Institutional Foundations of Comparative Advantage*, Oxford: OUP: 1–68.

Hughes, M., Scott, J. and Mackenzie, J., (1977), 'Trends in interlocking directorates: an International Comparison', *Acta Sociologica*, **30**, 3: 287–292.

Kadushin, C., (1995), 'Friendship among the French financial elite', *American Sociological Review*, **60**, April: 202–21.

Knez, M. and Camerer, C., (1994), 'Creating expectational assets in the laboratory: coordination in "weakest link" games', *Strategic Management Journal*, **15**: 101–119.

Laird, P.W., (2006), *Pull: Networking and Success since Benjamin Franklin*, Cambridge MA: Harvard University Press.

Le Wita, B., (1994), *French Bourgeois Culture*, translated by J.A. Underwood, Cambridge: CUP.

Laughlin, R. and Broadbent, J., (1998), 'Resisting the "new public management": absorption and absorbing groups in schools and GP practices', in *Accounting, Auditing and Accountability*, **11**: 403–435.

Maclean, M., (2002), *Economic Management and French Business from de Gaulle to Chirac*, Basingstoke: Palgrave Macmillan.

Maclean, M., Harvey, C. and Press, P., (2006), *Business Elites and Corporate Governance in France and the UK*, Basingstoke: Palgrave Macmillan.

Maclean, M., Harvey, C. and Press, J., (2007), 'Managerialism and the postwar evolution of the French national business system', *Business History*, **49**, 4, July: 531–551.

Maclean, M. and Harvey, C., (2008), 'The continuing diversity of corporate governance regimes: France and Britain compared', in Jackson, G. and Strange, R., (eds), *International Business and Corporate Governance*, Basingstoke: Palgrave Macmillan, 208–225.

Marceau, J., (1989), 'France', in Bottomore, T. and Brym, R.J., (eds), *The Capitalist Class: an International Study*, London: Harvester Wheatsheaf: 47–72.

Oakes, L.S, Townley, B. and Cooper, D.J., (1998), 'Business planning as pedagogy: language and control in a changing institutional field', *Administrative Science Quarterly*, **43**: 257–292.

Oh, H., Chung, M.-H. and Labianca, G., (2004), 'Group social capital and group effectiveness: the role of informal socializing ties', *Academy of Management Journal*, **47**, 6: 860–875.

Palmer, D., Friedland, R. and Singh, J.V., (1986) ,'The ties that bind: organizational and class bases of stability in a corporate interlock network', *American Sociological Review*, **51**: 781–796.

Portes, A. and Sensenbrenner, J., (1993), 'Embeddedness and immigration: notes on the social determinants of economic action', *American Journal of Sociology*, **98**, 6: 1320–1350.

Schmidt, V., (2003), 'French capitalism transformed, yet still a third variety of capitalism', *Economy and Society*, **32**, 4: 526–554.

Scott, J., (1991), 'Networks of corporate power: a comparative assessment', *Annual Review of Sociology*, **17**: 181–203.

Scott, J., (2002), 'Social class and stratification in late modernity', *Acta Sociologica*, **45**, 1: 23–35.

Solomon, M.R., (1983), 'The role of products as social stimuli: a symbolic interaction perspective', *Journal of Consumer Research*, **10**, December: 319–29.

Suleiman, E., (1978), *Elites in French Society: The Politics of Survival*, London: Princeton University Press.

Swartz, D., (1997), *Culture and Power: The Sociology of Pierre Bourdieu*, Chicago: Chicago University Press.

Useem, M., (1982), 'Classwise rationality in the politics of managers and directors of large corporations in the United States and Great Britain', *Administrative Science Quarterly*, **27**: 199–226.

Wacquant, L., (1989), 'Toward a reflexive sociology: a workshop with Pierre Bourdieu', *Sociological Theory*, **7**: 26–63.

Whitley, R., (1999), *Divergent Capitalisms: The Social Structuring and Change of Business Systems*, Oxford: OUP.

# Central bankers in the contemporary global field of power: a 'social space' approach

## Frédéric Lebaron

In the context of the financialization of the global economy, and the importance of financial elites (see Savage and Williams in this volume) the role of central banks has become particularly important. The financial crisis of August–September 2007, (the 'sub-prime mortgage crisis') has given a new illustration of the growing functional importance of these central banks, which are in charge of monetary and financial stability through their particular daily interventions on the markets. As 'lenders of last resort' in case of declining confidence between banks or financial actors and, more generally, 'custodians of monetary stability' as they are often described, central bankers determine the general level of confidence in the set of monetary and financial instruments which have developed in recent years, and contribute highly to the production of macroeconomic decisions, and financial dynamics.

Behind the opaque walls of central banks, well known to be very secretive institutions, particular social agents appear to be a new economic and political elite. Their role, action and beliefs have become determinant for the reproduction of the economic and social order as a whole. This specific 'financial' elite is related to the state bureaucracy (from which it frequently emanates), to the political field and to the dominant actors of the financial markets. In Europe, the creation of the European Central Bank (ECB) has objectified this process by putting the so-called 'independent' governing council of the ECB at the centre of monetary policy but also of macroeconomic policy in general. In the very recent period, European central bankers have been put under political pressure by French politicians, condemning the high level of interest rates and above all the over-evaluation of the Euro, resulting from the specific actions of the ECB.

In this situation, knowledge of the social trajectories which lead to the position of central banker in different parts of the world is a first step to understanding the social reality behind the emergence of these new global elites. It will help for example to determine the degree of homogeneity of this group and its internal structures; this knowledge will also give an understanding of the social 'embeddedness' of monetary and macroeconomic decisions, otherwise seen as structural macro-conditions without any social content. In this sense, the sociology of central bankers is a specific contribution to economic sociology, especially to the understanding of the political-institutional basis of the functioning of markets (see Fligstein for an approach centred on this question).

In the next section, I present the centrality of the space of central bankers in the global field of power and its particular structure. I then focus on comparative analyses about the social properties of the members of monetary policy councils in the three most influential central banks (from the United States, Europe and Japan), using specific Multiple Correspondence Analysis.

My results suggest that part of the differences in the strategies of central banks is related to specific social characteristics of their 'leaders' and that, more generally, the social structure of the space of central bankers provides a key for understanding the economic behaviour of central banks.

## Towards a sociology of central bankers

There are at least two competing viewpoints in the main discourses about central banks. The first one, dominant in the academic field, is provided by economics, which describe central banks as units of rational choice, involved in a game essentially made of strategic actions and reactions (for elements of syntheses see Blinder, 2004). The central banks are only more or less 'independent' according to various criteria – legal, behavioural, etc.; the preferred functions of the central bankers are more or less 'conservative' (reluctant to inflate) according to the personal tastes of the governor(s). But the behaviour of central banks is above all supposed to be essentially inspired by a universal economic rationality (produced by a scientific discipline: economics); when the differences in the environment are controlled, the strategies of different central banks seem then very close (see for a recent example of this conception of the European Central Bank: Gerdesmeier *et al.*, 2007).

The second viewpoint is provided by journalists (and actors of financial institutions). Central banks are described as places where singular individuals, usually 'governors' (sometimes called 'president' or 'chairman'), defined by their personal psychological and technical dispositions, are largely the origins of decisions made by the banks: interest rates cuts or rises, economic and monetary strategies in general. An extreme illustration of this second type of discourse is the common journalistic spin regarding Alan Greenspan, the well-known chairman of the Federal Reserve Bank of the United States between 1987 and 2006. This long-lasting central banker is usually taken to be responsible for a period of no-inflation growth, productivity rise, the success of the 'new economy', ups-and-downs of the financial markets; see for example Woodward, (2001): 'Greenspan, an old-school anti-inflation hawk of the traditional economy, is among the first to realize the potential in the modern, high-productivity new economy – the foundation of the current American boom (. . .) who has become the symbol of American economic pre-eminence.'

The first type of discourse lets individuals disappear inside a rational entity (the central bank), whereas the second reduces central bankers to exceptional personalities (governors). This double symmetrical reduction leaves a – largely empty – space for analyses inspired by economic sociology (for a short synthesis on economic sociology and money, see: Swedberg, 2003: 151–154). Central banks can also be defined as particular economic administrative and political organizations, defining social spaces that are rooted in historical-cultural contexts. Their decisions are made by social agents, who discuss, argue, and interpret the (economic) world and who try to convince each other (for a detailed sociological study of the minutes of the Federal Reserve Bank, see Abolafia, 2006).

## Councils as social spaces

My own analysis, based on biographical data analysis, stresses the importance of these councils ('monetary policy council', 'committee', 'governing council' . . .) as specific social spaces, shaped by legal-institutional rules, where different types of capitals, accumulated by individuals, are at stake. These spaces are inserted inside a more global field, what I call the global field of power. By field of power, I mean, following Bourdieu (1989), a space where agents possessing a relatively high volume of different sorts of capitals compete and struggle with each other to determine their value (for a recent discussion and application using Geometric Data Analysis, see Hjellbrekke *et al.*, 2007). One of the consequences of the current internationalization of fields is the constitution of a global field of power where agents from various national spaces relate to each other across borders. The space of central bankers has a specific position inside this global field. My analysis is therefore a response to Savage and Williams's call in the introduction for Bourdieusian analyses to re-invigorate the study of elites.

This perspective allows me to avoid another usual reduction, which is the assimilation of central bankers' decisions to the simple motive of global financial class interests (as is still often done in the Marxist tradition). In my perspective, the following sociological arguments are decisive:

- the social space of a monetary policy council is inserted in the global field of power;
- this social space is relatively autonomous; 'independence' and belief in independence are related to the characteristics of its members;
- in this social space, various species of capitals are at stake, in a dominant or a dominated role;
- it is a place of symbolic struggle, where language plays an important part (any decision being first 'debated' and 'argued' inside the arena of the council's meetings before becoming the official decision of the bank);
- the strategies of the central banks (monetary policy but also budget discourse, economic position takings, etc.) depend on these symbolic struggles;
- central banks are also inserted in a more global political, economic and financial context.

These arguments also complete and, to some extent, nuance, the description of an 'epistemic community' ('global community') of central bankers (Marcussen, 2003), who are supposed to share a common definition of monetary policy and orthodox economic conceptions all over the world. The group of central bankers is clearly dominated by a neo-liberal creed (on which see Lebaron, 2006) but the precise monetary and budgetary strategies, economic policy models, and conceptions of which 'structural reforms' to implement can vary highly inside this world, and these variations may explain different patterns of behaviour and/or discourses between the central banks. National specific conceptions, traditions or dispositions toward monetary policy also differ according to contexts and modalities of insertion inside the global field of power. The social networks described among the central bankers are themselves embedded in more constraining social structures.

More concretely, in this empirical investigation, my aim was to study the space of central bankers as a sub-space of the global field of power, with three main questions:

1) What are the principal dimensions of this space, looking not only at the governors but also at the members of the three main councils of monetary policy?
2) Are there sociological differences between the three largest central banks (ECB, Fed and BoJ)?
3) Are these differences sociologically consistent with differences in a central bank's strategies and behaviours?

## Methodology

The beginning of this project was a case study of the appointment of the nine members (one governor, two alternate governors, six members) of the first 'conseil de la politique monétaire' (Council of monetary policy) by the French government, which occurred after the decision to make the *Banque de France* 'independent' from political power in 1993 (applied in 1994), following the conditions of the Maastricht treaty voted by the French citizens in 1992 (Lebaron, 1997). Since this first study, I have collected biographical data about 94 central bankers: governors (chairmen / presidents), alternate governors and members of the councils. At this point, I have not included high civil servants of the central banks (general directors, alternate general directors, etc.), who can nevertheless have a very important practical and decisional role inside the organization, but who do not take part formally (namely, with voting rights) in the main economic and political decisions of the banks, the decisions on leading interest rates.[1]

It might seem relatively easy to find biographical information about central bankers. Different professionals from the financial institutions understand very well the strategic importance of knowing more concretely the persons in this field. 'Buba'-watchers, European Central Bank-watchers, the economic and financial media practically scrutinize *who is who* in the councils and, especially, who the persons just nominated are and what the possible consequences of their nomination might be for the implementation of the monetary policy of the bank. This practical interpretative work rests on a sort of biographical spontaneous inference: some members are, for example, supposed to be 'hawks' or 'doves' (which means more or less concerned with inflation and close to economic-monetary orthodoxy), according to their various successive positions takings in the press, their institutional and professional backgrounds, their social networks, etc.

As main sources of our own research, we used:

– publications and newsletters of Central Banking Publications Ltd, especially the *Who's Who in Central Banking?*, published by Morgan Stanley Bank.
– the official Web-sites of the Central Banks;
– other diverse Web-sites of Central Bank-watchers;
– national and international *Who's Who* (accessible, for example, at the library of the European Commission in Brussels);
– journalistic articles and books;
– interviews.

Biographical information, of course, is dependent on the official production of biographical data. It has been noted by various scholars that the media and the political field contribute to the social construction of individuals through a collective and individual strategic work on the biographies (Collovald, 1988). This requires me to be prudent in the use of biographical data coming from these kinds of sources; but the direct collection of data through surveys being difficult if not impossible in this field, we are forced to rely mainly on these data.

The statistical method used in this work is Geometric Data Analysis, and more precisely, specific Multiple Correspondence Analysis (Le Roux and Rouanet, 2004, 369–384). This is the method used by Bourdieu in *Distinction* which seeks to array a range of modalities (variables) in geometric space, using a version of principal components analysis. It is a method that can be used to display the positions of agents within a field, in keeping with the field being researched (according to sociological understandings of the kinds of factors relevant). This allows me to *construct a social space*. The more that individuals differ on a large number of questions and on rare modalities, the more they are distant from each other in the resulting multidimensional cloud. This cloud – the central object in GDA – is projected on the axes according to the criteria of maximizing variance along each axis (applying spectral analysis theorem). Resulting axes are orthogonal to one another. The first axes give a summary of the main distances in the overall cloud: one has to determine the number of axes to be interpreted and providing the best summary, through the use of eigenvalues and (modified) rates of variance. Two related clouds are then studied using relative contributions of questions and modalities to the axes: the cloud of individuals (which contains all relevant information) and the cloud of modalities (which can be seen as a synthesis of mean properties of the space).[2]

Finally, supplementary elements (i.e., further questions which are not used to construct the space itself, but which may be associated with it) are projected onto the space. This makes it possible to interpret the axes through looking at what kind of additional factors appear to be related with the organization of social space.[3]

This method is consistent with my interest in exploring the nature of inter-individual variability in a social space structured by dominant oppositions. It has been successfully used, for example, in the study of the French space of company managers (Bourdieu, 1978). This approach can be seen as a complementary alternative to social network approach in the sense that it considers fields as strong social structures resulting from the unequal distribution of various social resources. Rather than focus on the networks linking members of elites, it allows us to assess how similar or different they are in terms of a range of relevant attributes, such as their education and career trajectory.

## The space of governors in the world around 2000: a first global picture

As already stated, the space of central bankers can be described as a sub-space of the global field of power, which is the field of dominant agents in contemporary global society. This sub-space is even relatively 'central' in the structure of the global field; it is composed of very diverse forces representing most of the main poles of the global field of power: the economic and political powers, the university, the media, etc. These forces compete inside the field defined by the institution of the central bank to impose a certain direction to the monetary (and macroeconomic) control of the economy. The central bank is a State institution controlling the rules and some of the conditions of the monetary market, which makes it a very particular – and to some extent central – player in the global economic field. The precise conditions of its interventions vary, of course, according to national history and specific legal and political conditions; but it is relatively homogeneous now in the context of the liberalization of financial markets since the second half of the 1980s.

A specific MCA was performed, with 10 active questions and 37 modalities. More detailed results are described in Lebaron (2000). Three headings have been chosen to construct the social space: educational trajectory (8 modalities), career (10) and professional trajectory (19). This last heading contains 19 active modalities, which means it comprises more than half of the total number of active modalities. An important role in the construction of the space is therefore played by the set of institutions that an individual went through, besides the dominant traits of his (all the individuals here are male) educational trajectory and career, which contain 18 modalities, well balanced between both aspects. To summarize, the following modalities are used to construct the social space

- Educational trajectory (8): Discipline (4), Diploma (4)
- Career (dominant) (10): Place of the career (3), Sector (7)
- Professional trajectory (19) has had a position in the following institutions: Central Bank (2), Private Sector (3), Other administration (3), University (3), International Organization (5), Political Field (3).

Four axes have been retained for the complete statistical and sociological interpretations of the MCA (see Table 1). The first four axes represent 31.3 per cent of the total variance of the cloud, ie a modified rate of 79.7 per cent. We will centre in this synthesis on the first principal plane (axes 1 and 2).

The cloud of individuals resulting of this specific MCA has a triangular form in plane 1–2 (see Figure 1). Among these individuals, one can locate well-known personalities: Alan Greenspan (Federal Reserve Bank), a bit down on axis 2, Jean-Claude Trichet (who is now president of the European Central Bank after having been the governor of the Banque de France) on the right on axis 1, Ernst Welteke (then governor of the Bundesbank) and Wim Duisenberg (then president of the ECB), on the top of axis 2.

The relations between these agents can of course also be analysed in terms of social networks (Marcussen, 2003) they are members of certain institutions, which create various institutional or professional links between them. But we can also see that they occupy positions which are structurally impossible to reduce to ties inside a social network, and which relate to variations in their types of social trajectories, and to the specific sorts of capital they have been accumulating. Their position in a social space is not based on the structure of ties in a network but on distances between sociological properties. As Bourdieu noticed, networks are grounded on a kind of 'interactionist' view of social relations. For him, people who never meet each other are nevertheless objectivly related, through the different volumes and compositions of assets they possess. Social capital can not be seen as entirely independent from other sorts of capital and, on the contrary, it tends to the reproduction of unequal positions (Bourdieu, 1989).

Figure 2 shows the properties associated with these individuals. The first axis separates the insiders (who made their career inside the central bank, at the International Monetary Fund, or at the World Bank, which appear to be closely related to a career in the central banks) and 'personalities' who were appointed at the head of the central bank after a mainly academic, political or economic

**Table 1:** *Eigenvalues and rates of variance*

|  | Axis 1 | Axis 2 | Axis 3 | Axis 4 |
|---|---|---|---|---|
| Eigenvalues (λ) | .239 | .220 | .199 | .190 |
| Raw rates of variance | 8.9 | 8.1 | 7.3 | 7 |
| Modified rates | 30.2 | 22.1 | 15.1 | 12.3 |
| Cumulated modified rates | 30.2 | 52.3 | 67.4 | 79.7 |

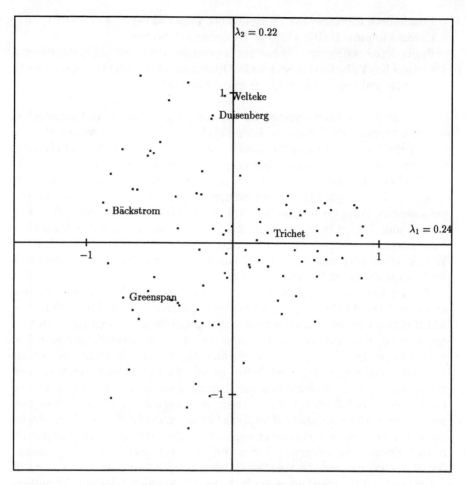

**Figure 1:** *The Space of Governors with personalities. Cloud of individuals in plane 1-2.*

trajectory and whose symbolic capital has been accumulated inside the global field of power but *outside* the bank. This first axis corresponds to competing definitions of economic excellence, which depend on the length of time with national and international public monetary and financial institutions: the position of governor can be described as the end of a specifically achieved internal career or can be, by contrast, a position invested by political, academic or financial actors at a certain moment of their personal trajectories.

The second axis corresponds to the opposition between the universe of global private finance and private enterprise on one side and the university and politics on the other, between individuals with a Bachelor of Arts (less educational capital) and the ones with a PhD. It is an opposition between an intellectual-political definition of excellence and a more pragmatic one, which can be observed as a principle of definition in many debates concerning monetary policy.

Figure 2 therefore shows that one can interpret the characteristics of an agent as personal structural properties. The position of an individual in the cloud of

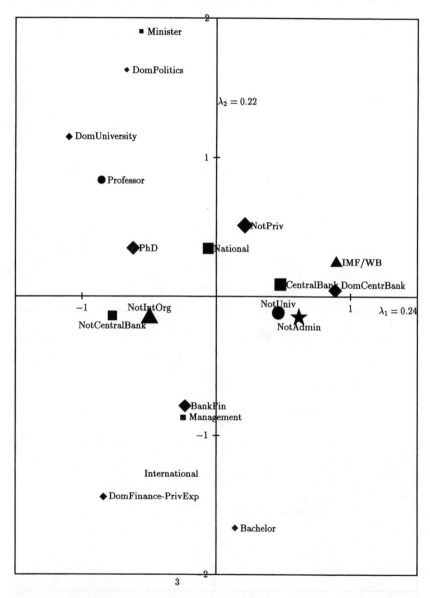

**Figure 2:** *The Space of Properties of the Governors. Cloud of modalities in plane 1-2. Modalities contributing the most either to the first or to the second principal axis.*

modalities lays at the barycentre (centre of gravity) of its own modalities. We see for example in Figure 3 that Alan Greenspan accumulates properties which are often opposed, like the links with the political field, the highest academic degree (PhD in economics) and a career of economic expert on the financial markets. This may help to explain the exceptional structure and volume of his

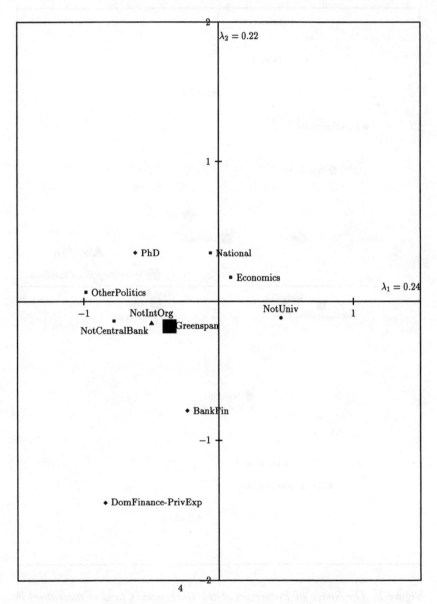

**Figure 3:** *Greenspan in the space of his properties. Cloud of Greenspan's modalities in plane 1-2 with mean-point.*

symbolic capital, which made him one of the most powerful economic actors in the 1990s, especially through his 'influence' on the world financial markets.

Differences between the regions of the world, projected as supplementary elements of the MCA, also appear, mainly on the second axis, with an opposition between Europe (eastern and western) and Latin America on one side (political) and other regions on the opposing side (see Figure 4). This opposition is

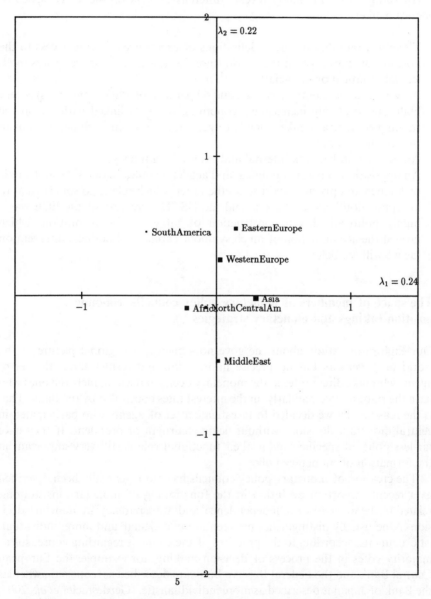

**Figure 4:** *Regions of the World. Supplementary modalities in plane 1-2.*

interesting, since it has often been said that Latin America is a place where the central banks were an important political target investigated by academics with political orientation (the 'money doctors'). Europe (East and West) is also more clearly on this politico-academic side. This study also shows the differentiation of economic excellence according to regions. This should be the subject of a more in-depth investigation with the help of new data.

To summarize, this study reveals different aspects of the social space of central bankers:

- There is a plurality of social definitions of excellence allowing access to the position of 'governor' in the World (more or less internal more or less intellectual, political or financial);
- the weight of economics (with around 40 per cent of PhD economists) is very high, and probably increasing: economics, which is linked with law in the training of central bankers, tends to get a monopoly in leading positions in the recent period;
- An opposition between internal and external legitimacy;
- An opposition between a political and academic pole, on one side, and a pole of finance and private expertise on the other, which relates to some extent to an opposition between Europe and the US. The creation of the ECB was a highly politically-driven construction of an economic institution, which needed the accumulation of much symbolic capital and political intervention (as we will see below).

## The space of members of monetary policy councils: eonomic position-takings and monetary strategies

Our exploratory study about the governors gives a first global picture of the world of governors but no precise information and results about the set of agents who take direct roles in the monetary decision itself, namely the ones who have the right to vote regularly on the interest rates controlled by the Bank. That is the reason why we decided to investigate a set of agents who participated in central monetary decisions without being chairman or president. If they have far less political specific capital, their functional role is still very important in the formation of monetary policy.

The creation of monetary policy councils has more generally been described as a recent important evolution in the functioning of monetary institutions, related to the move toward 'independence' and 'transparency' in monetary decisions. One usually distinguishes between more 'collegial' and more 'individualistic' councils, according to the practices of the councils regarding consensus or majority votes in the process of decision making; for example, the European Central Bank and the Federal Reserve Bank are described as 'collegial', whereas the Bank of Japan is described as more individualistic. (Gerdesmeier *et al.*, 2007; Chappell *et al.*, 2005).

In a more in-depth perspective, biographical information was collected about the members of the French *Conseil de la politique monétaire* (CPM, 'monetary policy council'), which existed between January 1994 and the end of 1998 as an independent central bank council (it was not abolished after this period but it lost its decision-making role over the interest rates); and, more recently, about the three councils which manage the three dominating currencies of the World, namely the Federal Open Market Committee (Fed), the Council of the Bank of Japan (BoJ) and the Governing Council of the ECB.

*The 'Conseil de la Politique Monétaire': under the control of 'énarques' (alumni from Ecole Nationale d'Administration) and of the Treasury*

Is there a French specificity in the definition of monetary excellence as it is objectified by the nomination in the council of the central bank? To answer this question, information about the members of the CPM was collected mainly through the *Who's who in France*, the press (mostly the economic press) and interviews (an interview of a former member and interviews of members of the staff or economists). A comparison was made between an 'ideal' council, proposed by an economic newspaper (*Le Nouvel Economiste*) a few months before the appointment of new members, and the real council which was finally constituted (after a decision by the prime minister Edouard Balladur).

The main conclusion of this monograph assesses the strong stability of the definition of monetary excellence in France, even after important changes like the beginning of European monetary unification. Still in leading positions are the Ecole Nationale d'Administration (ENA), the *'grand corps'* of the Inspection des finances and the Treasury, as the heart of financial administration. These still dominate in the banking sector, as shown in Bauer and Bertin-Mourot, 1997). Weaker in contrast is the more academic definition of economic excellence, which tends to be defined by the PhD in economics and a career trajectory in the universities in the Anglo-Saxon world. This leads us to the question of the competition between the French type of bureaucratic 'economics' capital and the Anglo-Saxon definition of practical economic expertise, in a context of the globalization of economic institutions. The social trajectories of the members also seem defined by a rapid social ascension, predominantly inside the public sector but sometimes in the corporate world. The study describes the central bank council of the Bank of France as a *'lieu neutre'* (neutral place), in the sense of Bourdieu and Boltanski (1976), which means a place where different dominant social interests are discussed, confronted and synthesized. This actually corresponds to the official ideology of the colleges, defined as pluralistic, apolitical, independent of parties. I have shown that the structure of the field of power is present, with a particular refraction, inside the specific space of the French central bank.

*Frédéric Lebaron*

## The space of council members in the world

I now report a more systematic account of the variations between different councils. In order to construct a space of the world-leading monetary policy councils, more diverse information than that collected about the governors was necessary: information about the symbolic capital of agents; socio-demographic data; indicators of position-takings (including textual data). We used the *Who's who in central banking*, European and national *Who's Who*, information and texts on various websites. A global indicator of symbolic capital of the members (coded in three positions: + / = / −) was constructed after a specific study of citations in the two journals *Le Monde* and *The Financial Times* over a definite period covering the 1990s (which probably over-represents the symbolic capital of Europeans).

In the exploratory study presented above, a small number (n = 39) of individuals have been retained. They are the voting members of the three leading monetary councils in the World: Federal Open Market Committee, Governing Council of the European Central Bank, and the Policy Council of the Bank of Japan. The period of study is the beginning of 2003.

The composition of the population is the following: Federal Open Market Committee, 12 members: 7 members of the Board of Governors and 5 members of the district banks (who are permuting regularly, except the representative of the Federal Bank of New York); Council of governors of the ECB, 18: 6 members of the Directory and 12 governors of National Central Banks; Policy Council of the Bank Of Japan 9: 1 governor, 2 alternate governors, 6 members. This structure gives more weight to the members of the ECB, who are twice as numerous as the members of the BoJ. But our aim was to integrate only the agents having a right to vote on interest rates during the period of data collection. This composition also gives an idea of the institutional differences between the three councils, which can be more or less federal, give more or less formal independence to the bank, etc.

A Specific MCA was performed, with 10 active questions and 28 active modalities (with 'unknown' information put as passive modalities). The headings, active questions and active modalities of the specific MCA were:

*General trajectory*

− socio-demographic characteristics (age [3] 1 = born before 1940; 2 = between 1940 and 1950 (not included); 3 = 1950 and after).

*Symbolic capital*

− symbolic capital (presence in the *Who's who in Central Banking 1997* [3] and symbolic capital indicator [3]: 1 = strong (+); 2 = intermediate (=); 3 = weak (−)).
− number of years in the position (years [3]): 1 = 2000 and after, Seniority − 2 = 1998 and 1999, Seniority =; 3 = 1997 and before, Seniority +)

134 © 2008 The Author. Editorial organisation © 2008 The Editorial Board of the Sociological Review

*Professional trajectory*

– academic trajectory (diploma [5]: 1 = PhD in Economics 2 = Master in Economics 3 = BA in Economics 4 = law and political science 5 = management)
– professional trajectory (enterprise [4]: 1 = banking sector, finance 2 = expertise, consulting, journalism 3 = industry, public enterprise 4 = No enterprise], university [2], administration out of CB [2], CB [2], political field [2], for a total of 12 modalities).

The first axis of the analysis is defined by the questions *Who's who in Central Banking* (.242), symbolic capital (.212), seniority (.160) and diploma (.138). It is an axis of specific symbolic capital.

One finds on the first axis (see Figure 5) an opposition related to the volume of symbolic capital, the level of seniority and between political trajectories and academic ones. On one pole, agents are characterized by their high level of symbolic and institutional capital, acquired during a long period on the council, and on the other one, they are newcomers into this space, which have more recent and scholastic resources. This axis opposes a political pole (on the side of accumulated and established capital) to a more academic one (on the side of the newcomers).

On the second axis (see Figure 6), the questions that contribute the most are diploma (.347), corporate trajectory (.185), academic trajectory (.153) and age. It is an opposition between industry, practical competence (relatively distant from economics), and scientific expertise. We have here an opposition between an economic-practical (industrial) and an intellectual-academic pole inside the field of power. This opposition, already somewhat evident in the global field of governors (esp. on axis 2) is more clear-cut here. Maybe we find here a

**Table 2:** *Eigenvalues and rates of variance*

|  | Axis 1 | Axis 2 | Axis 3 |
|---|---|---|---|
| Eigenvalues ($\lambda$) | .2663 | .19425 | .18648 |
| Raw rates of variance | 14.7% | 10.7% | 10.3% |
| Modified rates | 50.8% | 16.3% | 13.7% |
| Cumulated modified rates | 50.8% | 67.1% | 80.4% |

**Table 3:** *Contributions of headings*

|  | Axis 1 | Axis 2 | Axis 3 |
|---|---|---|---|
| General trajectory | .20 | .50 | .38 |
| Symbolic capital | .62 | .16 | .22 |
| Professional trajectory | .18 | .34 | .40 |

**Table 4:** *Relative contributions on Axis 1*

| Relative contributions (Ctr) | Left side | Right side |
|---|---|---|
| Symbolic capital + | | .171 |
| Who's who in Central Banking | | .167 |
| Seniority − | .100 | |
| Master in Economics | | .083 |
| Not Who's who in CB | .074 | |
| Political trajectory | | .073 |
| Academic trajectory | .049 | |
| Seniority − | .040 | |
| Symbolic capital − | .036 | |

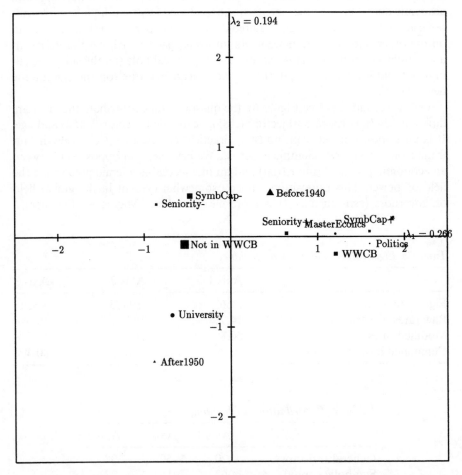

**Figure 5:** *The Space of Monetary Policy Councils. Cloud of modalities in plane 1-2.*

**Table 5:** *Relative contributions on Axis 2*

| Relative contributions (Ctr) | Left side | Right side |
|---|---|---|
| BA in economics | | .152 |
| Industry | | .119 |
| PhD in economics | .119 | |
| Academic trajectory | .110 | |
| Born after 1950 | .102 | |
| Symbolic capital = | .057 | |
| Born before 1940 | | .046 |
| Symbolic capital − | | .045 |
| Not academic | | .043 |

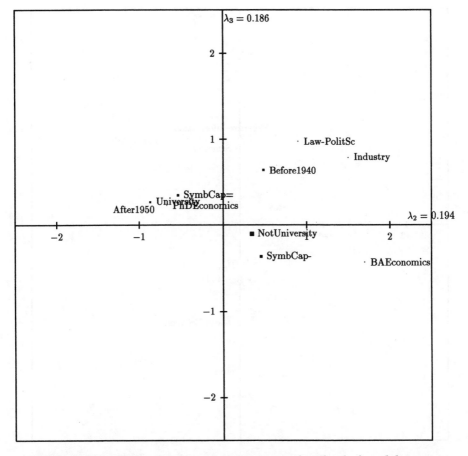

**Figure 6:** *The Space of Monetary Policy Councils. Cloud of modalities in plane 2-3. Interpretation of axis 2.*

first basis for the opposition between pragmatics and 'dogmatics', doves and hawks, which is attested in the general literature about central banks: academics appear closer to the economic dogmas than the more practical economists. The position of notorious 'hawks' like Ben Bernanke (now chairman of the Fed), or Otmar Issing, seems to go into that direction. But more information on the social origins and the position-takings of the individuals should be added here.

Axis 3 (see Figure 7) opposes private expertise accumulated in the longterm corporate world and trajectories which are more recent and more related to the political field or the world of central banks itself. This axis opposes two models of trajectories related either to the private or the public sector (including the political field).

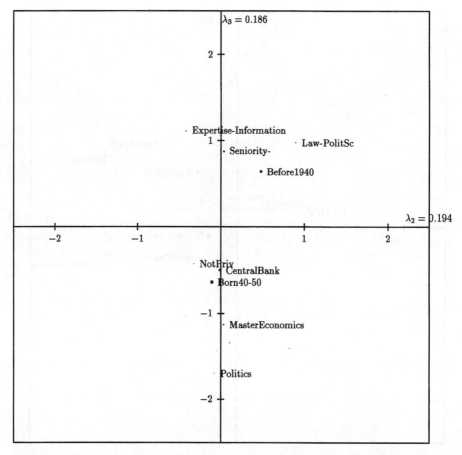

**Figure 7:** *The Space of Monetary Policy Councils. Cloud of modalities in plane 2-3. Interpretation of axis 3.*

**Table 6:** *Relative contributions on Axis 3*

| Relative contributions (Ctr) | Left side | Right side |
|---|---|---|
| Political trajectory | .119 | |
| MA in economics | .106 | |
| Seniority + | | .105 |
| Born between 1940 and 1950 | .096 | |
| Born before 1940 | | .084 |
| Expertise, consulting and journalism | | .068 |
| Law and political science | | .066 |
| Not corporate | .061 | |
| Trajectory in central bank | .046 | |

It is well-known that the three leading central banks have many institutional and practical differences, which make a systematic comparison complex (Gerdesmeier *et al.*, 2007). An important discussion has taken place about the differences in their monetary behaviour. It is usually stated in the economic press and among many economists that the ECB is more dogmatic and anti-inflationist than are both the Fed and the BoJ. The BoJ is less independent and still more related to the networks of industrial powers in Japan; its policy, in a context of deflation, was very expansionist (zero percent rate).

For some scholars of the ECB (Gerdesmeier *et al.*, 2007), referring to so-called 'Taylor-rule estimations', there are no important differences between the Central Banks' recent monetary behaviour. If this point is still a matter of debate, it seems nevertheless very difficult to deny any difference, since the relatively high interest rates in the Eurozone combine to very low inflation and to a structural and long-lasting over-evaluation of the euro. The 'real' consequences of this policy are another point.

We have studied the variable 'central bank' (3 modalities: ECB/Fed/BoJ) as a structuring factor in the space of individuals (on structuring factors in GDA, see Le Roux, Rouanet, 2004:214, 237). As figures 8 and 9 show, the sub-clouds and the modality mean-points of the central banks occupy different positions in the space. On the first axis, the ECB is on the side of higher levels of symbolic capital. Both other councils are on the other side. On the second axis, the BoJ appears on the side of 'practical' and industrial legitimacy, whereas both other banks are more 'academic'. The third axis (see Figure 9) opposes the ECB, on the more political and internal side, and the Federal Reserve Bank much closer to the private sector. This result is consistent with our previous findings about the space of governors.

I conclude that the governing council of the ECB is composed of agents with a higher level of symbolic capital than the other councils, which is

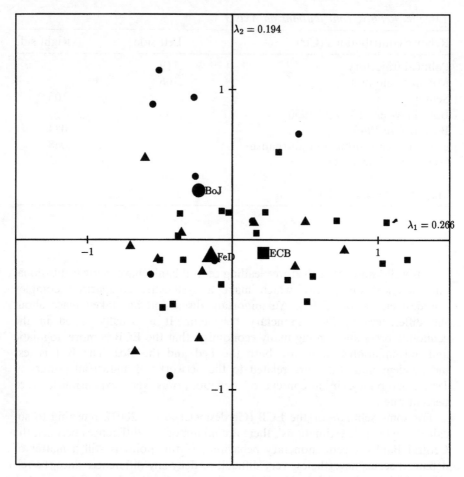

**Figure 8:** *The Space of Monetary Policy Councils. Cloud of individuals in plane 1-2 with mean-points of the Central banks.*

consistent with the idea that the ECB had first to accumulate its legitimacy in the first years of its existence, which was by no means the case for the Fed.

A second aspect here is the specificity of the Bank of Japan as (still in 2003) closely related to industry, which is rooted in the particularities of the Japanese industrial historical model of development, the monetary policy being subordinated in the long term to the industrial strategy and its specific elites. In the period of study, the central bank, though reformed and made more 'independent', has adopted a very 'accommodating' monetary policy

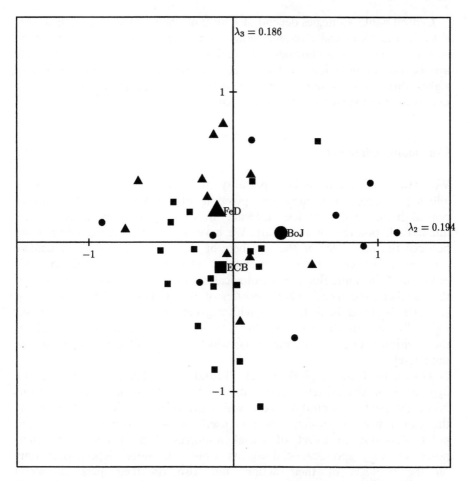

**Figure 9:** *The Space of Monetary Policy Councils. Cloud of individuals in plane 2-3 with mean-points of the Central banks.*

(with zero percent rates) in order to get out of a deep and long-lasting recession and deflation. This behaviour was completely opposed to that of the ECB, which since its creation has tended to adopt an over-reactive anti-inflationist behaviour.

The differences between the ECB and the Fed may also be founded on the particular politico-administrative mood of the ECB as opposed to the more markets-flexible attitude at the Fed, and which could be related to the trajectories of its members, professionally younger and closer to private economic and financial expertise.

Central banks strategies depend of course on their global environment, that is to say the social and economic situation and the strategies of other central banks and economic authorities in general. But the practical sense of economic agents, their more or less 'tacit knowledge' of the economy and the monetary stakes, their national and professional habits, also seem important factors in understanding the global strategies of banks.

## Concluding comments

We have seen that there is a plurality of social definitions of excellence allowing people to occupy the position of 'governor' in the World's central banks (more or less 'internal' in the organization, more or less intellectual, political or financial). We have also seen that the comparison between the properties of the members of three councils reveals systematic differences between three main banks, very probably related to their economic behaviour. But the sociological relation between the properties of the members, the specific characteristics of the councils and their monetary strategies is still difficult to assess with any certainty on this empirical basis, especially due to the lack of direct and comparable information about the position-takings of the members, which are not all made public at the same level.

The general sociological model illustrated in this paper stresses the hypothesis of the existence and stability of socially structured oppositions inside the field of central bankers, which are related to its insertion inside the global field of power, which is itself divided between fractions and poles according to a set of social resources. Central banks are com-posed of very specific social agents whose decisions depend not only on the contexts of their action, but also on their personal social properties.

Reference to the social 'embeddedness' of economic actions and decisions can then be extended to macroeconomic policy-making and to the structural conditions in which economic practices take place, which do not reduce to ties in a network. This economic-sociological approach is a way to integrate inter-individual variability in the understanding of economic processes and to uncover social regularities and structures inside (dominant) social fields.

## Notes

1 Specific MCA consists of putting certain modalities of active questions as 'passive modalities' (which means that they do not create the distance), without disturbing the main properties of symmetry of the method.

2 Readers not familiar with multiple correspondence analysis may find it useful to refer to the worked through example by Modesto Gayo-Cal, Mike Savage, and Alan Warde, (2006) where the method is unpacked for a non-expert audience.

3 In a recent study about members of the European Commission, French scholars focus, on the contrary, on the intermediate administrative high-level (General Directorates and Alternate General Directorates, see Georgakakis, de Lassalle, 2007) more than on the corresponding level of the Commissioners.

# References

Abolafia, M., (2006), 'Interpretive politics at the Federal Reserve', in K.K. Cetina, A. Preda (eds), *The Sociology of Financial Markets*, Oxford: Oxford University Press.

Bauer, M. and Bertin-Mourot, B., (1997), Collaboration de C.Laval, *L'ENA est-elle une Business School? Etudes Sociologiques sur les Enarques Devenus Cadres d'entreprise de 1960 à 1990*, Paris: L'Harmattan.

Blinder, A., (2004), *The Quiet Revolution: Central Banking Goes Modern*, New Haven: Yale University Press.

Bourdieu, P., (1989), *La Noblesse d'Etat. Grandes écoles et Esprit de Corps*, Paris: Minuit.

Bourdieu, P. and Boltanski, L., (1976), 'La production de l'idéologie dominante', *Actes de la Recherche en Sciences Sociales*, 2–3, Juin: 4–73.

Chappell, H.W.Jr., McGregor, R.R. and Vermilyea, T.A., (2005), Committee decisions on monetary policy, Evidence from historical records of the FOMC. Cambridge Mass: MIT Press.

Collovald, A., (1988), 'Identité(s) stratégique(s)' *Actes de la Recherche en Sciences Sociales*, **73**: 29–40.

Gayo-Cal, M., Savage, M. and Warde, A., (2006), 'A cultural map of the UK, circa 2003', *Cultural Trends, 58/59.*

Georgakakis, D. and de Lassalle, M., (2007), 'Genèse et structure d'un capital institutionnel européen', *Actes de la Recherche en Sciences Sociales*, Mars: 166–167.

Gerdesmeier D. *et al.*, (2007), 'The Eurosystem, the US federal reserve and the bank of Japan, Similarities and differences', working paper series, ECB.

Hjellbrekke J. *et al.*, (2007), The Norwegian field of power anno 2000, *European Societies*, Vol. 9, 2: 245–273.

Lebaron, F., (1997), 'Les fondements sociaux de la neutralité économique. Le conseil de la politique monétaire de la Banque de France', *Actes de la Recherche en Sciences Sociales*, 116/117, Mars: 69–90.

Lebaron, F., (2000), 'The Space of Economic Neutrality. Trajectories and Types of Legitimacy of Central Bank Managers', *International Journal of Contemporary Sociology*, **37**, 2, October: 208–229.

Lebaron, F., (2006), *Ordre monétaire ou chaos social? La BCE et la révolution néo-libérale*, Bellecombe-en-bauges: Croquant.

Le Roux, B. and Rouanet, H., (2004), *Geometric Data Analysis. From Correspondence Analysis to Structured Data Analysis*, Amsterdam: Kluwer.

Marcussen, M., (2003), 'Knowledge, power and monetary bargaining: central bankers and the creation of monetary union in Europe', *Journal of European Public Policy*, Vol. **10**, 3, June: 365–379.

Swedberg, R., (2003), *Principles of Economic Sociology*, Princeton: Princeton University Press.

Woodward, B., (2001), *Maestro. Greenspan and the American Boom*, New York: Simon & Schuster.

*Frédéric Lebaron*

*Programmes*

Specific Multiple Correspondence Analysis is a programme of the ADDAD library written by Brigitte Le Roux and Jean Chiche
Download: http://www.math-info.univ-paris5.fr/~lerb/
The figures were created with LaTeX. Our thanks to AsTeXassociation and especially to Michel Lavaud.

# What do heads of dealing rooms do? The social capital of internal entrepreneurs

*Olivier Godechot*

One well established phenomenon today is the return of inequalities during the late 20th century and the rise of a new elite – called the *working rich* by Atkinson and Piketty (2007). Wealthy chief executive officers (CEOs), who more or less directly set their own pay at higher levels each years (Bebchuck *et al.*, 2002), are not solely responsible for this trend. As Savage and Williams argue in the introduction to this volume, financial intermediaries play an important part, especially in financial centres. What is more, inequalities grow not only between finance and the rest of the economy but also within financial firms (Godechot and Fleury, 2005). In one of France's leading banks, Societé Générale, the differential ratio between the shares of the best paid 10 per cent and the worst paid 10 per cent increased from four times in 1997 to eight times in 2006. Higher up the ladder, the trends are even more marked. The average compensation (fixed wage and bonus) of the ten best paid persons in Societé Générale moved from 760,000 Euros in 1994 up to 6 millions Euros in 2000.[1] The top ten best paid includes many who are neither CEO nor chief financial officers nor, strictly speaking, 'traders' or 'sales' managers, although they are often designated by these terms. They are generally 'Head of' some activity or department, as in Head of Dealing Rooms, Head of (big) desks, or Head of Departments such as 'Equities', 'Equity Derivatives', 'Credit Derivatives'.

Such a shift is not well explained by the common neoclassical hypothesis of biased technological progress, which raises the demand for, and hence the price of, rare and productive skills. (Murphy and Zábojník, 2004). Other explanations need to be explored. In our previous work (Godechot, 2006; Godechot, 2007), we have shown how elite financial workers gain power through the appropriation of productive assets within the firm. First, this implicit property provides the legitimacy for claiming the fruits of 'their' assets. Second, employees benefit fully from any moves they make (or could potentially make) through this dynamic labour market since they carry with them intangible assets, like know-how or customer lists, that are difficult to protect, (Godechot, 2006).

In this chapter we would like to detail the importance of social capital for workers in finance, especially for the Heads of Dealing Rooms. Several studies have already shown the importance of social capital in this sector as well as its impact on compensation (Burt, 1997; Burt, 2006; Gargiulo *et al.*, 2006). Lacking precise analysis of how labour markets function, however, previous research has concentrated solely on certain dimensions of social capital, like how information circulates in an organization or the mechanisms of selective matching leading to pay disparities between men and women (Roth, 2006). In order to understand the effects of social capital more broadly, it is important not to rely solely on formal and managerial relations, as described in HR 360 evaluations and such like. One must also analyse carefully what heads of dealing rooms really do. To make some progress in this direction, we undertook three years of mixed methods fieldwork on compensation in the financial industry between 2000 and 2002 mainly in Paris but secondarily in London. During this fieldwork, a hundred interviews were conducted with diverse actors in the financial industry. In one bank, I was able to make direct observations as a trainee in the internal HR service that had to manage the bonus pool process. In a second bank, with the help of a trade union, I distributed a questionnaire to employees in order to measure their subjective feelings about bonus and obtained 80 answers. In a third bank, after HR insiders gave me access to wage data, I could study the compensation structure. Financial and social annual reports (*les bilans sociaux*) were collected as well as corporate press releases.

One important issue concerns how social capital relates to workforce flows in the labour market. Some senior employees are able to use the leverage of their accumulated social capital and take their teams with them whenever they change employers, seemingly mobilizing diversified contacts and relatively tightly-knit groups towards this end. Multiple employee moves from one company to another may be hard to measure statistically but they do appear frequent in this world. We counted around a dozen in our survey of the Paris financial sector. We observed that collective moves were particularly beneficial to the person organizing this operation, usually the Head. In 1999, for example, the Head of an Equity Derivatives group and his deputy resigned together, giving their employer, a large bank, just 48 hours to match a rival offer they had received. During the ensuing negotiations, they used the threat of leaving the bank with their entire team. Hence, they could use their social capital to move the scheme along. Their new contracts earned the Head and his deputy €10 million and €7 million respectively in 2000 (Godechot, 2006).

Analysing the relational structure underlying team moves can help us to trace the making of a financial elite. But it also enables us to develop our understanding of social capital. In recent years, many studies on social capital (Granovetter,1995; Burt 2005; Godechot and Mariot, 2004) have tried to link two contradictory aspects of relational activities: profits generated by the diversification and the non-redundancy of relationships (Burt, 1992); and profits relating to network closure and group cohesion (Coleman, 1988). Diversified relationships make it easier to build entities that are larger but more fragile in nature. Cohesive relationships create team spirit but also generate a lateral control system that makes it harder for a leader to emerge. To study these questions, we need to analyse what Heads of Dealing Rooms do to produce a system of relationships that is profitable both in the workplace and also in the labour market. Towards this end, we suggest that these people are internal entrepreneurs, similar to the proto-industrial 'bosses' described by Marglin (1974). Like them, Heads of Dealing Rooms try to create a central lynchpin role for themselves by subdividing and recombining work. In addition, they must be able to get the whole group to move en masse – raising questions as to the stability of a firm's boundaries when, as is the case in finance, social capital-based internal entrepreneurship has started to emerge.

## The head of dealing room as an internal entrepreneur

Heads of Dealing Rooms seem to be in a privileged position in financial dealing rooms. Statistical analysis of pay in the finance sector has revealed the rising compensation of these Heads (Godechot and Fleury, 2005). In terms of legitimising the appropriation of profits, a Head of Trading or Head of Sales running a financial products team, and to an even greater extent a Head of Dealing Room, occupies a position akin to a first-tier contractor and original promoter of the activity (Godechot, 2007). Changes in financial organization have also tended to increase the Heads' power to capture profit by concentrating it in their hands. It is more than a suggestive metaphor to call the Heads entrepreneurs. In this extreme example, we may very well discover certain basic characteristics of entrepreneurship, traits that are more visible when the entrepreneurship is in its embryonic phase, that is, when other entrepreneur functions have not yet started to mask the prime function of capturing profit.

Reading Bernard Mottez's (1960, 1966) history of the different forms of wage-earning, one is struck by the formal similarity between the position of a Head of Dealing Room, who is technically an employee, and the 'hagglers' or subcontractor who used to practice 'bargaining' in the early 19th century. The Head of Dealing Room monopolizes most of the power to recruit. He negotiates the bonus system for the whole of the room and presides over its distribution. Usually the Head is in the practical position of being able to determine, via a budget, how much a subordinate is supposed to be paid. The company provides capital, equipment and a back office. The Head of Dealing Room provides a team of professionals.

Stephen Marglin (1974), an astute observer of the early Industrial Revolution, has analysed the embryonic forms of capitalist firms under '*the putting-out system*' and characterized, in a famous article entitled 'What do bosses do?' the essence of entrepreneurial activity. Reversing the technological determinism found in some of Marx's texts, he has tried to show how technology is a consequence of social order and not a cause thereof. In his opinion, the division of labour was not adopted because of its greater efficiency but because it dispossessed workers of any control over their work and turned entrepreneurs into coordinators who by becoming indispensable to production acquire a situation of power in which they could earn greater profits and pursue a capital accumulation logic. The entrepreneurs' strategy is therefore to '*divide and conquer*' (Marglin, 1974: 35).

By transforming complex work into simple work, entrepreneurs shift the rent generated at the level of the individual self-employed craftsperson into the hands of the entrepreneur-coordinator. The division of labour is a strategic option, not as much because it makes it possible to produce things in a more technical fashion but because it modifies the locus where rent is captured. The entrepreneur who dispossesses the workers of their work can pay them less and can force them into competition with less skilled workers. Marglin alludes to imperfect competition, which probably plays a major role in this mechanism. A product market is protected by entry barriers, seemingly unlike an unqualified labour market. This means that entrepreneurs are capturing the rents that self-employed craftsperson used to possess. At the same time, entry barriers protect entrepreneurs from the transfer of this rent to consumers via some kind of price mechanism. Under these conditions, the resulting division of labour is politically optimal for the entrepreneurs alone: it is neither a technical optimum nor a social one.

This comparison of recent changes in the finance sector with the beginnings of the Industrial Revolution may appear odd and forced. It brackets employees in very different circumstances, the miserable conditions of manual industrial workers contrasting with the opulence of financial traders and executives who are empowered to conduct negotiations. But there are suggestive similarities between the processes at work, despite the differences in context. In our case, it is not so much the capitalist entrepreneur per se who pursues the 'divide and conquer' strategy but an employee, the Head of Dealing Room. The Head is tantamount to a workforce subcontractor who appropriates some of the subordinates' rent by subdividing, re-combining and managing the assigned workload to ensure his own indispensability. Pay in the finance sector may have globally increased in recent years, due to a sharp rise in volume, but this has been accompanied by greater hierarchical disparities. This chapter explains how basic financial traders or salespeople have been appropriating a relatively smaller share of increased profits, with Team Managers appropriating a relatively larger share.

## Subdivide and recombine

The political division of labour is an emerging effect, because the multiple effects that the division of labour produces often become visible only over time. In a new activity in finance, people always start out with the idea of subdividing work so as to increase efficiency, then occupy the terrain and mine the ore for as long they can before the competition attacks. A division is initially organized, sometimes euphorically, and everyone is keen to take part. It is only at a much later stage that people notice that the division of labour has been a process for managing interpersonal competition and that it conveys pre-determined forms of value sharing. The history of the division of financial labour is a recurring one of product discoveries by development teams, company launches as with hedge funds, and back office re-organizations; and all of these have emerging effects.

For instance, the Head of a Sales team at Mars Bank became very successful in a short period of time by promoting a range of derivative products tailor-made for customer needs. The team he put together to build on this success, however, was not comprised of peers or apprentices to whom he might communicate the whole of the business. The exceptions were team members located abroad, colleagues of equal seniority and peers he could not really control whom he described as 'free options'. But, more generally, any newcomers brought in were specialists in fields like tax, law, financial engineering or marketing, so that individuals had a particular set of competencies and undertook a series of tasks that the Head of Sales alone was in a position to re-combine:

> I've got guys now who are doing pure structuring [ie designing financial products] so my commercial staff can concentrate on sales and nothing else. (. . .) What I've done is separate the work into two so that some guys' job is to have ideas and produce brochures, whereas others are supposed to become best friends with CFOs who are potential customers.

The division of labour here possesses a Smithian dimension of efficiency as well as a Marglinian political dimension that is not necessarily intentional but whose force is augmented precisely because the former dimension masks the latter. By positioning himself in the middle of a division of labour that he orchestrates, the Head of Sales can keep the lion's share of a rent whilst enjoying the legitimization of its distribution (as he said, 'If you ask me, I've made a positive contribution'.

The political division of labour is not always an unintentional effect of a Smithian division of labour. If we retrace the division of labour in the derivative products area from the mid-1980s until the mid-1990s, we note that the division of labour has also been viewed as a political instrument for preventing autonomous financial actors from capturing an activity. The main organizer of the Saturn Bank's Options Department designed its development in opposition to the 'trader' model prevalent at the time in other banks, which he criticized for poor change management and for inability to devise a lasting activity. He also explained that he always wanted to avoid the kind of financial handicraft that relies on the juxtaposition of autonomous crafts persons:

> There was an inherent weakness in the old way of doing things: these were individual performances, not group ones. (. . .) What was really bad was how this personalized the work. At times we had a star system, with just one person dominating the whole marketplace. But it's impossible for a single individual, lacking the support of a group or a particular methodology, to last.

Individual performance cannot be relied upon long term because it is safe neither from adverse economic conditions nor from the possibility that the person in question will leave one day. This former Head of Options said about his experience at Saturn Bank that his aim had been to create a 'collective rent'.

This ex-engineer educated at one of France's top schools, after working a few years for banking information system was given the opportunity in 1985 to construct an options trading operation. He immediately realized then that this new product 'offered both leverage and safety' and sensed an opportunity to 'build an empire'. With a process background acquired during the reorganization of the bank's information system, he came into this new product area firmly committed to creating an entity that would be both technically and socially integrated:

> Our policy was to develop our own software and buy nothing . . . we wanted significant integration between our processes, back office, accounting, front office, etc. We also wanted to be responsible for sorting out any problems, if possible by applying a standard of maximum excellence.

To counter any departures that might have undermined his new structure, he tried to promote, via an advanced division of labour, what Durkheim called 'organic solidarity' (Durkheim, 1998 [1893]), that is a solidarity rooted in differentiation, which is more robust than mechanical solidarity when social norms weaken.

In the end, it was this outsider to finance who began to promote an industrial conception of finance (Clark, Thrift, 2005) that could not really come from more traditional activities like stock-broking, portfolio management in Equities or the '*cambists*' in Foreign Exchange. His approach was based on starting from scratch with the models he wanted to use; creating his own software; training his own employees who were recruited directly upon graduation from the best schools; and, above all, being sceptical about past techniques or actors, bearers of an individual rent that could not be merged with the collective rent he was trying to create. Describing Saturn Bank's Options Department, Uranus Bank's Executive Officer would later say:

> They began to develop software to allow them to manage Foreign Exchange options or any other kind of option. As a result, they took two years longer than we did to launch their options business. But when they finally got going in 1985–1986 they were quite successful.

The goal for the Saturn Head of Options at the time was to create an 'engineering bank' that unlike 'commercial banks' or 'marketing banks' would try to 'to have perfect control over the whole of the risk management and manufacturing process'. Commercial activity was only embarked upon when information technology, modelling, trading and arbitrage processes were all ready. One symbol of such integration was that Saturn Bank was the first to set up rolling Foreign Exchange option books, trade for 24 hours a day and pass from Paris to New York and on to Tokyo.

This modus operandi should be compared with the way that competitors like Uranus Bank constructed their own options trading groups. Uranus opted to acquire blocks of activity that already had a large market presence by buying in teams, software, etc. It took less time for them to become productive – but they were easier to spin off and formed a less durable collective activity. The strengths of Saturn Bank's advanced integration and division of labour should not be exaggerated, however. Despite in-house software and processes, the different elements comprising the entity managed by Saturn's Head of Dealing Room were easy to detach and there was always the threat that a not insignificant proportion of the business could go missing at any point in time. Our ex-manager spoke bitterly about American 'arbitrag*e*' banks (as opposed to the 'innovative' bank he was running) systematically hiring away entire teams with the help of English head-hunters. By taking his employees, they were eating into his collective rent.

Nevertheless, and despite its imperfect efficiency, this is the kind of work organization process that all of the banks surveyed would ultimately end up adopting, and it helped to shift the level at which rents were being capturing. A Head of Dealing Room (and to a lesser degree, a Desk Manager) is there to subdivide, recombine and orchestrate, personally crystallizing a lion's share of a trading division's total value creation. The specialists working below the Heads are often more competent in their own area of specialization but possess little awareness of what is being done on other desks, and even less knowledge of the back or middle offices. In reality, thanks to this divide and conquer strategy, the Head of a Dealing Room is theoretically in a position to break a room's secret value, at least partially, down into simple elements. The manufacturing of these elements can be delegated, but the Head is the only person in a position to recombine them. This is why some, like Saturn Bank's Head of Equity Derivatives group, under whose orders this particular product area had been developed, considered himself:

> lucky to have never had to specialize . . . It would have been completely counterproductive for me to get tied to one area, to settle into it, to say, 'I need to read up on new models', etc. Others could do that. My job was to fit the pieces of the puzzle together so that things ran harmoniously and we could grow as quickly as possible.

Top-down coordination is, de facto, inevitable even when it is disputed. A Head of Dealing Room ends up monopolising the rents that the traders used to split amongst themselves. The Head of Options at Saturn Bank was sufficiently powerful to suggest to Senior Management that a partnership should be set up, a specialist options subsidiary autonomous from the parent company, jointly owned by Saturn Bank and its dealing room managers on a partnership basis.

## Engineering a collective move

Hence organizing work and managing subordinates is not only a technical process undertaken in order to enhance material productivity. It is also a way of managing social capital and building an indispensable position inside the group. This process of centralization is, to a certain extent, similar to the whole structural aspect of social capital described by Burt (1992). But if we were to view it only in this way, we would focus solely on the exercise of power within the group and ignore the power of the group itself when it copes with other groups. An understanding of social capital requires us to link both dimensions.

Bourdieu (1980, 2) is generally cited for his emphasis on group closure because he stresses the durability and permanent nature of relationships and the strong interconnectivity of agents. These are all factors that are likely to engender a strong group when it interacts with other groups. When, on the other hand, Bourdieu affirms that 'it is the same principle that produces a group instituted to enhance the concentration of capital and infra-group competition for the appropriation of social capital' (1980, 3), he is distancing himself from the idea of a jointly-owned form of capital and adopting a more balanced strategic perspective that is closer to Burt. Studying kinship inside Kabyle clans, Bourdieu (1977) showed that the homogeneity and the size of the group was, for its leader, both a positive strength (for harvests or local wars against other clans) and a threat, because it generated costly consumption, risks of schism within the clan and a resulting division of the clan's property. The leader of the clan tries to maintain an equilibrium favourable to his power by constraining its members to appropriate types of marriage (inside or outside the clan). In parallel, Burt's most recent studies (2005) seem to attribute a greater role to group cohesion. He still sees diversification as the main vector of 'value added' (Burt, 2006) but now specifies that the group's cohesion enables trust to develop, reputations to stabilize and the group to line up behind an 'entrepreneur'.

In finance, Heads of Dealing Rooms are powerful not only because they can organize their primacy within the group but also because they build strong groups that can act in their favour. The most striking manifestation of their power is that they can threaten to take all of their subordinates with them if ever they jump ship. The opportunity to redeploy collective assets in the finance business increases the power that the Head acquires through a *divide and conquer* strategy. He can therefore re-allocate groups of people ruling a range of tangible or intangible assets (market share, products, software, customers, etc.). The advantage inherent in a Head of Dealing Room position is organizational, structural and statutory.

The following analytical schema of networks can illustrate and specify our point about the power to engineer a collective move (see Graph 1). A Head of Dealing Room is best placed to get the whole of the floor to move. It would be much harder for a subordinate financial trader to offer a team for sale because coordination costs would be much higher; and it would be even harder to sell the Head or the whole of the dealing room because this would require a reversal in existing subordination and asset allocation relationships.

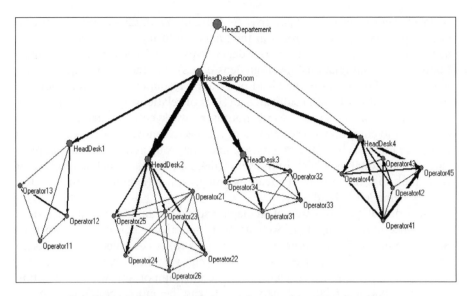

**Graph 1:** *Collaborative Relationships within a Dealing Room.*

The Head of a Market Department is generally not well placed to organize a transfer of activities, for several reasons relating both to the history of markets and to the organization of work. Department Heads like Jean-François Lepetit (2002) are often individuals who supervize a market's development without doing any real trading themselves. They often suffer from a lack of legitimacy and above all from a lack of control over actual assets in the form of customers, market share, etc. For these individuals, it is more a case of approving subordinates' sharing of assets than of granting their own assets. In addition, Heads of Department often supervize the activity from afar. They work in an office, isolated and protected by ranks of secretary desks and their interactions with the Heads of Dealing Rooms remain sporadic. On the contrary the Head of Dealing Room works directly in the dealing room, interacting on a daily basis with all subordinates, engaging in both business and informal discussions. The Head of Dealing Room will make connections that are both strong and diversified. The work organization will ensure that the centrality lying at the heart of the organizational chart is an effective one. Due to this relational centrality, the Head of Dealing Room is better placed to engineer a collective move. He becomes an indispensable intermediary between contacts separated by 'structural holes' (Burt, 1992), among whom he can develop competition in his favour.

But the Head of Dealing Room must take care to preserve also some redundant contacts so as to circumvent, if need be, any second-in-command who may be insufficiently loyal or cooperative. As Gargiulo *et al.* (2006) demonstrate so clearly, to maximize your profits in the finance industry it can be useful to act as the necessary go-between for your dependents (low density ties) whilst entertaining redundant relationships (high density ties) with the persons upon whom you depend. For instance, the Head of Dealing Room on one of the floors we observed (Godechot, 2001) cultivated all sorts of relationships beyond his direct subordinates. Moreover, an overly porous network could weaken the group dynamic and compromise the chances of a collective move. Closely-knit, united teams are more likely to move en masse, since the group as a whole will put pressure on individual members. Employees will be all the more inclined to leave if they think that the bulk of the team is going, with little more than a skeleton activity being left behind.

The originality of this way of managing social capital is that it incorporates the connections' strength as well as their selectivity, density and porosity. Strong connections are more effective than weak ones when the aim is to engineer a team move. To free up the time to cultivate these crucial connections, a Head has to decide which players are the most important, whilst delegating secondary players' relational networks. It can be more economical to get Desk Heads to organize their own teams' departure than to try to strike up a relationship with every single subordinate and then with their subordinates etc. To become a lynchpin, the Head of Dealing Room must also take care to maintain a modicum of relational porosity. If Desk Heads are in a position to move a whole market group without needing the Head of Dealing Room, the latter becomes surplus to requirements. But at the same time, it is also dangerous for the Head of Dealing Room to depend excessively on the Desk Heads' ability to get their own teams to jump ship.

Rising trading volumes have changed the balance of power in dealing rooms. Where a financial activity is still run by a small team of four or five traders, everyone interacts with everyone and the Team Manager has no significant structural advantage over anyone else. The manager has a kind of statutory privilege, and it is hard to imagine a manager accepting a subordinate position at the team's new company. At the same time, where a manager's style has displeased a team, the latter may well decide to jump ship without him. Larger activities encompassing several teams and reporting levels are marked by a more differentiated power structure. What can happen here is that a subordinate trader may well decide to jump ship along with a few colleagues, possibly accompanied by some outsiders, the manager of the group's largest desk and possibly another desk as well (if the individual in question relates well to the other desk managers). The only person capable of moving the whole trading floor, however, is the Head of Dealing Room, who becomes the key element in engineering collective moves due to the fact that he is the person who coordinates and subdivides the work.

During our investigations (based on nearly 100 interviews covering this and other topics), we heard many stories of collective moves, including:

- In 1990, after Drexel Burnham Lambert went bankrupt, its ex-Head of Futures negotiated with Indosuez the recruitment of a 60-person team (Lepetit, 2002: 115);
- A market-making team resigned en masse from Neptune Bank because members refused new risk control measures;
- An equity derivatives team resigned en masse from a London investment bank, starting up a rival firm in Dublin where contractual non-compete clauses did not hold;
- In 1999, a Head of Equity Derivatives and his deputy threatened to leave with the entire floor if the bank employing them did not accede to their pay demands (Godechot, 2006).

These stories are often swapped nonchalantly and can be old and second-hand. Better to understand the mechanisms by means of which a Head of Dealing Room will mobilize a group, it is also useful to undertake a detailed analysis of some failures.

## Limitations on the power to mobilize

It is risky for the bank to organize the replacement of a quitting Head of Dealing Room. Either the Head's successor finds it hard to get along with the teams under his direction and cannot stop people from leaving, or he gets along well with everyone and de facto replicates the ex-Head's structural position including any associated bargaining power. These difficulties about replacing a quitting Head of Dealing Room are especially acute where the successor is apt to show similar secessionist tendencies in the future. But the organization of a succession often provides the bank with an opportunity to gain time and to lock-in company assets.

Some of these issues can be illustrated by considering the story of a failed proposal for internal reorganization in Saturn Bank and the confrontational resignation of Saturn Bank's Head of Options. In 1990 and 1991, facing mass defections by traders head-hunted by English or American banks, this manager's reaction was to try and invent a new institutional form, a partnership that would be 75 per cent owned by Saturn Bank and 25 per cent by 20 or so partner employees. The purpose of this new system was to a stabilise staffing and develop long-term incentives for those who hoped to become a partner. The project's eventual failure was due, according to the Head of Options, to several factors. The Head of Fixed Income and Head of Equities were impatient rivals who wanted to break up his empire. The young Co-Chief Executive Officer, a newly appointed former government inspector, showed little understanding because he was primarily concerned with maintaining the unity of the bank he hoped to chair one day. Finally, the Head of Options did not have the time to promote his project internally. Trusting in his own power and empire, he tried to bulldoze his way through opposition partly by threatening resignation: 'To me this was paramount so I threatened to resign if I didn't get what I wanted'. His miscalculation may have been to think that his department's success was attributable to him personally, when his real power lay in his ability to engineer collective moves.

To combat the impending resignation and staunch the haemorrhaging, the bank organized what its HR managers described as 'a real putsch'. HR allegedly made a surreptitious promise to promote all of the Head of Options' direct subordinates so to prevent them from resigning along with their boss and leaving behind a 'burnt-out shell'. When the Head of Options finally did threaten to resign in 1992, he had not yet developed a credible project in another bank and could offer his team no other host structure if it followed him. It took him a year to put together an alternative project, finally concretizing his partnership idea in the subsidiary of a German bank and taking around a dozen colleagues from Saturn Bank to this new venture. But most of the financial power in the old Options Department, a total of around 300 or 400 employees, stayed put at Saturn.

The ex-Head of Options' rivals were the Heads of Equities, Fixed Income and Foreign Exchange who split up the Options Department so that each ran the options teams associated with their own cash product. Some of the Head of Options' subordinates were promoted to Desk (and even Dealing Room) Manager role and offered a chance to run a relatively autonomous derivative products section within the confines of departments defined by the underlying asset classes. More specifically, three direct subordinates of the ex-Head of Options were put in charge of the Equity Derivative Products group that would by the late 1990s become Saturn Bank's most profitable financial activity as the three subordinates rose hierarchically and revolutionized the pay scale. The ex-Head of Options would still talk about the trio with affection but others called them 'traitors'. Certainly, the ex-Head of Options had taken too much time to engineer a collective departure. By the time he made his move it was too late because the bank had already promoted the key figures he was counting on, realizing that they would be less inclined to leave if they felt attached to the old structure. The ex-Head of Options had lost his ability to take Saturn Bank's assets with him to the new structure.

It is not true that the ability to engineer a collective move automatically increases proportionately with the size of the team involved or the volumes traded. Higher volumes imply the mobilization of a bigger area but also diminish the intensity of mobilization. Going further up the hierarchical scale and dealing with larger volumes connects activities that are more distant and heterogeneous with less intense connections. Governance is done at a distance here and less time is spent with each individual. Leaders can easily fall prey to the counter-manoeuvring of direct subordinates who may hope that the boss will go to make room for their own rise. In the late 1990s, the most strategic structural position for engineering collective moves seems to have been the Head of Dealing Room. After 2000, 15 or so years on from their arrival in the finance industry, these Heads of Dealing started wondering how they might secure their ascent by attaining a status that would finally legitimize their astounding economic success. The lack of any clear response to this meant a whole array of career trajectories took shape within an organization where up to 2001 in the astute judgement of an R&D team manager 'no one questioned the hierarchy established [here] in the 1990s'. After the Head of Options left in 1992, his second-in-command inherited the Equity Derivatives Department, with the original number three becoming Head of Trading and the original number four Head of Sales. Two or three years later, the original second-in-command was promoted to run a financial products subsidiary in Asia, with the original number three replacing him as Head of Equity Derivatives and the original number four becoming his deputy.

The career trajectory of the original third-in-command is particularly interesting. By late 1999, he had been promoted to co-manage, working alongside an American, the whole of the Equity and Investment Department (stock brokerage, equity derivatives, financial analysis and IPOs) and got onto the firm's Executive Committee. The doors to the bank's highest echelons, traditionally closed to market professionals, seemed finally to have opened. Yet this was a risky ascent since it meant that the man being promoted was losing control over the Equity Derivatives group where his former deputy was now responsible. In other words, promotion put a distance between the manager and the entities that had first helped him to gain power. Two years later, the rise of the Equity Derivatives group was consecrated in a new reorganization. It became a distinct and autonomous department at exactly the same level as the equity department that the original third-in-command headed. Hence, this man definitively lost control over the Equity Derivatives group he had originally used as a springboard. He did take over some of the M&A activities that had heretofore escaped his clutches but lost out on control of the more powerful department. His remaining activities, like stock brokerage or M&A, were generally smaller earners at Saturn Bank and were substantial loss makers during the 2001/2002 recession.

Financial traders describing this case talked about how the original third-in-command had been duped, since his former assistant 'did him in' a claim which some traders softened with the reminder that 'it's the least thing to do in this business'. One year later, this former Head of Equity Derivative Dealing Room, had been isolated to the point where he left the bank and indeed the finance business. Unable to control his assets and teams, he had lost much of his power and legitimacy. He had been incapable, during the course of his risky rise, of converting market capital into a different kind of organizational capital.

In the early 2000s, banks were also looking for new contractual limitations on collective moves. But such retention policies have perverse effects and loopholes. The first solution was to try to grant financial operators a deferred bonus or 'golden handcuffs' because the bonus in cash or stocks will be paid only if the employee is still working for the bank. Traders and heads may have good salaries but may be reluctant to move because, if they move to another employer, they will lose accumulated bonuses from previous years. In 2002, a trader from Syrius Bank was trying to build a hedge fund with former colleagues from his bank but did not want simply to resign and abandon his deferred compensation: with the help of his father, an important lawyer, he was successfully fighting to have his bank fire him and therefore pay him his two million Euros of deferred bonus, instead of resigning and abandoning part of his past compensations. In another bank, I was told, some traders were trying to get fired in order to claim deferred bonus. The second solution was to tie employees with non-compete clauses. But the enforceability of such clauses is generally difficult in the courts of law of most countries. Their validity is generally limited in terms of time and space; and it is always possible for a team to escape non-compete clauses by moving from Paris to London, or from London to Dublin. If contractual limitations are not very effective at present, they may become more efficient in the future. But banks will also have to cope with traders and Heads' inventiveness as they try to circumvent them.

This section has demonstrated three kinds of constraints restricting Heads' ability to engineer collective moves in financial dealing rooms during the 1990s: circumstantial constraints as when the Head of Options jumped ship; structural as when the original third-in-command was run out a decade later; and contractual limitations through deferred bonus and non-compete clauses. This analysis of constraints also delineates the forces at work here. A Head of Dealing Room has to manage social capital in a way that is both practical and strategic, an art that cannot be reduced to a mere set of principles. Not only must Heads manage their social capital in a way that will enable them to engineer collective moves but also, in their relationships with their own bosses, they must transform it into a symbolic capital. They must get their own managers, top bank executives in the traditional sense of the term, to believe that they are basically the delegates of a closely-knit team of traders who are all ready to set sail if their conditions aren't met; and that belief in cohesion is often more important than the real cohesion of the team in question. The Head of Dealing Room appropriates the power of the group when speaking with the senior executive in the name of the trading group. At the same time and to maintain primacy, the Head of Dealing Room must add to the number of divisions, distribute privileges, get people to show patience, reward them and avoid being replaced by some alternative coordinator.

## Social capital, the frontiers of the firm and the dynamic of capitalism

We have drawn a highly political portrait of financial activities, which will help us to understand both the concentration of corporate assets in an individual at one point and the advent of internal entrepreneurs, formally categorized as employees but similar to Marglin's (1974) entrepreneur-capitalist. The character of these actors is both capitalist and anti-capitalist. Like traditional entre-preneurs, they accumulate a capital that they will be basically lending to another company or investing in a new business like a hedge fund. But, of course, such capital-intensive accumulation is detrimental to the company employing them and its formal owners (Folkman *et al.*, 2006). It transgresses the traditional boundaries of the firm and the idea of capital as shareholders' exclusive prop-erty (Rajan and Zingales, 2001). Through their social capital, internal entrepre-neurs get control over a substantial part of the firms' productive assets. Since they can move such assets to another firm, they become their practical owner. Hence, the concept of the boundaries of the firm, already shaken by human capital's greater impact (Zingales, 2000), is going to be further undermined by the rising power of social capital which lies even further outside of shareholders' control.

If this expropriation mechanism locally undermines the boundaries of the firm and shareholders' power, is it a threat for capitalism? Not exactly because internal entrepreneurs, with sufficient power and self-confidence, can turn into classical entrepreneurs and true capitalists. With the assets accumulated through working for employers in finance, they can launch a hedge fund. On the ruins of their previous employers' firm, they give birth to new capitalist structures. For instance, John Meriwether had been Head Bond Trader at Salomon Broth-ers before he founded the giant hedge fund Long Term Capital Management, whose 1998 bankruptcy was a front page item. Meriwether launched this fund in 1994 with a team of ex-Salomon colleagues (MacKenzie, 2003). More recently, John D. Arnold was cited by the newspapers as the most highly paid trader who was said to have earned two billion dollars in 2006. But he is no longer an ordinary 'trader' but now a full entrepreneur.[2] Originally, Arnold was one of Enron's biggest traders. After the company's bankruptcy, he founded *Centarius* hedge fund using his 2001 bonus of eight million dollars bonus and hiring former colleagues who accounted for half of his 17 traders in 2006. While many shareholders and workers lost money in Enron's collapse, part of its elite was able to reinvest Enron's intangible assets (team workforce, clients, knowl-edge of trading techniques) in new firms for their own interests. Hedge funds are therefore not just a new class of financial actor or asset class but also a kind of appendix to the traditional banking industry. They are the locus where elite financial workers, raised by traditional banks, gain their autonomy and become new capitalist players.

In a sense, we can see this dynamic as a creative destruction process (Schumpeter, 1943). As Marx says in the Communist Manifesto, 'the bour-geoisie cannot exist without constantly revolutionizing the instruments of pro-duction, and thereby the relations of production, and with them the whole relations of society' (Marx, 2000) Sudden access to wealth is difficult to explain without requiring some form of unequal exchange, some loopholes in the exchange of equivalents against equivalents. The transgression of the bound-aries of the firm thanks to social capital provides the basis for one of these unequal exchanges.

# Notes

1 Salaries are given in constant euros 2005.
2 See for instance Barrionuevo, A., 'Energy Trading, Post-Enron', *The New York Times,* January 15, 2006.

# References

Atkinson, T., and Piketty, T., (2007), *Top Incomes Over the Twentieth Century: A Contrast Between Continental European and English-speaking Countries*, Oxford: Oxford University Press.
Bebchuck, L.A., Fried, J., and Walker, D., (2002), 'Managerial power and rent extraction in the design of executive compensation', *The University of Chicago Law Review* **69**: 751–846.
Bourdieu, P., (1980), 'Le capital social. Notes provisoires', *Actes de la Recherche en Sciences Sociales* **31**: 2–3.
Bourdieu, P., (1977), 'Case study: Parallel-cousin mariage', in Bourdieu P., *An Outline of a Theory of Practice.* Cambridge: Cambridge University Press: 30–71.
Burt, R., (1992), *Structural Holes, The Social Structure of Competition*, Chicago: University of Chicago Press.
Burt, R., (1997), 'The Contingent Value of Social Capital', *Administrative Science Quarterly* **42**: 339–365.
Burt, R., (2005), *Brokerage and Network Closure*, Oxford: Oxford University Press.
Burt, R., (2006), 'Second Hand Brokerage: Evidence from Managers, Bankers, and Analysts', Communication for the 2005 annual meetings of the Academy of Management.
Clark, G., Thrift, N., (2005), 'The Return of Bureaucracy: Managing Dispersed Knowledge in Global Finance', in Knorr Cetina, K., Preda, A., *The Sociology of Financial Markets*, Oxford: Oxford University Press.
Coleman, J., (1988), 'Social capital in the creation of human capital', *American Journal of Sociology* **94** (suppl. 1): 95–120.
Durkheim, É., (1998 [1893]), *De la Division du Travail Social*, Paris: PUF.
Folkman, P., Froud, J., Johal, S., and Williams, K., (2006), 'Working for themselves? Capital market intermediaries and present day capitalism', University of Manchester/ Open University, *Working paper no.25, Centre for Research on Socio-Cultural Change.*
Gargiulo, M., Ertug, G., and Galunic, C., (2006), 'Network Structure and Individual Performance in Investment Banks', 22nd Egos Colloquium, Bergen, 6–8 July.
Godechot, O., (2001), *Les Traders*, Paris: La Découverte.
Godechot, O., (2006), Hold-up en finance. Les conditions de possibilité des bonus élevés dans l'industrie financière, *Revue Française de Sociologie* **47** (suppl. 2): 341–371.
Godechot, O., (2007), *Working Rich: Salaires, bonus et appropriation du profit dans l'industrie financière,* Paris: La Découverte.
Godechot, O., Fleury, C., (2005), 'Les nouvelles inégalités dans la banque', *Connaissance de l'emploi* Centre d'Études de l'Emploi, **17**.
Godechot, O., Mariot, N., (2004), 'Les deux formes du capital social. Structure relationnelle des jurys de thèse et recrutement en science politique', *Revue française de sociologie* **45** (suppl. 2): 243–282.
Granovetter, M., (1995), 'The Economic Sociology of Firms and Entrepreneurs', in: Portes, A. (ed.), *The Economic Sociology of Immigration*, New York: Russell Sage Foundation Publications.
Lepetit, J.-F., (2002), *Homme de Marché*, Paris: Economica.
MacKenzie, D., (2003), 'Long-Term Capital Management and the sociology of arbitrage', *Economy and Society* **32** (suppl. 3): 349–380.
Marglin, S., (1974), 'What Do Bosses Do? The Origins and Functions of Hierarchy in Capitalist Production', *The Review of Radical Political Economy* **6** (suppl. 2): 33–66.

Marx, K., (2000 [1848]), *Manifesto of the Communist Party,* http://www.marxists.org/archive/marx/works/1848/communist-manifesto/index.htm

Mottez, B., (1966), *Système de Salaire et Politiques Patronales: Essai sur l'évolution des Pratiques et des Idéologies Patronales,* Paris: CNRS.

Mottez, B., (1960), 'Du marchandage au salaire au rendement', *Sociologie du Travail,* **2** (suppl. 3): 206–215.

Murphy, K., Zábojník, J., (2004), 'CEO pay and appointments: a market-based explanation for recent trends', *American Economic Review* **94** (suppl. 2): 192–196.

Roth, L.M., (2006), *Selling Women Short,* Princeton: Princeton University Press.

Rajan, R., Zingales, L., (2001), 'The Firm as a Dedicated Hierarchy: a Theory of the Origins and Growth of the Firm', *Quarterly Journal of Economics* **136** (suppl. 3): 805–851.

Schumpeter, J., (1943), 'The Process of Creative Destruction', in *Socialism, Capitalism, and Democracy,* London: Allen and Unwin: 81–86.

Williamson, O., (1985), *The Economic Institutions of Capitalism,* New York: The Free Press.

Zingales, L., (2000), 'In Search of New Foundations', *The Journal of Finance* **50** (suppl. 4): 1623–1653.

# Everything for sale: how non-executive directors make a difference

*Julie Froud, Adam Leaver, Gindo Tampubolon and Karel Williams*[1]

a motive tends to be one which is to the actor and to the other members of a situation, an unquestioned answer to questions concerning social or lingual conduct. (Mills, 1940: 907.)

I do not think the board should be selling at this price. It is not a premium to where the shares were trading a few weeks ago. Sir Nigel Rudd [non-executive chairman] knows what he is doing. (Anonymous shareholder on how the Pilkington board should and would refuse a low bid from Nippon Sheet Glass, *Financial Times*, 8 November, 2005)

In 1940 the *American Sociological Review* published an article by the young C. Wright Mills who tried to rescue the concept of motive from psychology and claim it for sociology. Mills argued that motives were not individual springs to action but 'typical vocabularies (that) have ascertainable functions in delimited societal situations' (Mills, 1940: 904). He saw a motive as the social actor's 'unquestioning answer to questions of social conduct'. Consider, in 2005, an anonymous fund manager's view of the Pilkington board's response to Nipon Sheet Glass's (NSG's) first low offer in a takeover bid. The fund manager, presumably unknowingly, used motive in the precise Millsian sense, when he observed that Sir Nigel Rudd, non executive chair of Pilkingtons 'knows what he is doing'. As our second quotation indicates, the fund manager was confident that Sir Nigel was motivated to rebuff NSG's first low offer while indicating that the Pilkington Board was open to a higher one with a bid premium.

This Millsian usage is conceptually important because motive is the precondition of coherent elite group action; but it is empirically problematic because the effects of motive are hard to demonstrate. The classic literature on business elites, for instance, Useem (1984) and Scott (1997) rarely engages in empirical studies which convincingly show how elite social motives make a difference. If we are to resume elite studies and restore them to their central place in radical social science, we have to demonstrate motive. This chapter takes up the call made in the introduction to deploy appropriate methods, which in our case combine network analysis with historical case study of outcomes.

As discussed by Savage and Williams in this volume, we are interested in groups who do not occupy the traditional 'power elite' positions as chief executives at the apex of giant firms. We have elsewhere emphasized the growing importance of financial intermediaries (Folkman *et al.*, 2007) and in this article we turn to consider outside directors in giant companies (ie, those directors who do not have an executive position in the companies on whose boards they serve). The motives of this group have been discussed inconclusively in an older political economy literature on interlocking directors and in a new corporate governance literature on non executive directors (NEDs). New terms like NED both describe and con-stitute our world taken for granted; they are also about material outcomes and how motivated social actors could, should and do change the world. In the current literature on corporate governance, outside directors are always described as non-executive directors, using a term which has only passed into general use and acquired its current meaning with the UK Cadbury Report in 1992. Within this framing, NEDs are supposed to represent shareholders and solve the kind of agency problems analysed by mainstream finance authors like Jensen (1993) and Fama (1980). This replaces earlier discussions in older political economy litera-ture (eg Scott, 1979, Useem, 1984) about interlocking directorates and elite net-works.[2] Here, interlock directors represented the interests of finance capital, embodied in the dominance of banks and insurance companies, as originally analysed by Hilferding (1910) and Lenin (1917). Both literatures make strong assumptions and assertions about what outside directors should and could do to make capitalism work in different ways; but significantly both accounts of motive failed to convince 'so what' sceptics (see, for example, Pettigrew, 1992) that outside directors had any significant effects. This echoes the maverick British business-man Tiny Rowland who famously observed that boardrooms contained potted plants and NEDs and, in his experience, the potted plants were more useful.[3]

The unresolved question is whether outside directors are a motivated elite that makes a difference. Put another way, the question is whether the exchange of senior management and board level personnel between giant companies has any definite effect and, if so, how we might observe and demonstrate it. This chapter takes up these issues in three sections.

The first section introduces the framing of these issues in governance dis-course and political economy and explains how and why their evidence and argu-ments about motive are inconclusive. The second section considers whether and how current patterns of exchange of personnel in giant British companies are different from those analysed in the classic political economy literature by Scott and others; empirics and network analysis on a sample of several hundred NEDs suggests that interchange now takes the form of a general recycling of (current and former) senior managers between FTSE 100 and 250 companies so that the typical NED would now be a retired former FTSE 100 senior executive.

The third section explores how NEDs affect outcomes, by reporting a case study of Pilkington in the buildings materials sector, where changing board com-position has made a great difference to the way that directors respond to exter-nal bids to acquire the company. In the mid 1980s, the board joined in successful public resistance to a takeover bid by BTR; whereas in 2006 a NED-dominated board efficiently extracted the highest price when it sold the company on to Nippon Sheet Glass.

We show that exchange and interlock are now about cultural homogenization around the corporate norm that everything is for sale (at the right price) when assets and companies are routinely bundled and re-bundled. Here, the outsiders now defined as NEDs do not serve the new epochal interests of finance capital in any direct way, but enforce the changing conjunctural priorities of financialization. In an economy of permanent restructuring, the demand before the credit crunch of 2007 was always for delivering (short term) value to shareholders through buying and selling companies and divisions (see also Folkman *et al.*, 2007). The idea of the conjuncture is important because it recogizes that conditions such as liquidity and interest rates can change every 5 or 7 years in ways which will make it possible and/or necessary to generate returns to investors in different ways in successive conjunctures (Erturk *et al.*, 2008). Our broader cultural frame connects with Useem's (1984) classical concept of 'business scan' if scan is taken to mean not only horizons but also practices and norms of appropriate behaviour.

## Outside directors: from interlocks in political economy to NEDs in governance

In giant British companies since the early 1990s, the outside director has been constructed as a NED through corporate governance discourse, formalized in the Combined Code (1998, 2003, 2006), which emphasizes the director's responsibility in representing shareholder interests in the boardroom. At the same time, mainstream finance provides an historical backdrop with its generic problems about ensuring that manager/agents serve the interests of shareholder/ principals. Outside directors, now known as NEDs, were previously identified as interlocking directors in political economy studies of managerial elites, many of which focused on bank and insurance company representatives sitting on industrial company boards, and drew on theories of finance capital. This section considers how both literatures made unproven assumptions and assertions about the role of outsiders and neither literature convinced sceptics who accepted that outside actors and networks existed but doubted whether the outsiders had the desired effect or made much difference.

Since 2003, best practice includes the recommendation that NEDs should make up at least half the board of British public companies and there are also increasingly stringent requirements about how outsider NEDs have to pass tests of independence which exclude those with previous employment or other connection with the company, for instance as a supplier or consultant (Combined Code, 2003). Almost all FTSE 100 giant companies and FTSE 250 mid-sized public companies now conform to these combined requirements through separating the offices of chief executive and chairman, and by institutionalizing proceduralized governance through audit and remuneration committees chaired by outsiders (*Financial Times*, 18 June, 2007). This represents a significant break in board composition, practice and terminology. As early as 1973, the Watkinson Report for the Confederation of British Industry (CBI) argued for more non-executive directors on the boards of public companies; at this time, only 35 per cent of companies in the *Times 1000* in 1975–76 had more than two NEDs and a quarter had none at all (Tricker, 1978:77). An influential 1978 study significantly used the term NED in the subtitle of a report titled 'the independent director' and highlighted the lack of clarity about their role and responsibilities when many NEDs were 'insufficiently involved in financial matters' (Tricker, 1978:51–2).

The break came in the 1990s after a series of corporate scandals, including the Maxwell fraud, which were attributed to passive boards, and more NEDs, operating within proceduralized governance systems of audit and remuneration was seen as the solution. The seminal Cadbury Report of 1992 led to the UK's first corporate governance code which recommended that boards should have a minimum of three NEDs (the majority of whom should be 'independent' of management). Their role was to provide independent views on corporate strategy, performance, resources, appointments and standards of conduct, though there were continuing concerns about whether there were sufficient suitably-qualified individuals available to play what was deemed to be an important though still under-specified role (Solomon and Solomon, 2004:69–70).

Subsequent reports and codes continued to assert the primary importance of NEDs in the governance of public companies (Hampel, 1998; Combined Code, 1998), but it was corporate scandal in the USA, and in particular the collapse of Enron, which prompted a fresh look at NEDs. The Higgs Review commissioned by the Department for Trade and Industry (DTI) in 2002 was tasked with not only providing a picture of the current population of NEDs in the UK but also assessing their effectiveness and producing recommendations for improving their quality, diversity and independence.[4] The 2003 Higgs Report was met with considerable hostility by UK business groups (Solomon and Solomon, 2004:73–4; Maclean *et al.*, 2006:81), though its recommendations were hardly radical, since the report uncovered considerable problems in the recruitment and use of non-executives against a background of public concern about the risk of corporate failure. The main recommendation was that independent NEDs should make up at least half of company boards and that a senior NED on each board should have direct responsibility for communicating with shareholders.

If proceduralized governance with NEDs at the centre was a British invention, American mainstream finance theory (Jensen, 1993; Fama, 1980) encouraged the expectation that corporate performance benefits could follow, well beyond the prevention of Maxwell type fraud. Finance theory emphasized how the separation of ownership and control in public companies had created generic agency problems because the shareholder-principal faced costs and other difficulties in monitoring the manager-agent. In acting as the representative of the shareholder interest in the boardroom (including in the task of setting executive pay and incentive contracts), a diligent NED should help to reduce the extent of agency costs through better aligning manager and shareholder interests. The implication was that NEDs could restrain management pursuit of the quiet life, wasteful expenditure on executive perks like private jets, as well as empire building or following discretionary objectives through mergers or the refusal to return cash to shareholders.

There is no clear evidence, however, that corporate performance improved when companies acquired more NEDs with clearer responsibilities. Empirical studies in the UK and USA have produced mixed and confusing results when trying to examine the general relationship between governance measures and performance outcomes. Recent reviews and meta analyses of this empirical work emphasize the difficulties about sampling, specification of variables and relating changes in corporate performance to any one particular set of organizational changes. (See, for instance, Dalton and Dalton, 2005; Roberts *et al.*, 2005; Larcker *et al.*, 2005). In our view, it is inherently unlikely that organizational changes such as the number of NEDs or the separation of chairman and chief executive would strongly influence a complex outcome like performance, which has many other drivers. Predictably, when Dalton and Dalton reviewed 69 studies on the effects of separating the chair and CEO roles, they came to an agnostic verdict and finally concluded negatively that 'in sum, structural independence does not equal performance advantage' (p. S93). The sense of disappointment is reinforced by the general findings on other aspects of corporate governance reform (see, for example, Tosi *et al.*, 2000 or Barkema and Gomez-Mejia 1998), which suggest very weak links between executive pay and corporate performance. Indeed, in the UK proceduralized governance systems, of remuneration committees staffed by NEDs may have contributed to a general ratcheting up of executive pay levels (Ezzamel and Watson 1998; Erturk *et al.*, 2005).

If NEDs and corporate governance have by the mid-2000s acquired an aura of empirical disappointment, some 20 years before, in the 1980s, a similar kind of disillusion had enveloped the political economy of corporate networks and board interlocks. This analysis had two primary foci: first, the socio-economic background of company directors and, second, the extent to which individual directors sit on the board of more than one company. There is much of enduring value in this now-unfashionable literature; in particular, in Useem's classic *The Inner Circle*, which has influenced our own work. As well as inferences from networks, his analysis is also based on US and UK interviews with executive directors and NEDs. Partly in consequence, Useem rejects the dominant economic control interpretation of interlocks as way of exercising influence over other corporations (Useem, 1984:41–3). Useem instead suggests that 'the central driver is the efforts of giant companies to achieve an optimal 'business scan' of contemporary practices and the general business environment' (1984:45). Within this frame, Useem also found that ambitious executives were advised to find non-executive positions in other firms to improve their understanding of the business environment, as well as to access networks populated by other multiple directors, thus providing a short cut to contemporary business knowledge and sensibilities. Windolf (2002) similarly describes directors networked through membership of a least two corporate boards as 'big linkers' (p. 100) and explores various reasons for such links.

The mainstream approach to interlock in the 1970s and 1980s is exemplified by Scott, and emphasized the significance of shared elite social backgrounds and the representation of a 'constellation of interests' that operated through board interlocks. Whitley's sociological work, based on a sample of 40 industrial and 27 financial UK companies in the early 1970s, covers educational background and membership of exclusive London clubs. The key finding is that 'very large industrial and financial firms do recruit their Board members from a narrow segment in the population. These directors undergo a remarkably similar educational experience and, to some extent, have similar social circles' (Whitley, 1974:80). Scott provides the classic historical study of the informal British variant on finance capital as he argued that 'British banks stood at the centre of loose and overlapping groups of enterprises created through primary interlocks' (Scott, 1997:121), with the result that at the heart of the British economy was an inter-corporate network in which 'City' enterprises were closely aligned with 'non-financial enterprises'. Scott's key concept was of 'control through a constellation of interests', characteristic of 'the Anglo-American economies, where a specific structure of banking and credit has encouraged the building of large financial intermediaries' (Scott, 1997:51).

But these arguments elicited a 'so what?' response from management researchers like Pettigrew (1992) who questioned how interlocks actually changed firm behaviour and whether shared social backgrounds had any significance on their actions. Such problems have long been acknowledged: for example Whitley (1974:80) concludes by posing the unanswered research question of how 'the culture of the financial-industrial elite' 'will mediate structural exigencies of developed capitalism'. Researchers identified some general behavioural differences between groups of interlocked and non-interlocked firms (see, for example, Mizruchi's, 1996 analysis of political contributions in the USA). But the 'so what' question is still relevant because behaviours like political contributions do not address the fundamental issue of business performance. Pettigrew (1992) suggests that ethnographic investigations provide a second way of resolving these issues and Hill's (1995) interview-based investigation of how boards work and how directors see their role provides a good example of the value of such an approach. There are huge access problems, however, because the conduct and reasoning of NEDs on boards, in committees and in meetings with large institutional investors is mainly private. In effect, the chairman remains the only NED with a public speaking part and academic access to the discussions of the full board or its committees remains restricted.

The history of research into interlocks in the 1970s and 1980s prefigures that of research into governance in the 1990s and 2000s; but there is the same imbalance between assertions or assumptions and empirics about how capitalism works.

## Patterns of exchange: from banking interlocks to the recycling of FTSE executives as NEDs

This section addresses the question of what is new and different about the current pattern of exchange of personnel at board level. We first use sociograms which visually show the pattern of interchange of all NEDs within and beyond the FTSE 100 in 2005. Secondly we report a sample study of the backgrounds and careers of some 150 NEDs in FTSE 100 companies in 2005.[5] This randomly selected sample accounts for some 25 per cent of the total population of NED directors and provides a solid basis for inference about background and career patterns in the whole group. Let us begin with a preliminary review of the finance-dominated pattern of exchange some 30 or 40 years ago.

Between the 1960s and the 1980s, academic researchers established empirically that the pattern of exchange in Britain was finance dominated. Personnel from leading banks and insurance companies often sat as outside directors on the boards of industrial companies. In 1966, just under half of the directors of top 120 British companies were classed as 'finance capitalists' by Barratt Brown (1968:45). The significance of a financial company background for outside directors was confirmed by Scott and Griff's 1976 study (see Table 9.1). This shows the background in terms of primary interests of those directors of top 250 firms who were considered as 'multiple directors' (Scott, 1997:208–9) and who would now be classified as NEDs. Of this outsider group, around 37 per cent were current or retired senior members of the top 50 financial firms, which together accounted for almost as many multiple directors as the top 200 non-financials. Financial companies were disproportionately generous with their executives: on average each top 50 financial firm contributed 1.9 of their 'insiders' to other boards, while for non-financials, the average was only 0.6 (Scott, 1997:209).

**Table 9.1:** *Scott and Griff's 1976 Analysis of the Primary Interests of Multiple Directors of the top 250 British Enterprises*

| Primary interest of directors | Number of directors | per cent of directors |
|---|---|---|
| Top 50 financials | 97 | 34.4 |
| Retired from top 50 financials | 7 | 2.5 |
| Top 200 non-financials | 112 | 39.7 |
| Retired from top 200 non-financials | 17 | 6.0 |
| Other financial | 14 | 5.0 |
| Other industrial | 13 | 4.6 |
| Other | 22 | 7.8 |
| Total | 282 | 100.0 |

*Source: Scott and Griff 1985, table 12.5, reprinted in Scott (1997) table 53, p. 209.*

Does finance still dominate director exchange? Our sample data for 2005 permits us to see whether NEDs in the FTSE 100 have a financial background. The answer depends on how finance is defined. The classic studies from the 1960s to the 1980s defined finance narrowly as banking and insurance because these were then the leading sectors which sustained giant companies in finance. After a period of marked innovation in wholesale and retail markets, however, we define finance more broadly to include fund management, private equity and investment banking as well as retail financial services. On this broad definition, our sample of 150 NEDs included 13 (9 per cent) currently employed in finance. Less than half come from traditional retail financial services in banking and insurance; by 2005 a NED in our sample is just as likely to be employed by a private equity fund as by a bank. A total group of 29 NEDs in the sample (19 per cent) had a previous spell of at least five years in a senior position in a financial sector organization; 18 of them had experience at a mid-to senior level in the banking industry (retail or investment). Overall, 33 of the 150 NEDs (22 per cent) were currently or previously employed in financial services suggesting that, in simple headcount and percentage terms, a finance background is rather less important in the 2000s than 40 or 20 years ago.

The decline in the percentage of outside directors from the financial sector over the past 30 years is all the more striking if we recall that over the same period financial services has dramatically increased its share of activity within the group of giant firms. As Froud *et al.* (2006) demonstrate, the number of financial services companies within the FTSE 100 does not increase between 1983 and 2002, while the share of financial services in FTSE 100 employment has increased from 11 to 18 per cent but remains modest overall. But, as table 9.2 shows, the 24 financial services companies of 2002 account for a larger share of FTSE 100 capital employed and, a much greater share of FTSE 100 profits. Between 1983 and 2002, the finance company share in FTSE 100 capital employed increased sharply from 24 to 38 per cent and the finance company share of pre-tax profit profits more than doubled from 18 to 42 per cent.

The power of finance and the old distinction between financial and industrial companies has been reworked. Finance is no longer a controlling interest, though it has become a profit centre in its own right and is now established as

**Table 9.2:** *The Significance of Finance (SIC class 6) in the FTSE 100 in 1983 and 2002*

|  | No. of companies in financial services SIC class | Financial services: per cent share of the FTSE 100 in terms of | | | |
| --- | --- | --- | --- | --- | --- |
|  |  | Employment | Pre-tax income | Capital employed | Market value |
| 1983 | 24 | 11.0 | 17.7 | 23.5 | 18.6 |
| 2002 | 24 | 18.0 | 41.7 | 37.7 | 27.4 |

*Source: based on Froud et al. (2006) p. 18 (originally derived from Datastream)*

the main source of profit for the British giant firm sector. Nevertheless, there is a clear break: finance has moved from being an over-represented source of outside directors in the 1970s and 1980s to being an under-represented source of NEDs today. Given that personnel exchange between finance and industry is in decline, this raises a more general question about whether British giant firms in the 2000s are now much less densely networked and bound together through exchange of outside director personnel. The decline of tight networks is a major theme in historical studies of other advanced capitalist countries, especially Carroll's (2004) insightful work on Canada. This appears to be confirmed by evidence on British NEDs produced for the Higgs Review in 2002, which drew attention to the very limited pool from which existing NEDs had been drawn when most non-executives were white, male, late middle-aged members of the business classes (Higgs 2003: 42). But the evidence obtained on listed company directors from Hemscott for Higgs suggested that the interlocks that had pre-occupied an earlier generation of academic researchers were now completely marginal. For example, only 6 per cent of executive directors in all listed UK companies also held a non-executive position in another company and only 8 per cent of NEDs were also executive board members elsewhere. Overall, 80 per cent of NEDs sat only on one board so that bridging and linking between companies via their boards was a minority activity (Hemscott, 2003). The data suggests that UK plc appeared to be in the middle of an experiment in running national capitalism without board interlocks.

The Higgs evidence covers all listed companies, and the picture might be different if we narrow the focus onto giant firms within the FTSE 100 which were traditionally considered to be the privileged locus of networking and insider/outsider exchange. Figure 9.1 shows the extent to which board members

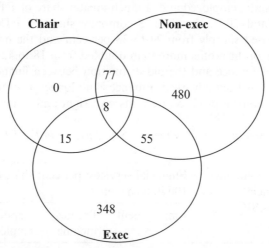

**Figure 9.1:** *The extent of interlock amongst FTSE 100 board members in 2005, including executive and non-executive members.*
*Source: CRESC Elites database, derived from Hemscott.*

of FTSE 100 companies have more than one appointment. For example, if we take all 620 NEDs in the FTSE 100 in 2005, 77 are also chair of another board, 55 hold executive positions in other companies and 8 manage to combine all three roles; however, a majority (480 directors or 77 per cent) hold no other board position in UK listed companies. Likewise, most executive directors do not have seats on the boards of other companies. Figure 9.1 also shows, by way of contrast, that all of the FTSE 100 chairs in 2005 also held another position, most usually as a non-executive.

Although chairs stand out as pluralists, the overall story of Figure 9.1 seems to be that the extent of interchange of personnel has become rather limited by 2005. Figure 9.1 presents a rather static and limited view, however, which under-plays the extent to which there has been exchange between boards. The analysis that follows is based on three sociograms reporting patterns of exchange within the FTSE 100, between the FTSE 100 and 250, and between FTSE 100 firms and charities, quangos and not-for-profit organizations. In the sociograms in Figures 9.2 to 9.4, nodes represent companies and links show personnel in common. The overall picture that emerges is far more interesting than that which would be drawn from figure 9.1: large numbers of active FTSE senior managers are now being exchanged before retirement through NED posts; just as important, the sample survey of careers then shows how governance has opened new NED career options for such executives after retirement; equally, the world of the FTSE 100 is not hermetically sealed because it connects through exchange of personnel with mid caps and not-for-profit organizations.

The conclusion is that the snapshot pattern for all NEDs in 2005 is one of significant exchange of outsiders within a relatively dense network of FTSE 100 giant firms and, interestingly, there is also outreach from this network of FTSE 100 firms into the FTSE 250. Figure 9.2 shows significant exchange between giant companies in the FTSE 100 in two ways. First, 60 per cent of FTSE 100 companies have an executive from another FTSE 100 company sitting on their board as a NED; second, over 40 of the members of the FTSE 100 share at least one NED with another company in the index. Interestingly, the new sphere of exchange is not limited to networking within the FTSE 100. Figure 9.3 also highlights a different kind of exchange *de haut en bas* where FTSE 100 executives from giant firms are recruited as NEDs in FTSE 250 mid-cap companies: in 2005, 30 per cent of FTSE 250 companies have an executive from the FTSE 100 sitting on their board, implying a kind of colonization by senior executives from giant firms. Equally, exchange of one kind appears to create or reinforce exchange of another so that FTSE 100 executives are more involved in charities and quangos if their home company has dense internal FTSE networks via its NEDs, as Figure 9.4 shows.

These exchange relations also have a temporal dimension absent in Figure 9.1, which can, however, be explored through the sample survey of 150 NED careers. In addition to those who are contemporaneously executives in one FTSE 100 company and NEDs in another, there are also recently retired executives from one FTSE100 company who are NEDs in another. The sample

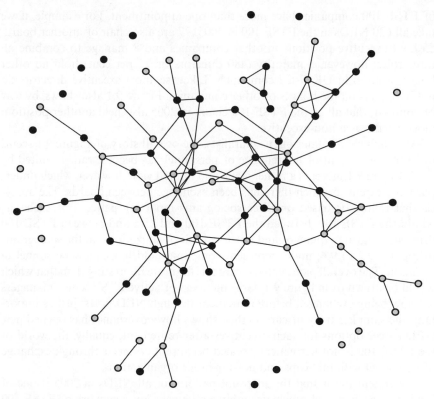

**Figure 9.2:** *Sociogram to show the extent to which FTSE 100 firms have executives from other FTSE 100 companies as their Non-Executive Directors (NEDs), November 2005.*

*Notes:*

1. Each node in the sociogram is a FTSE 100 firm.
2. A link between two nodes signifies that at least one NED sits on both firms' boards, ie where two FTSE100 companies have at least one NED in common. Over 40% of FTSE100 companies have a NED who also has a NED position on another FTSE 100 board.
3. Firms which have *executives* from other FTSE 100 firms as their NED are marked in black. 60% of FTSE 100 firms have a NED who is also an executive director at another FTSE 100 firm.

Source: CRESC elite database.

survey of NED careers broadly confirmed the judgement of the senior partner in a pay and remuneration practice who recently told us that, for retired giant company senior execs, 'the NED job is what you do between 50 and 70'. Overall, Table 9.3 shows that 45 per cent of 150 FTSE 100 NEDs were not in full time employment. Of the retired NEDs, around 80 per cent had backgrounds as cor-

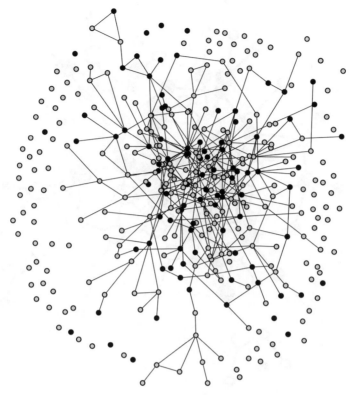

**Figure 9.3:** *Deepening or increasing the influence of FTSE 100 executives outside the FTSE 100 (1): NEDs on FTSE 250 boards, November 2005.*

*Notes:*

1. Each node in the sociogram is a FTSE 250 company
2. Lines between nodes show where a FTSE 250 company has the same NED as another FTSE 250 company.
3. The black nodes are those FTSE 250 companies that have as one of their NEDs someone who is also an executive member of a FTSE100 board. The sociogram shows that 30per cent of FTSE250 firms install FTSE100 executives as NEDs.

Source: CRESC elite database.

porate executives and no less than 59 per cent specifically had worked in FTSE 100 companies; if accounting, law, consultancy and other professions would seem to generate skill sets relevant to the NED role, surprisingly few (20 per cent) NEDs come from such professional backgrounds. For retired business executives with 20 years to fill, multiple and serial non-executive directorships represent a new kind of post-retirement career portfolio which has opened up since the early 1990s. In our sample of 68 retired NEDs, nearly 80 per cent were

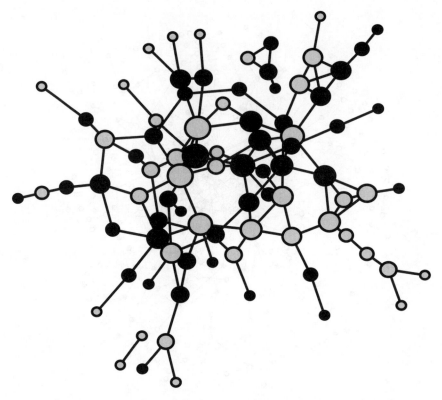

**Figure 9.4:** *Widening or increasing influence outside the FTSE 100 (2):*
*FTSE 100 executives in NED positions outside public companies,*
*November 2005.*

*Notes:*

1. Each node in the sociogram is a FTSE100 company
2. Lines between nodes represent shared NEDs (as in Figure 9.1)
3. Black nodes are those FTSE 100 companies with other FTSE 100 executives serving as
   NEDs on their board (as in Figure 9.1)
4. A larger size node (black or grey) indicates that one or more executives of the FTSE 100
   company also holds a patronage position (eg chair or other non-executive) in a charity
   and/or a governor position in a quango. This was determined by cross-checking the list
   of executives of FTSE100 firms against executives, chairs, patrons and governors of
   the largest 500 charities and 400+ quangos. The extent of such links is indicated by
   increasing the size of the node, so that a company with two executives on the board of a
   charity or quango will have a larger node than another company with only one executive
   in such a role.

Source: CRESC elite database.

**Table 9.3:** *Background and Activities of a Sample of FTSE100 NEDs, 2005 [figures in parenthesis are percentages]*

|  |  | FTSE 100 NEDs sample N = 150 | Of which: NEDs currently in full-time executive employment, N = 82 | And: NEDs in retirement, N = 68 |
|---|---|---|---|---|
| A. Is/was the NED ever employed in an executive role in: | (a) a FTSE 100 firm | 75 [50.0] | 37 [45.1] | 38 [58.5] |
|  | (b) another British public company | 86 [57.3] | 45 [54.9] | 41 [63.1] |
|  | (c) foreign Firms | 82 [54.7] | 46 [56.1] | 36 [55.4] |
| B. Is the NED: | (a) also currently NED at another plc (NED pluralism) | 93 [62.0] | 40 [48.8] | 53 [79.1] |
|  | (b) previously NED at another plc (NED succession) | 73 [48.7] | 31 [37.8] | 42 [62.7] |
| C. For those who are currently Chairs of FTSE100 companies, have they previously been: | (a) Chair of another public company | 48 [32.0] | 20 [24.4] | 28 [41.8] |
|  | (b) NED in another public company | 37 [24.7] | 20 [24.4] | 17 [25.4] |

*Source: CRESC elite database, derived from Hemscott.*

holding more than one NED post and exemplify *NED pluralism* in Table 9.3, while 65 per cent had also previously served as a NED at another company which exemplifies *NED succession* in table 9.3. For those who have not retired, executive responsibilities presumably limit the ability to hold multiple non-executive positions and less than half of full time executives qualify as plural-ists by holding more than one NED post. Serving FTSE executives with one non-executive position, however, could simply be represented as on the first stage of a new portfolio career, which combines and recombines executive and non-executive roles in a variety of ways over time as part of a general recycling of senior personnel.

This recycling of FTSE executives as NEDs before and after retirement manifestly interconnects FTSE companies which would otherwise be much more like self-contained executive silos, because there is still only limited recruitment of senior executive management from outside the company in many FTSE 100 companies. Direct external recruitment is increasing and our analysis of FTSE 100 CEOs showed that 25 per cent had been externally recruited in 2005; but the internal career is still more important as the route to the top: 41 per cent of FTSE 100 CEOs in 2005 had had served for at least ten years within the company before internal promotion to the top job.

In the light of this data, can we now meet the challenge which defeated earlier generations of researchers, and show that these patterns of exchange influence corporate behaviour and performance?

## So what?: *everything for sale* in building materials and the Pilkington case

Figures 9.2 to 9.4 only describe the current, recently established pattern of recycling FTSE executives as NEDs. The difficulty is to demonstrate that this has definite effects and in some significant way changes outcomes. *A priori* we would hypothesize that the pattern of exchange outlined in the previous section would have cultural effects in the homogenization of business culture and the limiting of attachment to anyone firm. But the extent of these cultural effects and their second order behavioural consequences cannot be determined *a priori* or read off the sociograms and this takes us back to the impasse in the earlier literature about whether interlocks implied control or influence with significant outcomes. Our novel approach in this section is to add a case study of a sector and a company so that we can infer the vocabularies of NED motivation by focusing on observable behaviour and outcomes at key decision points, such as hostile takeover, which distinguishes the British capitalist game from those of continental European countries. We focus on hostile takeover in the buildings materials sector, where all the major British PLCs have recently sold out to foreign buyers, and then on one company, Pilkington, whose board joined a spirited defence against takeover by BTR in 1986 but made a calculated sell off to NSG in 2006.

The British economy is one of permanent restructuring and churning of ownership. By 2003, only 23 of the original 1982 FTSE 100 companies survived after two decades of acquisitions, demergers and other kinds of ownership change. One indicator of commitment to restructuring is that over the period 1980 to 2003, for every pound spent on productive assets, FTSE 100 firms collectively spent nearly 80 pence on buying other firms (Froud *et al.*, 2006). If hostile takeover by other FTSE 100 companies was historically the major driver of this process, more recently private equity funds and foreign public companies have been active buyers of blocks of assets and whole British companies, especially those in the FTSE 250. In Continental Europe, loud voices and political actions resist cross border hostile approaches as in the case of the French (official) reaction to the attempt by Mittal to buy Arcelor, or the Spanish reaction to the EON bid for Endesa. But the identity of the purchaser is barely an issue in the UK where, as Will Hutton observed after $60 billion of recent or proposed foreign takeovers of British companies (*Observer*, 12 February, 2006), there was no public debate, controversy or resistance. Interestingly, in the UK, there was some hostility to the sale of public companies to private equity (Folkman *et al.*, 2008), but apparently a general lack of concern about sale to overseas buyers.

The passivity of both the UK government and the business community in response to foreign takeover reflects a normalization of the City precept that assets and companies are and should be for sale (provided the price is right). This is the editorial line in the City's newspaper, the *Financial Times* which in early 2006 argued that a wave of foreign acquisitions of UK major companies 'should be a cause for celebration, not gloom' because shareholders were being offered generous deals and it reflected well on Britain 'as an attractive place to do business' (11 March, 2006). In the post-Thatcherite world, the firm as a bundle of saleable assets is, like labour market flexibility, an operating principle, which, it is assumed, makes markets work better and improves competitiveness. But the normalization of this precept depends on several material preconditions. Discursively, politicians across all parties have reformatted the economy so that national success is no longer indicated by production, employment and trade balance but by consumption, labour market flexibility and financial market priorities (such as asset price stability or low inflation); the post-Thatcher consensus depends on all this because the national economy remains a failure by pre-1979 productionist standards (Elliott and Atkinson, 2007). Restructuring also depends on eager institutional shareholders who, in the 1990s bull market, bought the index and were willing to sell a share if offered a premium of 20–30 per cent over yesterday's close. More recently, some investors have been actively encouraging restructuring by taking public views on the next value-creating strategic move; for instance in 2006, a national newspaper carried the suggestion by a leading institutional investor (Brandes, an American 'value investor') that ITV, the main UK national independent TV broadcast company, should split itself into two parts, production and broadcasting (*The Observer* 5 February, 2006).

But this world of 'everything for sale' has a third key precondition because it requires motivated company directors who understand unquestioningly how to behave when auctioning the company. This typically means efficiently holding out for the highest price for shareholders when faced with friendly overtures or hostile takeover, and then endorsing acquisition without questions about industrial logic, the effects on other stakeholders or any reference to the mass of empirical research on how mergers usually destroy value. Our argument is that the exchange of personnel in the NED role secures this outcome. We can demonstrate this by considering first the absence of resistance in NED-dominated boards in the buildings material sector and then the change of behaviour at Pilkington.

It is striking that NED-dominated boards did not resist foreign takeover of all the British building materials firms which once accounted for 10 per cent of the FTSE 100. Table 9.4 lists the major deals since 1997 which took out Redland, Tarmac, Blue Circle, RMC, BPB, Pilkington and, most recently, Hanson. In several cases, these were not distress sales: British Plaster Board, Pilkington and Hanson were productively credible and financially viable on a stand-alone basis. But in all these cases the directors made a recommendation and sold out without protest after efficiently extracting a higher price for shareholders and thus serving their role of representing the interests of shareholders on the board, albeit interpreted in a very narrow way. The only standout against this process of restructuring has been Don Young, the vigorously renegade former director of Redland, whose web site and book questions the logic of what is going on from a traditional productionist view point (Young and Scott, 2004). Interestingly, Redland was the first and earliest of the foreign acquisitions and Don Young was an old school executive director with a long career in industrial relations/human resources who sat on the Redland Board by virtue of his role as head of organization and human resources.

While the general absence of resistance to foreign takeover in NED-dominated boards is revealing, the observation is hardly decisive when hostile takeover was well established long before the idea of the NED was formalized in the Cadbury report of 1992. Hence the special interest of the Pilkington case, where we can see how the successful hostile bid from NSG through a series of offers from November 2005 to February 2006, played very differently from the

**Table 9.4:** *Restructuring and Ownership Change in the British Building Materials Sector*

| Company | Acquired by | Date | Value of transaction |
|---|---|---|---|
| Redland | Larfarge (France) | 1997 | £1.8bn |
| Tarmac | Anglo American (UK) | 1999 | £1.2bn |
| Blue Circle | Larfarge (France) | 2001 | £3.1bn |
| RMC | Cemex (Mexico) | 2005 | $5.8bn |
| British Plaster Board (BPB) | St Gobain (France) | 2005 | £3.9bn |
| Aggregate Industries | Holcim (Switzerland) | 2005 | £1.8bn |
| Pilkington | Nippon Sheet Glass (NPG) (Japan) | 2006 | £2.2bn |
| Hanson | Heidelberg Cement (Germany) | 2007 | £9.5bn |

unsuccessful offer by British conglomerate BTR in 1986. Pilkington was always a special case in the British context because of the involvement of the founding family, its provincial base in St Helens and the technical excellence symbolized by the company's invention of the float glass process in the 1950s, which was subsequently licensed world wide.

This animated the successful resistance by community, politicians, management, board and major shareholders when BTR made a bid for Pilkington in 1986. As the company's web site explained, the BTR offer was publicly fought off as 'the company mobilised employee, community, city and parliamentary opinion to back its long termist approach to running its business' (pilkington.com, 'about pilkington'). 'BTR is regarded as an insensitive axeman, closing factories down readily' (*Financial Times*, 26 November 1986), even though Pilkington also had a record of cutting jobs and had shed some 20,000 workers worldwide over the 1981–86 period. As the press reported at the time, BTR's bid led to 'frank, bordering on direct, exchanges in the House of Commons' (*Financial Times*, 16 December, 1986), while in St Helens 'the unions were drawn into an alliance with management and there was co-operation between local politicians of all parties (*The Times*, 16 January, 1987). Nationally, discussion about the future of Pilkington was articulated in policy debate about 'short termism' in the City's treatment of industry: 'the BTR bid has been widely seen as a glaring example of how British manufacturing industry is increasingly falling prey to 'City slickers' with no long term commitment to industry's well being' (*The Times*, 16 January, 1987). The Pilkington Board led with a no-surrender position under the chairmanship of family member Anthony Pilkington who argued that the BTR bid was 'entirely lacking in logic for Pilkington's business, its shareholders, employees, customers, and the United Kingdom' (*Wall Street Journal*, 21 November, 1986). This trouble-making persuaded Pilkington's largest shareholder, Standard Life, to support the incumbent management (*Daily Mail*, 2 December, 2005) despite its weak financial performance.

Some twenty years later, the context of the national debate was very different, as are the specifics of the deal and the role of Pilkington's board in the bid process. Here we can identify three key differences: first, the financial position and prospects of the company; second, the conduct of the board; and, third, the changed composition of the board and the careers of the NEDs.

In 2005/6, Pilkington was a financially viable and productively credible firm facing an opportunist bid from a smaller rival. Considered as a stand alone operation, Pilkington in 2005/6 was in a much stronger defensive position than it had been 20 years previously. When NSG bid in autumn 2005, Pilkington was two-thirds of the way through a restructuring plan where it had met every financial target for cost reductions and return; it was a long-established world leader in glass technology with presence in a range of world markets. The offer from NSG was opportunist because the Japanese firm was much smaller and its bid was leveraged, (ie heavily debt financed) on the back of very low Japanese rates of interest, which NSG accessed as a member of the Sumitomo group. In summary, there was no business reason for Pilkington's board to recommend

NSG's offer to shareholders except for the bid premium which NSG might offer. But, in 2005/6, the Board raised no questions about industrial logic, financial records or the risks of leverage but focused only on raising the bid price for shareholders.

The Board in 2005/6 said nothing in public except that the initial offer and two subsequent offers were too low: for example, the first offer of 150 pence a share 'materially undervalued' the company according to non-executive chairman Sir Nigel Rudd (*Financial Times*, 19 November, 2005). This is now a more-or-less standard response in a well understood game of holding out for a higher bid and was subsequently, for example, used by the board of Hanson in response to an opening offer from Heidelberg Cement. In this new order, Pilkington's PR advisers focused on the investment community and in 2005/6 addressed fund managers, ignoring the public who had been so important in 1986. Thus, financial journalists in November 2005 spread the message that, as the Lex column in the *Financial Times* put it, offers had been refused but 'relations (with NSG) remain cordial and Pilkington is clearly for sale at the right price' (4 November, 2005). The Board and its chair in 2005/6 had the confidence of City investors who agreed that 'Sir Nigel Rudd knows what he is doing' (*Financial Times*, 8 November, 2005). The board extracted a final price of 165p in return for its recommendation; this represented a 39 per cent premium on the share price of October 28th, before NSG's interest was disclosed, and was considered a good outcome for the shareholders (*Financial Times*, 11 March, 2006).

This striking change in the board's conduct is clearly connected with changes in its composition because the Pilkington board of 2005 was decisively different from that in 1986, when family members and long-term employees were in the majority, and only four of the eleven were non-executives, as table 9.5 shows. At the time of the NSG bid twenty years on, the NEDs were now in a majority (five out of eight, in keeping with best practice corporate governance) and the NEDs had careers where limited attachment to any one firm was demonstrated by movement between firms, distance from operations and closeness to the culture of the corporate deal.

The key non-executive player at Pilkington in 2005/6 was Sir Nigel Rudd as chairman, whose *curriculum vitae* epitomizes the culture of the deal. He is formerly chief executive of Williams Holdings, the acquisitive conglomerate that Rudd helped to build into a FTSE 100 company; and since 1990 he has been non-executive chair of Pendragon, the acquisitive dealer chain spun out of Williams, which in 2006 beat Lookers to make a successful bid for the Vardy dealer chain. More recently, since 2003 he has been non-executive chair of Boots which first merged with Alliance and only a year later, in early 2007, was bought by private equity firm, Kohlberg Kravis Roberts (KKR), becoming the first UK FTSE 100 company to fall into private equity ownership. He had been non-executive chair of Pilkington since 1995 during which time the company has been the subject of much bid speculation. Barclays, where Nigel Rudd has been non executive deputy chair since 1996, is in many ways a standout in that, since the acquisition of investment banking business de Zoete Wedd (with a

**Table 9.5:** *Composition of the Pilkington PLC Board of Directors, 1986 and 2006*

(a) 1986

| Name | Position on board | Year of birth (where available) | Year appointed | Other positions include |
|---|---|---|---|---|
| Anthony Pilkington | Chairman | 1935 | 1980 | Previously chair of Flat Glass Europe division |
| D. Cail | Deputy Chairman | | 1975 ED; 1980 Deputy Chairman | Joined Pilkington in 1947; chairman of the Ophthalmic division in 1976; joined board in 1975. |
| G.N. Iley | ED | | 1976 | |
| Lord Croham | NED | 1917 | 1979 | Fomer head of Home Civil Service; chairman Guinness Peat Group and Anglo-German Foundation for the Study of Industrial Society; President Institute of Fiscal Studies and British Institute of Energy Economics. |
| D.N. Cledwyn-Davies | ED | | 1979 | Joined Pilkington 1956; previously chairman of Flat Glass division. |
| H. Kopper | NED | 1935 | 1983 | Non-exec chair at Flachglas AG; member of management board Deutsche Bank AG; chairman of H. Albert de Bary NV and Kali-Chemie AG; board member of various other European companies. |
| D.E. Cook | ED | | 1984 | Previously chairman of Pilkington Brothers South Africa (Pty.) Ltd |
| P.H. Grunwell | ED | | 1984 | Previously group chief accountant. |
| F.R. Hurn | NED | 1938 | 1984 | Chief executive Smiths Industries; NED OceanTransport & Trading plc; council member British Institute of Management; governor of Henley management college. |
| Sir Peter Thompson | NED | 1928 | 1985 | Executive chairman National Freight Consortium; previously on the board of Granville & Co Ltd and Kenning Motor Group plc. |
| Sir R Nicholson | ED | | 1986 | Previously Chief Scientific Advisor to the Cabinet; senior positions in Electro-Optical and Ophthalmic divisions. |

**Table 9.5:** *Continued*

(b) 2006

| Name | Position on board | Date of birth | Year appointed | Other positions include |
|------|-------------------|---------------|----------------|-------------------------|
| Sir Nigel Rudd | Non-executive Chairman | 1946 | NED since 1994; chair since 1995 | Also non-executive chair Boots Group and Pendragon; deputy chair (non-executive) Barclays plc. Formerly CEO Williams Holdings; non-exec chair at East Midlands electricity and NED at Gartmore Value Investments. |
| Stuart Chambers | ED (Group CEO) | 1956 | Appointed to board 2001; Group CEO since 2002) | Joined Pilkington in 1996 as group vice-president Marketing & Business Development, building products. Also NED at Associated British Ports. |
| Norman Lyle | NED | 1947 | 2005 | Also NED at Standard Chartered Bank of Hong Kong Ltd. Previously group FD Jardine Mathieson Holdings. |
| Iain Lough | ED (Group Finance Director) | 1947 | 2002 | Joined Pilkington 1993 as group financial controller. Also NED of Wilson Bowden. |
| Pat Zito | ED | 1949 | 2002 | Joined Pilkington 1985 as finance director of Australian operations. Currently President, Automotive OE Europe and North America. |
| Oliver Stocken | NED | 1941 | 1998 | Also non-executive chairman Rutland Trust plc, non-executive deputy chair 3i Group plc and NED at Rank Group, GUS, Stanhope and Standard Chartered. |
| James Leng | NED | 1945 | 1998 | Also non-executive chairman Corus Group and IMI. NED of Alstom SA and Hanson. |
| Christine Morin-Postel | NED | 1946 | 2003 | Also NED at 3i Group, Alcan Inc and Royal Dutch NV. |

*Source: Pilkington Annual Report and Accounts, various years.*

significant part subsequently sold to Credit Suisse First Boston), the bank has generally steered clear of acquisitions. Nigel Rudd has previously held board positions at Kidde and at East Midlands Energy as non-executive chair and at Gartmore Value Investments as NED (*The Times*, Power 100).

The four other Pilkington NEDs had arrived since 1998 and two of the four had been appointed since 2003. Their connection with the company was recent and their careers represent the same culture of the deal as Rudd: two were currently also NEDs of 3i, the British venture capital firm, and another was the senior independent NED of Hanson PLC, another firm with a highly acquisitive past. Unsurprisingly, some of these other NEDs were clearly well networked with Nigel Rudd: the longest serving Pilkington NED was finance director of Barclays Bank, between 1993 and 1999, where Sir Nigel served as NED after 1996. For figures like Sir Nigel and his NED colleagues, the prospect of selling one corporate bundle of assets and buying another is something that they are both familiar with and practised at. In 1986 the 'barbarians were at the gate' and it was a question of saving Pilkington from the values of acquisition and divestment represented by BTR the external predator; in 2005/6 these values were enacted in the career of Sir Nigel Rudd who chaired the board and whose everyday role seems to be to manage the selling of the company at the best price possible.

This vignette of difference between 1986 and 2006 is compelling because after 20 years the NEDs were not only sympathetic to the notion of *everything for sale* but also well-practised in running an auction. The vocabularies of motivation are rehearsed in NED careers where the sequence of executive and non executive roles in different companies provides socializing practice and preparation for the current game of corporate restructuring. This provides a means of understanding how the recycling of FTSE execs and the dominance of NEDs produces different corporate decisions and outcomes. The NED of 2006 represents, not the interests of a particular fraction of finance capital but, rather, the imperatives of financialization, where EDs and NEDs are part of a broader business community which provides career opportunities for executives beyond the single firm and may include a variety of post-retirement roles such as in private equity.

## Conclusion

Our aim has been to demonstrate how business elite research could be renewed through mixed methods research which here shows the outcomes of the new exchange of elite personnel established by the corporate governance system. Our conclusion is that elites research needs to be renewed in a conjuncture of changing financialization, which motivates new actors like NEDs or financial intermediaries.

The sociograms and sample survey of NEDs show how the exchange of elite personnel at board level remains an important aspect of corporate capitalism in the UK. But this now operates within a new financialization frame which is partly defined by proceduralized corporate governance and party defined by the changing ways of realizing shareholder value from one conjuncture to the next. It is important to underline the point that elite exchange is not simply a phenomenon within the largest public companies in the FTSE 100 in the UK, because it can also be observed between the largest firms and the mid-caps in the FTSE 250. Similarly, the exchange involves retired as well as current executives of the FTSE 100, which increases the pool of available motivated players. The exchange of personnel is also a way in which private sector norms may be enacted in other domains like charities, quangos and the public sector through the NED system. As for the case study of Pilkington in the building materials sector, one case is not conclusive but it is suggestive both about effects and about the possibility of new kinds of research into how exchange of personnel and group motivation makes a difference.

Motivation is not the same as behaviour because it leaves scope for discretion and judgement. If in principle everything is for sale, then NEDs have the practical responsibility for auctioning the company and for deciding which offer to accept and which to reject because the bidder's best and final offer is too low. The London Stock Exchange (LSE) is an interesting case because here (with the support of institutional shareholders including activists) the senior executives and the board turned down a series of friendly approaches and hostile offers from Deutsche Börse, Macquarie and NASDAQ. The LSE is an exception, however, because we can think of no other company that has seen off so many foreign would-be purchasers. The more usual story is that the UK target company goes to the first corporate buyer who is prepared to offer a significant premium over the undisturbed price and last week's close. And when rumours of bids begin to circulate, it is generally assumed that NEDs in the target company will not be a problem and indeed are motivated to sell at the right price because, like Sir Nigel Rudd, they 'know what they are doing'. Thus, by autumn 2007, the UK financial press regarded brewery company Scottish and Newcastle (S&N) as a bid target after much international consolidation among competitors. With characteristic worldliness, the Lex column of the *Financial Times* discounted the possibility that the S&N board would reject the rumoured joint bid by Carlsberg and Heineken because the Scottish and Newcastle NEDs were motivated and practised in selling the company:

> . . . anyone expecting a Braveheart style propensity towards independence should take a look at S&N's board. The non-executive directors are a Who's Who of recently sold mid-size UK companies with veterans of Scottish Power, Allied Domecq and Hilton among others (18 October, 2007).

## Notes

1 The authors would like to thank Zhong Chen and Xingfei Liu for their research assistance on the NEDs and Stefanie Pauwels for research on the Pilkington case.

2 Rather confusingly, several classic texts (especially Scott, 1979) have been reprinted and empirically updated (Scott, 1997) but, interestingly, the basic conceptual frame dates from the 1975–85 period and there has, in recent years, been a huge expansion in governance-based research on NEDs while elite network research has been relatively neglected except by those using a Bordieusian frame (eg Maclean *et al.*, 2006).
3 See Simon Caulkin's *Observer* column, 'Are they just bums on seats?' 20 January 2002.
4 See also the 2003 report by Tyson for the DTI.
5 The data on NEDs comes from the Hemscott database, which provides the names and positions of public company board members. Supplementary biographical information on the sample of NEDs, especially on career histories, was obtained through internet-based searches on named individuals.

# References

Barkema, H.G. and Gomez-Mejia, L.R., (1998), 'Managerial compensation and firm performance: a general research framework', *Academy of Management Journal*, **41**(2): 135–46.
Barratt Brown, M., (1968), 'The controllers of British industry' in Coates, K., (ed.), *Can the Workers Run Industry?* London: Sphere.
Bebchuk, L. and Fried, J., (2004), *Pay Without Performance: The Unfulfilled Promise of Executive Compensation*, Cambridge, Mass: Harvard University Press.
Cadbury, A., (1992), *Report of the Committee on the Financial Aspects of Corporate Governance*, London: Gee & Co.
Carroll, W.K., (2004), *Corporate Power in a Globalizing World. A Study in Elite Social Organization*, Ontario: Oxford University Press.
*Combined Code, The*, (1998), London Stock Exchange: London.
*Combined Code on Corporate Governance, The*, (2003), London: Financial Reporting Council.
*Combined Code on Corporate Governance, The*, (2006), London: Financial Reporting Council.
Dalton, C.M. and Dalton, D.R., (2005), 'Boards of directors: utilizing empirical evidence in developing practical prescriptions', *British Journal of Management*, vol.**16**: S91–97.
Elliott, L. and Atkinson, D., (2007), *Fantasy Island*, London: Constable.
Erturk, I., Froud, J., Johal, S. and Williams, K., (2005), 'Pay for corporate performance or pay as social division? Rethinking the problem of top management pay in giant corporations', *Competition and Change*, **9(1)**: 49–74.
Erturk, I., Froud, J., Johal, S., Leaver, A. and Williams, K., (2008), *Financialization at Work: Key Readings and Commentary*, London: Routledge.
Ezzamel, M. and Watson, R., (1998), 'Market comparison earnings and the bidding-up of executive cash compensation: evidence from the United Kingdom', *Academy of Management Journal*, **41(2)**: 221–31.
Fama, E.F., (1980), 'Agency problems and the theory of the firm', *The Journal of Political Economy*, vol.**88**, no.2: 288–302.
Folkman, P., Froud, J., Johal, S. and Williams, K., (2007), Working for themselves: capital market intermediaries and present day capitalism, *Business History*, vol.**49**, no.4: 552–72.
Folkman, P., Froud, J. and Williams, K., 'Private equity: levered on capital and/or labour', *Journal of Industrial Relations* (forthcoming).
Froud, J., Johal, S., Leaver, A. and Williams, K., (2006), *Strategy and Financialisation: Narrative and Numbers*, London: Routledge.
Hampel, R., (1998), *Committee on Corporate Governance: Final Report*, London: Gee.
Higgs, D., (2003), *Review of the Role and Effectiveness of Non-Executive Directors*, London: Department of Trade and Industry, Online. Available HTTP: <http://www.dti.gov.uk/cld/non_exec_review/pdfs/higgsreport.pdf> accessed 20 February 2005
Hilferding, R., (1910), *Finance Capital*, (reprinted 1981), London: Routledge and Kegan Paul.
Hill, S., (1995), 'The social organization of boards of directors', *British Journal of Sociology*, **46(2)**: 245–278.

Jensen, M.C., (1993), 'The modern industrial revolution, exit and the failure of internal control systems', *The Journal of Finance*, vol.**48**, no.3: 831–880.

Larcker, D.F., Richardson, S.A. and Tuna, I., (2005), 'How important is corporate governance?' mimeo, University of Pennsylvania: The Wharton School.

Lenin, V.I., (1917), *Imperialism. The Higher Stages of Capitalism*, (reprinted 1966), Moscow: Progress Publishers.

Maclean, M., Harvey, C. and Press, J., (2006), *Business Elites and Corporate Governance in France and the UK*, Houndmills: Palgrave Macmillan.

Mills, C.W., (1940), 'Situated actions and vocabularies of motive', *American Sociological Review*, vol.**5**, no.6: 904–13.

Mizruchi, M., (1996), 'What do interlocks do? An analysis, critique and assessment of research on interlocking directorates'. *Annual Review of Sociology*, **22:** 271–98.

Pettigrew, A., (1992), 'On studying managerial elites' *Strategic Management Journal*, **13:** 163–82.

Roberts, J., McNulty, T. and Stiles, P., (2005), 'Beyond agency conceptions of the work of the non-executive director: creating accountability in the boardroom,' *British Journal of Management*, vol.**16:** S5–26.

Scott, J., (1979), *Corporations, Classes and Capitalism*, Oxford: Oxford University Press.

Scott, J., (1997), *Corporate Business and Capitalist Classes*, Oxford: Oxford University Press.

Scott, J. and Griff, C., (1984), *Directors of Industry. The British Corporate Network 1994–1976*, Cambridge: Polity Press.

Solomon, J. and Solomon, A., (2004), *Corporate Governance and Accountability*, Chichester: John Wiley & Sons.

Tosi, H.L., Werner, S., Katz, J.P. and Gomez-Mejia, L.R., (2000), 'How much does performance matter? A meta-analysis of CEO pay studies', *Journal of Management*, **26(2):** 301–39.

Tricker, R.I., (1978), *The Independent Director. A Study of the Non-Executive and of the Audit Committee*, Croyden: Tolley.

Tyson, L., (2003), *The Tyson Report on the Recruitment and Development of Non-Executive Directors*, Report for the Department of Trade and Industry, London: London Business School.

Useem, M., (1984), *The Inner Circle. Large Corporations and the Rise of Business Political Activity in the US and UK*, New York: Oxford University Press.

Whitley, R., (1974), 'The City and Industry: the directors of large companies, their characteristics and connections', *Elites and Power in British Society*, London: Cambridge University Press.

Windolf, P., (2002), *Corporate Networks in Europe and the United States*, Oxford: Oxford University Press.

Young, D. and Scott, P., (2004), *Having Their Cake. How the City and Big Bosses are Consuming UK Business*, London: Kogan Page.

# Section 3
# Cultural Elites and Consumption of Elites

# The end of the English cultural elite?

*Dave Griffiths, Andrew Miles and Mike Savage*

In his autobiography, *Our Age* (1990) Lord Noel Annan, the distinguished Cambridge don, intellectual historian, first Vice-Chancellor of the University of London, and leading cultural broker between the 1950s and the 1970s, offered a heartfelt and emotional account of the rise and fall of the intellectual and cultural elite, a group with which he claims affinity. Drawing on his research on the rise of intermarriage and family connections amongst Oxbridge dons from the later 19th century (reprinted in Annan, 1999), he argues that in the immediate post war years, this intellectual and social elite came to dominate its age. The expansion of universities, the success of the BBC, the effective deployment of state funding for the arts and culture, and the deference of government and public opinion, led him to define the cultural elite as *the Generation that Made Post-War Britain.*

Annan made no bones of the fact that this was an elitist, gentlemanly formation. Expanding on the definition provided by the Oxford don Maurice Bowra, he saw this as consisting of 'those who make their times significant and form opinion'. He goes on, 'It goes without saying that he [Bowra] expected them to come from the upper or middle classes, to grow up in a public school and go to Oxford or Cambridge. He should have added the London School of Economics. These were the three places where ideas fermented' (Annan, 1990:3–4). He was emphatic that it drew upon an old, 'aristocratic', culture.[1] Nonetheless its liberal and bohemian formation allowed it to play a leading role in shaping cultural trends in post-war British culture, allowing a commitment to artistic and intellectual values, and a belief in cultural excellence. This is a picture painted with love.

The final part of Annan's book takes on sombre tones. He traces the eclipse of this elite. He attributes this partly to a lack of resolution as it faced the challenges of the 1960s and later. It was divided over whether to champion comprehensive education or whether to defend grammar schools (Annan, 1990:496). Its distinctiveness was eroded by the decision of the Robbins report to fund new universities as generously as the older ones, so questioning Oxbridge supremacy (1990:505). It failed to recognize the geo-political marginalization of Britain in the post-war years. But ultimately, in Annan's view, the 'death of the Dons' can be attributed to one person – Margaret Thatcher, Conservative Prime Minister between 1979 and 1990. 'She rejected practically all their beliefs and practices. It was she who led the hissing as my generation made their exit from the stage' (Annan, 1990:574). She rejected the compromising rationalism of the dons, replacing it with a policy-driven zeal and central control which undercut academic and intellectual expertise. The book ends wistfully:

> By 1990 only a handful of us were still able to imagine that they might mould the future. We were dying. . . . For us the owl of Minerva had folded its wings. All we could do was comfort ourselves with Shakespeare's reflection that, though there was never yet a philosopher that could endure the toothache patiently, a few of us had 'writ the style of the gods and made a push at chance and sufferance' (Annan, 1990:610).

Annan's account is personal, yet it resonates with sociological accounts. It accords with Nikolas Rose's (1999) and George Yudice's (2002) analyses of the way that neo-liberal governance accords a different kind of expertise, where culture becomes subject to 'instrumental' intervention, and can be shown to lead to specified outcomes. It strikes a chord with Zygmunt Bauman's (1989) excavation of the crisis of the 'legislative intellectual'. Whereas in earlier phases of 'modernity', intellectuals could legislate through being allowed to differentiate right from wrong, now their expertise was called into question as market logic allowed a different mechanism for allocating resources and values. From the other side of the Atlantic, Steven Brint (1993) showed how professions who had traditionally justified their social and economic advantages through their claims to 'status', especially through the respectability and social value of their calling, increasingly justified them in market terms. Doctors defended their high income not in terms of the social importance of medical care, but in terms of the scarcity of their skills. Other chapters in this volume, for instance du Gay's account of reform in the Civil Service, resonate. Annan's account represents, in palimpsest, the sociological orthodoxy which argues that neo-liberalism has undermined the power and authority of the traditional cultural elite.

Yet, despite the currency and power of this argument, there are no sustained studies of the organization of the English cultural elite which assess whether the 'rise and fall' argument can be sustained. Our chapter uses prosopographical data and social network analysis based on a comprehensive study of the Board members of 'cultural' quangos to assess, empirically, whether the sway of gentlemanly intellectuals has been transformed as radically as Annan claims. Our argument is that, despite important changes in the organization of cultural organizations and activities, it is too simple to see these as marking the wholesale erosion of the old cultural elite. We agree that the 'neo-liberalization' of cultural governance entails the end of the ascribed power of an old boy network, but our analysis reveals a process where traditional intellectual elites have proved able to remake their authority through playing key roles as brokers in more dispersed social networks. We argue that, within this process, a distinctive 'metropolitan formation' continues to be highly strategically effective in the organization of cultural life.

We begin, therefore, with a theoretical and historical elaboration concerning the post-war English cultural elite. In Section two, drawing on a comprehensive study of the personal characteristics of all board members of quangos working within the jurisdiction of the Department of Culture, Media and Sport, we show that although members of the old elite are over-represented, they no do not monopolize such key positions. We then use a case study of historical change amongst board members of the Arts Council of England to demonstrate a certain – though by no means overwhelming – 'democratization' of membership. In the third section, we use social network analysis to explore the composition of board memberships in 2007. We show how, in a relatively fragmented network, it is the old elites who are positioned strategically to connect otherwise fractured quangos. We theorize this dominance through arguing for the importance of a culturally imprinted and socially connected metropolitan formation' at the heart of this process.

## The historical power of the English intellectual elite

Annan's account of the post war dominance of the upper class, Oxbridge, intellectual elite can most effectively be seen as a re-iteration of the arguments made by the American sociologist, Edward Shils, in a famous article in the CIA funded journal, *Encounter*, in 1955. He argued that

> The re-establishment of amicable and harmonious relations between the intellectual and British society has really been the unification of the intellectuals with the other groups of the ruling elite . . . the culture which has now regained moral ascendancy is not an aristocratic one in the sense that it is the present culture of an active aristocracy . . . it is the culture traditionally inspired by those classes, the culture appropriate to certain institutions allied to these classes . . . it is pluralistic culture within itself; it has room for politicians, for sportsmen, for travelers, for civil servants and judges and barristers and journalists, for artists and writers of different persuasions. It is an unbourgeois culture' (Shils, 1955).

Like Annan, Shils insists that in Britain intellectuals did not reject aristocratic power, as happened in France for instance, but embraced it. Gentlemanly institutions such as the public schools and Oxbridge became devices for training new generations of intellectuals within a gentlemanly institutional shell.[2] Whereas in France, intellectuals railed against the wealthy old guard, so spawning what Pierre Bourdieu (1985) saw as a cultural tension between 'intellectuals' and 'industrialists', in Britain, it was actually an aristocratically intellectual group, notably that associated with Bloomsbury, which championed cultural modernism and the values of 'pure intellect' (see Rose, 2000; Savage, 2008). Sociologically, what is important about Shils' claim is the idea that the aristocratic intellectuals were not some traditional status residue but were active and vital forces in a forging post war English society. There was no contradiction between a modern, even meritocratic society, and the power of the aristocratic intellectuals.

A central aspect of this process was the enthusiasm of this group for working with state institutions to expand its remit and claim jurisdiction over the 'apparatus of cultural governance'. It is well known that the effectiveness of Oxbridge supremacy did not rely on its ability to deploy its own investments and private funds (as was the case in the American Ivy league, by contrast) but in securing state funding to underwrite its elite mission. The long-term interlinkage between the British state, its cultural apparatus, and the British intellectuals has been traced in Corrigan and Sayer's *The Great Arch* (1985) and we can see the pertinence of their emphasis by looking at Table one, below. This lists all the 50 Executive Quangos and Public Corporations which in 2006/07 were under the jurisdiction of the Department of Culture, Media and Sport, with their initial date of formation listed. These agencies employ 48,000 individuals and spend around £6.5 billion a year (Public Bodies, 2006). The details are revealing.

Table 1 reveals the long history of public cultural bodies, dating back to the Royal Armouries Museum (now situated in Leeds), in the 17th century. Most of the established, metropolitan museums were formed by 1860s, with the Tate and the V&A following by the end of the 19th century (see generally, Fyfe, 2000). The BBC, formed in 1922, proved a path-breaking model, and the Arts Council in 1946. We can also see more museums being founded, though with the exception of the Imperial War Museum these do not have the stature of the older museums. We also see the first intervention in the area of 'commercial' culture with the formation of the Tote in 1929.

Annan's account, along with that of other commentators, especially focuses on the role of the BBC and the Arts Council as allowing the remit of the intellectuals to be writ large. One of Keynes's last acts before his death in 1946 was to preside over the formation of the Council for the Encouragement of Music and the Arts (CEMA) in 1942, which was to become the Arts Council in 1946, and he succeeded in placing his Bloomsbury contacts on the commissioning panel whilst marginalizing the older and more traditional Royal Academy establishment (Skidelsky, 2003:728). The Arts Council grew out of a longer-term intersection between the British state and cultural brokers. The 1916 Entertainment Act had levied taxes on all entertainments, sports, racing and films (except for those organizations which were set up for charitable and educational purposes) but had allowed exemptions for those forms of entertainment deemed 'partly educational'. Before 1934 the commissioners had construed the words 'partly educational' pretty strictly but in that year the Law Officers gave an opinion (primarily with reference to the Old Vic and Sadler's Wells) that 'improving and educating taste in the drama is an educational purpose within the meaning of the above quoted section'.

The result was to make it difficult to find criteria to refuse 'partly educational' status, whereby any 'serious' company was permitted to claim exemption. By 1943, the Treasury reckoned it was losing £100,000 in London alone through these exemptions: 'in effect, it has come very close to ruling out only farces and musical comedies'. This led the Treasury to incorporate cultural intellectuals into its own decision-making apparatus, when in 1943 a special committee was formed to decide which performances were 'partly educational' and hence tax-free.[3]

**Table 1:** *DCMS Executive Quangos and Public Corporations, 2007, with date of initial formation*

| Date | Organization |
|------|-------------|
| 17th Century | 1 – Royal Armories Museum 1660 |
| 18th Century | 2 – Natural History Museum 1753; British Museum 1753 |
| 1800–1850 | 2 – National Gallery 1824; Sir John Soane's Museum 1837 |
| 1850–1899 | 4 – National Portrait Gallery 1856; National Museum of Science and Industry 1857; Victorian and Albert Museum 1897; Tate 1897 |
| 1900–1949 | 8 – Wallace Collection 1900; Horniman Museum 1901; Geffrye Museum 1914; Imperial War Museum 1917; BBC 1922; Tote 1929; National Maritime Museum 1937; Arts Council 1946 |
| 1950s | – |
| 1960s | 6 – Horserace Betting Levy; Museum of London; Museum of Science and Industry in Manchester [a]; Churches Conservation Trust; Gaming Board for Great Britain; British Tourist Authority |
| 1970s | 1 – British Library |
| 1980s | 6 – National Heritage Memorial Fund; Alcohol Education and Research Council; English Heritage; Public Lending Rights; Channel 4; S4C |
| 1990s | 10 – Football Licensing Authority; Historic Royal Palaces; National Endowment for Science, Technology and the Arts; UK Sport; Sport England; National Lottery Commission; Commission for Architecture and the Built Environment; UK Film Council; Community Fund; New Opportunity Fund |
| 2000s | 10 – 8 regional cultural NDPB's [b]; Museums, Libraries and Archive Council; and Olympic Lottery Distributor |

[a] Originally the North Western Museum of Science and Industry.
[b] Non-departmental Public Bodies.

A similar imbrication of the cultural elite with the state is evident in the BBC, most famously in the formation of the BBC's 'Third Programme' in 1946. Whereas 'highbrows' between the wars had largely scorned the radio as vulgar and plebeian, in the post war years, partly as a result of its wartime importance as vehicle of communication, there was growing interest in using it as a means of disseminating cultural values and, as Collini (2006) emphasizes, it also became a lucrative source of funds for the intellectuals themselves, with the fee of 20 guineas for a learned talk being amongst the best possible at the time. 'Broadcasting gave us the opportunity to popularize our views on a scale hitherto unknown to intellectuals' (Annan, 1990:291). The first head of the Third Programme, George Barnes, 'belonged to the intellectual aristocracy and married within it. . . . The Third became the patron of dons and sometimes appeared to be broadcasting solely to them. Nor was the Third Programme the only institution to be giving employment to intellectuals. The British Council and Arts Council began to grow in size' (Annan, 1990, 291).

The point here is that it was the ability of the intellectual aristocracy to entwine itself with state institutions, including ostensibly 'modern' ones, which marked out its ability to define itself as the decisive cultural vanguard. If we are to understand its subsequent fortunes, we need to place them within the context of recent restructuring of the state apparatus associated with neo-liberal reforms from the 1980s.

Here, we need to note, in the context of Annan's arguments about the more recent decline of the intellectual aristocracy, that there has actually been a marked expansion of the state's intervention in the 'governance of culture'. To be sure, there was something of a hiatus in the immediate post-war decades: no quangos were formed at all between 1946 and 1961. The remainder of the 1960s witnessed only a spluttering of life: the first regional museum (in Manchester), and also the development of the first quangos with governance and marketing roles. The 1970s and early 1980s saw little further intervention, and there is some evidence that Thatcher's government sought to reduce public intervention in this field. Even so, we need to question Annan's pessimism. No existing cultural quangos were actually closed down. The government grant to the Arts Council rose dramatically during the Thatcher years from £63 million in 1979–80 to £205 million by 1991–92 which, in terms of the 1994–95 Retail Price Index, was an increase from £117.8m to £179 million (Witts, 1998). Whatever the personal antipathies of Thatcher might have been to 'Our Age', it is not clear that they were severely undermined financially.[4]

Table one also indicates that from the mid 1990s there has been an intense wave of 'quango formation', possibly the most marked sustained state intervention in 'culture' which has ever been seen in the UK. Some parts of this are concerned with regulating the commercial aspects of intellectual property (Football Licensing Authority), others with intervening in popular culture and in forms of cultural promotion (notably in the arena of the Sports). Of particular importance is the development of the National Lottery as a major source of funding, which has led to the formation of a large public institutional apparatus for disbursing funds. Since 2000 the elaboration of a 'regional cultural apparatus', with an alliance between the Arts Council and the Department of Culture, Media and Sport, has been highly significant in leading to the emergence of regional cultural policy, and there has been a large absolute increase in public spending in this area.[5] Perhaps Annan's obituary to 'Our Age', published in 1990, was written too soon?

## Who are the quangocrats?

In this section we consider whether these new forms of investment have allowed the intellectual aristocracy to re-invent itself. Can we see the personnel involved in these quangos as representing the old cultural elite? Or are we instead seeing a new kind of cultural manager emerging, from a different kind of background? Do we now see a neo-liberal managerial elite with very little sympathy with the previous generation? In order to explore these issues we now turn to consider the profile of those acting as Board Members and chairs of these organizations in early 2007, before then examining historically whether we can detect changes in recent decades.

Members of all the boards of the 50 agencies listed above has been collected from *Public Bodies 2005/06*, the government's list of all non-departmental public bodies. Information has been obtained from publicly available sources from these bodies, such as management team profiles on their websites, press releases, board meeting minutes, annual reports and registers of members' interests. In the later two cases, these details have been obtained under the 2001 Freedom of Information Act if otherwise unavailable. Further research was gathered from biographical directories, including *Debrett's People of Today, Who's Who* and *Who's Who in Charities*. The data was collected between April 2006 and February 2007.

A total of 816 people sit on these boards, including 25 who sit on two each. Overall, 65 per cent of these individuals are male, with an average age of 57. 44 per cent are university educated, 40 per cent are listed within biographical directories (such as *Who's Who*), 36 per cent are charity trustees, 38 per cent are affiliated to a professional body, 29 per cent advise other quangos and 21 per cent hold corporate directorships, Smaller percentages have positions within professional bodies (18 per cent), hold quango directorships in other departments (17 per cent), are members of 'gentlemen's' clubs or sit on boards of educational establishments (16 per cent each), have official honours such as a MBE or have received honorary degrees (15 per cent each), advise companies (5 per cent) or sit in editorial positions, are shareholders in companies or hold visiting professorships (4 per cent each).[6] The relatively large numbers of members who are in gentlemen's clubs and who possess honours is prima facie evidence that they share some characteristics with an older elite. On the other hand, those who are university educated appear to be in the minority.[7]

The numbers of individuals per quango vary greatly, from 29 at the Imperial War Museum to just 5 each for Culture North West and Olympic Lottery Distributor. The demographics of the boards differ significantly as well. The average age of members ranges from 50 (UK Film Council) to 65 (Wallace Collection). Despite only 35 per cent of all directors being female, there are, fractionally, more women than men on three of the boards (Horniman Museum, National Lottery Commission and Olympic Lottery Distributor). Women, however, occupy less than 20 per cent of the positions on the Churches Conservation Trust, the Historic Royal Palaces, and the Horseracing Betting Levy Board and Tote). In some cases, such as Culture South East, half of the members sit on other quangos (whether inside or outside the department) whilst eight bodies have no members sitting on other boards.

While this demonstrates that these organizations differ in their profiles and composition, the data nevertheless indicates a clear predominance of Oxbridge and London University graduates among university-educated board members. Table 2 demonstrates the number of people who have attended various types of university and highlights how they have largely been educated at the top institutions. Of the 363 people who we know are university educated, more than a fifth in each case have been to Cambridge, Oxford or London. Over a quarter have been educated at overseas institutions, most commonly Ivy League or prestigious European institutions. In many cases, these people have been educated at more than one of these elite institutions.

The importance of academic pedigree is underlined when we consider board members who are university employees. Just as in Annan's day, university academics continue to form the single most important source of recruitment. Table 3, which shows the particular university affiliation of quango board members, indicates the central role of the older, more prestigious institutions, with London and Oxbridge staff predominating among the metropolitan museums, while those attached to provincial and newer institutions are more likely to sit on regional quangos.

A further piece of information that is illuminating here concerns the schools attended by these individuals. Table 4 identifies the schools most frequently listed by quango members. Although the absolute number of listed schools is small, and the individuals involved cannot be said to typical of board members, it is, nonetheless, the prestigious private schools that figure most strongly, especially amongst members of the London museum boards.

Finally, a total of 129 board members, amounting to one in six of those traced, frequent private member clubs. Of the 50 quangos, 42 contain at least one quangocrat who visits such establishments. By far the most popular among these is the Athenaeum, which caters for members of 17 different boards. Other popular clubs are the Reform (involving 11 boards, 4 of which were also connected to the Athenaeum) and Chelsea Arts (featuring on 7 boards, 5 of which were connected to the Athenaeum, and 3 with Reform). The striking thing about these findings, apart from the large number of individuals involved, is that these are all elite institutions located in the London heartland, thereby reinforcing the impression that there continues to be a socially distinctive, metropolitan dynamic in the governance of the cultural world.

**Table 2:** *University Attended by DCMS Board Members*

| Institution | No. of Quangocrats |
| --- | --- |
| University of London | 80 |
| Oxford University | 76 |
| Cambridge University | 77 |
| Other Russell Group universities | 97 |
| Overseas institutions | 98 |
| Other UK universities | 151 |
| Professional or military colleges | 19 |

**Table 3:** Universities which Employ more than one DCMS Board Member

| University | No. of Quangocrats | Organization |
|---|---|---|
| London | 14 | Alcohol Education and Research Council, English Heritage, Heritage Lottery Fund, Imperial War Museum, National Gallery London, National Museum of Science and Industry (2), National Portrait Gallery, Natural History Museum (3), Tate, Victoria and Albert Museum |
| Cambridge | 8 | BBC, British Museum (2), Living East, National Maritime Museum (2), National Museum of Science and Industry (3) |
| Oxford | 4 | British Museum, English Heritage, National Maritime Museum, Natural History Museum |
| Manchester | 3 | Commission on the Built Environment, Heritage Lottery Fund, Museum of Science and Industry Manchester |
| Newcastle | 3 | Arts Council England, Culture North East (2) |
| Oxford Brookes | 3 | Alcohol Education and Research Council, National Gallery London, Tate |
| Cardiff | 2 | BBC, Natural History Museum |
| City | 2 | Museums, Archives and Libraries Commission, National Endowment for Science, Technology and the Arts, National Portrait Gallery |
| De Montfort | 2 | Culture East Midlands (2) |
| Leicester | 2 | British Library, National Gallery London |

**Table 4:** *Most Popular Schools Attended by DCMS Quangocrats*

| School | Total No. of Quangocrats | Quangocrats by Type of Organization | | |
|---|---|---|---|---|
| | | London museums | National boards | Regional boards |
| Eton | 8 | 4 | 3 | 1 |
| Wellington College | 6 | 4 | 2 | 0 |
| Haberdashers' Aske School | 5 | 4 | 1 | 0 |
| St Paul's Girls' School | 5 | 4 | 1 | 0 |
| Cheltenham Ladies' College | 4 | 2 | 1 | 1 |
| Fettes College, Edinburgh | 4 | 2 | 2 | 0 |
| Rugby | 4 | 3 | 1 | 0 |
| Dulwich College | 3 | 1 | 2 | 0 |
| Shrewsbury School | 3 | 3 | 0 | 0 |

The analysis hitherto can be interpreted in two ways. On the one hand, we see in the composition of the UK's cultural quangos a clear over-representation of old elite schools, clubs, and universities, which is especially marked amongst the most prestigious national museums. We also see clear evidence of metropolitan bias. Yet at the same time, we need to recognize that the sphere of cultural governance is by no means the preserve of a closed elite. Whereas Annan (1990) argues that 'Our Age' was defined entirely through graduation from Oxbridge or London Universities, only 23 per cent of our quango board members appear to have been educated in this way. There does seem to be evidence of the opening of the corridors of power to a wider and more representative constituency. We can also see how the proliferation of quangos necessarily creates a more dispersed and fragmented structure. The older museum-based bodies appear to be the most 'gentlemanly' whilst the regional bodies are more open.

The question arises, therefore, as to whether, if we simply focused on the older bodies alone, we would find evidence of 'democratization'. We have examined this issue by conducting an exhaustive study of the board members of the Arts Council. This is probably the decisive body to focus on, because of its role in funding activities in the arena of 'high culture' (notably opera) and in co-ordinating cultural provision across England and Wales. Based on biographical abstracts in *Who's Who 2007* and *Who Was Who 1897–2006*, we compared the characteristics of those council and panel members who began their service in the 1960s and 70s with those who began their service in the 1980s and 90s.[8] This comparison allows us to test Annan's account of the fall of his generation.

What this indicates is that there was indeed something of a shift in the composition of the Arts Council executive around the Thatcherite axis of the late 1970s and early 1980s. Nevertheless, according to this evidence, the Arts Council remained, on the eve of the new millennium, very much an 'establishment' agency, strongly influenced by a male, Oxbridge-educated, academic/literary elite.

The clearest evidence for democratization is in the gender profile, where the proportion of women doubles, from 11 per cent to 23 per cent between the 1960s and the 1990s. The story is similar for those ACE board members reporting honours. Among the older generation, 72 per cent could claim an honour of some sort, a figure which declines to 43 per cent in the later cohort. The number of peers falls from 15 per cent to 8 per cent, the proportion of knights and dames also halves from 24 per cent to 12 per cent and the number of CBEs drops from 38 per cent to 26 per cent; only the relatively lowly OBEs hold up, declining only slightly from 12 per cent to 10 per cent.

There is also a decline in those belonging to private clubs, from 41 per cent to 25 per cent. Preferences for club type remain the same, with a clear domination by the Garrick and the Athenaeum, but there is more diversity in the range of clubs attended over time. This doesn't equate to less exclusiveness, however. While the Groucho establishes more of a profile, so does White's, Brooks's, and the Savile, and there is also greater presence from some of the more political and sport-focused elite establishments, like the Carlton and the Reform clubs, the Royal & Ancient, Hurlingham, and Leander.

We can see particularly interesting shifts in the occupational composition of board members (see Table 5). There is a decline in artists and artist academics, the kind of people who Keynes recruited in the 1940s. 46 per cent of members in the 1960s and 1970s were primarily prominent artistic producers, a figure which halved to 24 per cent amongst the later cohort. By contrast, academics retain their profile though the range of their disciplines diversifies: in the first cohort they were virtually all from English and Art History, but in the later cohort it included specialists in economics and business studies, social science, medicine and engineering. This is indicative of a growing influence of businessmen and financiers, professionals, and the civil service.

It seems then that even just taking the Arts Council, which, given its history and profile, is perhaps more likely than most to attract traditional groups, there is evidence of democratization. The major qualification to this point, however, concerns the educational background of its members, where there has been much less of a shift. In terms of schooling, the independent sector dominates throughout, although the numbers from state grammar schools rises slightly. Amongst the entire sample, just one individual (from the later cohort) was educated at a secondary modern school. The profile of the major public schools declines but they remain very important. In the first cohort 37 per cent had been to one of the 'top schools', 20 per cent to one of the original 'elite' Clarendon nine, and 10 per cent to Eton alone. After 1979, these numbers are 27 per cent, 12 per cent and 6 per cent respectively.

**Table 5:** *Occupational Backgrounds of Arts Council Board Members (percentage rounded by cohort)*

| Occupational group | Period of tenure at Arts Council | |
|---|---|---|
| | 1960s & 70s | 1980s & 90s |
| Literary[a] | 24 | 15 |
| Artists[b] | 15 | 8 |
| Artist academics[c] | 7 | 1 |
| Academics | 14 | 14 |
| Arts executives[d] | 13 | 16 |
| Lawyers | 6 | 1 |
| Media | 6 | 8 |
| Politicians | 5 | 3 |
| Businessmen | 5 | 10 |
| Civil servants | 1 | 4 |
| Architects | 3 | 4 |

Notes: a) editors, writers publishers; b) mainly painters, actors, musicians; c) e.g. musicians who become professors at the Royal College of Music; d) museum, theatre directors etc.

**Table 6:** *University Attendance of Arts Council board members (percentage rounded by cohort)*

| University | Period of tenure at Arts Council | |
|---|---|---|
| | 1960s & 70s | 1980s & 90s |
| Oxbridge | 47 | 40 |
| London | 6 | 8 |
| Edinburgh, Cardiff, Durham, Civics | 8 | 8 |
| Elite arts institutions (e.g. RADA) | 14 | 8 |
| Other universities | 1 | 8 |

Table six lists the changing University affiliations of Arts Council board members, where there is the least indication of change compared to any of the attributes we have studied. Oxbridge graduates remain very prominent. Elite arts institutions decline in importance and 'other' universities become slightly more important. these newer universities, however, notably Bristol which is more important in the later cohort, continue to be establishment oriented.

Within these broad patterns, we can also detect subtle shifts here. Cambridge becomes more important in the 80s and 90s (Trinity College being always important), challenging the previous dominance of Oxford (where University College had previously been very important). London associations become more diverse – from predominantly University College to include Queen Mary College, Bedford College, Birkbeck and more of LSE.

## Social networks of board members

The evidence above offers qualified support to Annan's arguments. The old, intellectual, gentlemanly elite is still somewhat over represented amongst board memberships as a whole, and especially amongst the older metropolitan and core cultural bodies, but they clearly do not monopolize membership. Even the Arts Council shows shifts towards more open recruitment. We need to be cautious, however, in extrapolating from these findings. As discussed in other chapters in this volume (Savage and Williams, 2008; Carroll, 2008), we must consider the paradoxical effects of the loosening of elite interlocks in actually making specific links and ties relatively more important. As discussed by Burt (1992), the thinning out of elite networks creates increasing strategic value for those individuals who can span the 'structural holes' that differentiate people in different sectors or boards. In a world of dense elite connections, the absence of any one individual would make relatively little difference to the networks. But where connections are sparse, particular individuals might come to command increased strategic power because they are unique in being able to connect groups which in their absence would be disconnected. This is a shift towards an individualized elite formation, within which individuals can act as brokers and intermediaries in a complex and differentiated array. We now, therefore, need to assess whether we can detect such brokers amongst the fractured cultural elite of contemporary England and if, we can, to consider what kinds of people they are. This will allow us to assess whether the power of the Annan generation's heirs lies not in their background per se, but in terms of whether their profile allows them to tie together an otherwise dispersed arena – a case of gentlemen brokers, perhaps.

Let us pursue this idea through the case of one individual, which our social network analysis shows to be one of the most 'connected', sitting on two boards (Culture North West and National Museums Liverpool) and having recently sat on two others (leaving his role at Museums Libraries and Archives Council and Museum of Science and Industry in Manchester during 2006). This is Loyd Grossman, OBE. He represents, in interesting ways, the old and the new. On the face of it, one would not expect Annan to have greeted him warmly, as he is distinctly 'arriviste'. He is American by background and spent his undergraduate years at Boston University. His expertise lies in popular journalism and television, as restaurant critic and 'foodie' (for instance in 'Masterchef'). His television programme 'Through the Keyhole' brought the homes of minor celebrities into public view and his range of best-selling sauces underpins his fortune. Yet at the same time, he has a relationship with the older formation that Annan celebrates: he was, after all a postgraduate at the LSE, and has worked for *Harpers and Queen*, and *The Tatler*, both of which defer to gentry idioms, and he is a Fellow of the Royal Society of Arts, the Society of Antiquaries (general and Scottish branches) and the Royal Society of Medicine. He frequents traditional private member clubs, including the Athenaeum and Chelsea Arts. But he is, above all, a broker, with a remarkable range of cultural engagements. He is a member of the Liverpool Culture Company, responsible for the 2008 European City of Culture celebrations, and part of the strategy group of the award-winning Another Places iconic art piece in Sefton. He is on the boards of many museum sector agencies, including 24 Hour Museums, Campaign for Museums and the Public Monuments and Sculptures Association. He is the Chair of the Better Food Panel within the NHS and sits on charities concerned with hospital patients and workers as well as health and social problems. He is also part of English Heritage's Blue Plaque Advisory Group, helping to determine which individual's home are worthy of special heritage status. He is a non-executive director of a production company and has previously sat on the boards of a further three quangos. He is certainly aware that this allows him a certain cachet: indeed, he is 'for sale'. A website (www.gordonpoole.com) offers his services as after dinner speaker at a rate between £5,000 to £10,000. Is he an emblem of the new cultural elite?

Let us explore how sparse networks facilitate the rise of brokers using a simple example. We have seen that relatively few current board members appear to have been to elite private schools. If, however, we consider the number of boards which are linked through having a member who has been to the same school, a very different picture emerges. Using the criterion of school attended,

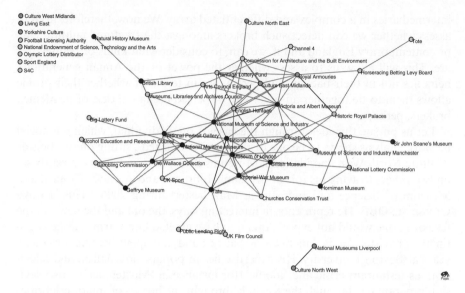

**Figure 1:** *Network of Quangos Linked through Schooling of Board Members.*

Figure 1 shows a very closely-knit network in which most boards are connected. Within the network, the nodes have been colour coordinated so that the grey nodes are regional bodies, the dark nodes London-based museums and the lighter nodes national organizations.

Figure 1 shows that those isolated organizations which are not linked through having members at shared schools are predominantly regional organizations or are sports related. By contrast London museums such as the V&A, the Science Museum, the Imperial War Museum, the Tate and the National Portrait Gallery are very well connected through having members from the same schools. When we look at which schools are creating these links, it is noticeable that there are few instances of any non-fee paying school having more than one former pupil sitting on a quango. As we saw from Table 4, however, a number of distinguished private schools have several former pupils on their boards, and it is in fact these schools that connect the boards. If we look at which particular types of organizations such private school members are involved with, we see that most are museum directors, with very few sitting on regional boards. In short, in a sparse network, it is possible for relatively unusual attributes to become relatively more important in connecting networks.

We can see more formally how specific boards are linked to each other in Figure 2, which reports interlocks of board members. There are 20 isolates – a considerable number – which do not share directors with any other organization. These are predominantly national regulatory organizations, though the British Library and Natural History Museum are also included. There are six instances of two organizations only interlocking with each other, and in every

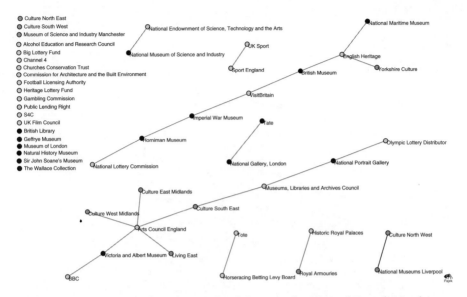

**Figure 2:** *The Interlocking Network of Quangos by Mutual Board Members.*

case one can detect an elective affinity between them, based on sport (UK Sport and Sport England), art (Tate and National Portrait Gallery), North Western interests (National Museums Liverpool and Culture North West), science (National Endowment of Science and National Museum of Science and Industry), horseracing (Tote and the Levy Board), and ancient Royal connections (Armouries and Palaces). There are also two large blocs. One consists of eight organizations, from which only English Heritage has links to more than two others. This links several large museums, the Lottery, English Heritage, Tourist interests and one regional bodies, and appears. It has no connections with the other bloc, which contains 10 institutions, centred around Arts Council England which has links to four regional cultural agencies, two museums, and two other national regulatory body. We can see here, evidence of two different powerful networks within a spare structure, one dominated by the Arts Council, the other by English Heritage. The relative power of these two organizations comes not from its multiple ties, since we can see that members of ACE Board only interlock with five other organizations, and English Heritage three, but lie in their relative position compared to other organizations who are either isolated or have fewer contacts.

Whereas Figure two looks at the overlapping membership of Boards, we can also see whether members of different boards share common membership of private clubs, making it possible for them to meet in such informal surrounds. Figure 3 shows a denser network: There are only three national institutions, and no museums, which fail to have any members of such clubs.

At first glance, it appears as though club memberships allow the regional organizations to link with multiple, London-based organizations (as the

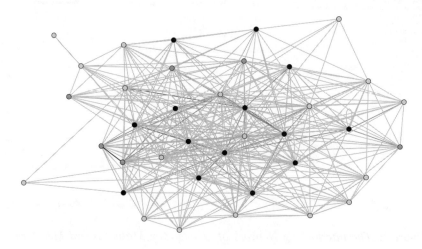

**Figure 3:** *DCMS Quango Network by Directors' 'Gentlemen's' Club Membership.*

example of Grossman would suggest). In fact only five of the ten regional bodies hold positions in this network. It is noticeable, however, that whilst the London-museums are all very central to this network, there are many national regulatory bodies that either do not connect with other institutions or only connect with those which are relatively unpopular. This again suggests that the national regulatory bodies do not share the same social spaces as the museum directors.

This pattern is even clearer looking at university education. Of the 50 bodies, 35 have London alumni, 33 have a Cambridge alumni and 24 have an Oxford alumni. Museums stand out as having graduates of all three leading Universities – of the 17 museum quangos, 11 have board members educated at Cambridge, London and Oxford. The only museums which does not have members educated at more than one of these, The Wallace Collection, still holds an impressive list of alumni including Cambridge, 2 other Russell Group establishments, 3 Ivy League institutions and the Louvre. In contrast, only 6 of the 24 national bodies and 2 of the 11 regional institutions include alumni of the three leading institutions.

This general pattern can be seen consistently across the various network types. However, what it interesting is that this mutual occupation of social space by the museums does not appear to be nepotistically creating quango positions. If we look at the entire network of DCMS quangos, linked by the 25 aforementioned interlocking directors, we see very little interaction between the museums. This suggests that there is a certain 'type' of individual who is sitting on those boards, rather than there being a group of individuals who know each other, who sit on multiple boards.

We can consider this issue further by looking at the average closeness centrality scores. Closeness centrality measures how connected the boards are to all others in the network. Those with high centrality share many common characteristics with well-connected institutions. Those with a low centrality are distant from the trends and nature of the network as a whole. Table 7 shows the average closeness centrality of the overall network, and each of the three categories.

These values clearly demonstrate the distinctive patterns of the London museums who report the highest score on nearly every dimension. The charities network is the only one in which they do not have the highest average value (though even there they are very close to the national bodies). The national quangos only have an above-average centrality score relating to charities. The regional boards are only above-average with regards to employment and the interlocking DCMS network. By contrast, the London museums never hold a below-average centrality score.

One way of specifying the dominance of the London museums is to consider where the biggest variations from the cross-quango average scores occur. In these terms, this sector is much more central than national or regional bodies when it comes to associations with private member clubs, possession of hon-

**Table 7:** *Average Closeness Centrality by Network and Quango Types*

| Network type | All Quangos | London-based | National | Regional |
|---|---|---|---|---|
| Member of professional institution | .828 | .908 | .787 | .808 |
| University attended | .678 | .760 | .656 | .615 |
| 'Gentlemen's' clubs | .458 | .644 | .428 | .267 |
| Honorary degree | .384 | .602 | .365 | .128 |
| Quango advisory position | .365 | .437 | .322 | .361 |
| Previous quango appointments | .255 | .360 | .245 | .136 |
| School attended | .246 | .348 | .240 | .123 |
| Charity trusteeships | .203 | .203 | .207 | .193 |
| Other Quango boards | .165 | .194 | .147 | .164 |
| Educational boards | .144 | .206 | .121 | .110 |
| Employer | .134 | .167 | .107 | .146 |
| Professional body | .128 | .199 | .083 | .128 |
| DCMS interlocking directorships | .043 | .060 | .029 | .052 |
| Corporate directorships directorship | .018 | .025 | .017 | .013 |

orary degree from elite institutions, private school education, sitting on educational boards and membership of professional institution boards. In other words the distance between the London institutions and the two other principal sectors of the cultural quangocracy is greatest when it comes to the most exclusive network types. This certainly suggests that elite reproduction of cultural capital is evident on the boards of these particular institutions.

Regional organizations, by contrast, are far removed from the UK and London-based bodies. They are much less central than their London counterparts in terms of school attended, honorary degrees awarded, charities and previous quango appointments. The marginal status of these institutions within the schools network suggests that the cultural capital evident within the museums carries little weight in the regions. Geography could explain why in other respects the regional bodies lack centrality, as it is clearly easier for somebody in London to sit on a local school, charity or hospital board as a fellow Londoner than someone in Liverpool, Leicester or Leeds. This raises the question, however, of whether the national boards are really national given how closely they are connected to London-interest groups and how simultaneously distant they are from the rest of the UK.

The positioning of the national regulatory organizations is different again. Whilst they are similar to the museums in terms of the social capital of connections through membership of charities, they are distant in terms of the companies they are directors of, professional bodies they are members or directors of, the quangos they sit on and the educational institutions they represent. Similarly, the positioning of the national bodies as distant from the London and regional bodies in terms of educational background, membership of 'gentlemen's' clubs and employment suggests that they share elements with both of the other two kinds of quango. Whilst they share a common geographical location with the London museum bodies, they occupy different social spaces, and while they occupy similar social positions to the regional boards they differ in social background. We need to recognize, however, that these regulatory organizations are not a cohesive group. They contain lottery funding bodies, sports institutions, film council and alcohol research bodies, for instance, and there is little reason to believe that the knowledge, background and experience required to sit on the board of the ombudsman of football stadiums and on an arts funding body should be the same. For this reason, it is possible to break these organizations down into those which allow access to elite circles (English Heritage, BBC and Royal Historic Palaces) and those which do not (the sporting national bodies).

## Conclusion: A fragmented but connected cultural elite

We can begin by agreeing with Annan that 'Our Age' no longer holds universal dominion over the cultural arena, yet we can also suggest that its power lives on, in the interstices of the complex social and institutional networks which now characterize the governance of cultural activities in the UK. Indeed, the picture we have traced is one that is not amenable to a simple interpretation. Instead we must recognize how complexity and fragmentation can also foster the significance of new kinds of elite connection. Let us recap on our main points in conclusion.

First, we need to understand there has been no simple 'marketization' of cultural initiatives but, rather, a hybrid process in which the nature and remit of government quangos have been extended into an increasing range of arenas, spanning forms of popular culture, through the disbursement of new kinds of funds, to regional initiatives. This extension provides an unprecedented arena for powerful individuals to have a role in the public governance of culture, in ways quite unforeseen even twenty years ago. Annan's account of decline might better be seen in terms of proliferation and hybridization.

Secondly, the expansion of such positions, as well as changes in the recruitment process to boards, has entailed a significant social pluralization of membership. 'Our Age' no longer monopolizes the 'governance of culture' in the UK, in the way it largely did even as recently as the 1960s and early 1970s. Whatever elite criteria one wishes to take as a marker of an elite background – attendance at private schools, education at Oxbridge, membership of gentleman's clubs – will only apply to a minority of board members.

Thirdly, and in contrast to Annan's lament, this process does not entail the simple decline of traditional elite powers but their reworking, so that they now provide the key 'bridges' and 'connections' in a much sparser network of power. In a fragmented cultural world, the individuals with traditional elites backgrounds are unusual in being able to span areas of jurisdiction, so making it possible for them to be key brokers. We might interpret this, in Bourdieu's terms, by noting that it is possible for any specific cultural sub-field to be relatively open to those who are expert within it (see the discussion in Savage and Williams, 2008). It is very rare, however, for an individual to straddle such cultural sub-fields, and those who do nearly always rely on expertise or 'capital' exogenous to that field. We have seen that it is mainly those who come from elite backgrounds who perform this linking and straddling role. Of course, in our analysis, we are only able to trace the potential for these individuals to link institutions: it would be necessary to examine ethnographically and through appropriate case studies, how such connections might be significant in practice.

Fourthly, we see, in powerful terms, the continued dominance of what we might term 'the metropolitan formation'. The traditional London-based museums embody a strong and engaging brand of social capital. Not only do they link with organizations relevant to their work, they also connect to organizations that appear to have the right 'cachet'. These include, for instance, sports clubs (rowing, cricket), theatre and the arts (even for the Natural History Museum), professional bodies and religious groups. Prestige organizations, such as those with 'National' or 'Royal' in their titles, appear particularly favoured. Indeed, the directors of London's museums are more likely to be part of a charity and other social organization that works outside of the UK than one working in the UK outside of London. It appears that there is a certain cultural framework inhabited by these individuals, with those moving amongst the most privileged circles particularly welcomed. Here we see the potential for the consolidation of elite strategic power, whereby the elaboration of a more dispersed and fragmented network bestows greater relative power on those few institutions which are central, and so underwrite a dispersed yet effective elite formation.

Finally, we should note the need for further research on the actual processes of connection which exist in the relatively sparse network we have found. We have found more evidence of connection between these quangos when looking at the informal arenas in which members might meet each other (notably clubs) or in terms of a shared background (at school and university) than in terms of their formal roles (compare Figure 2 with Figures 1 and 3). This mapping does not allows us to assess how links deriving from informal channels or a shared background actually work in practice: presumably not all members of the Athaneum know every other member. To address these issues, further research is required.

## Notes

1 'How did one get accepted as a member of Our Age? In the same way that most people have always got accepted – by ability, by family connections and knowing somebody' (Annan, 1990: 9). All page references to *Our Age* are to the 1995 paperback edition.
2 On the historical formation of this 'gentlemanly' culture and its mediation through the public school and university systems see Cain and Hopkins (1993) and Rubinstein (1999).
3 In classic British bureaucratic form, there were attempts to develop 'criteria' to assess whether performances were 'partly educational'. In 1944, the Advisory Committee specified its criteria which emphasized a notion of the plays' likely 'survival value'. The advisory committee used four categories. Firstly, 'all Shakespeare's plays are regarded as entitled to exemption. We have not accepted all the plays of any other writer as *automatically* entitled to exemption'. Secondly, all plays over one hundred years old were 'normally' exempted, 'particularly if they had been reproduced with some frequency in the meantime and had therefore become part of the country's general dramatic repertoire'. Thirdly, for plays written within one hundred years 'we have regarded *survival value* as providing an important consideration', requiring 'a fairly regular and continuing revival over a fairly long period of years. Further, plays, relating to historical or national events, or illustrating customs and ideas prevalent when they were written, or representing some well-known class of dramatic art, etc, would normally qualify for exemption'. Finally, for 'modern' plays, where survival value could not be applied, there was an attempt to consider potential survival value. All these details are derived from archival sources in the Public Record Office, and we thank Shinobu Majima for making these details available to us.
4 This seems to have happened despite Thatcher's intentions. A retrospective account of a 1986 enquiry – the Cork enquiry on theatrical arts – published as a short article in 1996 explains that although this enquiry which was seen as part of the budget-cutting exercise by the Thatcher government, it made major financial miscalculations and ended up presiding over significant increases.
5 This point is amplified if we also recognize the significance of devolution in Scotland, Wales, and Northern Ireland which has further expanded the role of cultural bodies in these nations (though since they are not formally under the jurisdiction of DCMS, they are not considered here).
6 This data has been collected from publicly available sources, which have been compiled by the individuals themselves. Some people might also fit these criteria despite not declaring so in the sources used.
7 It is likely that the true numbers attending university are greater than 44 per cent who actually revealed this.

8  Full Arts Council of Great Britain membership (Arts Council England after 1994), so leaving out those who were confined to the Scottish, Welsh and Irish Committees (later independent Councils) who have a rather different profile.

# References

Annan, N., (1990), *Our Age*, London: Fontana.
Annan, N., (1999), *The Dons: Mentors, Eccentrics and Geniuses*, London: Harper Collins.
Bauman, Z., (1989), *Legislators and Interpreters*, Cambridge: Polity.
Bourdieu, P., (1985), *Distinction*, London: Routledge.
Bouckaert, G., and Peters, G. B., (2004), 'What is available and what is missing in the study of quangos?' in Pollitt, Christopher, and Talbot, Colin (eds), *Unbundled Government: A Critical Analysis of the Global Trend to Agencies, Quangos and Contractualisation*, Abingdon: Routledge.
Brint, S., (1993), *An Age of Experts*, Berkeley: University of California Press.
Burt, R., (1992), *Structural Holes: The Social Structure of Competition*, Cambridge: MA.: Harvard Univeristy Press.
Cabinet Office, (2006), *Public Bodies 2005/06*, London: Cabinet Office.
Cain, P. J., and Hopkins, A. G., (1993), *British Imperialism: Innovation and Expansion 1688–1914* (Vol.1), London: Longman.
Carroll, W., (2008), 'The Corporate Elite and the Transformation of Finance Capital: a view from Canada', (this volume).
Collini, S., (2006), *Absent Minds: Intellectuals in Britain*, Oxford: Oxford University Press.
Corrigan, P., and Sayer, D., (1985), *The Great Arch: English State Formation as a Cultural Revolution*, Oxford: Blackwells.
Du Gay, P., (2008), 'Keyser Süze Elites: Market populism and the politics of institutional Change', (this volume).
Fyfe, G., (2000), *Art, Power and Modernity: English Art Institutions 1750–1950*, London: Leicester University Press.
Marr, A., (1995), *Ruling Britannia: The Failure and Future of British Democracy*, London: Michael Joseph.
Rose, J., (2000), *The Intellectual Life of the British Working Class*, Yale: Yale University Press.
Rose, N., (1999), *Powers of Freedom: Reframing Political Though*, Cambridge: Cambridge University Press.
Rubinstein, W. D., (1993), *Capitalism, Culture, and Decline in Britain. 1750–1990*, London:.Routledge.
Savage, M., (2008), 'Affluence and social change in the making of technocratic middle class identities: Britain, 1939–1955', *Contemporary British History*, forthcoming.
Savage, M., and Williams, K., (2008), 'Elites: remembered by capitalism and forgotten by social science', this volume.
Scott, J., (1985), *Corporation Classes and Capitalism*, London: Hutchinson, second edition.
Scott, J., (1997), *Corporate Business and Capitalist Classes*, Oxford: Oxford University Press.
Shils, E., (1955), 'The intellectuals: (1) Great Britain', *Encounter*, **4:** 5–16.
Skelcher, C., (1998), *The Appointed State – Quasi-Governmental Organizations and Democracy*, Buckingham: Open University Press.
Skelcher, C. and Davis, H., (1995), *Opening the Boardroom Door: The Membership of Local Appointed Bodies*, London: LGC Communications.
Skidelsky, R., (2003), *John Maynard Keynes, 1883–1946: Economist, Philosopher, Statesman*, London: MacMillan.
Useem, M., (1984), *The Inner Circle*, Oxford: Oxford University Press.
Witts, R., (1998), *Artist Unknown: An Alternative History of the Arts Council*, London: Little Brown.
Yudice, G., (2002), *The Expediency of Culture: Uses of Culture in the Global Era*, London: Duke University Press.

# Elite consumption in Britain, 1961–2004: results of a preliminary investigation

*Shinobu Majima and Alan Warde*

## Introduction: changing patterns of consumption

> In a pecuniary world . . . especially in any community where class distinctions are
> somewhat vague, all canons of reputability and decency, and all standards of con-
> sumption, are traced back by insensible gradations to the usages and habits of thought
> of the highest social and pecuniary class – the wealthy leisure class. (Veblen, 1925
> [1899]: 104).

In a magisterial survey, Daloz (2007) demonstrates the lack of a satisfactory
theoretical account of elite consumption. Most sociological approaches offer
partial analyses, being residual deductions from more general theories of consumption which pay insufficient attention to the specificities of the behaviour of
the rich and powerful. On the basis of comparative empirical observation Daloz
demonstrates that the markers of elite distinction vary greatly between societies
and may be founded upon possession of prestigious goods, access to personal
services, lavish ceremonies or an entourage of dependants. What in one society
is a source of symbolic superiority is, in another, a sign of vulgarity. Thus,
for example, rich Norwegians conceal their wealth, 'conspicuous modesty'
being a collective ethical imperative; Americans are much more likely to make
material display of their personal opulence; while the ostentation of the 'Big
Men' of Nigeria serves to express the collective standing of their clients.
Daloz argued that the principal sociological theories – of Simmel, Elias, Veblen
and Bourdieu – fail to appreciate the full range of possible strategies and
tend to see the behaviour of elites through the lens of the national system
with which they were most familiar. Theoretical progress, then, requires more
observations across time and space. About Britain there is currently little information; to our knowledge, apart from some schematic descriptions of the
lifestyle of the established upper class in the mid-20th century (eg Scott, 1982),
the consumption patterns of the elite have not been subject to systematic social
scientific analysis. This chapter takes one small step forward by looking in detail
at changes in the consumption behaviour of members of the economic elite
in Britain since 1961.

Following the advice of Daloz, we seek to make new research bear cumula-
tively on older theoretical insights, thereby also to establish their limits. Over

a century ago, Veblen showed that consumption is one means by which elites mark their position in advanced capitalist societies. We speculate that his work has residual value in understanding the changing significance of elite consumption in the second half of the 20th century. His ironic *Theory of the Leisure Class* (1899 [1925]) was the first to give a systematic sociological account of how people mark the social position and economic standing of their family household through their consumption habits. For him, in industrial and urban societies, wealth replaced free time as the primary indicator of social status. Since people do not flash their bank statements at one another, however, wealth, if it is to act as a claim to social prestige, must be revealed through publicly visible signs – bodies and bodily adornment, presence in particular places and at particular events, and perhaps especially the possession of goods.

The *Theory of the Leisure Class* received acclaim in the middle of the 20th century as it helped drive economic historians debates about the birth of the consumer society (see McKendrick *et al.*, 1982) and serving as an example for economists of the role of non-rational impulses behind consumption (eg hyperbolic discounting, Offer, 2006). Veblen's reputation was subsequently eclipsed by Bourdieu, following the publication of *Distinction* (1984 [1979]). This was not only a matter of the greater sophistication of an account written sixty years later, but because of his recognition of the intricate and complex matter of the formation and operation of cultural taste. In a world which spawned cultural studies as an academic discipline concerned with the semiotics of material culture and the importance of the encoding and decoding of the symbolic meaning of cultural products and practices, a sociological approach which insisted on the inextricable imbrication of cultural processes with class was unsurprisingly deemed analytically superior. For while Bourdieu agreed that possessions were important, as his concept of objectified cultural capital attests, he also considered embodied characteristics like deportment and accent, and competence and familiarity in understanding legitimate culture, as at least as important in establishing, reproducing and marking position in the social hierarchy. Pecuniary status, or economic capital, was insufficient alone to explain social standing or to grasp the unequal structuring of the space of lifestyles, which was manifested as differential patterns of taste.

Though some of his critics disagreed, Bourdieu, when he latterly deigned to make mention of Veblen, implied that their accounts were irreconcilable (see Daloz, 2007). One possible reason was that refined taste and sophisticated aesthetic appreciation was an attribute not so much of the wealthy bourgeoisie, the dominant fraction of the dominant class, but of a highly educated section of the middle class endowed with the largest volume of cultural capital. Coulangeon and Lamel (2007), however, on the basis of recent studies of cultural consumption in France, show that the radical separation of tastes between intelligentsia and bourgeoisie no longer appear as a principal division within the dominant class, while Gayo-Cal *et al.* (2006) and Van Eijck and van Oosterhout

(2005) imply the same for Britain and the Netherlands respectively. Goods, especially branded goods, are widely thought once again to be principal signifying objects of the social game (eg Holt, 2004). Molnar and Lamont (2002), for instance, show that, at least in the USA, material possessions currently play a major role in signifying social differences. Veblen may yet be vindicated.

We refer to Veblen, however, not in order to join the recent band of authors seeking to restore his reputation (eg Edgell, 2001; Mestrovic, 2003), nor to resurrect his theory of elite consumption – the criticisms of Slater (1997), Fine and Leopold (1993) and Daloz (2007) are trenchant – but because our data lend themselves to a re-consideration of some of the themes in *Theory of the Leisure Class*, particularly of 'pecuniary canons of taste'. The expenditure patterns of the rich and very rich identify items which, in their time, conferred distinction and which highlight continuities and discontinuities in the history of consumption in Britain. When the rich change their priorities, their earlier preferences may enter common circulation. With the expansion of a commodified culture of consumption, and its promotion of popular culture, the rich may alternatively find new items to convey distinction in previously ignored quarters. Therefore we explore how categories of consumption that at some time distinguish those in privileged and elevated position traverse the space of lifestyle. Because we use income as a proxy for elite membership this chapter makes no direct contribution to debates about elite formation; elite members have high incomes, but the converse is not true. Our diagnosis is more precisely of 'the pecuniary class' and the effects of its changing consumption on national patterns.

## Data and methods

The Family Expenditure Survey (FES), though far from perfect for our purpose, is unique in offering detailed data on households and their expenditure over half a century. From it can be gleaned the structure and content of spending for various groups in the population. Used with care, it can provide information to compare systematically patterns of change in consumption. It is a repeated annual survey of British households. Respondents keep a diary record of their outgoings over a period of two weeks and they also provide information about other larger irregular payments (mortgage payments, pensions and insurance) as well as their income and other household characteristics at a face-to-face interview. We report here on the datasets drawn from the diary records only for 1961, when the FES was first digitized, for 1981, and the most recent available, 2004.[1] FES records diary expenditure in several hundred categories (240 in 1961, 352 by 2004). These are not entirely comparable over time. Indeed only 81 of the detailed headings were included in all three years that we analyse. Detailed categories are combined by the FES, in a broadly consistent way over time, under aggregated headings, for example 'Transport and Vehicles' and 'Food', which also we report occasionally.

The analytic strategy of the paper has two components. First, we look *descriptively* at disproportionate expenditure by the Very Rich (highest one percent of incomes) and the Rich (the next nine per cent of households by income) in the years 1961, 1981 and 2004. The distinguishing features of the expenditure patterns of the Very Rich and Rich are described primarily by the proportion of their own household income that they devote to particular items in comparison to the mean for the population as a whole. This permits a sketch of the distinguishing features of the consumption patterns of rich households.

We would anticipate that a pecuniarily advantaged class will spend more on everything than those who are on average incomes. They more or less do so.[2] To investigate their priorities, we concentrate on those categories where the Very Rich and the Rich spend not just more than average but even more than the mean ratio of the general advantage that they hold. That is to say, in 1961, the Very Rich spent 3.42 times more than the average Briton, which we call their *ratio of advantage*. For many items, which they particularly value or *prioritize*, they spend in excess of that ratio. The assumption is that the greater the excess, the more the items involved are prized, being either symbolically or practically of greater value. Sometimes the excess is small, sometimes large. We have chosen two multiples to examine in this chapter: those where they spend between half as much again and twice as much, which we term *precedented*; and where they spend proportionately more than twice as much we talk of *superior* items.[3] Because the Very Rich are few in number (only 34 households in 1961, about 70 thereafter) care is required to ensure that exceptional large expenditures by one household do not give a misleading impression of the norms of the period. True, some exceptional expenditure may be on items by which the Very Rich seek to distinguish themselves from only slightly less opulent rivals but, unless they are also favoured by the much larger group of Rich respondents, we regard them as probable outliers. Hence, for the most part we restrict our interpretation to items which not only the Very Rich register as superior or precedented, but to which the next nine per cent, the Rich, also devote at least a greater proportion of their expenditure than does the population as a whole.

Second, we examine systematically all the categories (81 of them) which were reported in an identical fashion in each of the three years, ie 1961, 1981 and 2004. We processed the data using Factor Analysis, one of several multivariate methods that have been favoured by psychologists, sociologists and market researchers. Factor Analysis computationally calculates the relationship between budget shares of items that were purchased by the elite consumer and budget shares of items that were purchased by other consumers in the sample, and produces scores for factor 1 on the horizontal axis and factor 2 on the vertical axis. The scores function as ratios that relativize the expenditure level of each item in relation to the expenditure level of all the other items, and condense the relativized positions into a single scale. The position of each item is determined by the relative importance of each item in the household budget in relation to the priorities of other households, based upon the percentage of a household's total weekly expenditure devoted to that particular item. Factor analysis offers powerful visual representation in the form of maps of consumer tastes for 1961–2004, where are plotted the percentage of household expenditure on particular items, for example jewellery, beef, restaurants, new automobiles. We interpret the distances between items in a two dimensional space – analogous to what Bourdieu (1984) would term 'the space of lifestyles'. We see that the relative positions of items change over time. We can also superimpose 'supplementary variables' onto the same axes – we use measures of income, occupational class and age of 'head' of household – to help interpret the revealed patterns. In this chapter we use this information primarily to inspect the movement of those items which have been preferred by the Very Rich across the space of lifestyles.

## The pecuniary class: who are the Rich and Very Rich?

It is well documented that inequalities of income and wealth, which had been in decline in Britain since the 1930s, began to increase again in the 1980s and continue to grow. The Very Rich had more excess income to spend, as inequalities that had been in decline since the 1930s increased again in the 1980s (Atkinson, 2002). Disparities between the Very Rich and the average household are currently growing with potential consequences for new consumption priorities, though also for social cohesion (Lansley 2006). Figure 1 shows the relative levels of income for households at different points in the income structure over the period since 1961. The top ten per cent increased its share of income sharply from the mid-1980s. In the same period the income of the top one per cent increased in parallel until the mid-1990s, after which it took a larger proportion than ever of gross household income. Shifts in relative household expenditure patterns were less pronounced, but ran roughly parallel to income.

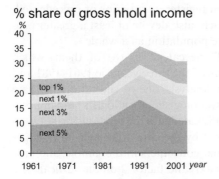
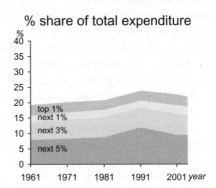

**Figure 1:** *Shares of income and expenditure of richest 10 per cent of households, 1961–2004.*
*Data source*: Family Expenditure Survey 1961, 1981, 1991, 2001 and Expenditure and Food Survey 2003–04. Figures represent the calculation by the authors.

The shifts reflect complex changes in the political economy of Britain. The impact of the governments of Margaret Thatcher after 1979 appears highly significant. The previous two decades had seen a consolidation of the welfare state, a shift towards higher taxation to support public services, an extension of free and subsidized welfare services, more state employment, and strong trades unions. During the 1980s all these trends were reversed, direct taxes were reduced, welfare services were deemed not only unaffordable but also potentially harmful to personal autonomy, state assets were sold off, entrepreneurship and competitiveness were encouraged, and trade unions were confronted and defeated. Greater inequality ensued from the revision of economic incentives, personal and corporate. The composition, orientation and reward structure of economic elites changed (see other articles in this edition).

The social characteristics of the households containing the Rich and the Very Rich changed to some degree over the 43 year period that we are considering (see Table 1). In 1961, Very Rich households were all headed by a man, whereas by 2004 over 20 per cent had a female head. Though recording categories make precise comparison impossible, households headed by employers, professionals and senior managers were a substantial majority of the Very Rich at all three dates. A few households headed by manual workers are represented at the earlier dates, though none in 2004. Among the Rich households, however, those headed by manual workers comprised almost half in 1961, over a quarter in 1981, but less than 10 per cent in 2004. The mean age of heads of Very Rich households fell from 53 to 45 and a parallel but slightly less strong tendency can be seen among the Rich. Rates of marriage remained constant, with about 9 in 10 of well-off households being couples, while the rate for the population as a whole fell from 76 per cent to 59 percent. Hence, the Very Rich, as estimated from those having the highest incomes, have typically been headed by a married male, who is an employer, senior manager or professional. The typical household head is now a little less likely to be male, is a few years younger and is never associated with manual employment. Perhaps, then, we see a shift from the rentier and owners of small businesses in the manual trades to the working rich occupied in higher managerial and professional positions.

The new Thatcherite economic formation generated much speculation about the pursuit of distinctive and individually chosen 'lifestyles' from among the varied offerings of a burgeoning 'consumer culture'. The reality of the connection between the much augmented resources of the very rich and their patterns of expenditure is documented below.

## Elite expenditure, 1961–2004: what do the Very Rich spend money on?

*1961*

In 1961 the Very Rich had a normal gross household income a little more than 5 times that of the average household, and spent about 3.5 times as much (£56

**Table 1:** Social characteristics of the Very Rich (top 1%), the Rich (next 9%) and all households

| 1961 | top 1 | % | next 9 | % | all | % |
|---|---|---|---|---|---|---|
| Male headed | 34 | 100.0 | 293 | 93.6 | 2834 | 81.3 |
| Female headed | | | 20 | 6.4 | 649 | 18.6 |
| Married | 31 | 91.2 | 285 | 91.1 | 2650 | 76.0 |
| Single, widowed, divorced, separated | 3 | 8.8 | 28 | 8.9 | 831 | 23.8 |
| Unemployed, retired | 4 | 11.8 | 32 | 10.2 | 857 | 24.6 |
| Employers professionals own account | 7 | 20.6 | 7 | 2.2 | 125 | 3.6 |
| Professional and managerial workers | 17 | 50.0 | 71 | 22.7 | 280 | 8.0 |
| Teachers | 1 | 2.9 | 15 | 4.8 | 64 | 1.8 |
| Officers HM forces police fire services | 1 | 2.9 | 2 | 0.6 | 8 | 0.2 |
| Clerical workers | 1 | 2.9 | 29 | 9.3 | 286 | 8.2 |
| Other ranks in HMF police fire services | | | 2 | 0.6 | 33 | 0.9 |
| Shop assistants | | | 2 | 0.6 | 61 | 1.7 |
| Manual workers | 3 | 8.8 | 152 | 48.6 | 1652 | 47.4 |
| Own account workers | | | 1 | 0.3 | 110 | 3.2 |
| Total | 34 | 100.0 | 313 | 100.0 | 3476 | 100.0 |
| Mean age | 52.6 (yrs) | | 50.0 (yrs) | | 50.6 (yrs) | |

| 1981 | top 1 | % | next 9 | % | all | % |
|---|---|---|---|---|---|---|
| Male headed | 72 | 96.0 | 657 | 97.0 | 5851 | 77.8 |
| Female headed | 3 | 4.0 | 20 | 3.0 | 1673 | 22.2 |
| Married | 69 | 92.0 | 617 | 91.1 | 5147 | 68.4 |
| Single, widowed, divorced, separated | 6 | 8.0 | 60 | 8.9 | 2377 | 31.6 |
| Unemployed, retired | 2 | 2.7 | 30 | 4.4 | 2331 | 31.0 |
| Professional and technical workers | 34 | 45.3 | 183 | 27.0 | 738 | 9.8 |
| Administrative and managerial workers | 30 | 40.0 | 166 | 24.5 | 782 | 10.4 |
| Teachers | 2 | 2.7 | 53 | 7.8 | 188 | 2.5 |
| Clerical workers | 1 | 1.3 | 46 | 6.8 | 503 | 6.7 |

|  | top 1 | % | next 9 | % | all | % |
|---|---|---|---|---|---|---|
| Manual work skilled | 4 | 5.3 | 134 | 19.8 | 1809 | 24.0 |
| Manual work semi-skilled | 1 | 1.3 | 53 | 7.8 | 852 | 11.3 |
| Manual work unskilled | 1 | 1.3 | 7 | 1.0 | 249 | 3.3 |
| Member of HM Forces |  |  | 5 | 0.7 | 27 | 0.4 |
| Total | 75 | 100.0 | 677 | 100.0 | 7524 | 100.0 |
| Mean age | 47.2 (yrs) |  | 45.9 (yrs) |  | 50.3 (yrs) |  |

| 2004 | top 1 | % | next 9 | % | all | % |
|---|---|---|---|---|---|---|
| Male headed | 55 | 78.6 | 503 | 79.3 | 4406 | 62.5 |
| Female headed | 15 | 21.4 | 131 | 20.7 | 2642 | 37.5 |
| Married, cohabitee | 62 | 88.6 | 582 | 91.8 | 4147 | 58.8 |
| Single, widowed, divorced, separated | 8 | 11.4 | 52 | 8.2 | 2901 | 41.2 |
| Unemployed, retired | 1 | 1.4 | 12 | 1.9 | 1922 | 27.3 |
| Higher managerial | 16 | 22.9 | 123 | 19.4 | 337 | 4.8 |
| Higher professional | 26 | 37.1 | 143 | 22.6 | 451 | 6.4 |
| Lower professional | 9 | 12.9 | 115 | 18.1 | 764 | 10.8 |
| Lower managerial | 8 | 11.4 | 93 | 14.7 | 435 | 6.2 |
| Higher supervisory |  |  |  | 4.1 | 199 | 2.8 |
| Intermediate | 1 | 1.4 | 24 | 3.8 | 496 | 7.0 |
| Small employer | 4 | 5.7 | 16 | 2.5 | 91 | 1.3 |
| Own account | 5 | 7.1 | 22 | 3.5 | 370 | 5.2 |
| Lower supervisory |  |  | 25 | 3.9 | 360 | 5.1 |
| Lower technical |  |  | 9 | 1.4 | 203 | 2.9 |
| Semi-routine |  |  | 17 | 2.7 | 730 | 10.4 |
| Routine |  |  | 9 | 1.4 | 690 | 9.8 |
| Total | 70 | 100.0 | 634 | 100.0 | 7048 | 100.0 |
| Mean age (years) | 44.9 (yrs) |  | 45.2 (yrs) |  | 50.9 (yrs) |  |

Data source: Family Expenditure Survey 1961, 1981 and Expenditure and Food Survey 2003–04. Figures represent the calculation by the authors

per week). As recorded by the highly aggregated categories, they spent most money on, in order of magnitude, food, transport, services and clothing and footwear (see Table 2). Table 2 also shows that transport and vehicles and durable goods are the greatest aggregate priorities at this time.

Examining all the 240 detailed expenditure categories in the 1961 survey we find a considerable number of superior items for the Very Rich, ie upon which spending exceeds by almost seven times that of the average household (see Table 3). These included new cars, expenditures on animals and pets (other than pet food), new televisions and radios, and exceptional holiday expenses. On all of these items a substantial amount was spent in a week, but these were not items upon which the Rich spend a disproportionate amount. They may be items distinguishing the plutocrat from the merely wealthy, but we need to be wary lest they indicate simply an exceptional large expenditure by a single household in the diary recording period.

Of the items on which the Rich also at least spent proportionately more than their own ratio of advantage, which was 1.72 in 1961, the most superior item for the Very Rich was repairs to furniture, upon which they spent 38 times more than the national average. Household fittings and hardware purchases were prominent too. Women's outerwear, an expenditure that Veblen thought symbolically very significant because women dressed to mark vicariously the status of the family, featured as a superior item upon which the Very Rich spent five per cent of its weekly income. Recall Veblen's (1925: 131) pithy observation that 'The blending and confusion of the elements of exclusiveness and beauty is, perhaps, best exemplified in articles of dress and of household furniture.' Transport figured significantly. Private cars in particular were important, for this was a period when cars, especially new cars, were rare and highly prized, but rail fares and taxis also figured among precedented items. Travel for holidays also registered, with water travel and hotels on the list of priorities. Domestic service was a major superior item of expenditure, a continuation of the earlier more widespread habit of the middle class employing servants. Financial provision was also extensive, with longer term savings, cash gifts and charitable donations suggesting priorities on family financial security and patrician orientation. Alcoholic drink, notably wine but also spirits were among the superior items of routine expenditure, as was an item of food, fresh cream, representing sources of traditional pleasures. Recreational activities registered in participant sports admissions, implying exclusive club membership, and hobbies, though absolute expenditure was small, suggesting limited engagement in commercial sources of leisure.

Summing up, the Very Rich were distinctive in respect of their financial transactions, travelling, taking expensive holidays, keeping servants, drinking wines and spirits, and conserving their property and their furniture. They bought comparatively expensive durable goods, including new cars, televisions and audio equipment. A little in advance of the explosion of mass consumption, it would be reasonable to think, since 'durable goods' was a precedented aggregate category, that these possessions were highly valued at the time and that many

**Table 2:** *Very Rich Households (top 1 per cent), Ratio of Advantage and Weekly Expenditure, Aggregate Categories, 1961, 1981 and 2004*

| | 1961 | | 1981 | | 2004 | |
|---|---|---|---|---|---|---|
| | Ratio-to-average | Shillings per week | Ratio-to-average | £ per week | Ratio-to-average | £ per week |
| Transport and vehicles | 6.54 | 177 | 4.79 | 90 | 3.37 | 239 |
| Motoring expenditure | | | | | 3.32 | 206 |
| Fares and other travel | | | | | 3.71 | 33 |
| Durable goods | 5.54 | 93 | 4.07 | 38 | | |
| Household goods | | | | | 3.94 | 139 |
| Personal goods & services | | | | | 4.26 | 68 |
| Leisure goods | | | | | 2.11 | 43 |
| Services | 5.99 | 157 | 4.58 | 63 | 5.06 | 408 |
| Household services | | | | | 3.58 | 88 |
| Leisure services | | | | | 5.83 | 316 |
| Alcoholic drink | 4.69 | 60 | 2.91 | 18 | 1.81 | 23 |
| Miscellaneous | 3.83 | 5 | 2.59 | 2 | 3.30 | 10 |
| Other goods | 3.70 | 98 | 3.15 | 30 | 2.11 | 50 |
| Clothing and footwear | 3.64 | 123 | 2.73 | 25 | 3.75 | 84 |
| Housing (net) | 3.05 | 105 | 2.30 | 46 | 2.93 | 198 |
| Fuel and light | 2.75 | 56 | 1.72 | 13 | 1.82 | 22 |
| Tobacco | 2.72 | 57 | 0.93 | 3 | 0.36 | 2 |
| Food | 1.82 | 199 | 2.13 | 58 | 2.00 | 129 |
| Total expenditure | 3.42 | 1121 | 3.07 | 385 | 3.28 | 1354 |
| Other expenditures | 3.91 | 95 | 5.64 | 287 | 8.59 | 1470 |

Note: Blank cells indicate that the data were not available.
Data source: Family Expenditure Survey 1961, 1981 and Expenditure and Food Survey 2003–04. Figures represent the calculation by the authors

other people would desire them too. The desire for a set of products that would make life easier signifies the relevance of material values. Goods that might be displayed for public attention figure more prominently in the 1960s than later, suggesting that there was some empirical basis for Veblen being the most commonly cited sociological theorist of consumption. At this time, the Very Rich do not only, if they do at all, claim superior status through their aesthetic tastes.

**Table 3:** *Superior and precedented items in the budgets of the Very Rich 1961*

| | Very Rich *top 1%* | | |
|---|---|---|---|
| | Ratio-to-average (Times) | Actual amount (Shillings) | Reference to Rich *next 9%* |
| **SUPERIOR ITEM** | | | |
| *Clothing undefined* | *65.68* | *3.05* | |
| *Other expenditure on animals and pets* | *44.33* | *24.35* | |
| *New cars and accessories* | *39.34* | *105.81* | |
| **Repairs to furniture** | 37.78 | 5.67 | * |
| *Second-hand coverings* | *36.57* | *3.06* | |
| *Other vehicle* | *27.87* | *1.46* | |
| *Stamp duties* | *24.32* | *1.53* | |
| *Participant sports subscriptions* | *22.31* | *6.67* | |
| *Second-hand furniture* | *21.85* | *9.18* | |
| *Sports goods* | *20.68* | *6.31* | |
| *Holiday expenses not allocated elsewhere* | *18.28* | *27.57* | |
| **Other repairs** | 18.26 | 1.69 | * |
| **Domestic services** | 17.74 | 37.39 | * |
| *Coke* | *17.55* | *17.74* | |
| *New radios televisions gramophones* | *17.15* | *18.64* | |
| *Group B frozen vegetables* | *16.53* | *0.11* | |
| **Fittings** | 16.13 | 7.15 | * |
| **Other household hardware purchase tax 25%** | 15.03 | 8.69 | * |
| *Other clothing charges* | *12.18* | *0.96* | |
| **Cash gifts and tips** | 10.98 | 28.17 | * |
| **Drink undefined** | 10.44 | 8.12 | ** |
| **Wines** | 9.69 | 11.70 | ** |
| **Charitable gifts** | 9.22 | 16.03 | * |
| **Water travel** | 9.15 | 0.97 | *** |
| **Fresh cream** | 9.05 | 1.47 | * |
| **Women's outerwear** | 8.98 | 65.20 | * |
| **Miscellaneous expenditure on goods** | 8.49 | 1.39 | * |
| **Participant sports admissions** | 8.49 | 1.79 | *** |
| **Motor vehicle repairs replacement of parts** | 8.36 | 10.08 | ** |
| *Private medical dental optical fees* | *8.31* | *6.93* | |
| **Spirits** | 8.26 | 18.14 | * |
| **Tools** | 8.18 | 0.64 | * |
| *Boys underwear* | *7.96* | *2.17* | |

**Table 3:** *Continued*

| | Very Rich *top 1%* | | |
| --- | --- | --- | --- |
| | Ratio-to-average (Times) | Actual amount (Shillings) | Reference to Rich *next 9%* |
| **Smokers requisites** | 7.88 | 2.00 | * |
| **Hobbies** | 7.58 | 0.50 | ** |
| *Payments to contractors for repairs etc* | 7.52 | 26.78 | |
| **Seeds plants flowers** | 7.46 | 12.13 | * |
| **PRECEDENTED ITEM** | | | |
| *Other household hardware purchase tax 0%* | 6.79 | 4.80 | |
| **Savings longer term** | 6.34 | 21.40 | ** |
| **Hotels and boarding houses** | 6.31 | 12.06 | ** |
| **Rail or tube fares** | 5.84 | 11.24 | * |
| **Taxis, inc hired driver** | 5.65 | 2.74 | *** |
| **China, glass, pottery** | 5.53 | 3.19 | * |
| *Subscriptions to friendly societies* | 5.38 | 3.30 | |
| **Food undefined** | 5.13 | 1.10 | * |
| **Total expenditure on all items in budget** | 3.42 | 1121.07 | 1.72 |

*Note*: For the Very Rich (top 1% income earner): **Superior item** = an average Very Rich spend more than twice as much on this item, compared to the ratio in excess of total average household expenditure on all items (i.e. more than 6.84 times in excess of average household expenditure in 1961). **Precedented item** = an average Very Rich spend more than one and half times as much on this item, compared to the ratio in excess of total average household expenditure on all items (i.e. more than 5.13 times in excess of average household expenditure in 1961).

For the Rich (next 9% income earner): ***Superior item = an average Rich spend more than twice as much on this item, compared to the ratio in excess of total average household expenditure on all items (i.e. more than 3.44 times in excess of average household expenditure in 1961). **Precedented item** = an average Rich spend more than one and half times as much on this item, compared to the ratio in excess of total average household expenditure on all items (i.e. more than 2.58 times in excess of average household expenditure in 1961). *Preferred item** = an average Rich spend more than the same proportion on this item, compared to the ratio in excess of total average household expenditure on all items (i.e. more than 1.72 times in excess of average household expenditure in 1961).

*Data source*: Family Expenditure Survey 1961, 1981 and Expenditure and Food Survey 2003–04. Figures represent the calculation by the author

*1981*

By 1981, the Very Rich were spending £385 per week on average, just over three times as much as the national mean. (The Rich were spending about twice the mean). Of the aggregate categories, 'transport and vehicles' had become precedented, while durables and services slipped down scale of the priorities (see Table 2).

Because the recording categories altered a perfect comparison between the two years at the greatest level of detail is impossible. Nevertheless, there are strong continuities. 10 items out of 30[4] in 1981 had been either superior or precedented in 1961: toys and hobbies, domestic services, savings, participant sports subscriptions, second-hand coverings, wine, holiday expenses, charitable gifts, rail or tube fares and taxis (see Table 4). Among the new items was eating out,

**Table 4:** *Superior and precedented items in the budgets of the Very Rich 1981*

| Item | Very Rich *top 1%* | | |
|---|---|---|---|
| | Ratio-to-average (Times) | Actual amount (Pounds) | Reference to Rich *next 9%* |
| **SUPERIOR ITEMS** | | | |
| *Other new second-hand vehicles* | *74.37* | *35.23* | |
| *New bicycles prams etc* | *61.47* | *35.48* | |
| *Footwear undefined* | *35.64* | *0.04* | |
| *PERMANENT SECOND DWELLING* | *15.80* | *0.74* | |
| *Second dwelling rent rates* | *15.80* | *0.59* | |
| **Hobbies** | 12.04 | 0.93 | * |
| **Domestic services** | 11.75 | 4.71 | * |
| **Savings** | 11.26 | 30.91 | * |
| **Participant sport subscriptions** | 10.82 | 4.70 | * |
| **Secondhand coverings** | 10.45 | 7.82 | * |
| **Meals out fruits?** | 9.06 | 0.03 | * |
| *Other expenditure on animals and pets* | *8.38* | *2.21* | |
| **Composite household durables** | 8.35 | 4.47 | * |
| **Other meals out** | 7.77 | 14.05 | * |
| **New furniture** | 7.21 | 10.37 | ** |
| **Theatres, concerts, circuses** | 6.96 | 1.09 | ** |
| **Non NHS spectacles** | 6.69 | 0.68 | * |
| **Mattresses** | 6.66 | 0.20 | * |
| **Wines other than bought by bottle** | 6.55 | 0.87 | * |
| **Air travel** | 6.35 | 2.40 | *** |
| **Holidays abroad** | 6.35 | 11.96 | ** |
| **Cleaning and dyeing** | 6.31 | 0.80 | * |

**Table 4:** *Continued*

| Item | Very Rich *top 1%* | | |
|------|-------------------------------|------------------------------|------------------------------|
|      | Ratio-to-average (Times) | Actual amount (Pounds) | Reference to Rich *next 9%* |
| **PRECEDENTED ITEMS** | | | |
| **Decorative fancy goods** | 6.12 | 1.77 | * |
| **Spares for TV radio gramophone** | 6.06 | 0.42 | ** |
| **Holiday expenses nae** | 5.97 | 12.13 | ** |
| **Hire of self-drive cars** | 5.89 | 0.52 | * |
| **Charitable gifts** | 5.82 | 2.10 | * |
| **Other subscriptions** | 5.68 | 0.69 | * |
| **Wines** | 5.39 | 4.61 | * |
| **Wines bought by the bottle** | 5.17 | 3.74 | * |
| **Misc expenditure nae** | 5.14 | 0.88 | * |
| **Other meals out and alcoholic drinks** | 4.97 | 0.79 | * |
| **Rail or tube fares** | 4.90 | 2.14 | * |
| **Jewelry, watches, clocks** | 4.80 | 2.67 | * |
| **Taxis inc hired cars with driver** | 4.68 | 1.19 | * |
| **Meals away from home** | 4.65 | 18.78 | * |
| **Total expenditure on all items in budget** | 3.06 | 385.43 | 1.93 |

*Note*: For explanatory note, see Table 3.
For the Very Rich: **Superior item** = more than 6.12 times in excess of average household expenditure. **Precedented item** = more than 4.59 times in excess of average household expenditure. For the Rich: ***Superior item** = more than 3.86 times in excess of average household expenditure. **Precedented item** = more than 2.89 times in excess of average household expenditure. *Preferred item = more than 1.93 times in excess of average household expenditure.
*Data source*: Family Expenditure Survey 1961, 1981 and Expenditure and Food Survey 2003-04. Figures represent the calculation by the authors

appearing under several different headings, which had become an important item of expenditure by 1981 (about £35 per week), evidence of it beginning to act as a marker of distinction (see Warde *et al.*, forthcoming). Wine remained a significant expense, but other alcoholic drinks had declined in their relative attraction. In 1961 it probably reflected simply having a taste for wine, while in 1981 it presumably signified that the Very Rich were paying a great deal more per bottle than the average punter. New domestic items included composite household durables (presumably early versions of fitted kitchens), new rather than second-hand furniture, spares for TV and gramophone, and decorative fancy goods. Air travel appeared as a superior item, along with rail and taxi fares which had appeared in 1961, now supplemented by car hire. Substantial amounts and large proportions of income were devoted to holidays, especially holidays abroad. Items for domestic use included composite household durables, new rather than second-hand furniture, spares for TV and radio. A few categories of items of personal property emerged as important: non-NHS spectacles, jewellery and watches, and cleaning and dyeing give a hint of the emergence of a greater concern with self-presentation. Also, unlike in 1961, the category of 'theatres, concerts and circuses' became a superior item, perhaps indicating a growing priority for spending on cultural events occurring in the public realm.[5] Nevertheless, the Very Rich continued to repair broken or damaged durable goods, including having their furniture re-upholstered.[6]

When compared with 1961, we conclude that the pattern of recurrent expenditure did not change radically. The Very Rich still spent heavily on many of the same items. They continued to save and invest in property and pensions to help ensure that they and their children continue to experience a comfortable material existence. Considered as innovators, they were early adopters of extensive air travel, and they were paying more attention to personal appearance. They perhaps also devoted relatively more of their resources to activities away from home, most obviously eating out, but also other recreational activities.

## 2004

By 2004, the 70 Very Rich households recorded in the expenditure diaries budgets of, on average, £1354 per week. In absolute terms, eating out, fares and petrol, drinking alcohol, jewellery, loans for car purchase and payments for domestic service were the largest diary expenditures.

The items of choice in 2004 include some that were prominent in the earlier years, but many that were new (see Table 5). Savings are joined by more financial items, including personal pensions and funds for dependants. Spending on children, on prams for babies and education for older children, appears. So too do payments for private medicine and dentistry, marks of the effects of the privatization of public services since the 1980s. Travel remains a marker of privilege, with internal air flights assuming new significance along with parking fees, bicycle accessories, and leather and travel goods. Taxis, rail fares and car hire, by contrast, are no longer priorities and, overall, relative expenditure on travel declined. Holidays abroad, as indicated by commissioned currency and amounts of money spent abroad, have high priority and absorb large sums. Also, as in 1981, eating out was a substantial superior item of expenditure. Rather more of the 29 items under consideration relate to personal care and appearance, including electrical appliances for personal care and men's outer garments, which add to superior items jewellery and watches and cleaning and dyeing. That wealthy households are now more distinguished by the dress of their male members than women is worthy of note, though the absolute sums involved remain higher for women than men (£32 for women's

**Table 5:** *Superior and precedented items in the budgets of the Very Rich 2004*

| | Very Rich *top 1%* | | |
| --- | --- | --- | --- |
| | Ratio-to-average (Times) | Actual amount (Pounds) | Reference to Rich *next 9%* |
| **SUPERIOR ITEMS** | | | |
| *Purchase of new motor caravan* | *100.69* | *1.43* | |
| *Further education (school trips, other)* | *63.33* | *2.77* | |
| **Widows/dependants/orphans funds** | 42.44 | 2.06 | ** |
| *Cash gifts to children* | *38.87* | *4.36* | |
| *Education (not definable)* | *32.42* | *1.46* | |
| *BBQ and swings* | *29.24* | *4.78* | |
| *Nursery, creche, playschool* | *21.33* | *12.85* | |
| **House extension etc, main dwelling** | 14.34 | 240.42 | * |
| **Personal pension** | 13.69 | 57.40 | * |
| **House extensions, second dwelling** | 13.47 | 8.33 | * |
| **Domestic services, inc cleaning, gardening** | 18.18 | 19.99 | * |
| **Jewellery, clocks, watches** | 12.11 | 27.04 | ** |
| **Leather and travel goods** | 11.58 | 7.17 | ** |
| **Commissioned travellers cheques and currency** | 11.29 | 0.66 | * |
| *Central heating installed, main dwelling* | *11.00* | *12.37* | |
| **Secondary education (trips etc)** | 10.80 | 1.54 | ** |
| *Legal fees paid to solicitors* | *10.56* | *3.64* | |
| *DVD purchase* | *9.78* | *0.78* | |
| **Money spent abroad** | 9.77 | 77.29 | ** |
| **Bicycle accessories, repairs etc** | 9.15 | 0.99 | *** |
| *Vacuum and steam cleaners* | *9.14* | *3.49* | |
| **Savings and investments (not AVCs)** | 8.56 | 51.21 | * |
| **Dry cleaners and dyeing** | 8.09 | 1.63 | ** |
| *Hire of equipment and accessories for sport* | *7.99* | *0.26* | |
| **Prams and pushchairs** | 7.76 | 0.79 | *** |
| **Private dental services** | 7.74 | 2.26 | * |
| **Parking fees, tolls, permits** | 7.70 | 4.67 | * |
| *Bottled gas – other* | *7.39* | *0.46* | |
| **Food away from home** | 7.13 | 34.68 | * |
| **Combined fares other than season tickets** | 6.97 | 0.74 | ** |

**Table 5:** *Continued*

|  | Very Rich *top 1%* | | |
|---|---|---|---|
|  | Ratio-to-average (Times) | Actual amount (Pounds) | Reference to Rich *next 9%* |
| **Medical insurance – total amount premium** | 6.94 | 10.22 | ** |
| **Purchase of dwelling/improvements** | 6.79 | 439.67 | * |
| **PRECEDENTED ITEMS** | | | |
| **Electrical appliances for personal care** | 6.55 | 2.20 | * |
| *Baby equipment (excluding prams and pushchairs)* | 6.49 | 0.46 | |
| *Infants outer garments (under 5)* | 6.35 | 4.38 | |
| **Cold food eaten off premises** | 6.24 | 2.05 | * |
| **Vegetable juices** | 5.75 | 0.05 | * |
| *Other household textiles, including towels, curtains* | 5.71 | 8.39 | |
| *Other fresh, chilled or frozen edible meat* | 5.56 | 0.03 | |
| **Air fares (within UK)** | 5.47 | 1.18 | *** |
| **Wood and peat** | 5.45 | 0.10 | * |
| **Equipment hire, small materials** | 5.34 | 8.49 | * |
| **Men's outer garments** | 5.27 | 22.44 | * |
| *Games toys etc (misc fancy, decorative)* | 5.26 | 1.82 | |
| **Personal computers, printers and calculators** | 5.07 | 8.74 | * |
| **Total expenditure for all items in budget** | 3.28 | 1353.83 | 2.02 |

For explanatory note, see Table 3.

For the Very Rich: **Superior item** = more than 6.58 times in excess of average household expenditure. **Precedented item** = more than 4.93 times in excess of average household expenditure. For the Rich ***Superior item** = more than 4.04 times in excess of average household expenditure. **Advantaged item** = more than 3.03 times in excess of average household expenditure. *Preferred item = more than 2.02 times in excess of average household expenditure.

*Data source:* Family Expenditure Survey 1961, 1981 and Expenditure and Food Survey 2003–04. Figures represent the calculation by the authors

outer garments compared to £22 for men's). The personal computer is the only category of durable domestic manufactured goods to be especially favoured by the Very Rich.

Regular expenditures in 2004 recorded under aggregated categories indicate that spending on 'leisure services', reached precedented levels. The shift in the structure of the economy from goods to services thus showed up as the altered priorities in the household budgets of the Very Rich. It is to services, particularly leisure services, that the Very Rich now particularly devoted their excess resources, confounding Veblen's (1925: 87) prediction that 'the present trend of development is in the direction of heightening the utility of conspicuous consumption as compared with leisure.' In a situation where they were richer relative to the rest of the population than in 1981, and where they were less likely to use public welfare services, their distinctiveness was in important part invisible, by virtue of measures to achieve security in the domains of health, finance and property. Tendential indications of this are evident in diary expenditures. For instance, medical insurance and private dental fees, and payments to widow's funds and cash gifts to children were superior items. So too was expenditure on second dwellings.

In 2004 priorities rooted elsewhere than routine household outlays became apparent. Indication of the increased priority of investments in social reproduction since 1981 – comparable figures were unavailable in 1961 – can be seen from irregular payments reported in the household interviews. Mortgages and improvements to houses, both first and second homes, registered as key aspects of elite differentiation. In 2004, extensions to houses, both main and second dwellings, were superior items. Purchase, mortgage and improvements to houses constituted a very substantial outlay, an average for the Very Rich of £860 per week, a sum additional to, but approaching the same magnitude as their routine expenditure on recurrent items (£1353 per week). Superior and precedence spending in 2004 dealt more than before with housing and financial security, including family reproduction.

Overall, between 1961 and 2004, common items of food and drink, still markers of wealth in 1961, disappeared, with one exception, eating out, which became a more important marker of distinction over time (Cheng *et al.*, 2007). Wine ceased to register. Generally, indulgence in traditional luxuries gave way, under pressure of greater concern with health and body management, to other priorities. By 2004 there were a number of items that attested to the importance of appearance, including care for clothes, though not clothes themselves, also jewellery, which had emerged by 1981 as a superior item, and leather and travel goods. It was not a matter of choice between goods or leisure, as Veblen had suggested, but of having both. Leisure services certainly became more central. Prudential financial investments became more important. There is also an unproven inference that domestic property investments became more prominent among the pecuniary class. These shifts accompanied continuing emphasis on travel, domestic comfort and the avoidance of menial domestic labour.

## The urge to distinction and processes of diffusion

In the second step in our analysis we sought to put the expenditure of the Very Rich into a wider context, locating them in relation to the culture of consumption of the population as a whole.[7] We examine systematically the 81 categories which were reported in an identical fashion in each of the three years. These items are located on a Factor Analysis Diagram (FAD), indicating the place in the overall pattern of expenditures for the population at each point in time. FADs allow us to compare the expenditure patterns of the Very Rich to those of the remainder of the population, their priorities being situated in the space of lifestyles at the three dates. This also allows us to inspect the movement of those items which have been preferred at any time by the Very Rich across the space of lifestyles, thus throwing some light on patterns of diffusion.

### 1961

Figure 2 identifies the superior and precedented items of the Very Rich. Almost all sit well to the left of the vertical axis, most lying in the North-West quadrant. They cluster fairly closely together and show the same substantive tendencies reported in section 3. When the supplementary socio-demographic variables are consulted (see Figure 3, panel a), and the locations of the households with the highest incomes and highest social class are identified, our interpretation is enhanced. Notable features of Figure 3 (panel a) are that class and income stretch out along the first (horizontal) axis. The Very Rich are positioned some considerable distance (to the North-West) from the rest of those with high incomes. A significant age effect appears on the second axis. The older Very Rich, all other things being equal, were more likely to spend extensively on domestic service, charity, cash gifts, women's outer-ware and spirits, while younger members joined sports clubs, had expensive holidays and used taxis and trains.

The diagram charts the general landscape of consumption in 1961. Poorer households spent proportionately more than others on food, suggesting the importance of 'the culture of the necessary' (Bourdieu, 1984), though some food items – poultry and coffee – remain middle-class priorities. The clustering of items at the bottom of the figure suggests a distinctive working-class culture of leisure, including watching football, drinking beer and betting, but also the payment of trade union dues. The items that distinguish the Very Rich can be seen clearly. Wealth was spent on wine, spirits, women's outerwear, domestic service, cash gifts, plants and flowers, animals, new cars, sports goods, sports club subscriptions, hobbies, air and water travel, coke (fuel), china, holidays, rail fares and taxis. This suggests a distinctive way of life with, especially for the older members, a domestic focus, which also involved much mobility and conspicuous consumption on women's clothing and new cars.

**Figure 2:** *The priorities of the Very Rich in societal context, 1961: superior and precedented items (selected categories) of Very Rich.*
*Note:* **Bold** = items which are superior for Very Rich. ***Italics bold*** = items which are precedented for Very Rich.
*Data source:* Family Expenditure Survey 1961. Figures represent the calculation by the authors.

*1981*

By 1981 the picture had not changed a great deal (see Figure 4). Items characterizing the Very Rich are similar. Restaurants, theatre attendance and jewellery were added, while plants, spirits, sports goods and subscriptions and women's outerwear lost their priority. Altogether fewer items among the 81 are especially prized.[8] This we should expect, since this step in the analysis ignores new categories of goods or services added to the portfolio of the elite in the interim period. The difference, however, is limited.

Some of the apparent difference between Figures 2 and 4 result from the different orientation of the socio-demographic variables to the two axes. As Figure 3 (panel b) indicates, age now runs diagonally from south-west to north-east, while that for class is aligned parallel to the second axis. The line for income runs, for the third to tenth deciles, parallel to the first axis, from right to left, but the two highest deciles are aligned with the vertical axis. Reading this suggests that the richer parts of the middle class consume disproportionately those items in bold to the north of the diagram, with the younger members preferring wine and theatre, the older domestic service and charity. The younger among the Very Rich indicated greater preferences for restaurants, toys and expenditure on animals and pets.[9] Items typical of the Very Rich clustered together slightly less closely than in 1961 and were beginning to show a stronger effect of age differences. The younger rich seemed to prioritize eating out, wine, theatre and jewellery.

The remnants of a working-class culture appear in the south-west corner of the diagram, but the items like trade union subscriptions and football match attendance grew distant from betting, cigarettes and sweets, the preferred luxuries of the poorer elements of the working class. The preceding decade of de-industrialization, high inflation and unemployment, probably produced greater material divisions within the working class. Leisure activities cluster in the south-west corner and are apparently less distributed according to social class; dancing, women's fashion, sports goods, football admission fees were becoming shared among younger cohorts, evidence of a spread of mass commodified consumer culture. Meanwhile food items were becoming ever more purely a function of income.

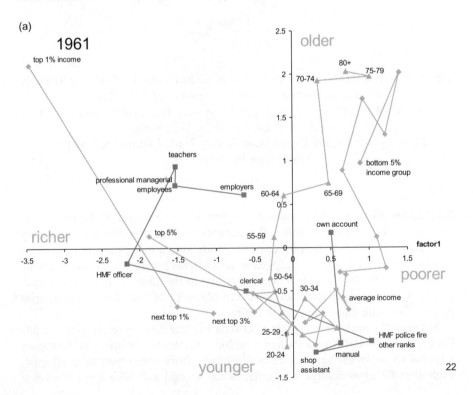

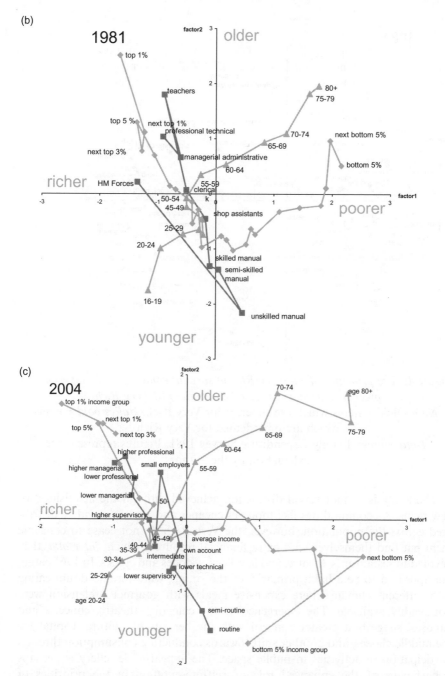

**Figure 3:** *Position of the Very Rich (the top 1%) in societal context: by income, occupational class and age, 1961, 1981 and 2004.*
*Data source:* Family Expenditure Survey 1961, 1981 and Expenditure and Food Survey 2003–04. Figures represent the calculation by the authors.

**Figure 4:** *The priorities of the Very Rich in societal context, 1981: superior and*
*precedented items (selected categories) of Very Rich.*
*Note:* **Bold** = items which are superior for Very Rich. ***Italics bold*** = items
which are precedented for Very Rich.
*Data source:* Family Expenditure Survey 1981. Figures represent the
calculation by the authors.

The analysis cannot reveal distinction achieved through the acquisition of
new items. As commodities like food get cheaper and are more widely distributed across the population, however, the Very Rich do not cease to consume
them but find themselves with extra financial resources which, *inter alia*, they
devoted to restaurants, theatre, and jewellery, watches and clocks. In 1961 eating
out appeared to be a habit primarily of the young, who were no doubt eating
in a different climate where expensive meals with gourmet pretension were
not readily available. The emergence of the category 'theatre, concerts and
circuses' suggests a greater concern with the benefits of cultural capital for
the middle classes, and another shift towards conducting consumption through
participation in activities in public space. The appeal of jewellery is perhaps
a harbinger of the enhanced role of self-presentation in the priorities of
the middle class and, as with restaurants, it was drawn from the south-west
quadrant of the 1961 diagram which characterized mainly the consumption
habits of youth.

*2004*

The patterns revealed by Figure 5 for 2004 suggest an accelerating rate of change. There is greater attrition. As demonstrated earlier, a substantial number of new categories come to be represented among the priorities of the Very Rich. The orientation of social groups to the axes is rather similar to that of 1981 (see Figure 3, panel c), with age positioned on the south-west to north-east diagonal, class running parallel to the second axis, and income running parallel to age along the first axis for those people over 50, but parallel to the second axis for those under 50. The implication is that having less income is largely a result of ageing, though there were also some very poor young working-class people. Class and income for those in the best position to participate in consumer culture runs from south to north-west on the diagram.

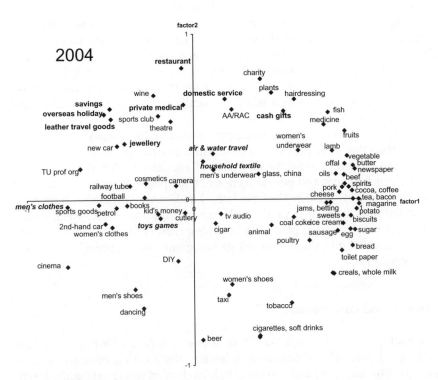

**Figure 5:** *The priorities of the Very Rich in societal context, 2004: superior and precedented items (selected categories) of Very Rich.*

*Note:* **Bold** = items which are superior for Very Rich. ***Italics bold*** = items which are precedented for Very Rich.

*Data source:* Expenditure and Food Survey 2003–04. Figures represent the calculation by the authors.

At the north-west tip we find disproportionate spending on savings, overseas holidays, leather and travel goods, private dentistry, jewellery and restaurants. Older Very Rich purchased domestic service, gave cash gifts and also travelled by air and water, younger ones bought men's clothes and toys. The diagram identifies nine superior items and three precedented. Rail travel, wine, theatre attendance and charitable giving had declined in importance since 1981. The reasons are likely to be different for each, but trickle-down effects – where it is the result of the rest of the population increasing their own expenditure in imitation of the elite – are unlikely to account for any of these. The possible exception might be wine, where there has been a change in tastes but accompanied by more robust supply and a drop in relative price.

The dispersion of items is quite broad, but perhaps less than in 1981, and (in this matter of dispersion) more similar to 1961. This suggests that there was probably something of a decline in the extent of the distance of the Very Rich from the rest of the population between 1961 and 1981, and a growing heterogeneity within the Very Rich. After 1981, the markers of distinction changed in such a way that it is difficult to determine whether the Very Rich were drawing further away from the mass of the population. The increasing impact of cohort differences on consumption behaviour, however, is probably one reason for change. Not only were the Very Rich younger on average by 2004, but it has also been remarked that there is a tendency for the habits of the young to be adopted by older groups, which might classically be seen in the spread of the use of restaurants.

Many more items clustered at the eastern margin by 2004, implying that some or many items that were part of the differential distribution of goods and services in 1961 did trickle down to the status of necessities. They thus appear as priority items for older and poorer sections of the population. Items that were inaccessible in 1961, because they were novel and/or very expensive, have been precipitated into the culture of the ordinary. Hairdressing, outer wear, china, animals and pets, as well as plants, fuel and almost every form of food have now been incorporated into the household spending and consumption of the mass of the population.


## Discussion and conclusions

The spending priorities of the Very Rich alter over time. In 1961 accumulating durable goods was still a distinguishing feature, along with comparatively high expenditure on transport and services. High levels of absolute expenditure were devoted to new cars and housing, first and foremost, but also to traditional luxuries, of food and alcohol. Concern with leisure appeared mostly as travel, involving staying at hotels and voyaging overseas. Also important were domestic items (furniture repairs, fittings) which, along with the purchase of coke presumably to stoke central heating boilers, a luxury at the time, might suggest a concern with a high standard of domestic comfort. Concern for financial security and investment germane to intergenerational reproduction was also apparent, in savings and cash gifts.

The pecuniary class of the early 21st century has dropped some previous indicators of distinction. A longterm shift occurred from concern with household goods to personal items like jewellery and luggage. Modes of premium travel were continuously revised as first the ownership of new cars, then air travel itself, and currently internal air journeys, were favoured. The priority of expensive foreign holidays grew. Proportionately, spending on sports club membership, durable goods, smoking requisites and alcoholic drinks declined. Luxurious items of drink or food no longer registered, though eating out became a strong sign of distinction and a means by which the Very Rich both saved their own labour and participated in commercial activities in public space. That did not, however, entail giving up domestic comfort or ease, payments for domestic service being one of the constant and primary distinguishing features of this group. Also constant, though probably accelerating, was engagement in more varied strategies for the reproduction of secure economic foundations for family life, through investments, savings, pensions, cash gifts and spending on children's education.

Accounts of the operation of contemporary consumer culture tend to suggest fast, repeated but rather unpredictable shifts in preferences. The process of change is probably best characterized as evolutionary. The FADs suggest that the waxing and waning of priorities was a rather smooth process. Items that cease to be superior tend, two decades later, still to be precedented, and vice versa. So, jewellery, watches and clocks moved up the hierarchy at each time point, but even in 1961 had been items preferred by the solvent younger middle class. Wine, though no longer a superior or precedented item by 2004, nevertheless appears on the diagram close to other items preferred by the Very Rich. Of course, this impression is partly an artefact of analysing items in categories that were identical in all three years, which are unlikely to present great surprises. Meanwhile, luxury foods, plants and flowers, spirits, furniture repairs and cruises ceased to be priorities of the Very Rich.

The process of constantly drawing new marks of distinction is an almost inevitable consequence of economic growth under capitalism characterized by processes of mass production. Some earlier priorities of the Very Rich automatically receded as the relative prices of items like cars, clothing and wine fall. It does not require the rich to go out consciously looking for new items for display to account for the fact that their spending priorities change. With that in mind, it is interesting to consider which items accrued to the superior category. Emergent were high expenditures on house purchase and improvements, including on second homes, on more personal items, and on leisure services. On balance, however, the shifts, relative to the mass of the population, were not radical.

Nevertheless, there was something of a watershed in patterns of consumption in the 1980s. This resulted partly from changing distribution of income as the Very Rich got relatively richer: the ratio of advantage in expenditure of the Very Rich which fell from 3.42 in 1961, to 3.06 in 1981 and rose again to 3.28 in 2004. But changes in state policies had an effect as certain public services were reduced or withdrawn. The reorganization of public services, particularly those that the middle classes had made full use of, like the National Health Service and education, resulted in the Very Rich devoting a greater proportion of their resources to private medicine and educational provision for their children. As we have seen this was part of a more general tendency to make even greater range of financial provision for old age and family members than before – though they always had done this disproportionately. If expenditure is the yard-stick, housing became a greater priority also, partly investment in second homes which became a superior item, but also in purchase and renovation of houses. Such items, which deserve greater attention, are partly prudent financial invest-ment, and partly a visible marker of status and taste. In addition there are changes that must be attributed primarily to taste. Some of the main priorities of the Very Rich are ones where selection is subject to aesthetic judgments. Per-sonal items of jewellery, holiday destinations and restaurant meals are all sym-bolical goods which play a major role in strategies of distinction. Many priorities, however, remain in areas of practical benefit and utility, while others that are increasingly important are financial investments. It would be easy to exaggerate the extent to which items conveying symbolic distinction have eclipsed concerns with comfort and security.[10]

The analysis adds something to our understanding of mechanisms involved in consumption. A process of the sedimentation of a shared culture of con-sumption is apparent, as some categories of expenditure which were priorities of the most opulent at one point in time, become less distinguished as wider sections of the population gain access. This is true of luxury foods, durable goods and clothing. As much as anything this probably results from changing prices for mass produced goods. There is no convincing evidence of trickle-up effects from the poor working class to the opulent, though instances would be hard to detect at this level of aggregation. Those items emerging in 2004 were never the provenance of the lower classes – multiple modes of saving, private health care and internal air flights have not been post-war niche consumption areas for the working classes. Those items that did rise up the hierarchy are mostly ones which have migrated from the household budgets of relatively comfortably off younger cohorts (as with eating out and personal items) into categories of higher priority for the Very Rich as a whole. In the cases of restaurant meals and foreign holidays the Very Rich may be engaging more frequently than before but probably are selecting options which are more expensive and of better quality. Indeed, the returns to wealth lie probably more in higher quality than in distinctive com-position of items. The evidence is far from perfect for adjudicating between theoretical positions on elite consumption, but it does suggest that Veblen's account was probably particularly effective in shedding light on differences in consumption in the 1960s.

Many of Veblen's themes resonate with the spending of the wealthy in a pecuniary society. Conspicuous consumption of furniture, clothes and personal possessions appear at different times as markers of wealth. Domestic service, with its intimation of distance from menial labour, is a permanent priority, as Veblen would predict. Also, his (1925:96) observation that 'Expenditure . . . in order to be reputable must be wasteful' should also give pause for thought to advocates of sustainability. Much has changed, however. The elite apparently live less leisurely lives. Their priorities are not only with items of conspicuous consumption. As the very rich find many of their preferences met relatively more cheaply than before, their excess resources will inevitably find new outlets. When Veblen argued that goods came to replace leisure he did not appreciate the extent to which commercial agents would begin to sell the opportunity to pass time unproductively through leisure services.

Our analysis provides no more than a background note to the sociology of elites. We have taken those households with the very highest incomes as a 'pecuniary class', mere proxy for an economic elite. The Very Rich come from different walks of life and their trajectories and current positions are likely to generate different priorities. Were we able to distinguish between households engaged in the cultural, political and corporate business fields we might uncover priorities of each separately, but alternative sources of data would be required to identify the differences made by affiliation to different fields. Our approach cannot capture symbolic differentiation *within* spending categories which is essential both to a rounded understanding of taste and to precise testing of theories of distinction and imitation which also require other data sources. Nevertheless, examining the priorities of the Very Rich systematically over time does take a first step towards describing the consumption patterns of those at the top of the British social hierarchy and showing how these change.

# Notes

1 Data about irregular payments have not been saved in the electronic files of the FES in 1961 and therefore we were unable to chart trends in expenditure on income tax, occupational pensions, mortgage payments or housing renovations. As will be commented upon below, these last two categories seem to have become much more important strategic items in recent years.

2 The ratio of proportionate expenditure of the Very Rich to the average is usually greater than one for they tend to consume common goods of superior quality. There are however some exceptions, some items are *disparaged* by the elite.

3 The term 'precedented' is used in the sense that some items are accorded precedence over others. The term superior is not used in the way that an economist would. It is not defined as luxury or by its elasticity. We are not considering luxuries and necessities. At the expenditure levels of the very rich the idea of necessity it is not helpful (even if it may be in other sorts of investigation.

4 These 30 were superior or precedented for the Very Rich and at least preferred by the Rich.

5 In 1961, this had been a precedented item for the Rich, but was unmarked for the Very Rich.)
6 Of these preferred items, those to which substantial sums of absolute expenditure were devoted included savings, eating out, holidays, new furniture and second-hand coverings.
7 In section 3 we distinguished whether the priorities of the Very Rich were also items upon which the Rich also spent a greater proportion than their ratio of advantage. In this section, all items which were superior or precedented for the Very Rich are represented, regardless of the patterns of expenditure of the Rich. This therefore records some additional items upon which the Very Rich spend excessively.
8 In 1961 there were 13 superior and 4 precedented items, in 1981 there were 9 superior and 4 precedented.
9 This category does not include pet food, therefore indicating purchase and perhaps stabling of animals. Veblen devotes several pages (1925:139–46) to the role in 'pecuniary repute' to 'domestic animals ... [which] are items of conspicuous consumption, and are therefore honorific in their nature and may legitimately be accounted beautiful'.
10 Of course no person needs very many symbolic items to communicate social position and cultural commitment; a few strategically selected symbols are sufficient.

# References

Atkinson, A., (2002), 'Top Incomes in the United Kingdom over the Twentieth Century', University of Oxford, *Discussion Papers in Economic and Social History*, No. 43.
Bourdieu, P., (1984 [1979]), *Distinction: Critique of the Judgment of Taste*, London: Routledge.
Cheng, S-L., Olsen, W, Southerton, D. and Warde, A., (2007), 'The changing practice of eating: evidence from UK time diaries 1975 and 2000', *British Journal of Sociology*, 58(1): 39–61.
Coulangeon, P. and Lemel, Y., (2007), 'Is "distinction" really outdated?: questioning the meaning of the omnivorization of musical taste in contemporary France', *Poetics*, 35 (2–3): 93–111.
Daloz, J-P., (2007), 'Elite distinction: grand theory and comparative perspectives', *Comparative Sociology*, 6(1–2): 27–74.
Edgell, S., (2001), *Veblen in Perspective: His Life and Thought*, New York: M.E. Sharpe.
Fine, B. and Leopold, E., (1993), *The World of Consumption*, London: Routledge.
Gayo-Cal, M., Savage, M. and Warde, A., (2006), 'A cultural map of the United Kingdom, 2003', *Cultural Trends*, **15**(2–3): 215–39.
Gronow, J. and Warde, A., (2001), *Ordinary Consumption*, London: Routledge.
Holt, D., (2004), *How Brands Become Icons: The Principles Of Cultural Branding*, Boston MA: McGraw Hill.
Lansley, S., (2006), *Rich Britain: The Rise and Rise of The New Super-Wealthy*, London: Politico's.
Molnar, V. and Lamont, M., (2002), 'Social categorisation and group identification: how African-Americans shape their collective identity through consumption', in McMeekin, A., Green, K., Tomlinson, M. and Walsh, V., (eds) *Innovation by Demand*, Manchester: Manchester University Press: 88–111.
McKendrick, N., Brewer, J. and Plumb J., (1982), *The Birth of a Consumer Society: The Commercialisation of Eighteenth Century England*, London: Europa Publications.
Mestrovic, S., (2003), *Thorstein Veblen on Culture and Society*, London: Sage.
Offer, A., (2006), *The Challenge of Affluence: self-control and well-being in the United States and Britain since 1950*, Oxford: Oxford University Press.
Scott, J., (1982), *The Upper Classes: Property and Privilege in Britain*, London: Macmillan.
Slater, D., (1997), *Consumer Culture and Modernity*, Cambridge: Polity Press.
Van Eijck, K. and van Oosterhout, R., (2005), 'Combining material and cultural consumption: fading boundaries or increasing antagonism', *Poetics*, **33**: 283–98.

Veblen, T., (1925 [1899]), *The Theory of the Leisure Class: An Economic Study of Institutions*, London: George Allen and Unwin.
Warde, A., Cheng S-L., Olsen, W. and Southerton, D., (forthcoming) 'Changes in the practice of eating: a comparative analysis', *Acta Sociologica*.

# A culture in common: the cultural consumption of the UK managerial elite

## Alan Warde and Tony Bennett

Historical analysis offers a number of different visions of the role of cultural consumption in the operation of social relations of power in modern western societies. There are perhaps four versions. In one, dominant social classes intervene to prohibit, sponsor or channel the pleasures and recreations of subordinate social classes with a view to achieving social stability and moral hegemony. Second, dominant classes engage in exclusive activities, marking their separation from other groups in society by their prestige and refinement. Cultural consumption organizes social distinction, the notorious example being Sumptuary Laws. Third, cultural practices express social divisions within the dominant classes. Cultural conflicts and competition – at Court, between the aristocracy and bourgeoisie, and later between people of business and intellectuals – mark divisions among fractions of the powerful. Fourth, cultural engagement is a means of establishing connections within the dominant classes, sealing the sense of belonging to an identifiable superior stratum of society. Cultural participation provides a platform on which to acquire and use social capital; meeting the right people lubricates the social life of members of the upper echelons of society. To be sure, this is a rather truncated functionalist schematization of processes that are complex and often ambivalent, and ones which moreover operated rather differently from country to country (Coulangeon, 2004).[1] Nevertheless, it is possible to see in this sketch a role for cultural consumption in the service of dominant groups in class societies.

All these accounts assume that classes with disproportionate power in society can be identified and that they are able to define and sustain a shared cultural universe, albeit sometimes contested, with consequences for other classes. What is unclear among the competing accounts are:

- whether the concept of cultural capital any longer has purchase in understanding the operation and distribution of cultural practices;
- whether there is any longer a legitimate culture whose boundaries can be determined, the command of which delivers social distinction;
- whether cultural taste has become a much more individualized property whose distribution no longer follows the contours of social class;

- whether the relationship between the elite fractions of the managerial class and the rest of the population has altered.

In order to explore these issues we conducted a small number of interviews exploring the cultural practices of people occupying powerful positions in British society as part of a larger study of the whole population, 'Cultural Capital and Social Exclusion' (for preliminary results see *Cultural Trends*, 2006). The aim of the chapter is to report on the general content and tenor of those interviews and thereby to describe the nature and distribution of cultural tastes among the managerial elite in prestigious positions in British business, politics and administration. This allowed identification of rarely addressed social and cultural differences. The chapter uses this evidence to analyse the distinctiveness of elite consumption and the role of people in powerful positions in the cultural field at the beginning of the 21st century.

In the first section of this chapter, we describe the study, our interviewees and the strategy of data collection. In section two, we explore the extent to which these people could be said to share a definite set of cultural tastes and commitments. In section three, we examine their reactions to 'popular' culture to explore the contemporary provenance of distinction. In section four, we describe the extent of their investments in cultural activity with a view to estimating the value of cultural capital. In section five we attempt to draw some conclusions about the implications of these features for the extent to which this managerial elite forms a cohesive and integrated group in relation to the rest of the professional and managerial classes and the wider population. When compared to other parts of the population this is a culturally highly active group, playing a significant role in the organization of, usually rather traditional, types of cultural activity. Their interests are wide-ranging and there is a good deal of variety in their leisure and cultural attachments, particularly in relation to gender. Nonetheless, these people have enough in common in terms of their preoccupations and tastes to justify seeing them as members of a shared culture. We also find a powerful role for social connections in determining the rhythms of their cultural practice, and show how their cultural life is embedded within work and social milieu.

## The study

This chapter arises from a study which systematically explores the organization and distribution of cultural capital in Britain, using focus-group discussions, semi-structured household interviews and a questionnaire, applied nationally to both a random sample and an ethnic boost sample, to examine the cultural tastes, forms of cultural participation and cultural knowledge of the population. It also involved interviews with eleven people who had achieved particular prominence in business, public service, political or academic life.[2] These interviews are the focus for our discussion here.

Semi-structured interviews were conducted with four women and seven men in the early summer of 2004. Our strategy was to find some people who fill positions that are unquestionably ones from which institutional power is exercised and to inquire about their cultural practices. The sample was opportunistic, derived from institutional and personal contacts of the research team. It included CEOs and a Finance Director of large corporations, proprietors and directors of large family businesses, very senior administrative staff of the Civil Service and Members of Parliament. Their average age – reflecting their achievements – was well above the main sample mean of 48: most were over 50 and some were in their 60s and 70s. Except for one woman, who had risen to political prominence through the trade-union movement, and one of the men, who did officer training at Sandhurst, all had university educations, to postgraduate level in some cases. Behind these common educational careers, however, were significant differences in social origins and background. While some of those we interviewed had ascended to prominent positions from working-class backgrounds, others had built their careers on the basis of their parents' middle-class social positions and, in two cases, had inherited property, a country estate in one case and a stake in a major family retail business in another.

In the terms of Savage *et al.* (1992), the interviewees were predominantly bureaucrats (managers) though three were propertied (two by inheriting family capital). Those who began as professionals early moved into more general management roles. We might therefore characterize the group as a managerial elite. They constitute an elite in the sense that they have power and influence that affects a large number of other people, including other members of their occupational class. We will see whether they deserve to be called members of a social class later.

Most interviews were held at some place of work, for although several were officially retired, they continued to hold positions in various organizations. Interviews asked questions about personal and family biography, cultural practice and taste, and roles in organizations responsible for the delivery of cultural services. In the first area interviews covered careers, family of origin and education and current domestic situation, including education of children. Regarding the second, interviewees were asked about their cultural activities and tastes, moving through television, cinema, visual arts, music, sport, reading, and other fine arts. They were also asked about collecting. In the third part, we asked about the organizations they belonged to and whether they played any role in the management or administration of arts organizations.

Analysis has been the product of several careful readings, organized by theme, with attention being paid to the range and distribution of the cultural activities that the interviewees participated in, the understandings supporting such activities, and the social contexts in which they were framed. We looked for similarities and differences in the experience of each individual and considered to what degree these could be understood as aspects of a shared social condition.

## Shared commitments

If one were to select eleven people at random from the British population and ask about their participation and their tastes, one would certainly find much greater heterogeneity than was revealed by our elite interviews. Both by way of norm and of practice they are strikingly similar in their tastes. Of course, there are personal deviations from their common cultural commitments, but it is the similarities that stand out.

One indicator of this was the taken-for-grantedness of the value of certain practices and artefacts. No one questioned the relevance of being asked to focus on the domains identified; no one seemed surprised about being asked about paintings or music. No one made disparaging remarks about the fields of the fine arts or high culture. On occasions people said that they were not very interested in some domain or other, but they never denied their validity. Moreover, there were few, if any, instances of one interviewee describing something as execrable while another attributed it great intellectual or cultural value.

A second indicator was the degree to which certain areas of cultural practice appeared to be obligatory. All read. Materials were varied. Newspapers and current affairs magazines were common. Several expressed a liking for non-fiction of a political or biographical nature. Some read very little, if any, fiction. But everyone read and many would have liked to read more. All bar one said that they liked classical music. Almost everyone went to orchestral concerts and, more significantly, everyone had at some stage of their lives been a regular visitor to the opera and, for some, this was a continuing involvement. In a couple of cases it had become less feasible because of living in a rural location. For another two, no longer attending was something of a blessing as they confessed to not liking opera very much and had done so mainly out of a sense of professional and social obligation. Timothy, a senior civil servant, was one such; he observed that 'it would be fair comment to say that a lot of senior civil servants meet each other at the opera and the ballet'. Cynthia, who was married to a Member of Parliament and, through her own career, held a number of non-executive directorships and was a member of several national regulatory bodies and commissions, reported that in the 1960s and 1970s, living in metropolitan political circles, exchange of invitations to the opera was a key form of sociability which resulted in very frequent visits. That only 15 per cent of the British population, as reported in the survey, ever go to opera and only 5 per cent with any degree of regularity, indicates its special significance for the elite. There is almost no doubt that it played a central role in the mobilization, organization and connections of this stratum, especially in London, in the second half of the 20th century. The same was true of their frequent visits to art galleries, concerts and the theatre, activities which formed a part of the regular social rhythms and expectations of their professional lives. To be an effective manager at a senior level apparently requires some engagement, in association with clients and contacts (but mostly not colleagues), in visits to the theatre and opera as well as to sports events and restaurants.

There thus appears to be an established core of practices which professional and corporate elites participate in, with some items more central than others. Classical music, painting and reading are more or less compulsory. Other activities attract quite a number of participants disproportionately – a liking for modern jazz being one of them – but are clearly optional. Everyone visited art galleries regularly, in London especially but also when travelling. As part of a work trip or a holiday, this group attended art galleries in foreign cities and were thus able to comment on, for example, the virtues of the Hermitage Museum in St Petersburg, the Van Gogh Museum in Amsterdam, and the Museum of Modern Art in New York.

A closer examination of the visual arts will allow us to probe the cultural practices of this group more deeply. What stood out most here was the strong preference for Impressionism which, for most of our interviewees, served as the organizing centre of the likes and dislikes – of types of art and of artists – through which the interviewees positioned themselves in the art field. This was partly a consequence of our showing the interviewees two pictures – J.M.W. Turner's *The Fighting Temeraire Tugged to her Last Berth to be Broken Up* (1838) and David Hockney's *Paper Pools* (1980) – and asking them whether they recognized the paintings, knew who the painters were, and whether they liked them. Turner's position as a precursor of Impressionism and, more generally, as the key mediator between earlier traditions of British art and European modernism, helped to bring Impressionism into the discussion if, which was rare, it hadn't been raised already.

The rate of recognition was, unsurprisingly, much higher for the Turner painting than it was for the Hockney, as was the rate of liking but in ways that differed in accordance with both age and gender. The response of Beverley – the CEO of a financial consultancy company, and in her late 50s at the time of the interview – was typical of many in linking a liking for Turner to a fondness for Impressionism:

> I like all the Turner paintings. I like them because they seem to me to be a combination of attention to detail, like the Salisbury Cathedral ones, and that kind of thing. But also with an almost Impressionist sort of ease so – you know, so I – well I don't have a lot of language I can use for art because again I'm not knowledgeable about it but I like that one. I like most of his paintings.

For James, a retired senior servant, a liking for Turner and for Impressionism flow seamlessly into one another:

> Yes, yes, all of the Impressionists yes is approachable, I get into that. I mean Lucien Freud, seen quite a lot of that once or twice recently, just to pick a modern artist. Wouldn't go a million miles to see that (the Hockney: AW, TB), a Turner, yes. I think the one, the Turner, Whistler, Monet Exhibition is a very interesting one to see.

Impressionism also occupies a central place in the tastes of Keith, a director of a family-owned national retail chain, providing the point of reference in relation to which he locates his other tastes:

Yes, well starting, I mean actually Impressionism because I covered quite a bit of that in History, the sort of Monets and Manets and what have you, I mean I do think that is particularly striking art. So I mean I enjoy Impressionism and if there's an exhibition on in London of an Impressionist painter, I'll try and go along. Landscapes, I find very stirring, I mean having grown up in such a bold landscape as . . . you know, which has got so many different types of geography so I enjoy sort of rural landscapes and paintings. I'm not particularly turned on by portraiture or indeed still life.

Ralph, 70 years old at the time of the interview, but still working part-time in honorary scientific positions after a career as a highly successful scientist and, later, a university vice chancellor, expressed his fondness for Impressionism in ways that connected with his professional interests:

Yes, I mean the ones that I guess I've liked for a long time and still do are the Impressionists where I'd go anywhere to see. And I, you know, I also feel that they got an insight into the physics of seeing things, and also when I look at them you know I also get an aesthetic thrill out of seeing them.

Responses to the Hockney and to modern art more generally were more ambivalent. Ralph recognized the painting but was lukewarm: he and his wife liked some of Hockney's paintings, but not others, just as they liked and owned some modern art but were also left cold by much of it 'especially if it's just a black, sort of black square or something'. Robert, the Cambridge-educated CEO of a major international company, and in his late 50s, was similarly open to the challenges of modern art while also wanting to keep the art itself at a distance. While intrigued by 'the Damien Hirst type stuff', he told us that 'I wouldn't have it in my own home, even if I could afford it' preferring, when it came to buying art, to stay with work influenced by the Impressionists. Alistair, also in his fifties and, by inheritance, a landowner, expressed a similar ambivalence in his reactions to the Hockney painting:

It's an interesting picture, – to be honest I haven't got a clue who it's by but I find it you know, I like the colours on that. But it's – it's something I wouldn't find easy to sort of live with but, it's something I would expect to see in what is it the Tate Modern or something.

James was more forthright, telling us that 'abstract art doesn't do anything for me and it doesn't inform me,' going on to say 'I'm traditional; I don't regard that as art'.

Keith, who was about 50 at the time of the interview, was the only one of the men who responded positively to modern art, welcoming the intellectual challenge that it posed.

When you get to somebody like Damien Hirst I find that, find his work quite extraordinary but thought-provoking at the same time. You know the sort of, is it The Cow in formaldehyde or something, and you just, I mean it clearly stirs one to think, well really what all that's about?

Like all of the men, however, he had little liking for the Hockney picture. By contrast, the women we interviewed were more open to Hockney and to modern art in general, and often in ways which stressed continuities with both Turner and Impressionism. Beverley, while saying that she didn't like modern art much, both recognized and liked the Hockney: 'I like the light, I like the light and Turner's sort of style but I like the colours and the broadness of it'. Caroline – who had risen to a position of political and public prominence through the trade union movement and the Labour Party – also instantly recognized and liked the Hockney, seeing a place for it in her bathroom. She also liked the Turner, seeing both pictures as having a strong visual impact, as did Cynthia who was absolutely bowled over by the Hockney ('Wow, yes. Yes.').

It is clear, then, that Impressionism occupies a distinctive position in the tastes of these interviewees as the most consistently liked art genre. Only Eleanor liked portraits, and still lifes were also unpopular. Attitudes toward modern art ranged from indifferent to hostile on the part of the older men interviewed, through a sceptical curiosity on the part of the younger men, to a more open response on the part of the women interviewees. With regard to named artists, Impressionist painters or related painters in the tradition of European modernism were the most frequently mentioned (van Gogh, Monet, Picasso, Magritte, Manet, Whistler, Munch, Gaugin) followed by artists with Renaissance associations (Titian, Raphael, Breugel and Rembrandt) and some modern British artists (Hockney, Spencer).

The survey data showed that a preference for Impressionism was second only to a preference for Renaissance art in strength of connection with regular art gallery attendance (several times a year or more), followed by modern art, but with weak connections in the case of still lifes, portraits and landscapes (see Silva, 2006: Figure 3). In class terms, Renaissance art was the most strongly connected to the higher professional and managerial classes, and was followed in this by Impressionism, while landscapes, still lifes and portraits did not generally recruit much support from these classes. Modern art stood out in being liked most by women and by younger members of the survey (see Silva, 2006, Table 2).

The strong interest in Impressionism, and the more divided views about modern art that we have reported above, are consistent with these wider tendencies. Where our interviewees might seem to be most at odds with these is in the relatively little attention they paid to Renaissance art. Yet, apart from the fact of not being prompted by the two pictures we showed, this perhaps also reflects the key historical role that Impressionism has played in the formation of the professional middle classes in Britain. While, as we have noted, there is plenty of evidence of a cosmopolitan involvement in art institutions internationally, the Tate, both Tate Britain and Tate Modern, is the most frequently cited, albeit in different registers. Tate Britain was usually referred to as a place for frequent visits – Robert and his wife were members – whereas, except for Eleanor, who lived nearby and often popped in for short visits, going to the Tate Modern was viewed more as an experiment, a voyage into new territory prompted by a sense that, while doubtful about the aesthetic merits of the art on display, one really ought to learn to like it.

This connection between a strong liking for Impressionism and a close relationship with the Tate is no accident. Between its opening in 1897 and its extension in 1926 the Tate served as the primary artistic site through which the meritocratic professional middle classes sought to distance themselves from the working classes while simultaneously laying a claim to independent cultural leadership and distinctiveness, differentiating themselves from earlier hegemonic fractions of the English aristocracy by claiming an exclusive title to, and familiarity with, European modernism, and French Impressionism in particular (Taylor, 1999). Impressionism has thus played a key role in organizing the historicity of the British art field. Michael Grenfell and Cheryl Hardy (2003) argue that this historicity takes the form of a division between a rear-garde (Titian, Michaelangelo, Poussin, Gericault, Goya), representing a class/art connection that is most deeply rooted in tradition, and a consecrated avant-garde consisting mainly of representatives of European modernism (van Gogh, Monet, Bonnard, Picasso, Mondrian, Duchamp) on the one hand, and two newer formations on the other: an American avant-garde (Hopper, Pollock, Rothko, Twombly, Koons, and Basquiat) and a British avant-garde (Sickert, Spencer, Moore, Hockney, Bacon, Gilbert and George, and Hirst). It is notable, and clearly a function of their age, that none of our elite sample made any reference to the American artists named here. They were instead most strongly related to the historical formation of the consecrated avant-garde. Their relation to the current British avant-garde was tentative and tremulous, combining a hesitant liking with recognition of how this art had constituted a disconcerting challenge to their tastes and of the role that this had played in their educational and social trajectories.

## Distinction and a commitment to legitimate culture

In the context of great controversy as to whether or not it now makes any sense to identify some tastes and practices as 'legitimate' (eg Coulangeon, 2004; Glevarec, 2006) we are wary of classifying items in terms of high and popular culture, or high and lowbrow taste. We did, however, using our survey data, calculate whether some items were more preferred by those with the highest institutionalized cultural capital. That is to say, we compared the practices and the tastes of those with degrees and those with no qualifications. From this we constructed a ranking of the legitimacy of cultural items in our survey. Table 1 identifies the cultural activities in which graduates were more likely to participate than were the unqualified.

This provides one context against which to consider the expressed preferences of our elite interviewees. Seven activities were 'legitimate' by the criterion that graduates were more than twice as likely to participate, namely: going to the opera; attending rock concerts; going to the theatre; attending orchestral concerts; visiting art galleries; engaging in body maintenance activity; and going to night clubs. The last was shown by correlation analysis to be unrelated to the

**Table 1:** *Cultural Participation*

| Activity | Mean (%) | Those with degrees (n = 366) as a % of all who do the activity (b) | Those with no qualifications (n = 419) as a % of all who do the activity (c) | Ratio (b/c) |
|---|---|---|---|---|
| Opera: go ever | 15.4 | 49 | 11.2 | 4.37 |
| Rock concerts: go ever | 31.1 | 37.2 | 10.9 | 3.41 |
| Art galleries: go ever | 44.7 | 38.4 | 12.6 | 3.04 |
| Orchestral concerts: go ever | 32.5 | 42.7 | 14.6 | 2.92 |
| Selected body management activities | 52 | 32.7 | 12.5 | 2.61 |
| Theatre: go ever | 56.4 | 34.3 | 15.9 | 2.15 |
| Night clubs: go ever | 36.3 | 27.3 | 12.7 | 2.14 |
| Practice any sport | 56.3 | 30.5 | 15.3 | 1.99 |
| Museum: go ever | 62.9 | 32.3 | 17.3 | 1.86 |
| Belong to any group or club | 9.4 | 36.7 | 20.4 | 1.79 |
| Cinema: go ever | 74.6 | 28.5 | 16.3 | 1.74 |
| Have paintings | 39.4 | 31.1 | 18.6 | 1.67 |
| Have read named books (eg Harry Potter) | 54.3 | 32.2 | 20.2 | 1.59 |
| Stately homes: go ever | 71 | 29 | 20.7 | 1.40 |
| Read books | 79.6 | 27.1 | 21.8 | 1.24 |
| Pub: go ever | 83.5 | 24.9 | 23.7 | 1.05 |
| Have seen works by named painters | 89.2 | 25 | 24.2 | 1.03 |
| Have videos | 90.4 | 23.7 | 24.1 | 0.98 |
| Have listened to any of named musical items (eg Chicago) | 95.4 | 24.1 | 24.7 | 0.97 |
| Eating out: go ever | 96.5 | 24.1 | 25.2 | 0.95 |
| Have CDs | 96.9 | 23.6 | 25.8 | 0.91 |
| Watches TV | 98.4 | 23.4 | 26.9 | 0.86 |
| Would make a point of watching specific TV events | 67 | 24 | 28.2 | 0.85 |
| Read a daily newspaper | 76 | 22.9 | 27.8 | 0.82 |

**Table 1:** *Continued*

| Activity | Mean (%) | Those with degrees (n = 366) as a % of all who do the activity (b) | Those with no qualifications (n = 419) as a % of all who do the activity (c) | *Ratio (b/c)* |
|---|---|---|---|---|
| Would make a point of watching any of the film directors | 59 | 20.5 | 28.9 | *0.70* |
| Receive any lessons in arts and crafts | 43.3 | 18.4 | 32.6 | *0.56* |
| Bingo: go ever | 14.2 | 13.5 | 37.7 N = 1564 | 0.35 |

Note: This table reports the mean levels of participation in selected activities. Respondents with degrees and with no qualifications are calculated as a percentage of those who ever participate.

rest and might be ignored. The other six formed a coherent cluster of activities: participation in one was likely to entail participation in the others. Our elite interviewees were very likely to be heavily involved in most of these. Of course, we should not be surprised that this group liked what graduates like, since all but two of them held degrees themselves. But, except for rock concerts, which are preferred by younger graduates, they were disproportionately likely to participate in these activities when compared to the average university-educated Briton. A strong commitment to legitimate culture is thus apparent. To the extent that command of legitimate culture signifies distinction, these are people of 'refined taste'.

Most of our interviewees also expressed a liking for some forms of popular culture, with James, a retired higher civil servant, the sole exception in having preferences exclusively for legitimate culture. James expressed a liking for opera, chamber music concerts, Impressionism and contemporary fiction while distancing himself from popular culture, prefacing his answers to specific questions, as did others, with a somewhat horrified series of 'No, no's. Thus:

> Do you ever watch TV during the day time or mornings?
> No, no.
> Have you ever been concerned with keeping fit and running or anything?
> Oh no, good gracious no.
> Is sport something that is important to you?
> Not at all. It is something to be avoided at all costs.

Among his explicit dislikes were jazz, musicals, abstract art, Damien Hirst, Harry Potter, Lord of the Rings. Other men also refused items vehemently. Thus Ralph:

> Home and Away?
> No, no. I don't even know what it is.
> Reality?
> No, and never.

And Timothy:

> Contemporary music of any kind, country and western?
> Not really, no.
> Harry Potter books?
> No, and almost as a matter of principle . . . no.
> You wouldn't watch soap operas or chat shows?
> No, or reality, awful.

Despite some of these perhaps predictable aversions, however, with the exception of James all had some overtly popular culture items in their portfolios of preferences.

The extent to which the interviewees sought explicitly to distinguish their cultural interests and practices from popular ones varied across different domains. The differences between the ways in which television and film viewing were described are significant in this regard.

A distancing from television was most evident in the rarity of television viewing among our sample. And even when television was watched, it was presented as if it were another kind of activity. Many of the men thus reported that they watched television a lot for sport, but in ways that suggested this was not really watching television – it was the sport they were interested in, not television, as if they were watching sport *through* television rather than actually *watching television*. As far as more general patterns of viewing were concerned, the response of Eleanor, indicating decreased viewing with age (in marked contrast to the overall tendency of our main sample in which television viewing increases significantly with age) was typical:

> I was one of the sort of people who would, if . . . I was at home on my own in the evening, I'd put the television on . . . I can't give you the moment when I stopped and for a long time I knew what was on television and then would switch the television on because I knew what was on. I've moved even further down that line so that now unless somebody says hey by the way there's a good programme on, you should watch it, I am very unlikely to turn the television on.

The distinction that is enunciated here between purposive viewing, as opposed to watching whatever happens to be on, is a recurring theme in the interviews and, as such, one which rehearses long-established divisions between practices of attentive viewing on the one hand and the allegedly distracted viewer of popular entertainment media (Crary, 2001). This is clear in the landowner Alistair's reflections on the subject in which he goes to some pains to make it clear that he and his wife 'are not addicts at all' and that, when they watch television, it will usually be to watch for a specific purpose citing news, current affairs programmes and documentaries as his favourite genres. Most of all, though, it was the fact of not watching much that he dwelt on most:

But I wouldn't class ourselves as big television watchers. We watch it when it sort of suits us and if there's something that we think might be quite interesting is on. We watch a little bit of, sometimes a little bit of sport, things like Wimbledon Fortnight we particularly enjoy. If (Local F.C.; Aw playing I might well watch that. But I don't watch, we don't watch a lot of television.

Preferences were consistently for BBC channels in both the terrestrial and digital environments – where history channels were also frequently referred to – and the preferred genres were history documentaries, news and current affairs, and television dramas with programmes like *Panorama, News Night, Question Time, University Challenge, A Touch of Frost, The Bill, Spooks, Absolutely Fabulous, Midsummer Murders, Pride and Prejudice* and *In the Footsteps of Churchill* being specifically mentioned, as also were satirical shows like *Have I got News for You* and *Dead Ringers*. Soap operas, however, were almost universally disliked. For Caroline, soaps were to be avoided in view of their potential to corrupt and degrade:

> I can't be doing for one iota with a soap or reality TV. I think reality TV is just banal, really and soaps, they're so...I was thinking to myself last night that *Eastenders*, I think it was, came on and before I switched over, they were having a row already, you know and I felt, you know, why doesn't somebody make a programme about people who are nice to each other, it's just so miserable and I think it has a huge impact on the way people behave, you know, just shouting at people's faces, that all becomes quite acceptable. One of my daughters won't let her girls watch it anymore because she says they pick up such awful bad habits and ways of speaking to people that it's not nice.

Robert had similarly strong aversions to reality television:

> I'll walk out of the room if my son has got Big Brother on or any of these bloody things where they vote for people who then get kicked off. I literally you know, walk out of the room and go read a book or get away from it, I can't handle it, right. I hate them, right, with a vengeance.

The opposition to reality television was not, however, universal. Indeed, Keith, who had been educated at Eton and, subsequently, at universities in Scotland and the United States, and had widespread cultural interests in the arts and theatre, found reality TV fascinating. Clearly a little perplexed as to why this should be so, he justified his interest in this genre as a form of learning, thus bringing it into line with his other television interests which had a strong documentary and current affairs accent.

There is plenty of evidence here, then, that, for our elite interviewees, all of whom had considerable resources of cultural capital, a sense of the division between 'serious' and 'improving' programmes on the one hand, and less respectable, 'trashy' and, in some respects, depraving programmes on the other, informed the choices they make.

The picture is more mixed with regard to their film preferences. James disliked going to the cinema because of the ways in which it bombarded the senses, leaving little room for the more critical mood he preferred when watching films. He described the atmosphere of the cinema as 'somewhat repellent', objecting to the smell of popcorn and the overwhelming noise. It was not just the occasion of popular cinema that James found offensive, but its content too, describing *The Lord of the Rings* as 'simply ghastly' and the *Harry Potter* films as 'awful' – mere 'spectacle, technological spectacle'. Just as averse to Hollywood epics and musicals, his preference was for films by European art directors. While Ralph also had a particular liking for French films, this European art director focus was not shared by the other interviewees. A more typical response was to opt for instances of comedy, literary adaptations or costume dramas. This was true for Eleanor. Her favourite films were romantic comedies – *Pretty Women, Four Weddings and a Funeral* and *Notting Hill* – or comedies, like *The Full Monty*. And neither Eleanor nor Alistair were guided in their film choice by any knowledge of film directors. As Alistair put it:

> Directors? No I'm not very knowledgeable about that, I'm afraid I'm the type of person who almost leaves when the credits flash up. And, no, I don't, we don't really go and see a film on the basis of a director, you do get to know of some of them but it's been something that's never really particularly interested me. As I say we go because we've heard the film's good or it's on a subject that we know we will like.

As was the case with their tastes in relation to art, where references were made to films or directors with high cultural associations, these were mostly European. America was identified primarily in terms of Hollywood, with little reference being made to contemporary American film directors who have challenged the hegemony of European art cinema (Hitchcock is referred to, but his role is similar to that of the consecrated avant-garde in the art field). We should note, however, that in this respect our elite interviewees were at odds with our main sample where references to American cinema were far more common than to European cinema, especially among younger managers and professionals (see Savage, Wright and Gayo-Cal, forthcoming).

This lack of interest in directors was also frequently accompanied by a disavowal of any serious purpose when going to the cinema. Although Keith and his wife went to the cinema only rarely, he told us that 'when we do I find it generally speaking terrific entertainment, a great sense of escape and we would typically go and watch the sort of, I suppose blockbusters and secondary blockbusters that are being advertised'. And Robert, who loathed reality television and who had quite high tastes in other areas – he was very knowledgeable about modern art, particularly about Impressionism, and went to the theatre regularly – had self-confessedly popular tastes in film citing *The Bourne Supremacy, Spiderman*, and, in contrast to James, the *Harry Potter* series and *The Lord of the Rings* as films he liked, and *The Return of the Jedi* as 'my favourite all time film'.

In summary, then, the evidence of these interviews suggests that a combination of high levels of cultural capital and significant levels of economic capital associated with senior management or professional positions is likely to result in a more distinctive set of relations to television than to film, where responses are more mixed and varied.

## Heavy investments

A third feature of the cultural habits of this elite group, hinted at already, is the extent of their participation. They go out to cultural events comparatively often, and even if not very interested, are fluent and have more than a smattering of knowledge about many forms of culture. They collect things. Almost all say they eat out often – and those who say it is a rare occurrence still mostly do so more frequently than the national average. They support cultural organizations. For example, they are likely to be supporters of arts organizations (eg. Friends of the Tate (several), the Royal Academy, the National Trust, English Heritage, the Royal Society of the Arts). They are occasionally trustees, by invitation, of arts organizations (Royal College of Music, Provincial Theatre and City Operatic Society) and their companies sponsor art events. That said, their charitable and public roles are at least as likely to be in their own professional world (Chair of Trustees of an educational charity, Institute of Directors) or in local good works voluntary associations (military cadets, organizations for deprived young people) as in culture and the arts. Despite being enormously busy otherwise, they invested heavily in a wide range of cultural activities – except, as we have seen, for television, which they said they rarely had time to watch.

Paradoxically, this extensive involvement appears not to be a consequence of any great commitment to culture for its own sake. One or two are specialists or enthusiasts. Theatre was a passion for Robert and for Eleanor. Robert explained how he and his wife had developed a passion for theatre, at one time, when in their 20s, watching ten Royal Shakespeare Company performances in six weeks. He had had his company become involved in sponsoring theatre, and now, in his 50s, he made theatre a priority: 'live theatre in London is a big part [of our recreational time]', having been 'thirty or forty times in the last four years [since returning from working abroad]'. Robert had also invested much time and effort in learning about painting. But Robert and Eleanor were exceptions. Indeed, in some ways the greatest apparent enthusiastic obsession was among men associating themselves with soccer and with the professional soccer clubs of their city of birth. Generally, however, culture was a high priority not as end in itself but, rather, as a corollary of work. (It should be noted that none of these people are primarily engaged in the culture industries; none were professionals or managers in the world of the arts.) The elite presents itself first and foremost as professionally engaged. Their jobs and careers came first; and not only because we asked questions about biography at the beginning of the interview. Even for the enthusiastic Robert, a good deal of his engagement was through his company with a view to entertaining clients. For the rest, culture was mostly a complementary activity, but none the less essential for that. The participation of some men was ensured by their partners (and to a much lesser extent their children). Men followed their wives tastes more, and often to a significant degree. Men reporting their preferences often said 'we', meaning themselves and their partners. Women, by contrast, always said 'I'. Ralph used 'we' so often that he felt obliged to define who 'we' were, attributing to his wife his own consumption of art objects, paintings, TV programmes, concert-going and novels. He relies on his wife to lead him beyond his conservatism in aesthetic matters, making him take more seriously trends in modern art he would otherwise dismiss out of hand, and also follows his wife's choice in the novels he reads; 'anything that my wife says "look, I really recommend that", I'll read'. Culture was a family business with primary responsibility for organizing it being delegated to their wives, surely a sign of its limited centrality for most of the men we interviewed.

One point of importance is precisely that the elite seem to recognize that they derive profits from the time invested in cultural activities. Their behaviour would be hard to understand if they did not believe that there is some gain from investing in the acquisition of cultural capital. They do not refuse opportunities for cultural participation, nor ever denigrate the value of culture. Rather they participate heavily. This seems to imply that they recognize the value of cultural capital. But is it part of a strategy of distinction through refined taste?

## Social integration

Probably taste is not what is primarily at stake. Rather is seems to be more a matter of connections. Frequent attendance at (selective) events outside the home implies some imperative to join in a cultural life in public. This may well be a prerequisite of networking. The webs of privileged connections deliver invitations to arts events: Robert said, 'as CEO you could spend your whole life going to the opera, going to ballet, going to the theatre'. Contacts provide opportunities to take up positions on voluntary bodies – sport, arts, young people, military and church – but also to ones beyond their main career which are paid. Almost everyone has some such position, and many have a large number. They are members of clubs and dining circles. They also boast connections to practicing artists. Painters, potters and sculptors are mentioned as parts of a network of friends or acquaintances, and their work is quite often purchased or collected (in small amounts) directly from such people. Connections are very important, and are different for this category of person, probably both in volume and capacity to deliver profits.

Thus it seems likely that the role which command of cultural capital plays in the formation and organization of managerial elites is primarily that it eases social relations within the stratum. Participation provides a platform upon which to acquire and use social capital; meeting the right people beyond the orbit of economic organizations does indeed lubricate the social life of the elite. Familiar cultural commitments serve, when necessary, as a repository of shared experience and a means of mutual recognition. What differences exist – and there are some differences between men and women, younger and older, and first and second generation middle class – are not obviously being used to mark internal cultural differences within the elite. This integration of members of the upper middle class offers them opportunities and secures privilege for them and also for their children.

Their integration is not, however, based upon condescension, or revulsion, towards members of other social classes. The evidence is not consistent with a view that higher classes express hostility towards lower classes through their cultural practice. Never did their occasional distaste for elements of popular culture spread over into condemnation of those people who had a consuming interest in reality TV or country and western music. This elite is also probably not very different in the content of its tastes and practices from other members of the professional and upper managerial classes. Professionals and executives are, according to our survey data, more likely than other classes to attend opera, concerts, art galleries, etc. The elite group. however, is more heavily engaged in cultural activities with tastes that are probably more attuned to legitimate culture than the rest of the middle class. More important, perhaps, they are themselves – as trustees and sponsors – actively involved in the processes through which official forms of cultural legitimation are organized and enacted. That this occurs for most in the absence of an enthusiastic orientation towards the fine arts suggests that Britain is more like the USA (where, according to Ostrower, 1998, participation in the arts is better explained by its role in the social organization of the elite) than France, where effortless command of legitimate culture is a powerful symbol of high social status (Bourdieu, 1984; Lamont, 1992). Nonetheless, their behaviour can be expected to reinforce a definition of legitimate culture, at least for their own generation.

It is important to note that our interviewees are of a particular generation and it may be that the cultural patterns are in process of change. Those born after 1945 have a greater smattering of popular and commercial culture in their repertoires, and this holds *a fortiori* for those who were also first generation middle class. But the shift is hardly momentous and it would seem that effective dominant class reproduction continues to make use of the symbolic items of legitimate culture. The experience of the upwardly mobile suggests though that it is possible to acquire and to learn the rudiments of that culture, perhaps through the shared experience of higher education, even if the formal curriculum is not responsible, and probably also through a process of occupational socialization associated with higher managerial positions. It would not be entirely wayward, then, to suggest that the lifestyles of the higher managerial positions in the occupational field includes the introduction and reinforcement of the value of culture, especially of legitimate culture as a set of practices they have in common. We would, though, be cautious about describing this as a shared habitus in view of the general difficulties that now beset this concept (Lahire, 2003, 2004; Bennett 2007).

## Conclusions

The eleven people we interviewed proved to be more homogeneous in practice and taste than might reasonably have been anticipated. An engagement with classical music was apparent in all but one case, and opera in particular seemed to play a strategic and obligatory role in the cultural portfolio of people in this stratum of British society. Universally they expressed interest in the visual arts and went to art galleries regularly, with visits to famous galleries in other countries part of their itineraries when on holiday and when travelling abroad for work reasons. Participating by attending live performances or visiting cultural sites was an especially prominent feature of their behaviour – all activities that we might reasonably describe as key elements of legitimate culture in Britain. They also shared other elements of lifestyle which, while not necessarily so symbolically distinctive, indicate a shared set of practices and values in the cultural domain. All travelled a lot, most had second homes, all but one ate out very regularly, all were members of cultural organizations and most held positions of authority in voluntary associations. While some of the above appeared almost to be obligatory for people in the sort of positions that they held, there were also some equally significant, if more optional, commitments.

There was some evidence of differences within the group being structural. There was some difference between those who were first generation middle class and those who had had parents in the upper middle class. The first generation had a tendency to be more heavily specialized in their most preferred activities, and to appreciate rather more elements of more recent culture, including modern art and rock music. Second generation interviewees seemed somewhat more comfortable with a wider range of legitimate culture. The differences, however, were not great. This supports Erickson's (1996) claim that secondary cultural socialization in adulthood is an important and effective process in acquiring tastes; and also probably an indication that being in a managerial position encourages, if not entirely requires, wider cultural engagement as a means of communication for work purposes. There were also some differences in tastes between men and women, though rather less than might have been predicted on the basis of their very different career trajectories.

A second key feature of the cultural activities of these individuals was the extent of their investment in cultural activities. This arose partly as a function of their work. Many of their cultural visits and engagements were with colleagues or clients, including cultural activities organized by firms for public relations or commercial purposes. Frequency of attendance at concerts, however, and visits to theatres and galleries was far above the British norm, and also well above the norm for those holding equivalent levels of institutional cultural capital. One explanatory factor is the coincidence of opportunities for accumulating and displaying cultural and social capital. One of the most striking features of this group was the extent to which those who had retired were invited to take on other jobs and projects, in the commercial, voluntary and state sectors. Another feature was the wide span of activities reported. Though we might not want to describe them as cultural omnivores on the basis of the composition of their tastes (they often avoided activities symbolic of popular taste, though mostly without disparaging or claiming to dislike the culture of groups less elevated in the social hierarchy), in terms of volume of engagement these were highly active people across the range of legitimate and mainstream culture. Moreover, culture was very much a family affair, with partners, and especially wives, clearly knowledgeable and committed, and devoting energy to organizing and validating cultural activity. Since the primary impression is that culture was not a burning passion of most of our interviewees, it is hard not to conclude that at least they believe that cultural capital is of value, that it is something that one might accumulate and expect to profit from in other avenues in life. If no one else does, the powerful believe that command of legitimate culture is a worthwhile form of investment.

A third conclusion is that these patterns of cultural engagement do confer and signal social distinction. We have seen that cultural capital is accorded value by this group. It generates social capital (jobs after retirement, invitations on the social circuit to opera, positions in voluntary associations). It is heavily loaded towards the inclusion of traditionally legitimate cultural items. And most notably the range and types of cultural activity that characterize this group are not widely accessed by the majority of the population, and even less so by the working and lower middle classes. These would seem to be exactly the conditions for the operation of distinction, in the terms proposed by Bourdieu. The picture is somewhat complicated, however, when we consider newer forms of culture, like television and cinema, where tastes are much more popularly shared. The image of an upper middle class repelled by the tastes of lower classes and rejecting them as vulgar or demeaning, was not much apparent. James's dispositions had echoes of this type of response to popular culture, but he was exceptional, for most interviewees expressed few strong or hostile dislikes of commercial popular culture. More significant perhaps was their failure to engage with contemporary music, modern art and American cinema, probably largely a feature of their age and generation, though it might equally be read as a defence of the most legitimate and orthodox cultural items. So it was less an overt expressed hostility, more a quiet and tacit avoidance of a range of the cultural options now available. Rarely if ever was there anything but silence regarding more popular working-class cultural pursuits – they would simply never think about playing bingo or going to watch a boxing match. *De facto*, their practices exhibit some real distinction; they do things which other people like them also do in disproportionately large amounts, things which are, if not denied to, then at least not encouraged among the subordinate classes. But this is not evidence of the sort of snobbery that once associated popular taste with social inadequacy. The elite hold particularly strongly to the tolerant cultural attitudes that are now common among the educated liberal professional and managerial classes.

Finally, though it may be controversial on the basis of interviews with just eleven individuals, it seems possible to draw some tentative conclusions regarding the implications of our findings for the four positions on class analysis with which this chapter began. These people constitute a stratum of top managers, a managerial elite. Although one or two had had professional careers, they had all been for some long period in the highest executive positions in large organizations. Shared understandings about culture and its qualities serve to bind this group together, allowing a sense of mutual belonging and respect even when coming from different economic fields. Culture produces affinities within the group without necessarily or intentionally excluding others. Nothing in our evidence suggests that their attachment to a dominant culture is an attempt to exercise social control over subordinate classes. Neither does our managerial elite seem to be engaging in activities which are exclusive to people in their very elevated social stratum. Their pursuits are neither rare nor arcane. They are ones shared, though probably less intensively, by other sections of the middle class. Nor does our evidence indicate the use of culture to mark divisions within the elite. Their preferences and practices are not uniform, to be sure. But there is a strong common core of activities in which they engage and value; some essential, some normal and some strategic among this group. Alongside these are optional tastes, some of which suggest distinctiveness, for example shooting, attending church and arts performances, and others which are unremarkable, including listening to Radio 4 and Classic FM and playing or having played sports. It would seem then that cultural consumption primarily serves to integrate the upper middle class, symbolizing their membership of a superior social stratum. It arises in the context of social connections offering opportunities to secure privileges. The overall picture is one of considerable cultural coherence at the top of the social and economic hierarchy.

## Acknowledgement

This chapter draws on data produced by the research team for the ESRC project Cultural Capital and Social Exclusion: A Critical Investigation (Award no R000239801). The team comprised Tony Bennett (Principal Applicant), Mike Savage, Elizabeth Silva, Alan Warde (Co-Applicants), David Wright and Modesto Gayo-Cal (Research Fellows). The applicants were jointly responsible for the design of the national survey and the focus groups and household interviews that generated the quantitative and qualitative date for the project. Elizabeth Silva, assisted by David Wright, coordinated the analyses of the qualitative data from the focus groups and household interviews. Mike Savage and Alan Warde, assisted by Modesto Gayo-Cal, co-ordinated the analyses of the quantitative data produced by the survey. Tony Bennett was responsible for the overall direction and coordination of the project.

# Notes

1 For a thorough review of competing theoretical accounts of elite consumption, supported by comparative historical evidence, see Daloz (2007).
2 The survey was administered to a main (random) sample of 1564 respondents. Data was collected between November 2003 and March 2004 by the National Centre for Social Research. See Thomson (2004) for the technical report. For preliminary analysis of the findings of the survey see *Cultural Trends* (2006).
3 This was in marked contrast to the focus groups and household interviews which we conducted, where we often found either opposition or indifference to these institutions and practices.

# References

Bennett, T., (2007), 'Habitus clivé: aesthetics and politics in the work of Pierre Bourdieu', *New Literary History*, **38**(1): 201–28.

Bourdieu, P., (1984), *Distinction: A Critique of the Judgment of Taste*, London: Routledge & Kegan Paul.

Bourdieu, P., (1996), *The Rules of Art: Genesis and Structure of the Literary Field*, Cambridge: Polity Press.

Coulangeon, P., (2004), 'Classes sociales, pratiques culturelles et styles de vie: le modèle de la distinction est-il (vraiment) obselète?', *Sociologie et Sociétés*, **36**(1): 59–85.

Crary, J., (2001), *Suspensions of Perception: Attention, Spectacle and Modern Culture*, Cambridge, Mass: MIT Press.

*Cultural Trends*, (2006), Special issue on 'Culture, tastes and social divisions in contemporary Britain' edited by Bennett, T. and Silva, E. **15**(2–3).

Daloz, J.P., (2007), 'Elite distinction: grand theory and comparative perspectives', *Comparative Sociology*, **6**(1–2): 27–74.

Erickson, B., (1996), 'Culture, class and connections', *American Journal of Sociology*, **102**(1): 217–251.

Gleverac, H., (2006), 'La fin du modèle classique de la légitimité culturelle. Hétérogénésation des ordres de légitimité et régime contemporain de justice culturelle. L'example du champ musical', In: E. Maigret and E. Macé (eds) *Penser les médiacultures. Nouvelles pratiques et nouvelles approches de le représentation du monde*, Paris: Colin/INA, 69–102.

Grenfell, M. and Hardy, C., (2003), 'Field manoeuvres: Bourdieu and young British artists', *Space and Culture*, **6**(1): 19–34.

Lahire, B., (2003), 'From the habitus to an individual heritage of dispositions: towards a sociology at the level of the individual', *Poetics*, **31**: 329–355.

Lahire, B., (2004), *La culture des individus: dissonances culturelles et distinctions de soi*, Éditions la découverte: Paris.

Lamont, M., (1992), *Money, Morals and Manners: The Culture of the French and American Upper-middle Classes*, Chicago Il: Chicago University Press.

Ostrower, F., (1998), 'The arts as cultural capital among elites: Bourdieu's theory reconsidered', *Poetics*, **26**: 43–53.

Savage, M., Barlow, J., Dickens, P. and Fielding, T., (1992), *Property, Bureacracy and Culture: Middle Class Formation in Contemporary Britain*, London: Routledge.

Savage, M., Wright, D. and Gayo-Cal, M., 'Globalisation, cosmopolitanism and consumption' (forthcoming).

Silva, E. (2006), 'Distinction through visual art', *Cultural Trends*, **15**(2/3): 141–158.

Taylor, B., (1999), *Art for the Nation: Exhibitions and the London Public*, Manchester: Manchester University Press.

Thomson, K., (2004), *Cultural Capital and Social Exclusion Survey: Technical Report*, London: National Centre for Social Research.

# Eating money and clogging things up: paradoxes of elite mediation in Epirus, North-western Greece[1]

## Sarah Green

This chapter concerns a few people in a rather remote part of mainland Greece who have, in recent years, become involved with funded European Union (EU) programmes aimed at encouraging the sustainable development of their region, Epirus. Epirus constitutes the north-west corner of mainland Greece, and it shares a substantial border with Albania; having experienced considerable economic and population declines in recent decades, the region has been defined by the EU as a high priority for development assistance, and that has provided access to considerable amounts of funding for the region in the last two decades.

In comparison with many of the elites discussed in this volume, it is questionable whether the people I focus upon here could be counted as elites at all: they are small town lawyers, village presidents, civil servants and similar people, who take a leading role in applying for and then managing EU funded development projects. They are not CEOs of major companies, nor the heads of dealing rooms in banks, nor one of the multi-millionaires working in the City of London. One aspect that they share with these others, however, is that their position is based on their role as key mediators, in this case between the European Union and the region of Epirus: for the most part, EU development funds flow from the EU into the region via these people. Moreover, there is a long history of the study of elite groups in southern Europe from the perspective of their position as mediators, including quite intricate studies of the social, political and economic relations involved. That provides an opportunity to compare past accounts of such groups with contemporary experiences and in particular, to look at how the possibilities of mediation are undergoing some changes.

Here, I will focus on how all those involved with the EU development programmes struggled with the difficulties caused by a particular form of social relations: one that involved making a strong distinction between peoples with whom you have a close relationship (seen as those who are synonymous with your interests), and those with whom you have no relationship (seen as those who will have interests that are different from your own). This extends an issue I have considered in earlier research in the course of exploring attitudes towards official statistics in Epirus (Green, 2005:ch. 5). There, I argued that most people in Epirus assumed that official statistics (eg from the Greek census) are always 'moulded' by 'interests' (Green, 2005:168). Within that perspective, there is no such thing as objective, disinterested data, because there is no such thing as objective, disinterested people: everyone has particular interests that inevitably become entangled in everything they do, say and represent. As I will discuss further later, people's interests are assumed to be based upon their dense networks of social relations, which places them in a particular, and inevitably partial, social location. In this sense, people are not conceived of as isolated, autonomous individuals, but as always already existing as part of a set of social relations.[2]

I made a brief point in that earlier research about how this meant that for Epirots, official statistics can never represent the whole – eg an entity such as 'society' – because statistics will always reflect the partial interests of the peoples who compiled, or commissioned, them (Green, 2005:188); so such statistics can only ever provide partial accounts – partial in both meanings of the term: both incomplete and subjective.[3]

I will draw on this here to explore how the assumption of inevitable self-interest and partiality became involved in both the use of, and expectations about, EU development funding in Epirus, and also to consider how that might be undergoing some change. All parties involved, including the European Union (as a distant and somewhat obscure participant, from the perspective of those in Epirus), were assumed to have their particular 'interests,' and it was not possible that all interests could be served simultaneously. This also carried the implication that the funding had to arrive via mediators, who could transform the interests of one entity (the EU) into those of another within Epirus. These mediators were a range of public officials, both elected politicians and civil servants; often, they also had a strong say in the design of the funded development projects, and a management role in the deployment of the funds.

The assumption that everyone acts partially and according to their interests meant, of course, that the mediators were expected to transform the interests of the EU into their *own* interests. Perhaps inevitably, this led to regular accusations of corruption (the idea that the mediators 'eat' the money). That is not, however, my key interest here: rather, I will explore how this assumption of partiality made it virtually impossible for the mediators to act in a way that would be perceived as being a success, even by themselves. Instead, and despite much energetic effort on the part of these mediators, projects rarely seemed to be completed and the reputations of the mediators rarely appeared to escape unscathed. In other words, nobody's interests appeared to be served, in the end. It is this paradox that concerns me here: how is it that this particular form of mediation regularly appeared to fail in the eyes of everyone involved, including those of the mediators? It would do an injustice to the participants in the research to suggest that actually, the activity succeeded in some obscure way: while it is possible to argue that on the grounds that despite everything, the mediation continued in much the same way as it had done, I am more interested in the fact that there was genuine and widespread discontent about the apparent inability to generate the outcomes that people hoped would occur.

I will suggest that this assumption of partiality itself generated an understanding of the situation that led to this paradoxical outcome. It led to a series of both social relations and expectations that made it both appear impossible that a successful outcome would result and also difficult to know what else to do. I also suggest that this assumption of partiality did not reflect a clash of 'cultural values' between the peoples of Epirus and the EU development project policies. Instead, it reflected a social difference, a difference in understanding the significance of people's social locations, which informed expectations of the future in Epirus, of what the outcome of any given project or activity might be. Most people I met in Epirus endorsed an ideal of statecraft which suggested that elected politicians, civil servants, and other people in positions of public office or influence, ought to act for the 'public good' rather than for themselves. Indeed, this ideal was most often represented as a self-evident moral value, one that Greeks (as nationals) have always already recognized.[4] Given, however, the additional inevitability that everyone must act from the position of their own partial interests based upon their social location, it was also assumed that, in practice, it was impossible for anyone to act impartially. The expectation, therefore, was that the EU would design development projects to reflect its own ('European') interests and not those of Epirus; that the elites who mediated between the EU and Epirus would do so in a way that reflected their particular interests rather than those of the EU or the majority of residents of Epirus; and that the outcome would be that the projects would not be completed as planned by the EU, and the reputations of the elites would be tarnished for 'eating' the money rather than using it effectively on behalf of Epirus and Epirots.

There was yet more to this. The position of the elites was partly dependent upon the assumption that their mediation was essential for there to be any chance of development in Epirus, because they were the only means to gain access EU development funds. In recent years, however, a series of political and economic changes next door in Albania has potentially challenged this assumption. The increasing presence of Albanians in Epirus, and the visibility of Albania since the collapse of socialist rule there in 1990 has led to the possibility that what might happen next is not as fixed or predictable as existing social relations and perceptions suggested. Albanian citizens had almost no direct access either to EU development funds or to the political mediators on the Greek side, and yet they were finding ways to 'develop,' both legally and illegally, and very rapidly at that. The implication is that what might happen next has become contingent, less predictable. And that in turn implies that the mediating role of the small elites in Epirus, already judged to be ineffective, might also be challenged as lacking the inevitability that it once had. This does not challenge the assumption of the inevitability of partiality; but it does challenge the idea that partiality is related to particular forms of mediation.

The remainder of this chapter explores this approach through first briefly reviewing past anthropological studies on elite mediators for this region of Europe, and then continuing on to some ethnographic material from the contemporary moment.

## Patronage revisited

In the past, the majority of anthropological discussions about elites in southern Europe concerned the issue of elite mediation between people and the state (eg Blok, 1974; Boissevain, 1974; Campbell, 1964; Davis, 1977; Gellner and Waterbury, 1977; Peristiany and Pitt-Rivers, 1992). There were a range of different approaches in this literature but a common issue they all addressed was that in many parts of this region in the past, there were few if any means by which people could directly access services that the state was officially supposed to provide. This was either because such services did not exist in practice or because, for one reason or another, the majority of people were blocked from having access to them. In such conditions, it was argued, a variety of mediators developed to fill in the gaps. These were people who used their personal social, political and/or economic positions either to mediate connections between socially excluded people and the state (eg Campbell, 1964), or who privately provided the services that the state was unable to provide or had been prevented from providing (eg Blok, 1972). Some researchers argued that over time, such mediators developed a power base that challenged, infiltrated and at times even restructured state processes, making the mediators indispensable to the functioning of the state.

There was a strong implication in parts of this earlier literature that there was something culturally distinctive about the southern European region that led to this situation (eg Banfield, 1958; Gilmore, 1982; Peristiany, 1976). This idea, however, of a 'Mediterranean culture' that leads to inefficient and corrupt states has been repeatedly and effectively critiqued (eg Herzfeld, 1980, 1984; Pina-Cabral, 1989). There were three main criticisms: first, there is no convincing evidence that the diversity of peoples living in the Mediterranean region have anything distinctly in common with one another in cultural terms; second, that blaming 'culture' (and thus people themselves) for ineffective state provision was to ignore the wider political, economic and historic conditions that made it difficult for peoples in this region of Europe to develop effective state structures (eg Herzfeld, 1992); and third, that embedded in the 'Mediterranean culture area' argument was the unexamined and ethnocentric assumption that there is a correct way in which to conduct statecraft, that being the one practised in northern Europe. This sustained critique of the earlier literature on southern European patrons, brokers, mafia and so on, rightfully led to the abandonment of any serious support for the idea of a Mediterranean 'culture' that results in inefficient or corrupt states.

Having said that, there are other elements of this earlier literature that have continued to inform more recent studies, and are worth examining, as they could contribute to the approach towards the study of elites that is represented in this volume – that is, considering elites 'not as fixed, traditional pillars, but as a group of intermediaries whose power rests on being able to forge connections and bridge gaps' (Savage and Williams, 2008:4). This approach encourages a view of elites as existing within networks, webs or constellations of relations that generate elite's position *as* elites. Similarly, the earlier anthropological literature on elite groups in southern Europe particularly focused on the way social relations were used to structure the interrelations between social, political and economic entities. This was partly an argument about culture but it was more of an argument about social structure: the idea was that the structure and logic of people's personal social relations (ie their kinship relations) was reiterated in relations with, and within, the state. A brief example from an earlier anthropologist of Greece, John Campbell, and a more recent one, Michael Herzfeld, outlines the significance of this for the contemporary study of elites as mediators.

John Campbell studied the Sarakatsani peoples during the 1950s. The Sarakatsani were, at the time, a group of nomadic shepherds living in Epirus; nowadays, a few Sarakatsani still seasonally move their flocks and herds around the region (mostly by truck than on foot) but the majority now live in towns and cities. In his book *Honour, Family and Patronage* (1964), Campbell argued that the only way the Sarakatsani could receive access to state services was via an intermediary such as a lawyer or village president, who took on the role of patron. This was mostly because, Campbell argued, the Sarakatsani had no personal social networks in the villages and towns, and it was only through such relations that access to state services was possible. Campbell describes the situation thus:

> The lawyer, or other patron, bridges the gulf of hostility and indifference created by the absence of relationship and the difference in status. [. . .] In effect, patronage converts impersonal and ephemeral connexions [*sic*] into permanent and personal relationships; for in Greek society it is, generally, only in established personal relationships, of which the archetypal forms are found in the family, that any considerable element of moral obligation exists. (Campbell, 1964:259).

Campbell also commented that as far as the Sarakatsani were concerned, the civil servants in the towns felt no obligation whatever to assist lowly and unrelated people such as these nomadic shepherds. Campbell concluded that the Sarakatsanos 'does not believe in the existence of any ethic of professional bureaucratic service to the community. "They are all *eaters*," he says in sweeping condemnation' (Campbell, 1964:257).

Although Campbell's perspective is infused with the implication that there were clear moral ideals that prevented the Sarakatsani from receiving direct access to state services, his main emphasis was on the way the structure of social relations in the region constrained the means the Sarakatsani had available to them to gain access to the state.

A more recent view, from the work of Michael Herzfeld, looked at this in terms of indifference on the part of people in state power, a lack of concern for those who had no power or personal relationship with officers of the state (Herzfeld). Herzfeld wonders why Greek bureaucrats appear to be particularly indifferent and self-serving, when in other spheres, Greeks appear to be amongst the most passionate and empathetic of people. Explicitly rejecting any argument that this is simply 'cultural' (Herzfeld, 1992:44), Herzfeld suggests it is related both to the way the Greek nation was conceived as being composed of peoples related to one another by blood,[5] and to the way the Greek state has remained economically and politically dependent upon a variety of international powers (Herzfeld, 1992:40–43). The idea of the nation as people 'of the same blood' ('the nation is a single enormous kin group' (Herzfeld, 1992:42)) generates an air of intimate connection between the state and people's own families, in the manner of Russian dolls: the nation is one huge family, and a person's own family is both an integral part of and a replication of that, only on a smaller scale. The accompanying implication is that the nation, like people's own families, are exclusive and particular: neither the nation nor the people of the nation can represent all views nor all interests equally; by definition they must be partial. Herzfeld argues that when this logic is combined with the long-term dependence of Greece on a number of external powers, which have often prevented the 'efficient' running of the Greek state, what has often happened is that local elites have stepped in to fill the gaps, taking on metaphors of kinship (dense and permanent social relations) to gather power around themselves. Herzfeld puts it this way:

> Greece has not developed a bureaucracy as free of patronage as some of its richer and more industrialised neighbours have in Europe. The reason for this state of affairs are embedded in Greece's continuing economic dependence and in the support that outside interests have always provided for privileged elites within. [. . .] When state efficiency fails to materialize at the local level, or is impaired by powerful mediating interests that protect local solidarities, the emotive symbolism of blood, body, and patriline may get far more play. (Herzfeld, 1992:42–43)

Herzfeld represents elites as both separate from, and often harmful to, the interests of others in Greece: both here and elsewhere (eg Herzfeld, 2002:903), he suggests that these elites have consistently been persuaded, ultimately against their own interests, to absorb and reproduce externally-generated discourses about Greece and its classical heritage (contrasted with its contemporary lack of such an impressive heritage) that ultimately renders the country dependent upon, and subordinate to, those external powers.

My focus is on rather different kinds of elites: not those ideological leaders at the top of the political hierarchy, but on those at a much lower level, who become involved in applying for and attempting to implement EU development projects. As I briefly discussed above, these people find themselves in the difficult position of attempting to mediate between what are understood as being mutually exclusive interests: those of the EU and those of some aspect of

Epirus. The funding cannot arrive in Epirus unmediated, for the EU is an external entity, unrelated in any direct way with Epirus and Epirots: the only way for it to arrive is through these mediators.

This points to an important difference between my focus and that of Herzfeld: rather than considering the aspects of the relation between elites and the external forces that is exclusive to them, I focus on the position of elites as local mediators, which renders more visible the aspects that cause elites trouble and also makes it more obvious that the elites depend upon their relations and mediating role in order to be elites in the first place.[6] Part of the reason for that shift in focus is that the sense of control by external powers over Greece and the Greeks that Herzfeld records tended to be replaced in Epirus by a sense of the indifference of such external powers, a point to which I now turn in moving towards the ethnography.

## Indifference, mediators, interests and eating

Epirus is one of those places where you can have the impression that most people do not suffer from illusions of grandeur. A common account given is that powerful entities have been generally indifferent towards the region and the peoples living there, rather than actively or deliberately exploiting and oppressing them (Green, 2005; 2006). This evokes an image of powerful entities being like over-large clumsy animals that occasionally stomp across Epirus on their way to somewhere else and pursue their own interests that have nothing to do with Epirus, not noticing the destruction they leave in their wake as they do so. That is quite different from the image of an evil uniformed authority deliberately applying the thumb screws on a place, evoked by a more common stereotypical account of recent Greek nationalist historiography, that draws on the notion that Greeks have been put upon by more powerful entities for a number of centuries, and certainly for the entirety of the modern period.[7] While there is a strong sense in Epirus, as I have outlined above, that all people are informed by their own partial interests, that tends to be interpreted as leading to a disinterest in and neglect of others, rather than any explicit or conscious attempt at domination or control.

In that context, the position of those who mediate between the funding provided by EU development projects and the Epirot region was a somewhat unenviable one: the development money will not have been designed with Epirus in mind and would be intended to pursue interests that were not those of people in Epirus; and the mediators, being people with their own interests, would inevitably 'eat' the money anyway – that is, use it to serve their own interests, rather than those of anyone else. A rather different but nevertheless related picture emerged from the people involved in the mediation, in which the problem was not caused by them but by both the conditions of the EU funding, which were difficult to translate (as it were) into the Epirot context; and by the behaviour of many of the residents of Epirus, who would inevitably pursue their own interests rather than that of the general good.

The notion that the people who mediate between the EU and Epirus end up 'eating' the money they bring to the region – an idea that was present even during John Campbell's time in Epirus – provided a strongly recognizable metaphor about the structural position and expected behaviour of the mediators. Nobody, of course, said that they themselves actually 'ate' any development money; but everyone understood the expectation that such money would almost inevitably be eaten. This was as much a prediction of a known future as it was a commentary on the fate of current development projects. Indeed, the expectation of the diversion of funds away from their formal intended purpose and into the sphere of somebody's particularistic interests (that is, the redistribution of the funds within the social networks of the mediator who secured them) was so strong that several presidents of villages complained that they found it almost impossible to convince people that at least some of the money genuinely had been used as it should have been. This is an important element of the assumption of the inevitability of the partiality of interests: that it generates an expectation, or even a sense of certainty, of what might happen next. Here, I am borrowing a concept from Stef Jansen, whose work on concepts of home and hope in Boznia-Herzegovena led to the insight that notions of the future often have as much of an effect in structuring the present as do accounts of the past (Jansen, 2007).

The idea of 'eating' the funds perhaps inevitably led to a sense that rather than generate anything resembling development, what occurred almost always seemed to result in a kind of inexorable slowing down or clogging up of activity. Equally, those involved in mediation often suggested that there was strong resistance to anything that did not appear to directly benefit people's own partial interests. This echoes the sentiments expressed in Clarissa de Waal's ethnographic research on problems with rural development in southern mainland Greece (de Waal, 1994). De Waal suggests that attempts at new developments in rural areas, with or without EU funding, were regularly and deliberately blocked by the developers' neighbours because of deep-seated jealousy: within that perspective, if someone had more, or was developing faster than, or differently from, the rest, that was bound to be the result of self-interested and probably illegal activity. Many members of the regional elites in Epirus asserted that precisely this kind of attitude was preventing them from being able to make headway with their development projects.

Moreover, many of the elected politicians with whom I spoke expressed genuine personal concern about the lack of 'something happening,' as it threatened their elite status – their position as people of importance in the region who could effectively mediate between the EU and Epirus. Given that these resources were widely regarded as being provided in order to pursue some particularistic interest of the EU,[8] the main job of those mediating these funds was to convert it into something that reflected the interests of people in Epirus. If they failed to do that effectively, failed to convert the funds into something that visibly demonstrated their powerful capacities (even if what was made visible was not what the EU intended to be done with the money), then they would lose face. In fact, this was part of the reason, according to many people with whom I discussed the issue, for the strong preference amongst many politicians in Epirus for development projects that literally leave permanent marks on the landscape – a new road, a large building, anything that cannot be ignored – despite the fact that most EU development programmes intended for remote, highly mountainous and depopulated areas such as Epirus encourage 'environmentally sustainable' projects – projects that are supposed to leave almost no mark on the landscape whatsoever.[9] In any case, the apparent impossibility of making anything actually happen – the greater the effort, the more things seemed to get clogged up – was in some senses even more of a problem for the mediators than it was for the rest of the population, many members of whom would enjoy regularly sitting in coffee shops and cynically commenting on the corrupt doings of their local power holders.

And as if that was not enough, the extremely slow pace of anything happening was made all the more visible in Epirus by the frenzy of activity (albeit frequently illegal) going on next door in Albania since the mid-1990s, a couple of years after the communist regime there collapsed and the border was reopened. If Brennan's suggestion that a key element in the logic of the kind of modernity brought about by late capitalism is an inexorable speeding up of tempo (Brennan, 2000), then all the activity on that score appeared to be occurring on the Albanian, not the Greek side of the border. Indeed, the most energetic activity on the Greek side of the border in terms of both development projects and other work seemed to be provided by the newly arrived (cheap) Albanian citizens, something I will discuss further below.

## The paradox of development and elite mediation

Having outlined the assumption that the interests of the EU would be different from the interests of people in Epirus, there is the additional issue that made the mediation, or at least the translation, between them particularly hard. Mediators often had to effectively represent themselves as being the guardians of Epirot cultural heritage and tradition to satisfy the requirements of the funding, while simultaneously demonstrating their thorough modernity, as people on a par with their interlocuters in the EU. In one sense, the situation reflected the dilemma also faced by *mestizo* regional elites studied by Penny Harvey in the Peruvian Andes. In that example, the 'codes' (of tradition and modernity) were combined, despite being apparently incompatible: the *mestizo* elites were reliant upon their ties with their particular region and its 'traditions' in order to be elites at all, and yet they lived in a world in which elites were expected to be cosmopolitan – to be those people, as Harvey neatly puts it, 'who are best able to avoid the constraints of location' (Harvey, 2002:75). In Epirus, the regional elites faced a similar dilemma, and it is one of the elements that made the idea of the 'eating' of EU funds particularly paradoxical. Being able to mediate sufficiently between the EU and Epirus so as to bring the funds into the social, political and economic networks of the region was the act of an elite person; but to use those funds for the purpose intended by the EU (ie for 'development' of an 'underdeveloped' region) would be doubly troubling: on the one hand, it would be regarded as following the partial interests of the external entity, the EU, rather than their own interests; and secondly, unless handled with extreme care, it would imply acknowledging being at a lower social position than the funding body, as the funding is provided for regions in particular need. Yet if the funds were diverted ('eaten'), which would avoid being regarded as simply following the EU's interests, it would also negatively affect the mediator's reputation, as he (it was almost invariably 'he') would be seen as being both too 'traditional' in his behaviour and also accused of being 'corrupt'. The point is that mediators in Epirus faced a multi-layered paradox that made it virtually impossible for them to use the EU funding money in any way, let alone for the purposes it was intended, while unambiguously maintaining their position as elites.

## The peculiarities of EU development money

Before going on to provide some brief ethnographic examples of this situation, it is worth pausing for a moment to consider the character of this money, the 'stuff' that mediators were drawing into the social networks of Epirus. In line with what I have described above about the pervasive assumption of partiality and interests, the money was not simply money; a rather different view was expressed in Epirus, one that reflected the argument of a number of more recent researchers on money, who suggest that money is best understood in terms of how money is related to, and entangled with, other things, and in terms of what it *does* within any given context, rather than suggesting it *is* something in itself, as such.[10] The money that was destined to be 'eaten' by mediators in Epirus was not just any money: it was EU money, and that made it different from other kinds of money. This distinction between types of money is similar to that found by researchers such as Sharon Hutchinson (1992) working with the Nuer peoples in the Sudan in Africa, and Viviana Zelizer (1997), who worked with working-class Americans on their relationship with money; both noted that people ascribed money with different characteristics according to how the money is obtained and relative to the relationship between the entities that give and receive the money. Thus, for example, Sharon Hutchinson (1992) reports how Nuer market traders made a stark distinction between the money they received for their cattle from other Nuer, and money they received for products they sold in a local market from complete strangers. Nuer traders called the money from complete strangers 'shit money' and it could only be used to pay taxes; such money could never be used to buy cattle, for example, which, to the Nuer, are the most important possessions anyone can have.

In those terms, most people in Epirus in the late 1990s and early 2000s considered EU development money to be markedly different from other kinds of money. First, it was strongly believed that only those who had good knowledge of European funding programmes, highly competent political skills, and appropriate political links in the capital city, Ioannina – ie, expert mediators – had any chance of receiving some of this money. In that sense, the money was axiomatically elite money, only available to those considered to be elites. This kind of money can only be brought in through mediation; and thus it immediately slots into the elites' social, political and economic networks of social relations and partial interests. The money has to be mediated in order to have any meaning. Second, there were complex bureaucratic procedures that had to be undertaken in relation to this money, both in applying for it and in accounting for its use, and these procedures were for the most part entirely baffling to the majority of the population in Epirus; again, only a small number of people with special skills could negotiate this minefield of paperwork. Third, before the introduction of the euro, the money was not recorded in the development project paperwork in the same currency as was used in Epirus: the paperwork used a notional European Monetary Unit (or EMU for short) that was not associated with any coins or notes in use anywhere, whereas Epirus used the Greek drachma. Even since the introduction of euro notes and coins (Greece is in the 'euro zone'), there was a widespread sense that this money is not the same kind of money as people in Epirus had experienced before. In this, Epirots agree with Dodd (2001; 2005) that the euro is, in terms of conventional theories of money, a peculiar variant indeed: it is not associated with any particular sovereign state, and it was unclear to many people in Epirus whether it was under the control of the European Union alone or of the Greek government as well. Either way, the peculiarity of this money made the external origins of EU development funding (and therefore its different interests) particularly explicit and visible. Finally, the sheer quantity of this money – the enormous amounts that were being spent, and the activities that they were supposed to fund – marked this money out as being very distinctive indeed.

To give a small sense of the scale and style of the provision of this money: just one major programme, which combined contributions from the European Regional Development Fund, the European Social Fund and the European Agricultural Guidance and Guarantee Fund, paid over €236 million in five years between 1994 and 1999 to development projects in Epirus. At the time, Epirus had a total population of around 340,000 (Green, 2005:449). Although this might appear to be reasonable expenditure in some parts of Europe, to most people in Epirus, it constituted unthinkable amounts of public funding, at least for the purposes that this money was intended: the EU document describing the programme suggested that the funding was provided in order to, 'develop the endogenous resources of Epirus, modernize the economic fabric and reduce the region's isolation'.[11] In short, the money was for general (perhaps even generic) 'development.' Of course, there had been very large development programmes directed at Epirus before:[12] the Marshall Plan after World War II[13] and the major efforts in rural development made by the military regime under Georgios Pap-padopoulos in the 1970s[14] are two of the most notable. The more recent EU money, however, was recognized as being somewhat different, in that control over the design and execution of development projects and their budgets was generally represented by EU documentation as being much more devolved down to small regional groups and organizations, and even to individuals, than the previous interventions such as the Marshall Plan had been (Ray, 2000). The Marshall Plan was widely understood as being heavily controlled by central government institutions based in Athens, or even international organizations, and controlled by Athens-appointed regional directors in Epirus (cf. note 13). In short, in contrast to these previous programmes, the new EU programmes were explicitly supposed to be in the hands of the regional mediators, who would be directly communicating with Brussels, rather than Athens.

This was, of course, closely related to the EU's policies of subsidiarity and regionalization (Harvie, 1994). It was supposed to give the impression that European regions were in control of their own development; but in Epirus, where there was a pervasive sense that powerful entities are indifferent towards this region and design their own policies in their own image and for their own purposes, what it meant in practice was that the regional mediators were now much more directly associated not only with the EU's money but also with the implementation of the EU's policies than they had been in previous eras. That formed an important part of the perceived power dynamics embedded within the EU development money: although regional elite groups had a greater and more direct mediating role (and control over budgets) than earlier development programmes had allowed them, there was a clear recognition amongst most people in this region (and amongst those the mediators themselves) that they were not the ones who designed the *policies* that controlled which development programmes should be funded, nor which ideals or visions of the future those development programmes should promote. In other words, the people of Epirus were not the ones who defined the agenda for development; rather, the regional elites would be the ones who would apply for money once the agenda had been defined, and they would be charged with implementing its vision.

## Metaphors of growth and destruction

To return to my earlier point, it is in this context that the 'eating' of EU money could make sense but also generates its own dilemmas. In part, by defying the wishes of the EU policies while also receiving the money could be seen, in some senses, as 'saving face.' Here, the metaphors that surrounded the idea of 'eating' development money were quite visceral. For example, the development money was very often represented by the EU policies and program manuals as 'seed money': in other words, money intended to be used to 'plant' something so it would grow into a fully formed entity capable of maintaining and perhaps even reproducing itself. These 'seeds' – the EU development money, constrained and defined by all the rules and regulations about how it should be used so as to pursue a particular policy – were key to the EU's concept of 'sustainable development'.[15] It is easy to see how people in Epirus related that to the idea of 'eating': 'eating' the seed money was explicitly understood as a means to destroy, rather than to help plant, these 'seeds'. 'Eating' development money was understood as an activity that caused the eater to get fat, while also destroying the (re)productive potential of the money, and thereby destroying any possibility of the EU policy 'bearing fruit.' In this sense, the act of eating demonstrated that the eater did not *need* 'developing': and it was also an assertion of agency, in that it constituted a rejection of the policy implications of accepting the money. It is what could be called a Catch-22 situation, from the perspective of the regional elites.

That paradox was part of the reason that nobody I met ever said that they themselves 'ate' EU money, but many of those identified as being members of the regional elite often expressed understanding for the dilemmas faced by those who did. This perspective was even expressed by civil servants who asserted that they themselves were attempting to do things differently. For example, an agronomist and development worker in Ioannina, whom I will call Georgios, spent several hours one afternoon explaining to me that he intended to change things in Epirus, because if he did not, nothing would never happen in the region. He spent some time criticizing some of his former colleagues for never leaving their offices in order to visit fields and animal stables, and for using development money to build extensions to their houses, rather than to develop more productive breeds of sheep or goats. 'They just sat on their behinds all day in their offices, "eating",' he said; 'I'm not like that, I want to do my job right.'

All of this critical talk could be seen as a means by which Georgios was demonstrating that he had more 'up to date' attitudes (and perhaps more importantly, moral values) than those of his predecessors – he occasionally explicitly said as much. At other points in the conversation though, he expressed sympathy for the attitude of those who 'eat' by strongly criticizing the people of Epirus whom he was trying to help to 'develop'. Having first complained that he had attempted and failed to get a fresh mushroom farm going because, he said, 'people here won't eat fresh mushrooms, they think it's poison' (implying that the residents of Epirus are not cosmopolitan enough in their culinary tastes), he then also talked about a visit he had made to the Florac region of France to see the way the farmers managed sheep and goats there. Florac, according to Georgios, had much the same landscape and very similar farming activities as in Epirus – mostly sheep and goat pastoralism. Georgios also made it clear that, in his view, even though the Florac region is quite a remote rural region of France, it was self-evidently much more central and European than Epirus. Georgios explained that he was stunned to see how much better the shepherds of Florac did things than they were done in Epirus. As an example, he described the sheep dogs he came across in France. He said that with one whistle from the shepherd, the dog rounded up the sheep and brought them to the fold. He contrasted this with the Epirot sheep dogs, which, he said, 'Hang about anywhere, are completely undisciplined and half wild, and are lazy, like their owners'. The proper way, Georgios said, should be for the shepherd to be actively in control of the dogs and the dogs to be circling and controlling the flock in line with what the shepherd commanded. In Epirus, Georgios complained, the shepherd often just wanders around – these days on a motorbike or in a truck; the sheep do what they like and the dogs go around either sleeping or biting people.

Georgios completed his statement by saying that that if he gave such lazy and undisciplined people (and their dogs) the EU development money, they would probably just 'eat' it by buying a better motor bike or building an extension to their home in the city, or spending it on one of their children to be sent abroad to get an education as a lawyer or doctor. When those children came back, he said, they would not be able to find any work because Greece was full of qualified lawyers and doctors, but had almost no professionally trained (ie 'state of the art' modern) farmers.

All of this can be seen as Georgios reiterating the view that everyone acts in their own partial interests, indifferent to the interests of a greater whole such as 'society' or 'the public' or even 'Epirus'. He was complaining that this prevented 'proper' development. Of course, the same people Georgios criticized – those shepherds living in the rural parts of Epirus with their apparently improperly trained dogs – had equally critical views about civil servants such as Georgios, reflecting the same understanding of partial interests. I repeated my conversation with Georgios to one such man, who had quite a large flock of sheep that he moved between the north and the south of the region with the seasons. He laughed bitterly, and said,

He said that, did he? Well, I expect my dogs *would* bite him; my dogs know when someone doesn't recognize – well, I should watch my language. And did you ask him, this great visionary of an agronomist who lives in the city, what he did with that money that he did not give to me because he thinks I'm lazy and backward, eh?

The shepherd drew the fingers of one hand together and gestured it towards his open mouth, implying that Georgios had 'eaten' it. He turned to see the reaction from the other people in the coffee shop where we were sitting, and noting that he had their attention, he added, 'Go tell him to move to France, if he likes it so much there. Maybe he could send me a poodle as a sheep dog'. And he burst into laughter at his own joke. Like most jokes, there was a note of bitterness in it. The shepherd recognized that he was being accused of being 'backward' in comparison to his French counterparts, and in making the poodle joke, he was not only taking a stereotypical poke at Frenchness; he was also implying that what works in France and for the French would not work in Epirus: different interests born of different contexts. In that sense, while Georgios could be said to be doing precisely what Herzfeld suggested that elites do in Greece (ie reiterate an external rhetoric about civilization and modernity that ultimately undermines the reputation of Greece and the Greeks), the shepherd who responded both resented and rejected its implications. But in addition to Herzfeld's point, I would suggest two other things were going on here as well: Georgios was also drawing on the assumption of the inevitable and universal expression of interests and partiality; and he was expressing his deep frustration at being unable to mediate the relation between the EU and the Epirot region in a way that he wanted to do.

This example outlines how the dilemmas faced by everyone involved in this situation tended to lead to the expectation that development projects which were supposed to speed things up, make things happen and draw Epirus out of its 'isolation' into a fast-moving, flexible Europe, would achieve precisely the opposite: generate the conditions for clogging things up and slowing things down. And unlike the case of the bureaucrats who gain much of their control through 'the suppression of time' (Herzfeld, 1992:162), forcing people to wait, queue, fill in forms and then come back next week, this slowness of progress of development projects was generally regarded as a lack of control on the part of the mediators: an inability to effectively mediate.

An example of what happened in the case of one particular development project will outline the interplay of expectations and relations in all of this a little more clearly.

### The Aristi-Doliana development project: the horse trail with no horses and the lake with no water

This project, which began in the late 1990s, was developed by two village presidents and concerned the two villages they respectively represented. One, called Doliana, was nestled among low hills just above a small productive agricultural plain, in an area not particularly noted for its tourist interest. The other was Aristi, a small village to the east of Doliana in the Zagori area, which is in the heart of the region most visited by tourists in Epirus.

The idea of the project was to encourage a new kind of tourism to the area. Both villages would have improvements to make them more attractive to tourists, including the 're-traditionalization' of their churches (the removal of 'modernizations' made during the 1970s) and the setting up of traditional hostels and so on. In addition, a horse trail would be developed linking the two villages. Tourists would be able to travel on horseback across a small plain and up into the mountains and forests to Aristi, stopping on the way at a lake in the middle of the plain. The lake did not yet exist; the project plan suggested that it would be dug and filled with water, after which, because this was a damp area, the lake would keep filled with water naturally. Trees would also be planted around this lake to make it attractive to the tourists. The president of Doliana divided his time between living in the village and living in Ioannina, and had in the past lived in Italy; the president of Aristi, a lawyer, lived most of the time in Ioannina. Both were strongly committed to the idea that they should proactively grasp opportunities made available by the EU on behalf of their respective towns; but both also strongly expressed the view that these funds required mediation, they needed to be 'moulded' to fit the conditions in Epirus, as the EU was pursuing its interests relative to its own network of connections, which would inevitably be different from those of the presidents and their social relations.

The reactions towards these plans by people living in the two villages were predictable. Even before any work on the projects began, most were convinced that the two presidents intended to use the funds in their own interests, both to make themselves (and their relatives) more wealthy and to enhance their regional reputations. This expectation was then confirmed in many people's minds by the fact that a failure to receive permission from the Forestry Commission to build the horse trail through the forest meant that this part of the project was stalled. All the workers who had been hired to build the horse trail were retained and made to clean up the villages regularly instead. People joked that their two villages had never been so tidy.

In addition, the lake was dug, but it was not very successfully gathering water. Moreover, the lake's location upset many people, as that area had been common land used to graze sheep and goats in the past, and this was no longer going to be permitted. Apparently, the sheep and goats would worry either the tourists and/or the horses upon which the tourists would be sitting. To many local people, this was simply proof that nobody who had designed the development plan had the faintest idea what traditional life in a largely pastoral area might involve. Finally, and perhaps inevitably, there was considerable overspending on some parts of the project, which meant that the few young people in both villages who had been hired to do administrative and other office work for the project were laid off early. These redundancies generated a deep sense of frustration among the young workers, along with bitterness and expressions of exasperation that once again, the money had been 'eaten' by already fat and powerful men and that there was nothing to show for the spending of all that money.

One of the ex-administrators from Doliana, a woman in her twenties, asserted that that most of the money had gone on improving just a single house in Aristi, which was to be an information centre (but that would now revert to being a privately owned house as the project had collapsed), and the rest of the money had gone to somewhere obscure known only to the president of Aristi. Her implication was that the president of Aristi had 'eaten' her salary and was now sitting in Ioannina doing nothing. She was extremely bitter about the whole situation.

An older man from Doliana, who was an agricultural vet, was more cynical rather than bitter. It was naïve of the young woman, he thought, to imagine that anything would have come of this project other than the aggrandisement of the two presidents. The vet had discovered recently, he said, that he was supposed to be in charge of the horses for the development project, but nobody had ever consulted him about this and no horses had ever appeared, which was exactly as he would have expected. He sat, on a warm Sunday afternoon drinking in the local coffee shop and dismissed all politicians and development workers as permanently engaged in what he called 'masa' (chewing or masticating) – by which he meant chewing on the development money for their own interests, in the way a cow constantly chews grass. 'Nothing ever happens here; people make sure of that' he said. The vet was expressing the firm expectation that what happens next in EU development projects is precisely nothing. In contrast to such projects, he represented himself as a man of integrity, a professional man who took care of farm animals when they were sick. But he also agreed that this was his partial interest.

From the perspective of the two presidents, the failure of this project was both deeply disappointing and also somewhat humiliating, as they had both identified themselves with it and had loudly promised that this project would be carried out using the most state-of-the-art techniques, the top water and lake engineers and landscape architects, the best specialists in horses and the best tour guides. The president of Doliana, whom I came to know better than the president of Aristi, predictably blamed the resistance of the local populations against anything 'new,' as well as complaining about the 'clogging up' caused by the complicated bureaucracy of the project – not only the Forestry Commission's resistance to the idea of a horse trail but also the multiple complexities and audits imposed by the EU to implement the project. In other words, the people who were controlling the bureaucratic tempo were the officers of the EU and the Greek state; they were not the mediators. Yes, the money had been 'wasted,' but that was not, the President felt, his fault.

## Challenging assumptions about what might happen next: Albania and Albanians

Here, I will return finally and very briefly to the contrast that Albania and Albanians were providing in this situation. They constituted an increasingly discomfiting 'absent presence'[16] here, given the rapid pace at which events were unfolding in Albania, as well as the increasing involvement of Albanian citizens in development projects in Greece.

Within the perspective of Greek nationalist rhetoric, Albania and Albanians lie completely outside any 'interests' and partiality within Greece, and thus have no way of securing mediation, because they are always already unrelated. Yet at the same time, there was a long-term disagreement about the correct location of the border between Greece and Albania, which makes the precise location of the boundary between those who are related and those who are not rather ambiguous. A part of southern Albania is known in Greece as Northern Epirus, with the implication that it constitutes the northern part of the region of Epirus – ie in this view, it is a contiguous part of the Greek nation, even though there is no longer any suggestion that it ought to be a part of the Greek state. The peoples who are associated with that region are referred to as Northern Epirots in Greece and are usually represented as being Greek, while they are also Albanian citizens. Northern Epirots are relatives, both literally (many are directly related to families living on the Greek side of the border) and in national terms.[17] That in itself was not problematic: there is no difficulty with the idea that the location of the nation and the location of the state rarely precisely coincide. The discomfort came from the very different way in which peoples from the Albanian side, whether Northern Epirots or 'Albanian Albanians,' were dealing with mediation. Excluded from both the local mediating networks and from most EU funding, people from Albania were finding other means, both legal and illegal, to 'develop'. They provided an example of a different way to do things, one that was not based on a dependence upon mediation. The implication of that was that the mediation of elites is not always necessary. The vision of what might happen next thus became potentially more contingent and unpredictable, and the stability of the social relations upon which the elites base their mediating role became less obviously inevitable.

There were things became visible about Albania and the people there that had been invisible during the Cold War and that were challenging the self-evident truths of the 'western' version of what is properly 'modern.' As Herzfeld notes, there was previously little challenge to the idea that communism was backward: 'Greece . . . more or less absorbed the American view that communism was incompatible with civilization' (Herzfeld, 2002:904). It was impossible to maintain that image once the borders opened. For a start, the speed with which things were occurring on the Albanian side of the border implied a reversal of one of the most common assumptions about tempo during the Cold War: ie, that communism slows things down, whereas capitalism speeds things up (Brennan, 2000). The collapse of the communist regime in Albania has certainly been associated with speeding things up in that country; but that has not been generally associated with some kind of wholehearted transition to a capitalist way of doing things, or at least a capitalist way of *thinking* about things. Rather, it has tended to be associated with a slightly modified communist way of doing things but without the moral sensibility of communist ideology and/or without the strong disciplinary controls of a Stalinist state to prevent things from running amok (De Waal, 2005). As Buroway and Verdery (amongst others) have noted, the shift away from socialism in many parts of what used to be known as 'Eastern' Europe implies neither some kind of radical break from the previous period nor a simple copying of the practices, let alone the attitudes, of capitalist parts of the world (Burawoy and Verdery, 1998).

The fact that Albania did not proceed headlong into a kind of mimicry of western capitalism when the communist regime collapsed there made the starkly evident difference in tempo on the two sides of the border particularly notable. Not all of this was represented positively in the Greek media – on the contrary, the usual story was that a state of near-anarchic criminal chaos had developed there. By 1997, when there was a popular armed uprising against the Albanian government over the government's failure to protect citizens from fraudulent banking schemes (pyramid schemes; another money issue that needs future analysis), most people in Epirus were convinced that Albania, which for almost half a century had become virtually invisible to the point of being almost forgotten about, was now one of the most dangerously out-of-control states in Europe: indeed, it was the kind of place where patronage relations and mafia (more in the sense that Gambetta describes, as businesses (Gambetta, 1993)) could potentially thrive, unencumbered by any dependence upon external forces. This place was not lethargic and it also did not subscribe to the visions of the European Union for 'Europe.' This was something else.

A very different, but related, image was emerging about the Albanian citizens who had moved into Greece in increasing numbers since the re-opening of the border (Northern Epirots and others; the distinction between them was rarely very clear). Media reports focusing on the criminal and violent activities of some of these newcomers were mentioned occasionally by people who lived around the border but, for the most part, this was restricted to discussions of organized crime, which in people's imaginations was based in Albania and in large cities such as Athens; such illegal entrepreneurs might pass through Epirus, but it was imagined that they, like all other external forces, would be on their way to somewhere else, more central. The talk about the Albanian citizens who lived in Epirus mostly concerned the way Albanian labour was rapidly altering the Epirot landscape – both literally and metaphorically. In recent decades, many Greek shepherds had stopped grazing their animals on the hills and had started to use stored fodder and to rear breeds of sheep and goats that could live in stables, rather than the older breeds traditionally used in the region. This had resulted in a severe overgrowth and reforestation of the mountains, which made the mountains look wild and uninhabited. With the arrival of (cheap) Albanian labour, it became cheaper to hire an Albanian worker to take the animals up the hills for grazing than it was to buy fodder and keep the animals in stables. As a result, much of the overgrown hillsides of the region began to be cleared of vegetation once again. In that sense, the landscape was literally changing as a result of the arrival of Albanians in Epirus.

In addition to the new Albanian shepherds, there were other Albanian citizens working in the region. They worked regularly as skilled and unskilled workers in cultural heritage development projects (particularly as stone masons amongst the men and as seamstresses amongst the women); they also worked as musicians in local festivals and weddings (the men) and at festivals of folk music and dance events (both men and women). Many of these cultural heritage projects were paid for by EU-funded development money, the purpose of which was to develop cultural heritage tourism in the region.

In sum, these newcomers in Epirus not only worked long hours for very little money, they also possessed skills that were associated with 'tradition' and 'cultural heritage' in the region; they had skills that had somehow been lost over the years on the Greek side of the border, as the younger people left for cosmopolitan cities and the older people had passed away. Somewhat ironically, perhaps, those people who had been overtaken by a Stalinist revolution in Albania had apparently maintained their 'traditional' values and skills much more effectively than the people on the Greek side of the border.

This account could be seen as being at the opposite extreme of the story about the Albanian organized crime lords. But in both cases, what the people in Epirus highlighted was that this was 'something else,' an alternative that made the inevitability of what would happen next much less certain than it had been before. Whether judged as good or bad, it pointed to the possibility of changing the tempo, and of shifting the parameters of the debate that had generated an expectation that what would happen next was nothing at all. In short, and despite its many negative aspects (both imagined and experienced) it was hopeful. It was too early to say, by the time my research ended, what the outcome might be for forms of mediation; but it was clear that the parameters of the debate, the way in which to measure what makes a person into one of importance, was in the process of renegotiation.

## Notes

1 This chapter is based on several years of in-depth ethnographic fieldwork carried out during the 1990s in Epirus. Included in this research was a study of several EU-funded development projects, mostly in Pogoni County and surrounding regions. The research was funded by DGXII of the European Commission of the European Union: Contract number EV5V-0021 (Archaeomedes I); EV5V-CT94–0486 (Environmental Perception and Policy Making); and ENV 4-CT95–0159 (Archaeomedes II). Full details of the research carried out can be found in Green (2005:ch.1).

2 This conception of social relations is not in any way limited to Epirus, of course (Strathern, 1988, 1996).

3 I am indebted to the work of Marilyn Strathern in developing this notion of partiality (Strathern, 1991).

4 Several scholars working on the development of the concept of the Greek nation have argued that this idea of timeless moral values of the people of the nation was an essential part of the development of the legitimacy of the Greek state (Gourgouris, 1996; Herzfeld, 1986; Kitromilides, 1994).

5 Herzfeld was drawing on the work of Roger Just here (Just, 1989).

6 This is a point made repeatedly in anthropology, including by Shore (2002: 2–3) and Piña-Cabral (2000: 2).

7 Herzfeld (1985, 1986).

8 In this respect at least, Epirot perspectives of the EU's policies quite closely reflect those of Cris Shore, who suggests that the bureaucratic institutions of the European Union is composed of an elite that is deliberately distant from the 'ordinary' people of Europe, and whose perspective on the world largely reflects their own political and social ideals, rather than anyone else's (Shore, 2000:18).

9 Baker, 1997; Jenkins, 2000; Poncelet, 2001; Ray, 2001.

10 Gregory, 1997; Hart 2000; Hart, forthcoming; Hutchinson, 1992; Leyshon, 1997; Thrift, 1994; Zelizer, 1997.

11 http://ec.europa.eu/regional_policy/reg_prog/po/prog_30.htm, last accessed 13.3.2007.

12 Kofas, 1989.

13 Hogan, 1987; Killick, 1997.

14 Andrews, 1980; Clogg and Yannopoulos, 1972.

15 The EU development web pages are littered with 'seed money' programmes, and whole manuals are written about 'seed money.' See, for example, INTERREG's 'Seed Money' application package; (http://www.bsrinterreg.net/projects/SeedMoney_app_pack.html; accessed 13.3.2007).

16 The phrase is not intended to echo the arguments of Herzfeld's article title concerning 'crypto-colonialism' (Herzfeld, 2002).

17 A detailed discussion of Northern Epirus and Northern Epirots can be found in Green, 2005: 15–16; 222–226.

# References

Andrews, Kevin., (1980), *Greece in the Dark: 1967–1974,* Adolf M. Amsterdam: Hakker.

Baker, Susan (ed.), (1997), *The Politics of Sustainable Development: Theory, Policy and Practice within the European Union,* London; New York: Routledge.

Banfield, Edward C., (1958), *The Moral Basis of a Backward Society,* London: Collier-Macmillan.

Blok, A., (1972), 'The peasant and the brigand: social bandity reconsidered', *Comparative Studies in Society and History,* **14:4**: 494–503

Blok, A., (1974), *The Mafia of a Sicilian Village. 1860–1960. A Study of Violent Peasant Entrepreneurs,* Oxford: Blackwell.

Boissevain, J. F., (1974), *Friends of Friends: Networks, Manipulators and Coalitions,* Oxford: Blackwell.

Brennan, T., (2000), *Exhausting Modernity: Grounds for a New Economy,* London: Routledge.

Burawoy, M. & Verdery, K., (eds), (1998), *Uncertain Transition: Ethnographies of Change in the Post-socialist World,* Oxford: Rowman & Littlefield, Lanham, MD.

Campbell, J. K., (1964), *Honour, Family and Patronage: A Study of Institutions and Moral Values in a Greek Mountain Community,* Oxford: Clarendon Press.

Clogg, R. and Yannopoulos, G. N., (eds), (1972), *Greece Under Military Rule,* London: Secker & Warburg.

Davis, J., (1977), *People of the Mediterranean: An Essay in Comparative Social Anthropology,* London: Routledge and Kegan Paul.

De Waal, C., (1994), *Urban Aspiration and Rural Development in Southern Greece,* Ph.D.: University of Cambridge.

De Waal, C., (2005), *Albania Today: A Portrait of Post-communist Turbulence,* London: I. B. Tauris in association with the Centre for Albanian Studies.

Dodd, N., (2001), 'What is "sociological" about the euro?' *European Societies* **3:1**: 23–40.

Dodd, N., (2005), 'Reinventing monies in Europe', *Economy and Society* **34**: 558–83.

Gambetta, D., (1993), *The Sicilian Mafia: The Business of Private Protection,* Cambridge, Mass.; London: Harvard University Press.

Gellner, E. and Waterbury, J., (eds), (1977), *Patrons and Clients in Mediterranean Societies,* London: Duckworth.

Gilmore, D., (1982), 'Anthropology of the Mediterranean Area', *Annual Review of Anthropology* **11**: 175–205.

Gourgouris, S., (1996), *Dream Nation: Enlightenment, Colonization, and the Institution of Modern Greece,* Stanford, CA: Stanford University Press.

Green, S. F., (2005), *Notes from the Balkans: Locating Marginality and Ambiguity on the Greek-Albanian Border,* Princeton, NJ, Oxford: Princeton University Press.

Green, S. F., (2006), 'From Hostile Backwater to Natural Wilderness: On the Relocation of "Nature" in Epirus, North Western Greece', *Culture and Society* **3:2**: 436–60.

Gregory, C. A., (1997), *Savage Money: The Anthropology and Politics of Commodity Exchange,* Amsterdam, London: Harwood Academic Publishers.

Hart, K., (2000), *The Memory Bank: Money in an Unequal World,* London: Profile Books.

Hart, K., (forthcoming), 'The persuasive power of money', in *Persuasion in Economic Life,* edited by S. Gudeman, Oxford: Berghahn Books.

Harvey, P., (2002), Elites on the margins: *mestizo* travers in the southern.

Peruvian Andes', in *Elite Cultures: Anthropological Perspectives*, C. Shore and S. Nugent (eds), London: Routledge: 74–90.

Harvie, C., (1994), *The Rise of Regional Europe*, London; New York: Routledge.

Herzfeld, M., (1980), 'Honour and shame: problems in the comparative analysis of moral Systems', *Man (n.s.)* **15**:2: 339–51.

Herzfeld, M., (1984), 'The horns of the Mediterraneanist dilemma', *American Ethnologist* **11**:3: 439–54.

Herzfeld, M., (1985), *The Poetics of Manhood: Contest and Identity in a Cretan Mountain Village*, Princeton N.J: Princeton University Press.

Herzfeld, M., (1986), *Ours Once More: Folklore, Ideology, and the Making of Modern Greece*, New York: Pella Publishing Inc.

Herzfeld, M., (1992), *The Social Production of Indifference: Exploring the Symbolic Roots of Western Bureaucracy*, Oxford: Berg.

Herzfeld, M., (2002), 'The Absent presence: discourses of crypto-colonialism', *South Atlantic Quarterly* **101**:4: 899–926.

Hogan, M. J., (1987), *The Marshall Plan: America, Britain, and the Reconstruction of Western Europe, 1947–1952*, Cambridge: Cambridge University Press.

Hutchinson, S., (1992), 'The cattle of money and the cattle of girls among the Nuer, 1930–83', *American Ethnologist* **19**:2: 294–316.

Jansen, S., (2007), 'Troubled locations: return, the life course, and transformations of "home" in Bosnia-Herzegovina', *Focaal*: **15–30**.

Jenkins, T. N., (2000), 'Putting postmodernity into practice: endogenous development and the role of traditional cultures in the rural development of marginal regions', *Ecological Economics* **34**:3: 301–14.

Just, Roger, (1989), 'Triumph of the Ethnos', in *History and Ethnicity*, E. Tonkin, M. McDonald & M. Chapman (eds), London; New York: Routledge: 71–88.

Killick, J. R,. (1997), *The United States and European Reconstruction, 1945–1960*, Edinburgh: Keele University Press.

Kitromilides, P., (1994), *Enlightenment, Nationalism, Orthodoxy: Studies in the Culture and Political Thought of South-eastern Europe*, Aldershot: Variorum.

Kofas, Jon V., (1989), *Intervention and Underdevelopment: Greece During the Cold War*, University Park; London: Pennsylvania State University Press.

Leyshon, A., (1997), 'Geographies of money and finance II', *Progress in Human Geography* **21**:3: 381–92.

Peristiany, J. G. and Julian Pitt-Rivers, (eds), (1992), *Honor and Grace in Anthropology*, Cambridge: Cambridge University Press.

Peristiany, J. G., (ed.), (1976), *Mediterranean Family Structures*, Cambridge (UK); New York: Cambridge University Press.

Pina-Cabral, J. de, (1989), 'The Mediterranean as a category of regional comparison: a critical view', *Current Anthropology* **30**:3: 399–406.

Pina-Cabral, J. and Antónia P. de L., (eds), (2000), *Elites: Choice, Leadership and Succession*. Oxford: Berg.

Poncelet, E. C., (2001), 'A kiss here and a kiss there: conflict and collaboration in environmental partnerships', *Environmental Management* **27**:1: 13–25.

Ray, C., (2001), 'Transnational co-operation between rural areas: elements of a political economy of EU rural development', *Sociologia Ruralis* **41**:3: 279–95.

Ray, C., (2000), 'The EU LEADER programme: rural development laboratory', *Sociologia Ruralis* **40**:2: 163–71.

Shore, C., (2000), *Building Europe: The Cultural Politics of European Integration*, London; New York: Routledge.

Shore, C. and Stephen N., (eds), (2002), *Elite Cultures: Anthropological Perspectives*, London: Routledge.

Strathern, M., (1996), 'Cutting the network', *Journal of the Royal Anthropological Institute* **2**:3: 517–35.

Sarah Green

Strathern, M., (1988), *The Gender of the Gift: Problems with Women and Problems with Society in Melanesia*, Berkeley and Los Angeles, CA; London: University of California Press.

Strathern, M., (1991), *Partial Connections*, Savage, Maryland: Rowman & Littlefield.

Thrift, N. J., (1994), 'On the social and cultural determinants of international finance centres: the case of the City of London', in *Money, Power and Space*, S. Corbridge, R. Martin & N. J. Thrift (eds), Oxford, UK; Cambridge, Mass: Blackwell Publishing: 327–55.

Zelizer, V. A., (1997), *The Social Meaning of Money: Pin Money, Paychecks, Poor Relief and Other Currencies*, Princeton, N.J.: Princeton University Press.

# Notes on Contributors

**Tony Bennett** is Professor of Sociology at the Open University, a Director of the Economic and Social Science Research Centre on Socio-Cultural Change, and a Professorial Fellow in the Faculty of Arts at the University of Melbourne. He is a Fellow of the Australian Academy of the Humanities. His publications include *Formalism and Marxism; Outside Literature; Bond and Beyond: The Political Career of a Popular Hero* (with Janet Woollacott); *The Birth of the Museum: History, Theory, Politics; Culture: A Reformer's Science; Accounting for Tastes: Australian Everyday Cultures* (with Michael Emmison and John Frow); and, most recently, *Pasts Beyond Memory: Evolution, Museums, Colonialism and New Keywords: A Revised Vocabulary of Culture and Society* (edited with Larry Grossberg and Meaghan Morris). T.Bennett@open.ac.uk

**William K. Carroll** is a professor at the University of Victoria, where he teaches in Sociology and in the Interdisciplinary Graduate Program in Cultural, Social and Political Thought. His research interests are in the areas of social movements and social change, the political economy of corporate capitalism, and critical social theory and method. He has won the Canadian Sociology Association's John Porter Prize twice: in 1988 for *Corporate Power and Canadian Capitalism* (UBC Press, 1986) and in 2005 for *Corporate Power in a Globalizing World* (Oxford University Press, 2004). Recent publications include 'Hegemony and counter-hegemony in a global field', *Studies in Social Justice* 1, 1, 2007: 36–66, and 'Global cities in the global corporate network', *Environment and Planning A*, 39, 10, 2007: 2297–2323. wcarroll@uvic.ca

**Paul du Gay** is Professor of Organizational Behaviour at Warwick Buisness School, and Adjunct Professor of Organization Studies at Copenhagen Business School. His research interests are located on the cusp of the sociology of organizational life and cultural studies. Recent publications include *The Values of Bureaucracy* (ed. OUP) and *Organizing Identity:persons and organizations after theory* (Sage). He is a member of the ESRC's Centre for Research on Socio-Cultural Change (CReSC). Paul.duGay@wbs.ac.uk

**Julie Froud** is Professor of Financial Innovation at Manchester Business School and a member of CRESC. Her current research interests include financializa-

Editorial organization © 2008 The Editorial Board of the Sociological Review. Published by Blackwell Publishing Ltd, 9600 Garsington Road, Oxford OX4 2DQ, UK and 350 Main Street, Malden, MA 02148, USA

tion and the development of financial innovation, the business of private equity and corporate narratives for the capital markets. Julie is also the editor of *Competition and Change*. julie.froud@manchester.ac.uk

**Olivier Godechot**, sociologist, is a research fellow at Centre Maurice Halbwachs (CNRS, Ecole Normale Supérieure). One of his main topic concerns financial industry. In his first book, *Les traders, 2001,* he develops a sociology of financial behaviours in trading rooms. In his second book, *Working rich, 2007,* he focuses on wages in financial industry and on the making of a financial labour market. He also studies networks in academic fields with a special interest in recruitment. olivier.godechot@ens.fr

**Sarah Green** is a Social Anthropologist working at the University of Manchester. Her work focuses on location, borders and places: on analysing how people locate themselves both in the world and in relation to themselves and others, and how that is informed by political conditions, as well as by imagination and diverse ways of knowing. She has carried out ethnographic fieldwork in London (on gender, sexuality and community); the Greek-Albanian border (on the ambiguities of location in the Balkans and development); in the Peloponnese (Argolid Valley; on environmental problems generated by citrus farming); in Manchester (on the uses of information and communications technologies on grassroots organizations); and most recently on the Greek-Turkish border in the Aegean (on the shifting relations across this border, focusing particularly on money and visibility). Her publications include *Urban Amazons* (Macmillan 1997) and *Notes from the Balkans* (Princeton University Press 2005). Sarah.Green@manchester.ac.uk

**Dave Griffiths** is a PhD research student within CRESC at the University of Manchester. His ESRC-funded project is entitled 'The Social Networks of Public Elites', and utilizes social network analysis to examine the board composition of the UK government's quangos. He has presented papers at conferences in the UK and Europe. david.griffiths@postgrad.manchester.ac.uk

**Charles Harvey** is Pro-Vice-Chancellor and Professor of Business History and Management at Newcastle University. He holds a PhD in International Business from the University of Bristol. Professor Harvey is author of numerous books and articles in the fields of strategy, management and business history. He is the co-author, with Sydney Finkelstein and Thomas Lawton, of *Breakout Strategy* (McGraw-Hill, 2007), which presents a complete strategy system based on the experiences of more than 100 of the world's most successful breakout companies. In 2006 he published, with Mairi Maclean and Jon Press, *Business Elites and Corporate Governance in France and the UK* (Palgrave Macmillan), a trail-breaking study of the exercise of power within two very different national business systems. Recent publications include contributions to the *Journal of Management Studies*, *Human Relations*, *Organization Studies*, and the *Economic History Review*. He is joint editor of *Business History*. Charles.harvey@strath.ac.uk

**Frederic Lebaron** is professor of sociology at the University of Picardie-Jules Verne in Amiens, head of the Centre universitaire de recherches sur l'action publique et le politique – Epistémologie et sciences sociales (CURAPP, CNRS-UPJV), and member of the Institut universitaire de France (IUF). He has recently published *Ordre monétaire ou chaos social. La BCE et la révolution néo-libérale* (éditions du Croquant), and a handbook, *La sociologie* (Dunod). flebaron@yahoo.fr

**Adam Leaver** is a Senior Lecturer in Financial and Divisional Innovation at Manchester Business School. He is co-author of *Financialization and Strategy: Narrative and Numbers* (2006) and co-editor of the forthcoming *Financialization at Work: Key Texts and Analysis*, both published by Routledge. In addition he has published work in The Sociological Review, Economy and Society and Review of International Political Economy. His current research interests are in financial innovation and its social impact, particularly in the housing market; developments in the pharmaceutical industry and elites in the financial and cultural industries. adam.leaver@manchester.ac.uk

**Mairi Maclean** is Professor of International Business in the School of Strategy and International Business, Bristol Business School, UWE. She holds an MA and PhD from the University of St Andrews, and an MBA from the University of Bath. Her interests include corporate governance, business elites, business history, business transformation and transition, and comparative organization studies. She has published widely in the field of international business. Her recent books include *Business Elites and Corporate Governance in France and the UK* (Palgrave Macmillan, 2006), written with Charles Harvey and Jon Press, and funded by the Leverhulme Trust and Reed Charity; and *Economic Management and French Business from de Gaulle to Chirac* (Palgrave Macmillan, 2002). She is the author of four books and editor of a further three, and has published more than forty articles in journals such as *Human Relations, Business History, West European Politics* and *Relations Internationales et Stratégiques*. mairi.maclean@uwe.ac.uk

**Shinobu Majima** is Associate Professor in Economic History at Gakushuin University, Tokyo, where she teaches the history of economic growth in Britain, Europe, America and China from a consumerist standpoint. She is currently working on a book entitled *Fashion Fever: Gender, Culture and Economy in an Age of Abundance* and on a project on the history of the UK Family Expenditure Survey. shinobu.majima@gakushuin.ac.jp

**Andrew Miles** is Senior Research Fellow in the ESRC Centre for Research on Socio-cultural Change (CRESC) at the University of Manchester. He was previously a Senior Lecturer in Modern Social History at the University of Birmingham. He has written widely on the stratification, mobility and the history of work, including *Social Mobility in Nineteenth and Early-Twentieth Century England* (1999) and (with others) *HISCO. Historical International Standard Classification of Occupations* (2002). His current interests are in the social and life course dynamics of cultural participation and in the development of social research methods for the cultural sector. Andrew.Miles@ manchester.ac.uk

**Michael Moran** is WJM Mackenzie Professor of Government in the School of Social Sciences, University of Manchester. His most recent book is *The British Regulatory State*, 2nd edition, Oxford University Press, 2007. michael. moran@manchester.ac.uk

**Mike Savage** is professor of Sociology at Manchester where he is also Director of the ESRC Centre for Research on Socio-Cultural Change (CRESC). His interests are in stratification, urban sociology, and cultural sociology, and his recent books include *Globalisation and Belonging* (with Gaynor Bagnall and Brian Longhurst, Sage 2005), and he is completing a study of *Class and Culture after Distinction* with Tony Bennett, Elizabeth Silva, Alan Warde, Modesto Gayo-Cal and David Wright. mike.savage@manchester.ac.uk

**John Scott** is Professor of Sociology at the University of Essex and has previously taught at the Universities of Leicester and Strathclyde. He has written on business ownership and control, social stratification and power, social network analysis, documentary research, and social theory. He is currently working on historical issues in the development of British sociology. His publications include *Social Theory* (Sage, 2006), *Power* (Polity Press, 2001), *Corporate Business and Capitalist Classes* (Oxford University Press, 1997), and *Who Rules Britain?* (Polity Press, 1992). He is the editor of *The Sociology of Elites* (3 Volumes, Edward Elgar, 1990), *Power: Critical Concepts* (3 Volumes, Routledge, 1994), and *Social Networks: Critical Concepts*, (4 Volumes, Routledge, 2002). scottj@essex.ac.uk

**Gindo Tampubolon** works broadly in the area of social change. Together with Mike Savage he investigates social mobility in Britain over the last quarter of the century, using latent growth models. This involves modelling dynamics of inter and intra-generational social class mobility. There is also an inter-cohort element, due to the use of two British cohorts: the National Child Development Study, 1958, and the British Cohort Study, 1970. A separate strand of his works draws ideas from social network analysis. This has been fruitfully applied to investigating the growth of knowledge in clinical innovations over the last 30 years. Gindo.Tampubolon@manchester.ac.uk

**Alan Warde** is Professor of Sociology at the University of Manchester and a member of CRESC. He works on the sociology of consumption and on social stratification. His most recent book is *Trust in Food: a comparative and institutional analysis*, with U.Kjaernes and M.Harvey, published by Palgrave, 2007. alan.warde@manchester.ac.uk

**Karel Williams** is co -director of CRESC and a professor at Manchester Business School in the Financial and Digital Innovation subject group. Since the late 1990s he has worked in a team with Julie Froud and others mainly on financialization and the remaking of capitalism. Their book on giant firm strategy (*Financialization and Strategy*, 2006) consolidates their arguments about the narrative and performative turn in corporate strategy; while the commentaries in their forthcoming reader (*Financialization at Work*, 2008) present a distinctive frame and conjuncture definition of financialization. karel. williams@man.ac.uk

# Index